Social work education Voices from the Asia Pacific

Edited by Carolyn Noble, Mark Henrickson and In Young Han

SYDNEY UNIVERSITY PRESS

Published 2013 by SYDNEY UNIVERSITY PRESS

Second edition

Sydney University Press
Fisher Library F03, University of Sydney NSW 2006 AUSTRALIA
Email: sup.info@sydney.edu.au

National Library of Australia Cataloguing-in-Publication entry

Title:	Social work education : voices from the Asia Pacific edited by Carolyn Noble, Mark Henrickson, In Young Han
Edition:	2nd edition
ISBN:	9781743320396 (paperback)
Notes:	Includes bibliographical references
Subjects:	Social work education--Pacific Area Social service--Pacific Area
Other Authors/Contributors:	Noble, Carolyn, editor Henrickson, Mark, editor Han, In Young, editor
Dewey Number:	361.3091823

Cover design by Miguel Yamin
Cover artwork by Carolyn Noble

Contents

Introduction

Why a second edition of this book? There are several reasons.

First, we remain excited about the growth of social work in the Asia Pacific. In this book you will hear stories about what is going on in many countries and regions of the Asia Pacific, and once you've read these stories we think you will be just as excited as we are.

Second, the Asia Pacific is a dynamic place. Nothing stays the same for very long, and the region remains the economic, political and social centre of gravity for the world. We want to give social work educators an opportunity to revise and update their contributions to the first edition, and to hear from new authors in places where social work education is emerging, and where social work issues are coming to the foreground.

Third, despite the astonishing diversity of the region in language, culture, philosophy, religion, economic systems and the way social work is taught and practiced, we believe that the social work environment is gradually becoming more cohesive. This emerging cohesiveness is a remarkable achievement, and is an acknowledgement of work of the regional social work educators' organisation in bringing together social work scholarship across the region into one vibrant and relevant organisation—the Asia Pacific Association of Social Work Educators (APASWE), which also provided seed funding for this book. Spurred on by the debates surrounding the revision of the definition of social work, social work educators from every country are having important and productive conversations with colleagues throughout the region. These conversations go to the heart of social work: What is social work, is it a profession, or discipline, or both? Are those differences meaningful? And how is social work practiced where you are? Does it matter there are differences? And what can we share from addressing these questions? As social work educators we must ask ourselves a further key question: How do we teach social work and prepare students for practice in an increasingly globalised, dynamic and culturally diverse environment?

With this book we hope to provide a resource for social work educators and students throughout the region to have those conversations.

We acknowledge again that English is the colonial language of this region, and while it remains the default language of international social work conversation, it also imposes a kind of epistemological hegemony, forcing people to think and communicate with English words and concepts. In the Asia-Pacific region English is not always an easy fit. In this book, each chapter is translated into Chinese, Japanese and Korean (in that order). Where the first language of the author is not English, the first language has also been provided: in most cases this will include regional languages such as Vietnamese or Fijian. The abstract in the first language of the author is included immediately following the abstract in English; this means that where the authors are Korean, or Japanese, for instance, the abstract order is changed to reflect those languages first. In this way we hope not only to communicate with people who are less confident in reading English, but also to express ideas and concepts that fit better in another language.

We are tremendously grateful to our translators whose work truly was a labour of love and commitment, since they worked without financial compensation. Translators worked in pairs, cross-checking and back-translating each others' work from the abstracts supplied by the authors. In some cases the authors provided their own first-language abstract. Chinese translators were students from Massey University-Albany's (New Zealand) Master of Applied Social Work program: they are Mengyi CAI, Yidan LI, Haiying SONG, Zenjiang HU, Yun CHEN, and Rong YING. Japanese translations were done by Shoichi Isogai, MApplSW, a graduate of Massey University, and Kana Matsuo, a chapter contributor to this book. Korean translations were done by In Young HAN, one of the editors of this book. Working on these translations was a valuable experience for all of us, and we hope you will also find them useful, even if only as a reminder that the Asia-Pacific region is a vast and complex place, where sometimes English is a not so welcome visitor.

This book is divided into four sections. The authors in the first section write from an array of cultural voices. Jun Sun HONG and In Young HAN write about the increasingly diverse and complex social welfare and changing population environment of the Republic of Korea, and how social work educators are addressing that new diversity. Lorraine Muller and Susan Gair tell us their story of the cycle of learning about an Australian Indigenous people's perspective from their respective cultural heritage and the curricula and interactive learning that this engendered. Murli Desai provides an overview of the contemporary scene in the Asia Pacific with respect to gender, and the progress—or lack of it—countries have made toward gender equity in education and other social indices. Mark Henrickson critiques the way social work educators replicate heteronormativity and continue the marginalisation of gender and sexual minorities if they do not take a critical stance with their teaching. And Moses Ma'alo Faleolo considers the thorny question of how social work educators consider and teach cultural validity, particularly in respect of indigenous cultures, using his Samoan heritage. His Samoan cultural knowledge provides another dimension to working cross-culturally with knowledge and sensitivity and provides a powerful insight into his culture and its wisdom for all to share.

The second section hears from national voices. In this section Kana Matsuo describes for us the conversation that has taken place in Japan about the definition of social work. Japan is a particularly fitting place for this discussion, because there has been a great deal of conversation and debate about social work—and professional social work—in Japan for quite a long time. Richard Hugman has been actively supporting the development of social work and social work education in Vietnam for many years, and together with his colleagues Bùi Thị Xuân Mai and Nguyễn Thị Thái Lan (these names are in traditional Vietnamese order with surnames first) offer us an on-the-ground perspective on the emergence of social work in Vietnam, and the challenges that social work educators are facing in that emerging and powerful nation. Joseph Leung writes about the explosion of social work in the economic power that is China, and the challenges that development has brought. And Keo Chanvunthy describes the sometimes overwhelming challenges and complexities of establishing a social work educational program in post-war Cambodia, a nation with so much to develop, yet so few resources to develop with. Bala Raju Nikku describes the development of social work in Nepal where the rapid growth of social work programs in both the State supported and privately funded Universities and Colleges has not been matched with professional oversight and the required resources. The demand for practitioners and educators in the country is also an unmet need that requires urgent attention.

The third section addresses curricula and practica concerns. Heather Fraser and Ksenija Napan both address their individual experiences of enhancing the classes they teach: Heather Fraser explores how in the classroom politics and emotions can both inspire and collide. Ksenija Napan takes a critical standpoint in relation to the politics of teaching and invites teachers and students to think critically about social work issues, curricula and values. Both show how this is possible in the classroom with classes of new students and provide valuable examples of how to teach critically and reflectively. Louise Coventry and Marty Grace describe how working cross-culturally with social work students and supervisors from different cultural backgrounds can be a rich and rewarding experience if attention to reciprocity and thoughtful engagement and exchange are put at the centre of this learning. Kate Saxton is an addition to this edition; she describes the challenges of educating students for a newly emerging social work discipline in a nation with a complex educational and political environment.

Finally, in the fourth section, policy voices, we hear from Carolyn Noble, who encourages us to critique western and post-colonial paradigms of social work from Asia Pacific perspectives; she tells us that the theories and models of social work are not universal, but rather local, and need to be understood and implemented in ways that take into account indigenous and local contexts. Deborah West and Dan Bashiera explore the practice-activism divide, outline an ethical discourse between social work and humanitarianism, and discuss how this discourse can provide a framework to consolidate and develop the knowledge base for evidence based practice in resource-poor, cross-cultural and remote environments. Nilan Yu explores the implications of labour migration for social work education in the Asia Pacific, and unpacks some of the related human rights and welfare issues at the local, regional and global levels. Finally, Linda Briskman discusses the issue of asylum seekers and their current treatment on arrival in Australia and the politics underlying their plight. She urges social workers to work with social movements to ensure that their human rights are fought for, secured and then protected as they try and make a new life for themselves and their families. If social work is concerned with social justice then this issue needs our full attention.

We finish this introduction as we did in the first edition by acknowledging the many indigenous communities, past and present, throughout the region for their care and custodianship of our lands and the abundance, diversity and resources of their domains, and for their willingness to share their knowledges with us in the development of this book. We are all the richer for this knowledge.

And, finally we are thankful to each other for the collegial collaboration and camaraderie we have shared in the production of this expanded volume. Again, enjoy!

Carolyn Noble, Sydney
Mark Henrickson, Auckland
In Young Han, Seoul
April 2013

1

Cultural voices

1

Call for incorporating cultural competency in South Korean social work education

Jun Sung Hong and In Young Han

In recent years South Korea has become multicultural with a rising number of foreign migrants, along with an increase in international marriages. Consequently, there have been several major social problems, which necessitate culturally competent social services in South Korea. This chapter examines the potentials for culturally competent practice in multicultural South Korea. We discuss the social problems and the lack of cultural competence in South Korean social work education, as well as the current programs and services for immigrants and non-Korean residents in South Korea. Suggestions for cultural competent education and practice in South Korea are discussed.

한국 사회복지교육에서 문화적 유능성 포함의 필요성

한국은 최근 외국인 이주자의 증가와 국제결혼의 증가로 다문화 사회가 되어가고 있다. 그 결과 여러가지 사회문제가 발생하였고, 문화적 역량을 갖춘 사회복지 서비스의 필요성을 대두시키고 있다. 본 장에서는 다문화 사회에서 요구되는 문화적 민감성을 가진 사회복지사를 키우기 위해 문화역량 교육의 필요성과 이에 따른 실천현장교육의 부족, 이민자와 외국인의 현존하는 프로그램에 대해 논하고 사회복지 교육에서 필요로 하는 문화역량 교육과 실천의 필요성이 언급되었다.

在韓國社會工作教育中，對于文化能力合作的需求

近幾年，日益增長的國際婚姻導致外來移民增多，從而使韓國文化更加多元化。因此，已經出現了許多主要的社會問

題，這些問題都使得文化能力社會服務在韓國變得不可或缺）。這一章調查了對于多元韓國下潛在的文化能力實踐。我們討論社會問題以及韓國社會工作教育當中文化能力的缺失，同時也會討論現有的課程以及對于移民和非韓國居民的服務。最後，我們也將討論對于在韓國文化能力教育和實踐的一些建議。

文化的な適性能力を韓国にあるソーシャルワーク教育に取り入れるための呼び出し

近年の韓国では、外国人移住者の増加に加え、国際結婚が増えたことで多文化になってきている。その結果、韓国では、文化的に適性能力のある社会福祉事業を必要とする幾つかの主要な社会問題が発生している。この章では、多文化な韓国での文化的適性のある実践の可能性を調査する。韓国の社会問題とソーシャルワーク教育の文化的適性の欠如、そして韓国に住んでいる外国人移住者と韓国人でない居住者の為の現在の政策と福祉サービスについて論じる。韓国でのソーシャルワークの文化的適性のある教育と実践を提案する.

Introduction

Globalisation in the 21st century resulted in rapid increase in migration and worldwide transfer of labour forces (Lee, 2008). Within a few decades, South Korea has been confronted with unprecedented rapid social changes. These changes include inflow of North Korean defectors and migrant workers from Third World countries, and rising number of 'international marriages'. South Korea was an homogeneous, agrarian-based society for centuries. However, the recent demographic features of South Korea reveal that the society has become diversified (Chun, 2008). According to the Korea Immigration Services of the Ministry of Justice (2011), the number of immigrants rose from 1,066,273 in 2007 to 1,395,077 in 2011. The number of marriage between South Koreans and non-Koreans also soared from 110,362 in 2007 to 144,681 in 2011. Today, immigrants and non-Korean spouses constitute two per cent of the country's entire population.

'Multiculturalism' and 'diversity' have been a major focus in South Korea. From a research standpoint, increasing number of migrant workers—both legal and illegal—prompted debates in South Korea concerning newly emerging social problems, such as discrimination, human rights abuse and exploitation. Despite a critical need for research, studies on multiculturalism, interracial marriages, and ethnic enclaves are relatively scant in South Korea. Interestingly, social science researchers in the US have examined globalisation, multiculturalism, and ethnic enclaves, while South Korean researchers have primarily examined issues such as the Korean diaspora and problems involving KOSIAN (children of Korean and other Asian parents; Cho and Kim, 2008). Likewise, there has been a dearth of research in South Korea that informs social work professionals about culturally competent practices and services for non-Korean residents.

This chapter underscores the importance of culturally competent education and practice in South Korea. We begin by investigating the scope of South Korea's multicultural population and problems experienced by four major groups: foreign migrant workers, foreign wives of South Korean men, mixed-race children, and North Korean defectors. We also examine how cultural competency has been conceptualised in multicultural societies, such as USA. We then offer suggestions for effectively incorporating cultural competency in South Korean social work education.

New arrivals and 'new' problems in South Korea

We begin our discussion by assessing some of the major changes in South Korean demographics. Previously an agrarian-based society, South Korea emerged as one of four newly industrialised countries (NIC), along with Japan, Taiwan and Singapore during the latter half of the 20th century. South Korea's emergence as an NIC was a direct result of a transition due to inevitable changes in the structure of the national economy (Lim, 2002). Its success story has earned its reputation as the 'Miracle of the Han River'. Today, South Korea is one of the world's leading countries in science, information and technology. Although the 48 million people are predominantly South Koreans, its burgeoning economy has attracted migrants from Third World countries who seek to be a part of the 'Korean Dream'.

Foreign migrant workers

> I heard a shout from my boss insulting/forcing me with verbal abuse to hurry so I was scared and I lost concentration so I was pulled by the machine. When the machine was switched off, I realised my fingers had been chopped off; so I was rushed to the hospital and that was the last time I saw my employer. (A migrant worker from Ghana, AMNESTY International 2008)

The number of people residing outside of their birth country is greater than ever, estimated at more than 200 million (United Nations Population Fund, 2007). South Korea has rapidly become a new arena of global migration that is linked to accelerating social trends that only a few decades ago were thought of as unlikely. Since the early 1960s when South Korean society shifted from agrarian-based to industrial-based, thousands of South Koreans migrated annually to other countries, such as Germany and the Middle East. During the 1970s and 1980s, about 30,000 South Koreans migrated to other countries to work in the construction sector. However, there was a notable transformation in the late 1980s, when South Korea experienced a severe labour shortage in the small and medium-sized manufacturing firms and a major decline in the labour force due to exhausted surplus in the rural areas. Furthermore, domestic manpower shortage in the labour market is reflective of South Korea's rising standard of living. Consequently, the relatively better-educated and wealthier South Koreans eschew low-paying and less prestigious manual jobs, particularly the so-called three-dimensional (dirty, difficult, and dangerous) factory jobs. To address the shortage of semi- and unskilled labour jobs, the South Korean government recruited migrant workers from foreign countries. In 1992, the government systematically enacted immigration policies to bring in foreign migrant workers (Moon 2000). Both foreign migrant workers and South Korean government perceived transnational labour migration as beneficial. For foreign labourers, migration to South Korea would provide opportunities for better standard of living; for the South Korean government, importing migrant workers would resolve the problem of worker shortage. In sum, South Korea shifted from a 'labour-sending' to a 'labour-importing' country (Moon, 2000).

Since the early 1990s, migrant workers came mostly from the People's Republic of China, South Asia and Southeast Asia. Even during the Asian financial crisis in 1997, when the government sought to deport foreign migrant workers, there were 370,000 foreigners residing in South Korea (Moon, p. 148). Interestingly, South Korea is the only industrialised nation in which undocumented workers far outnumber documented workers. To illustrate, 80% of foreigners in South Korea are undocumented workers (Seol and Skrentny, 2004). According to Amnesty International (2008), foreign migrant workers were estimated at 360,000, which comprised 1.5 per cent of the total labour force in South Korea in 2006.

In conjunction with the importation and the influx of foreign migrant workers, new social problems also emerged in South Korea. According to the Korea Immigration Service, foreign migrant workers have been confronted with prejudice and discrimination because of low educational attainment and low socio-economic status, as well as human rights violations and exploitation (Shin, 2004). In response to these emerging issues, the South Korean National Assembly passed the Act Concerning the Employment Permit for Migrant Workers in 2003. In reality, however, foreign migrant workers have limited legal protection from discrimination and exploitation. To illustrate, Amnesty International have documented that foreign migrant workers have not been paid and worked long hours for lower wages in comparison to South Korean employees in a similar job. Foreign migrant workers work in unsanitary and dangerous conditions. They are also prohibited from organising labour trade unions. In case of work-related injury, which is common, foreign migrant workers receive inadequate treatment and little or no compensation. To make matters worse, one-third of female foreign migrant workers receive considerably less pay than their male and South Korean counterparts. Female workers are frequently sexually harassed by their male employers or co-workers. Regrettably, limited Korean language skills and inadequate resources, along with fear of deportation hinder many foreign migrants from seeking legal assistance.

Foreign wives of South Korean men

In South Korea, the rapid population decline and the diminishing role in households in the rural areas have prompted local governments to assist rural men in finding brides from foreign countries. From 1990s, increasing numbers of rural, young South Korean women relocated to urban areas (mostly Seoul) where socio-economic conditions and opportunities were far better than rural areas. As a consequence, the number of bachelors in rural areas increased considerably, and the South Korean government began recruiting joseonjok (ethnic Koreans in China) women as prospective brides for unmarried rural men. Since the 1990s when the diplomatic relationship between South Korea and China was first established, the rate of marriage between rural South Korean men and joseonjok women has increased tremendously (Cha, 2008). From 1990 to 2005, the number of joseonjok women who entered South Korea for marriage with South Korean men had been estimated at 100,000 (Cha, 2008).

The number of Japanese women in South Korea who married South Korean men is estimated at 17,000, while the numbers of women from the Philippines married to South Korean husbands is approximately 6,000. The nationalities of foreign brides of South Korean men also include Vietnamese, Thai, Russian, and Uzbek. In 2005, about 160,000 out of 250,000 marriages between South Koreans and non-Korean consisted of South Korean men and foreign women (Lee, 2008), and one out of every four men in rural areas is married to non-South Korean women in 2006.

Similar to foreign migrant workers, many foreign women (mostly in their early 20s) eyed South Korea in seeking a better life. They married South Korean men (typically between 35 to 45 years of age) and unwittingly became a major participant in South Korea's 'international marriage trade'. Life in South Korea has been difficult for many foreign brides due to marital problems, such as being pressured by their husband's family to bear children (especially sons) and expectation that they submit to their husband. Many women are also forced by their husband and his family to assimilate. According to the Ministry of Health and Welfare, 58% of foreign women in South Korea experience marital hardships because of language and cultural barriers (Kim 2006), which results in verbal and physical abuse at the hands of their husband and his family. A study by Yang, Kim, Sohn et al. (2003) found that life in South Korea was difficult for foreign wives of South Korean men in Gwangju and Jeonnam because of cultural adjustment problems and spousal abuse. The Ministry of Gender Equality and Family estimated that in 2007, about 47 per cent of foreign women were victims of spousal abuse in 2007, and the Emergency Support Center for Migrant Women received over 13,277 cases of spousal abuse involving foreign wives of South Korean men (Kim, 2008). To make matters worse, several tragic cases of spousal abuse have been reported by the national media, such as a 19-year-old Vietnamese woman who was severely beaten and killed by her South Korean husband. Other cases include a 22-year-old Vietnamese woman who committed suicide by jumping off a fourteen-story building, and a 45-year-old Chinese woman who attempted suicide to end her life of abuse perpetrated by her South Korean husband (Cha, 2008).

Mixed-race children

> I long for a day when biracial people won't have to face discrimination and can be dignified no matter where they are. (A Korean/African-American girl, Pearl S. Buck International)

In addition to the increasing rate of international marriages between foreign women and South Korean men, the number of mixed-race children in South Korea has also increased in recent years. The Pearl S. Buck International estimated that as of 2003, there were 35,000 people of mixed racial/ethnic heritage in South Korea; of these, 30,000 have blood-ties with other Asian countries while the rest have ties with US and other Western countries. Also in recent years, mixed-race actors, musicians and athletes such as Hines Ward (an American football player for the Pittsburg Steelers), received a nationwide recognition, which changed people's perceptions of mixed-race people changed in South Korea—from outcast to hero. The South Korean government subsequently proposed creating measures to safeguard mixed-race people's human rights. In 1989, South Korea signed the UN Convention on the Rights of the Child, which prohibits discrimination against children regardless of their ethnic origin (Min, 2004). Researchers and the media also focused on South Korea's nationalism and pride in ethnic purity and homogeneity. This was a far cry from decades ago when mixed-race people in South Korea were shunned and discriminated against.

MIXED-RACE CHILDREN OF THE PAST

South Koreans have traditionally valued homogeneity and distrusted others, which stemmed from invasions such as the Imjin War (1392–1398), Japanese colonialism (1910–1945), and the US occupation of South Korea (1945–1948). Reinforcing this prejudice has been directed against people who were a reminder of South Korea's most desperate times—the Korean War (1950–1953) and its aftermath. Children in particular suffered tremendously during and after the war, as pillaging and ravaging caused major devastation across the peninsula. Already in 1951, the UN Korean Reconstruction Agency estimated that there were 100,000 orphans, and in 1953, there were 293,000 widowed women with 516,000 children (Hubinette, 2005).

About 60,000 US troops were stationed in South Korea to protect its security interests in the Asia-Pacific region, and sexual exploitation of Korean women took on a mass scale (Hubinette,

2005). Women who had sexual contact with US servicemen were disdained and stigmatised as they were perceived as violating female chastity, ethnic purity, and pure blood-lines. Consequently, many of the wives of US servicemen migrated to the US, which constituted 10–15 per cent of the first-wave of Korean immigrants in the US (Hubinette, 2005). About 12,280 babies and children of US servicemen and Korean women, known as 'Amerasians,' 'GI babies,' or 'mixed-race children' were abandoned by both parents; of these, about half were adopted to the US or other western countries (Hurh, 1972).

Living conditions in South Korea were particularly difficult for mixed-raced children in South Korea, as they were ostracised by the mainstream society. These children symbolised the physical boundary marker between the colonisers (US) and the colonised (South Korea). Consequently, issues concerning mixed-race children in South Korea were featured in the Western media, which prompted many organisations to take action. International children's organisations, such as the Christian Children's Fund and Save the Children in the US established orphanages and programs in South Korea. World Vision, a Christian relief organisation, also created a documentary about the deplorable living conditions of these children (Hubinette, 2005). Others individuals also followed suit, including Nobel Laureate author Pearl S. Buck, and US farmers Harry and Bertha Holt. Buck adopted seven mixed-race children from China and established the Welcome House, an adoption agency on for mixed-race children (this agency was later renamed Pearl S. Buck International). Harry Holt adopted eight mixed-race children from South Korea and later founded an adoption agency, which rapidly developed into one of the largest international adoption agencies in the world.

TODAY'S MIXED-RACE CHILDREN

Despite the South Korean government's efforts to end discrimination and protect the rights of mixed-race children of international marriages, mixed-race children in South Korea have frequently encountered problems in school due to adjustment difficulties (Shin, Doh, Hong and Kim., 2012) and social exclusion from South Korean classmates and teachers (Min, 2004). Findings from a limited number of nationwide surveys in South Korea revealed that bi-racial/ethnic children frequently experience peer rejection and victimisation in school although the prevalence rates vary. According to the National Human Rights Commission survey in 2003, which consisted of a sample of 98 bi-racial/ethnic children and their families, over half of these children reported experiencing peer victimisation and exclusion by their classmates and teachers in school (Min, 2004).

A more recent nationwide survey by the Ministry of Health, Welfare and Family Affairs also found that 11.5 percent of non-Korean and mixed-race children expressed having difficulty in getting along with their peers, and 5.3 per cent had experienced bullying (as cited by C. Kim, 2009). A more recent national survey of 1,725 South Korean elementary and middle school students in 23 school districts conducted by Cheongso'nyeon Huimang Jae'dan (2009), a government organisation, also found that slightly over half (52.9%) reported that they could be friends with mixed-race children. However, 37.7% were uncertain, while 9.3% were unwilling. Of the students who were unwilling to befriend a mixed-race child, 32.5% responded 'because they have different thoughts and lifestyle from me'. Others responded that 'their appearance and skin color are different' (24.2%), 'I would worry about being excluded' (16.8%), and 'I would be embarrassed to be their friend' (15.5%).

In addition to peer victimisation and social exclusion, mixed-race children are more likely than South Korean children to have low academic performance in school. For instance, Jo's (2008) ethnographical research, which was conducted with 17 mixed-race children in Seoul, Incheon, Jeonju, and Jeonbuk, found that these children are likely to perform poorly in school due to language and cultural barriers, learning difficulties, and social exclusion. Despite these problems, educational opportunities and programs that can enhance academic performances and social skills of mixed-race children in South Korea have been severely limited because of inadequate amount of government support and programs (Oh, 2007).

North Korean defectors

Since the demarcation of the Korean peninsula in the 1950s, North Koreans who were displeased with North Korean politics, economy and the social system, or those whose very existence has been in jeopardy fled to South Korea and other countries (Yoon, 2001, p. 2). The number of North Koreans defectors in South Korea increased rapidly during 1990s. Economic deterioration and worsening living conditions in the North, coupled with much higher living standards in the South motivated North Koreans to undertake a risky journey to the South. Prior to 1993, about ten North Korean defectors entered South Korea, and in 1994, the number increased to 52. Within three years, about 85 North Koreans defected to South Korea. By 2000, that number rose to 312 (Yoon, 2001).

Many North Korean defectors have experienced hardships and struggles in South Korea due to cultural differences between the two Koreas. Jeon's (2000) study, which consisted of semi-structured interviews with 32 North Korean defectors, identified four categories of adjustment problems, which include suspicion, different ways of thinking, searching for new sets of values, and discrimination. Some scholars also documented that many North Koreans in South Korea had suffered from post-traumatic stress disorder depression, and anxiety (Chang, Haggard and Noland, 2006; Kim and Kim, 2006; Lee, Lee Chun, et al. 2001). For instance, Lee et al.'s (2001) study, which consisted of 170 North Korean defectors, found that virtually all of the respondents had suffered from trauma, mostly due to water shortage (93%) and no access to medical care (89%). Ninety per cent of the respondents suffered from anxiety, and 81% were chronically depressed.

Summary

In summary, the increasing rates of foreign migrant workers, foreign wives of South Korean men, mixed-race children, and North Korean defectors in South Korea necessitates the development of programs and policies that effectively address the issues of prejudice, discrimination, human rights violation, adjustment problems, and mental distress among these populations. Furthermore, social work professionals in South Korea (and other Asian countries) are confronted with following challenges: (1) To what extent is the sociocultural context in their native country influenced by globalisation of American culture? (2) How can social workers interpret human rights and human needs in the sociocultural contexts in their own countries? (3) In what way or to what extent should social workers adopt the westernised social work practices? (4) In what way can social workers infuse their traditional culture into social work practice? (5) What types of social work exchange should social workers advocate for with other countries (Yip, 2005)? Nevertheless, question remains: What are some current programs and policies in South Korea?

Discussion

According to the Ministry of Foreign Affairs and Trade (MOFAT), there are 63 listed international NGOs and civic groups, which provide counseling and services for foreigners in South Korea. One is the Bucheon Migrant Workers' Welfare Center, which provides array of counseling, medical support, and educational support activities for foreign migrant workers. Others include the Nepal-Kyung Hee Goodwill Hospital, a branch of Kyung Hee University Medical Center; UNICEF Korea; and United Help for International Children, which provides medical and educational services for children of immigrants, foreign migrant workers and 'international marriages'. Government bodies and organisations in South Korea have also pulled together financial support for immigrants and multicultural families in their adjustment and Korean language educational programs. Many schools with high number of immigrant and mixed-race children have after-school Korean language classes. In additional, several major Korean universities, such as Yonsei University and Ewha Woman's [Women's] University also have provided scholarships and tuition-waivers for foreigners.

Several primary and secondary schools have also added multicultural curricula. These multicultural curricula are designed to expose South Korean children to different cultures through lessons and activities. Kim's (2001) study, which examined young South Korean children's exposure to multiculturalism, found that such curricula enhanced children's awareness and understanding of different cultures and reduced biases and prejudicial attitudes toward non-South Koreans. The author concluded that South Korean children need more opportunities to understand different cultures.

Understanding cultural competency

In pluralist societies such as the US, the aspiration to provide culturally relevant care to diverse populations is a standing ethical commitment (Wendt and Gone, 2012), and there have been growing demands for cultural competency in social work, as a result (Allen-Meares, 2007;). Cultural competence has gained considerable popularity in recent years (Wendt and Gone, 2012) and is one of the foundations for social work educational and practice in the US, and the National Association of Social Workers (NASW) Code of Ethics, which sets the ethical standards for social work profession in the US, includes evidence of social workers' growing recognition of the importance of cultural competency (Allen-Meares, 2007). A variety of theories and models of cultural competence and similar constructs, such as 'cultural sensitivity', 'cultural relevance', and 'multicultural practices' have emerged (Boyle and Springer, 2001), along with educational efforts (Betancourt, 2004).

Definition and conceptualisation

As previously mentioned, social work practice cannot be effective unless the social worker is culturally competent (Logan, 2003), which requires an understanding of the culture of their clients, and recognition that there is a complex interplay of the individual and his or her environment. According to the NASW Code of Ethics, cultural competence is 'a process by which individuals and systems respond respectfully and effectively to people of all cultures, languages, classes, races, ethnicites, nationalities, religions, etc. in a manner that recogni ses, affirms, and values the worth of individuals, families, and communities and protects and preserve the dignity of each'. An earlier philosophical framework by Cross, Bazron, Dennis, and Isaacs (1989) conceptualises cultural competence as 'a set of congruent behaviors, attitudes, and policies that come together in a system, agency, or among professionals and enable that system, agency, or those professionals to work effectively in cross-cultural situations.' Culture implies 'the integrated pattern of human behavior, which includes thoughts, communications, actions, customs, beliefs, values, and institutions of a racial, ethnic, religious, or social group,' while competence connotes 'having the capacity to function effectively' (Cross et al., 1989, as cited by Kim, Kim, and Kelly, 2006).

Research on cultural competence has identified dimensions of knowledge, values, and skills that are necessary for cultural competence practice with any size system (Gutierrez and Alvarez, 2000). Within the context of knowledge, cultural competence entails acquiring knowledge about particular group; understanding salient concepts, such as identity, culture, and inequality/oppression; and understanding of one's own social location (e.g., dominant privilege). Values is defined as an appreciation of the importance of the clients' standpoint and openness to different and opposing perspectives. In terms of skills, the service provider must be able to communicate effectively across differences, take the role of a learner, to be comfortable in situations that are uncomfortable,and build alliances between and among groups (Gutierrez and Alvarez, 2000).

Social work education in South Korea

Social work and social welfare educational programs in South Korea began in 1947 at Ewha Womans University, which offered classes in casework. Social work education in South Korea had been heavily influenced by social work education in the United States (Chon, 2004). It was not until 1980s that social work became recognised as a profession in South Korea. In the 1990s, demands for social work education have been growing and as of 2009, there are approximately 439 social work programs in four-year universities (an increase from 150 programs in 2002), of which 12,000 students are enrolled in a social work program (Korea Association of Social Workers, 2010). There are also 80 schools that offer non-traditional social work programs, which include two to four year online universities. The number of social work programs in South Korea is expected to increase.

Most recently, a number of social work programs in South Korean universities are including courses on international and multicultural social work in their curricula. The underlying mission is to educate social work students on the importance of cultural competency and international social work, social development and partnerships and collaborative exchanges with other countries, and to enhance students' awareness and understanding of international organisations and NGO activities. The Graduate School of Social Welfare at Ewha Womans University currently offers a Master's level classes entitled 'International Social Work', 'International Cooperation for Regional Development', 'Cultural Diversity and Social Work Practice', and 'Regional Study and International Volunteerism'. The doctoral program offers an elective course entitled, 'Seminar in Populations with Special Needs' of which ethnically diverse populations is the main focus. Social work and social welfare programs in other universities have also offered graduate classes and seminars, such as 'New Family Welfare & Social Integration', and 'Welfare Services for the Migrant Workers' at Yonsei University.

Unfortunately, social work educational programs in South Korea have also not adequately prepared students to meet the challenges of multiculturalism and globalisation of the social work profession because students have limited opportunities to work with people of diverse cultural backgrounds. Moreover, preparing social work students for the Level One or Level Two Social Work Licensure Examination has been the primary focus, and social work programs for the most part offer coursework in social work theory, human behavior in the social environment, social welfare policy theories, social welfare law, social welfare practice, survey of social work, social welfare organisation, community organising and practicum.

Suggestions for incorporating cultural competency in South Korean social work

Nonetheless, considering the recent demographic changes in South Korea, together with newly emerging social issues, there is a major need for services, organisations, and policies that are culturally relevant and evidence-based. Within the last few decades, globalisation, which was driven by economic forces from developed countries such as the US, has greatly affected the social and cultural context in most Asian countries (Yip 2005), including South Korea. As previously mentioned, social work education and training in South Korea have been influenced by Western models, particularly the US, which is not surprising considering that large number of social work scholars in South Korea have received their educational training in US social work programs. It is imperative that social work students and professionals are prepared to provide culturally relevant services for diverse populations. Effective culturally competent social work practice requires an empowerment-focused approach, which addresses the issue of dominant privilege and oppression. In addition, there is a critical need for joint collaborations and cultural exchanges in research, practice and advocacy.

Empowerment

Social work professionals working with racially and ethnically diverse clients need to consider an empowerment approach. Empowerment was originally developed in the US during 1960s and 1970s for African Americans, which moves away from 'hand-me-down' and 'handout' approach. Instead, empowerment is strategically built around the notion of strengthening the clients (Kim, McLeod and Shantzis, 1992). It is defined as intrinsic motivation manifested in four cognitions: meaning (a fit between the requirement of role and one's personal beliefs and values), competence (self-efficacy), self-determination (choice in initiating and regulating action), and impact (ability to influence the outcome) (Spreitzer, 1996). Mary Keegan Eamon argues that empowerment is one of the most frequently used, yet ambiguously defined concepts in the social work profession. Although the definition of empowerment varies, it is an essential element in social work practice and services, which assists clients in asserting their rights and privileges. Empowerment has been applied in both micro- and macro-levels, and vulnerable populations, such as racial/ethnic minorities have been the main targets (Eamon, 2008). The empowerment approach is also designed to increase power on the individual, interpersonal, and political levels, and raises the issue of oppression.

It is critical that social work educators in South Korea train students with in-depth understanding of the empowerment approach. To our knowledge, however, the empowerment approach is rarely discussed in social work classes and is primarily taught as a concept or theory rather than practice. For instance, participatory decision-making process is one type of empowerment-based approach, which provides clients the opportunity to partake in decision-making. Regrettably, social work practitioners and service providers in South Korea typically employ the abovementioned 'handout' approach and decision-making is left at the hands of service providers, rather than the client. It is essential that social work students in South Korea understand the practical aspects of empowerment-based approach. Practica and internships are integral parts of social work education in South Korea, as they are in the US. One possibly effective strategy is for instructors to train students on how to work collaboratively with their clients in accessing needed resources, which can assist clients in attaining self-determination.

Dominant privilege and oppression

The empowerment-based social work practice also goes hand-in-hand with the issue of dominant privilege. In recent years, Eurocentric practice and White privilege have been addressed in social work and counseling professions in the US (Spanierman and Poteat, 2005). White privilege refers to a system of unearned benefits and opportunities simply because of dominant status (Donnelly et al., 2005). Privilege is not recognised by those who benefit (Ancis and Szymanski, 2001), as it has been perceived as natural and maintained through process of denial and belief in meritocracy (Ancis and Szymanski, 2001). Systems of oppression are characterised by dominant-subordinate relationships in which the dominant members not only have greater social power but also set the norm (Goodman, 2001).

Social work professionals in South Korea need to be aware of their own dominant status. In the US, Janet Helms developed the White Identity Development Model as a process of moving towards a non-racist white identity and the abandonment of racism. She argued that as the individual changes from racist to non-racist, he or she recognises racism and become conscious of his or her identity. The individual then engages in development tasks necessary for a healthy racial/ethnic identity, which involves awareness of his or her benefits that stem from institutional and cultural racism (Evans, Forney and Guido-DiBrito, 1998). Social work students in South Korea need to also understand that their privilege as a dominant member of society can contribute to oppression of minorities. It is also imperative that social work programs in South Korea address the issue of dominant privilege and thereby raise students' awareness of their privileged status and how this can invariably affect their practices.

We recommend South Korean social work educators foster awareness of dominant privilege and oppression in the classroom in ways that transcend the traditional, didactical approach. South Korean social work educators need to create an atmosphere that facilitates students' understanding of dominant privilege and oppression. Educators must engage their students in activities that address dominant privilege and oppression through an experiential or hands-on approach. Activities should contain an educational component that presents new information or perspectives to students, as well as a psychological component designed to promote student's awareness of their attitude (Mims, 2007) and initiate dialogue. Students also need to be informed that the underlying premise of such activities is to be aware of their privilege and how that can affect their practice.

Joint collaborations

To incorporate cultural competency effectively in social work practices, exchanges of social work practices is also important. Considering the similar cultural values among many Asian countries, social work exchanges should not be confined to western countries and Asian countries, rather than among Asian countries (Yip, 2005). Most recently, several member countries of the Asia and Pacific Association for Social Work Education (APASWE) including Australia, Japan, New Zealand, South Korea, and Singapore have established joint collaborative projects with developing countries, such as Cambodia and Bangladesh. Through the Korea Project, Ewha Womans University has dispatched social work educators, professionals, and student volunteers to the Royal University of Phnom Pehn in Cambodia and Grameen Bank and Basdara Primary School in Bangladesh to assist these countries in developing social work education through consultation and exchange of ideas.

Joint collaboration and partnerships between APASWE member countries and Third World countries work in two ways. First, mutual understanding between and among Asia-Pacific countries has been enhanced through joint collaborative efforts. Second, these efforts have fostered a sense of community and solidarity among the citizens of the Asia-Pacific regions. Recognising the importance of social work education, both APASWE and the recipient countries have benefited mutually through exchange of ideas. Social work educators, professionals and students in South Korea have gained an understanding of the importance of culturally competent social work practice. Cultural competency can be best incorporated in social work education through joint collaboration and partnerships. Collaboration between social workers and organisations that offer services for diverse populations is essential. In recent years, social work programs in South Korea have provided these opportunities for students by actively forging collaborative ties with international organisations and civic groups that are dedicated to advocate on behalf of immigrants and minority populations. We also recommend social work programs to take one step further by establishing collaborative efforts with ethnic and immigrant communities. Social workers can work together with community representatives in determining programs and services that could effectively meet the individual and collective needs of diverse populations.

Social work educators and professionals can also actively recruit qualified minorities in social work educational programs (e.g., through funding) so that they can be an active part of providing needed social services to their communities in South Korea. To our understanding, South Korean social work programs have not established any sort of joint collaborations and partnership with ethnic and immigrant communities.

Conclusion

Twenty years ago, the idea of seeing a factory worker from Bangladesh walking in the streets of Seoul or a young Vietnamese woman living in rural areas were uncommon in South Korea. Twenty years ago, mixed-race children were virtually invisible in schools, and international marriages were met with glares. Today, South Korea has become a host to two million immigrants, refugees, and minorities. The key question in South Korea today is not whether it will become a land of immigration, but rather what kind of immigration country it will become (Lim, 2002). Incorporating cultural competence in social work education and practice is the first necessary step in the development of a healthy, multicultural society.

REFERENCES

Allen-Meares, P. (2007). Cultural competence: an ethical requirement. *Journal of Ethnic and Cultural Diversity in Social Work*, 16(3–4), 83–92.

Alvarez, A.R. (2000). Educating students for multicultural community practice. *Journal of Community Practice*, 7(1), 39–56.

Amnesty International (2008). Republic of Korea (South Korea): migrant workers are also human beings. Retrieved 17 April 2013 from lib.ohchr.org/HRBodies/UPR/Documents/Session2/KR/AI_KOR_UPR_S2_2008anx_Migrantworkersarealsohumanbeings.pdf.

Ancis, J.R. & Szymanski, D.M. (2001). Awareness of white privilege among white counseling trainees. *The Counseling Psychologist*, 29(4), 548–69.

Betancourt, J.R. (2004). Cultural competence: marginal or mainstream movement? *New England Journal of Medicine*, 351(10), 953.

Boyle, D.P. & Springer, A. (2001). Toward a cultural competence measure for social work with specific populations. *Journal of Ethnic & Cultural Diversity in Social Work*, 9(3), 53.

Cha, O.S. (2008, May). Multicultural social integration with a focus on victimised married migrant women. Paper presented at the Globalization and Households in East Asia Conference, Seoul, Republic of Korea.

Chang, Y., Haggard, S. & Noland, M. (2006). North Korean refugees in China: evidence from a survey. In S. Haggard & M. Noland (Eds). *The North Korean refugee crisis: human rights and international response* (pp. 14–33). Washington: U.S. Committee for Human Rights in North Korea.

Cheongso'nyeon Huimang Jae'dan (2009). Cheongso'nyeon Huimang Jae'dan. Retrieved 17 April 2013 from www.safeschool.or.kr.

Cho. H. & Kim, E.M. (2008). Global Seoul: social communication and development of foreign communities in Seoul. In Ewha Womans University (Ed.), *Proceedings of globalization and households in East Asia: policy implications for Korea* (pp. 63–68). Seoul: Ewha Womans University.

Chon, S.Y. (2004). A study of the relationship among the social work educations: values and advocacy. Masters thesis. Seoul Women's University, Seoul, Republic of Korea.

Chun, S.J. (2008). Multicultural education as a social integration mechanism. In Ewha Womans University (Ed.), *Proceedings of globalization and households in East Asia: policy implications for Korea* (pp. 95–107). Seoul: Ewha Womans University.

Cross, T.L. (1989). *Towards a culturally competent system of care.* Washington, DC: CASSP Technical Assistance Center, Georgetown University Child Development Center.

Donnelly, D.A., Cook. K.J., Van Ausdale. D. & Foley. L. (2005). White privilege, color blindness, and services to battered women. *Violence Against Women*, 11(1), 6–37.

Eamon, M.K. (2008). *Empowerment and cognitive-behavioral methods: empowering vulnerable populations* (p. 28). Chicago: Lyceum Books, Inc.

Evans, N.J., Forney, D.S. & Guido-DiBrito, F. (1998). Racial and ethnic identity development. In N.J. Evans, D.S. Foney & F. Guido-DiBrito (Eds). *Student development in college* (pp. 76–77). San Francisco: Jossey-Bass.

Goodman, D. (2001). *Promoting diversity and social justice: educating people from privileged groups* (pp. 1–233). Thousand Oaks: Sage.

Hong, J., Kim, Y., Lee, N. & Ha, J. Hubinette, T. (2005). Comforting an orphaned nation. Stockholm: Stockholm University Department of Oriental Languages.

Hurh, W.M. (1972). Marginal children of war: an exploratory study of American-Korean children. *International Journal of Sociology of the Family*, 2(3), 10–20.

Jeon, W.T. (2000). Issues and problems of adaptation of North Korean defectors to South Korean society: an in-depth interview study with 32 defectors. *Yonsei Medical Journal*, 41(3), 362–71.

Jo, H.Y(2008). Academic performance of migrants' children in Korea. In Ewha Womans University (Ed.), *Proceeding of globalization and households in East Asia: policy implications for Korea*. Seoul: Ewha Womans University.

Kim, C. (2009). Social challenges of multicultural society in Korea: focusing on directions of the multicultural education for Kosian. Masters thesis. Kyung Hee University, Seoul, Republic of Korea.

Kim, H.T. (2001). Young Korean children's social interactions in a multicultural society. *Journal of Child Educare Research*, 7(1), 1–18.

Kim. I.J., Kim. L.I. & Kelly. J.G. (2006). Developing cultural competence in working with Korean immigrant families. *Journal of Community Psychology*, 34(2), 149–65.

Kim, J.H. & Kim, T. (2006). Economic assimilation of North Korean refugees in South Korea: survey evidence (Paper No. 06–19). KDI School of Pub Policy & Management. Retrieved 22 April 2013 from ssrn.com/abstract=960640.

Kim, S., McLeod, J.H. & Shantizis, C. (1992). Cultural competence for evaluators working with Asian-American communities: Some practical considerations. In M. Orlandi (Ed.), *Cultural competence for evaluators: a guide for alcohol and other drug abuse prevention practitioners working with ethnic—racial communities* (pp. 203–60). Maryland, MD: U.S. Department of Health and Human Services.

Kim, T.J. (2008, April 29). Misunderstanding causes conflicts in interracial marriages. *The Korea Times*. Retrieved 17 April 2013 from www.koreatimes.co.kr/www/news/special/2008/04/242_23327.html.

Korea Association of Social Workers. (2010). Korea Association of Social Workers. Retrieved 17 April 2013 from www.welfare.net.

Lee. H.K. (2008). International marriage and the state in South Korea: Focusing on governmental policy. *Citizenship Studies,* 12(1), 107–23.

Lee. Y., Lee. M.K., Chun. K.H., Lee. Y.K. & Yoon. S.J. (2001). Trauma experience of North Korean refugees in China. *American Journal of Preventive Medicine,* 20(3), 225–29.

Lim, T.C. (2002). The changing face of South Korea: the emergence of Korea as a land of immigration. *The Korea Society Quarterly,* Summer/Fall, 16–21.

Logan, S.L. (2003). Issues in multiculturalism: multicultural practice, and cultural diversity and competence. *Social Work Encyclopedia Supplement.* Washington: NASW Press.

Mims, G.A. (2007). Privilege and oppression: two sides of the same coin. Paper presented at the Great Plains conference on teaching psychology, Univerity of South Dakota, USA.

Ministry of Justice (2011). *KIS STATIS 2011*. Seoul: Korea Immigration Services.

Min, S.J. (2004, April 26). Discrimination plagues migrant children. *JoongAng Daily.* Retrieved 17 April 2013 from koreajoongangdaily.joinsmsn.com/news/article/article.aspx?aid=2405349.

Moon, K.H.S. (2000). Strangers in the midst of globalization: migrant workers and Korean nationalism. In S. Kim (Ed.), *Korea's globalization* (pp. 147–69). Cambridge: Cambridge University Press.

Oh, S.B. (2007). A study of the instance of opportunities of education and its alternative policy for ethnic minorities' children born in intermarriage homes. *Journal of Anthropological Studies*, 2, 1–15.

Seol, D.H., & Skrentny, J. (2004). South Korea: importing undocumented workers. In Cornelius, W.A., Tsuda, T., Martin, P.L., & Hollifield, J.F. (Eds). *Controlling immigration: a global perspective* (pp. 481–513). Stanford, CA: Stanford University Press.

Shin. J.H., Doh. H. S., Hong. J.S. & Kim. J.S. (2012). Pathways from non-Korean mothers' cultural adaptation, marital conflict, and parenting behavior to bi-ethnic children's school adjustment in South Korea. *Children and Youth Services Review*, 34(5), 914–23.

Shin, S.I. (2004). Social welfare intervention for low-income foreign families. *The Journal of Social Welfare*, 27, 113–39.

Spanierman. L.B., & Poteat. V.P. (2005). Moving beyond complacency to commitment: multicultural research in counseling psychology. *Counseling Psychologist*, 33(4), 513–23.

Spreitzer, G.M. (1996). Social structural characteristics of psychological empowerment. *Academy of Management Journal*, 39(2), 483–504.

United Nations Population Fund. (2007). State of world population 2006. New York: United Nations.

Wendt. D.C., & Gone. J.P. (2012). Rethinking cultural competence: insights from indigenous community treatment settings. *Transcultural Psychiatry*, 49(2), 206–22.

Yang, C.H., Kim, Y.J., Sohn, S.Y., Yang, S.H., Shin, B.K., & Cho, J.H. (2003). A study on the human rights and welfare of foreign wives in the Gwangju and Jeonnam area. *Social Welfare Policy*, 16, 127–49.

Yip. K.S. (2005). A dynamic Asian response to globalization in cross-cultural social work. *International Social Work*, 48(5), 593–608.

Yoon, I. (2001). North Korean diaspora. *Development and Society*, 30(1), 1–26.

2

Respecting knowledge: circular movement in teacher/learner roles to advancing Indigenous social work education and practice

Lorraine Muller and Susan Gair

Euro-centric curricula is identified in the literature as contributing to Aboriginal and Torres Strait Islander students' lack of engagement with tertiary education. We—a non-Indigenous social work educator and an Indigenous PhD student—describe our quest towards curricula more respectful and inclusive of Australian Indigenous knowledges rather than solely reflective of colonialist constructions. The chapter begins with the second author revealing how she took on the role of learner under guidance from Indigenous community members, including the first author, her then PhD student. The first author details her roles as student, teacher researcher and beyond. She identifies the absence of a grounded theory of Indigenous practice in her work towards translation of oral Indigenous knowledge into an academic theory that can inform social work. We model one way for Indigenous and non-Indigenous educators (and practitioners) to work in partnership to uphold respect for Indigenous knowledges in social work.

教師/學生的角色輪換對本土居民社會工作教育和實踐的促進作用

各種文獻显示，歐洲為中心的課程使得托雷斯海峽島民學生和土著人民從高等教育畢業的的人數寥寥無幾。我們（一個本土社會工作教育者和一個本土博士生）認為，我們的課程旨在探索該如何尊重和囊括澳大利亞本土知識，而不是單純地探尋殖民風格的建築。文章的開始，第二作者闡述了她如何在本土社區成員的指導下進行的學習，以及第一作者為學習本土文化而由教師的角色轉變為第二作者的學生的經歷。她在研究中發現，口口相傳的本土知識轉化為學術理論的時候，會因為翻譯問題有所缺失。所以，我們建立了一個模型，幫助本土和非本土教育者（和實踐者）携手在社會工作實踐中保持尊重本土知識。

タイトル：知識の尊重：先住民のソーシャルワーク教育と実践を進めることへの教師/学習者の役割の循環

著者：ロレーヌ・ミュラー、スーザン·ゲール

高等教育を卒業する数少ない先住民とトレス海峡島民学生が受けた西欧中心のカリキュラムの貢献は各種の文献に示されている。先住民およびトレス海峡諸島の学生に向けた我々−非先住民のソーシャルワーク教育者と先住民である博士課程の学生は単なる植民地時代の遺風を反映したカリキュラムではなく、オーストラリア先住民に根付いている知識をより尊重しかつ包括的に組み込んだカリキュラム構築に向けた探求を述べる。この章では、第二著者によって、先住民コミュニティのメンバーたち(彼女の博士課程学生であり本稿の第一著者を含む)の指導下で、学習者としての役割をどのように果たしているかを明らかにすることから始める。第一著者は、学生としての役割、教師、研究者その他の役割を詳細に述べる。第一著者は、口述で伝えられてきた先住民たちに根付いた先住民知識をソーシャルワークの学術理論の中に翻訳するという彼女の研究を通じ、先住民に根付いた実践にグラウンデッド・セオリーが不在であることを明らかにする。先住民族と非先住民族の教育者(そして実践者)が、ソーシャルワークにおける先住民族に根付いた知識を尊重し、協力関係を構築する一つのモデルを提示する。

앎의 존중: 사회복지 교육과 실천 토착화를 위한 교육자/피교육자의 순환적 활동

본 장은 유럽 중심 교과과정에 실망하면서 고등교육을 받고 졸업한 Torres Strait 섬의 토착민 학생에 관한 이야기이다. 백인 교육자와 토착민 박사과정학생으로 모인 우리들은 식민지적 발상에서 벗어나 호주 토착민의 지식을 좀 더 존중하고 받아들여 교과과정에 반영하고자 하였다. 본 장은 공동저자가 주 저자였던 박사과정학생과 지역 토착민에게서 배워나가는 과정을 묘사하고 있다. 주 저자는 학생이면서 선생이었고 조사연구자였으며 토착민에 대한 실무관련 근거이론이 전무하다는 것을 파악하고 구두로 알게 된 고유한 지식을 이론화하여 사회복지에 접목시키게 하였다. 우리는 사회복지에서 토착민이거나 백인이거나를 불문하고 파트너쉽을 통해 토착민 지식을 존중하는 하나의 모델을 제시하였다.

INTRODUCTION

> Stories go in circles ... It helps if you listen in circles because there are stories inside and between stories ... finding your way through them is as easy and as hard as finding your way home. Part of finding is getting lost, and when you are lost you start to open up and listen. (Tafoya, 1995, p. 12)

> There is an eastern saying 'The teacher and the taught together create the teaching'. (Tolle, 2000, p. 85)

A growing body of literature highlights the inadequacy of Euro-centric curricula in higher education and there have been ongoing calls for foundational learning from an Indigenous worldview (Bessarab, 2012; Hart, 2008; Nash, Munford & Donaghue, 2005; Nakata, 2007; Walter, Taylor, & Habibis, 2012). For Indigenous Australian social work students, a colonial terrain must be navigated in order to graduate with skills and knowledge for social work practice (Green, Bennett, Collins, Gowans, Hennessey, & Smith, 2012). For non-Indigenous students, effective ways of working with Indigenous Australians are a necessity, while social work educators must teach all students how to uphold human rights and social justice (Boshier, 2006; Clark, 2000, Sinclair, 2004). In this chapter we use a simple, narrative format to tell our interwoven stories of circular teaching and learning, in order to promote Indigenous knowledges in social work education and support the advancement of Indigenous social work.

SUSAN—SOCIAL WORK EDUCATOR

James Cook University offers social work programs via the Cairns, Townsville and Mackay campuses and by distance education. The Cairns campus is located on the traditional lands of Gimuy Walabara Yidinji and Yirrigandji peoples; the Townsville campus is located within Wulgurukaba, Bindal and Biri country, and in Mackay the traditional owners include the Yuibera people. This geographical catchment, from where the university draws the majority of its students and, where the majority of graduates find employment, has an Indigenous population higher than the national average.

I began tutoring at James Cook University in 1991 after completing my social work degree as a mature age student. I secured a full time academic position in 1997 after completing postgraduate studies. Relating to Tafoya's (1995) words above, by 1999 I felt *lost*. There were at least two glaring deficits in my teaching. The first was that the content of subjects I taught was minimally useful to Indigenous students. Indeed, it probably contributed to them dropping out. The recommended readings and texts disrespectfully constructed Indigenous peoples within a white worldview and assumed them only to be 'the client'. The second deficit followed on from the first; my teaching did not offer frameworks for Indigenous students to build their practice skills and knowledge. I knew I needed to transform my teaching and students' learning.

TRANSFORMING CURRICULA—A LEGITIMATE ROLE FOR A WHITE WOMAN?

The legitimacy of non-Indigenous academics teaching about historical and contemporary Indigenous issues is contested (Bennett, Green, Gilbert & Besserab, 2012; de Ishtar, 2004; Gair, Thomson & Miles, 2005). Nevertheless, what I sought to do, in the absence of any Indigenous academic staff, was to improve my teaching and enhancing students' learning with content from an Indigenous perspective (Sonn, Bishop & Humphries, 2000). Additionally, I needed to develop my knowledge and skills to effectively facilitate all students' learning (Akerlind, 2007; Whitehead, 2008).

In 2001 I received funding for an action research project to increase Indigenous content in our curriculum. We undertook the project guided by Aboriginal consultant, Mrs Dorothy Savage. We had no Indigenous academic staff at that time. Together we planned, implemented and evaluated the changes (Gair, Thomson & Miles, 2005). We did not seek to focus on Indigenous people's stereotypical deficits (Cavanagh & Maskell, 2005), but rather to take a much broader view of listening, learning, respect and action for change. Despite positive outcomes from that project, further gaps in our curriculum were evident.

Lather (1998, p. 492) recommended a shift from 'one who knows' to a praxis of 'not being so sure'. In the past I had taught about Indigenous disadvantage in Australian society, but I was much less confident about my understanding, skills, knowledge, teaching ability, and legitimacy around preparing Indigenous students and non-Indigenous students for effective, respectful work with Indigenous Australians. At that time we undertook research that revealed our Indigenous student numbers had *decreased* by 60% over the previous decade (Gair, Thomson & Savage, 2005). Action was needed to arrest this trend. I asked my then Honours student (Lorraine) to help me connect with the Indigenous community so I could learn more about local Indigenous organisations, and how they supported their community.

From teacher to learner

In 2003 I negotiated to spend three months working as a volunteer—a learner—at an Aboriginal, traditional owner organisation in the North Queensland community where Lorraine lived. Lorraine acted as teacher and intermediary. Staff of the organisation and community members supported and advanced my learning. I accompanied the Executive Officer in the day-to-day business of this highly respected organisation, and when opportunities arose, I asked elders and community members about how to improve my teaching and increase Indigenous student numbers.

We talked about how I might change subject content so that it made sense to Indigenous students and would facilitate non-Indigenous students' learning about working respectfully with Indigenous colleagues and community members. These wise guides identified the lack of Indigenous educators and support staff as highly problematic. They suggested racism must be confronted in the classroom and they shared their experiences of racism from white professionals. They identified that non-Indigenous students needed to learn how to listen deeply, and that students needed detailed information about native title, human rights and Australia's hidden history. At this time I also pondered Dominelli's (2002) concept of 'dumping' —where non-Indigenous people expected and even demanded that Indigenous people teach them what they needed to know. While this may be legitimate criticism of my actions in seeking help from the community, I believe I respectfully sought learning through negotiation and by slowly building relationships. I also spent time with women in the community and I was in awe of their incredible strength in the face of huge adversity.

Progress in advancing Indigenous social work education and practice?

Reflecting on our social work curricula after returning to the university, I realised there was limited content on Indigenous organisations, Indigenous leadership, conflict resolution, theories, values, history, activism, and healing processes, to name but a few significant omissions. Further, almost all of the processes I had observed whilst in the community were collective and community-driven. Yet group work and community development in our curriculum were taught as narrowly defined modes of practice based on non-Indigenous models. Equally, I recognised a lack of content on working differently with men and women.

By 2005 I had incorporated many Indigenous authors into the subjects I taught including interpersonal skills, organisational practice, research methods, and working across cultures. In 2008, after robust debate in my Department, a new subject was developed—*Aboriginal and Torres Strait Islander skills and frameworks for practice*. This subject was developed through close collaboration with our Indigenous Advisory Group members, our Indigenous student support staff, and my new PhD student, Lorraine. The name of the subject, its content, structure, key concepts, learning outcomes, recommended Readings, and Study Guide were all developed under the direction of these advisors. In 2013 almost all of the teaching undertaken in that subject is by Aboriginal and Torres Strait Islander guest speakers, and our Indigenous Advisory Group continues to graciously offer valuable guidance.

Yet in 2013, Indigenous knowledges still do not seem to be highly regarded. At James Cook University (JCU) we have no permanent Indigenous social work academic staff. The appalling lack of Indigenous social work academic staff is a national issue and it has been reported that there are only 'four identified teaching and learning Aboriginal and Torres Strait Islander academics' working in Schools of Social Work in Australia (Bennett et al ., 2012, p. 214). Equally, a recent study undertaken by our Department revealed that Indigenous students experienced racism in classrooms and on field placement, and paradoxically, their cultural knowledge was welcomed yet devalued (Zuchowski et al., 2012). That study provides evidence of the need for ongoing listening, learning and action.

Revolving roles

Over time, my relationship with Lorraine was informed by new understandings of teaching and learning; this being a direct result of my knowledgeable community teachers and Lorraine's wise counsel. While I had a good working relationship with my other students, my relationship with Lorraine was continually evolving, revolving and reciprocal in these ways:

Teacher/student/learner—I had learned an immeasurable amount from Lorraine and the community. Equally, she was a university student and I was an educator.

Supervisor/supervisee—I was persistent in requesting Lorraine's next written drafts until the final document was submitted for examination and we celebrated the awarding of her PhD. We had embraced decolonisation theory for her PhD research and for our curriculum. Lorraine is an ongoing supervisor/mentor to me on Indigenous matters, and we have remained in contact as Lorraine continues research that shifts the lens onto non-Indigenous culture.

Colleagues—We have co-taught in social work subjects, and co-presented at national and international conferences. Lorraine and I also co-facilitated three women's writing groups between 2005–2007 at the request of a small group of women from the community.

Friends—and our families became friends.

Learning *cycles* and *circles*

Seminal literature identifies learning *cycles* including action learning, experiential learning, action research cycles, and ongoing deep reflection for lifelong transformative learning (Heron, 1996; Kolb, 1984; Schon, 1983). Yet, it seemed to me, reflective learning cycles could lead to insular and individualistic learning that may pay lip service to what might be learned from Indigenous colleagues, students and the community if they were respected as partners in learning (Bulman & Hayes, 2008; Noble & Henderson, 2008). Supporting this notion, Fullan (1993) identified that there can be a ceiling effect on how much we can learn from our own personal reflections.

Overall, my western propositional logic about how to teach, who can teach, who needs to learn, what needs to be taught, and what are the connections between lessons, has hindered the development of my professional practice as a social work educator (Heron, 1996). I felt connected to the words of Nias (cited in Butler, 1992, p. 235) that a journey of personal growth can take a monumental effort but will change one's professional practice. I have come to see teaching and learning in ways that were outside my consciousness, and that seem more empathic, circular, respectful, reciprocal and collective, and less dogmatic, individual, closed and disconnected, than was evident to me from the reflective learning literature (Romer, 2003). Elsewhere in the literature, learning in *circles* has been identified as respectful, shared, rotating or simultaneous teaching and learning processes. This process seemed more representative of my learning journey (Hart, 2008; Graveline, 1998; Bulman & Hayes 2008; Wilson, 2004).

RECOMMENDATIONS

My key recommendations for non-Indigenous educators and practitioners are: to ask for help to learn; and to be committed to becoming a wiser educator, researcher, supervisor, and/or social work practitioner for the benefit of Indigenous peoples. In words of Dr Karen Martin: offer respect, listen and learn (Martin, 2008), and 'lose the expert' role (Petersen, 2006, p. 9). Clark (2000) stated that a learner stance offers respect, and recognises the uniqueness of each individual. This may be considered different from dumping where Indigenous peoples are expected to educate others. Recognise and value the potential fluidity in teacher/learner roles and embrace opportunities to learn from (but not exploit) Indigenous colleagues, practitioners, students (who may be experienced practitioners) and clients. Be totally committed to the inclusion of Indigenous knowledges, worldviews and ways of working. Facilitate opportunities for increased inclusion of Indigenous staff, students, colleagues, consultants and clients for enriched social work programs, effective social work practice, and the advancement of Indigenous peoples

LORRAINE—CIRCULAR LEARNING

> It is not alpha and omega, beginning and end, but circular and reformative. (Fletcher, 2007, cited in Muller, 2010)

THE SWIRL OF GANMA

I respectfully draw on the Aboriginal concept of *Ganma* to explain the mutual and circulatory learning process of circular learning. *Ganma*, 'where a river of water from the sea (western knowledge) and a river of water from the land (Indigenous knowledge) engulf each other, flowing together and becoming one' (Watson & Chambers, 1989 cited in Hughes, 2000, p. 6). The entities of salt water and fresh water maintain their identities; one does not dominate or subsume the other and only in a certain state, for a short period, are the two waters as one. There are multiple layers of meaning available for interpretation in Ganma, as is common in Indigenous teaching, depending on the level of understanding a person has achieved at the time (Sveiby & Skuthorpe, 2006). Ganma is used by Hughes (non-Indigenous) when trying to articulate Indigenous methodologies and reflect on the unique reconciliation where a Western-trained intellectual seeks to learn from, not 'about', the 'oldest continuing intellectual tradition in the world' (2000, p. 2).

When saltwater meets freshwater, small swirls can form—carrying a hint that it could result in a whirlpool. Reflecting on the relationship of learning Sue introduced earlier, knowledge transfer can be challenging. Mutual respect steered us from conflict that could have threatened the circle of learning.

A swirl of Ganma developed as Sue and I became both teacher and learner in a two-way knowledge transfer. Sue's knowledge enabled me to understand more of the reality of non-Indigenous Australians. In turn, I was able to foster greater understanding for her on Indigenous ways of seeing. We each filled the role of cultural consultant for the other, sharing our understanding of our respective cultures and their differences, while maintaining separate identities.

Sue remained 'white' without forgoing her identity; like Ganma the fresh water flowing from the land does not make the sea water free from salt and whereas salt water may infiltrate the fresh water to a point, the water flowing from the land remains fresh. Sue is now a more knowledgeable and empathic 'white' academic. Sue did not enter into the identity crisis, the 'wannabe phenomenon' where non-Indigenous allies working with Indigenous people take on, or 'appropriate' Indigenous cultural discourse and mannerisms (Kincheloe & Steinberg, 2008, p. 141).

Circles—mutual learning

When people from disparate cultures seek to learn from each other, the circular style of working, similar in many Indigenous peoples' ways, is a natural progression (Wilson, 2004, p. 290). Circles are an integral way of working because when people are sitting in a circle it creates a sense of equality, where no one is higher or more important, no one has their back to another, and people gathered in a circle can evoke a greater sense of connectedness.

To explain how this circular movement of teaching and learning began, I use my way of seeing and my way of saying. Sue and I are very different people; our life experiences reflect dissimilar foundational 'ways of being' (ontology), 'ways of knowing' (epistemology) and 'ways of doing' (methodology) (Martin, 2008, p. 72). Although we have some similarities in our field of study, gender and grandmotherhood, we see things differently with different styles of expressing what we understand; that is, we have different ways of seeing, and ways of saying. Storying is a useful way to incorporate past events and it allows humour to lighten up a serious piece of learning. Telling our two different accounts of the same story helps demonstrate some of the complexities that we each experienced. Naturally, it is not appropriate to speak for another person so in this chapter we each share our 'way of seeing' the same story.

Collision of knowledges

When I finally got to university in my late thirties, I realised how different I was from the mainstream. My way of looking at the world did not fit the conventional social script. I was confronted by a worldview and cultural truths that clashed with my understanding of the world. When literature used the term 'we' I realised that generally it meant 'white/dominant class'; it did not include me. Colonialist interpretation of history and reality challenged me. I struggle to understand how the concept of patriarchy can be a 'truth' that is illuminated by feminist theory. I know patriarchy as a pestilent concept introduced with colonisation (Robertson, 2000). Conventional academic theories and models are based on foreign cultural assumptions and values. It was hard work to translate this knowledge to a form that was useful for me and my 'way of knowing'. It was clear to me that I was not 'white'.

The Aboriginal and Torres Strait Islander Women's Taskforce on Violence Report became my inspiration and treasured textbook because it contained a historical and theoretical base I could understand (Robertson, 2000). Indigenous writers discussed relatedness and spirituality that resonated within me (Atkinson, 2002; Martin, 2003; McLennan & Khavarpour, 2004).

After completing undergraduate studies, I remained unfulfilled. While it was recognised that Indigenous Australians have different ways of working, their ways of working remained relegated to that of the 'other' in welfare texts. I was conscious of the void in literature on theories that relate to the context, values, history and spirituality of Indigenous Social Health/Welfare practice.

Documenting knowledge

I am sure I was a challenging student, because I was confident in my ways of seeing the world. Trying to share this way of seeing with Sue, who in turn tried to guide me in Western academic 'ways of doing' increased the momentum of our two-way teaching and learning relationship. During my Honours research, Sue (supervisor) and

I gained some understanding of each other's 'way of seeing', while she guided me in the art of research and thesis writing. The divergence in our understanding of 'normal' cultural processes meant that I frequently had to explain my understanding and Sue had to explain hers. I was challenged to explain the what-why-how of the research, while Sue equally was obliged to explain the expectations and functionality of the academy. I was familiar and comfortable with this respectful circular sharing of knowledge. These discussions subsequently contributed to the focus of my first doctoral research; documenting Indigenous Australian Social-Health theory.

My first PhD research project found me as my colleagues and I discussed how the meta theory informing the practice of Indigenous social-health workers was absent from our course; it was an *oral theory* and unavailable to us as legitimate knowledge in the Western academy. Students and workers in the Indigenous health/welfare sector confirmed that the absence of accessible Indigenous theory was an enormous barrier to educational participation. We concluded that if our theory and praxis were documented, it could be available for Indigenous students in a written format. The task of translating the meta theory that informs Indigenous workers in the social, emotional and physical helping professions became my doctoral research. The collective origins of the research topic meant that the topic and research question remained unchanged throughout the project.

Translating an oral theory into an academic format suitable for use in the Western academy is no easy task and I had to demonstrate that I had the necessary respect and integrity to undertake it. Not only did I need to draw on the wisdom and knowledge of people who shared their knowledge with me, I needed to draw on the knowledge and wisdom of non-Indigenous people with whom I had strong connections.

I sought community approval for my choice of supervisors who were chosen for their specific wisdom, guidance, integrity and openness at the very beginning of the research project. The guidance provided by my second supervisor is valuable to me, but part of a different story that is hers to tell.

Reciprocating roles

I was surprised when Sue asked me to help find an Indigenous organisation where she could learn from Indigenous people. It was evident Sue was committed to building curriculum more inclusive of Indigenous knowledges even though Sue did not know what constituted that knowledge. I am sure when Sue asked me to help she did not realise what it entailed for me.

When I approached our local Aboriginal Corporation with the proposal of Sue's volunteering I was acting as a referee to her suitability. I gave assurance that she was no 'new ager' seeking to claim knowledge, but an accomplished academic, with a clear spirit, respectfully seeking an opportunity to learn. I knew that I would be accountable if she had failed. It was my responsibility to ensure Sue's foundational training and mentoring; that she knew basic protocols. (Fortunately, Sue was a good student, attentive, observant and respectful). Sue's academic qualifications were discussed briefly, but her learning goals and intentions were discussed in some detail, as were possible mutual benefits to be gained.

Functioning as teacher for Sue slowed my Honours progress but this delay was mitigated by what I learned from teaching. To be honest, I did baulk at the prospect for I suspected that, while 'Dr Susan Gair' was a respected academic, she did not know how little she knew.

At this point I had an obvious role change; I became the teacher/mentor while Sue became student. Foregoing the expert role, 'Dr Susan Gair', became 'Sue the student'. When non-Indigenous professionals are engaging with Indigenous people, they need to embrace reciprocal, two-way learning opportunities (Nasir, 2008). Conceptualising a white mentor (or teacher) as 'the 'knight in shining armour coming to the rescue', assuming that 'the purported rescue is needed and wanted and that the rescuer knows what to do and how to do it', Nasir suggests that 'to be effective the knight may need to get off his horse often—take off his armour and be prepared to learn from those he is "rescuing'" (2008, p. 9).

Educating Sue became a collective concern and her willingness to learn with humility gained her the respect of her different teachers. I learned a great deal about my own 'way of knowing' and 'way of being' from the process of teaching Sue. I had to unpick what I knew and examine in minute detail things I previously had never needed to question. At times, I acted as a translator between Sue and her teachers.

Sue's culture stems from being one of the beneficiaries of colonisation and for me it was difficult to understand. 'From the inside, a culture is "felt" as normative, not deviant. It is European culture which is different for an Aboriginal person' (Langton, 2003, p. 121). Colonisation, and its agent racism, is not always overt but is evident in many ways (Paradies, 2007). Just as it is difficult for a person who has not experienced racism to comprehend its effects, it was difficult for me to understand life without its influence.

Decolonisation, undoing the process of colonisation, is the framework used in my PhD research that enabled a safe space for our discussions. Poka Laenui (2007) explained the five stages of colonisation that he and Virgilio Enriques identified as Denial and withdrawal; Destruction/eradication; Denigration/belittlement/insult; Surface accommodation/tokenism; and Transformation/exploitation. Laenui (2007) further proposed five stages of decolonisation: Rediscovery and recovery; Mourning; Dreaming; Commitment, and Action. In addition to these stages of decolonisation providing a clear framework for my research, a new stage of decolonisation emerged in my research; a stage of Healing (Muller, 2013). De-colonisation is a process that involves the whole of society, where both the colonisers and colonised can shed the imposed doctrines that gives power to colonisation ideology.

RESPECT IN RESEARCH

Respect and mutual exchange of knowledge is central to my research approach. In my role of researcher I am a learner because if I knew, I would have no need to ask others to share their knowledge and wisdom with me. My research identified that for Indigenous

Australians, respect refers to a multiplicity of rules that dictate behaviour; it is a thread that is entangled with ancient law, philosophy, spirituality, and that informs an appropriate code of conduct (Muller, 2013). Respect is an essential element of circular learning. Juanita Sherwood explains that 'Respect means that you're open enough to acknowledge that there are many ways of being in this world and that they all have their own authority' (2010, p. 261). Sherwood notes that new ways of knowing can be produced through respectful research (p. 291).

An expert panel, which ensured protocol, respect and appropriate process was followed during the PhD, and that knowledge shared was accurate and appropriate, was a central feature of my research. These 'experts' are knowledgeable people within their areas but even they have an expectation of a circular motion of knowledge. In the process of sharing the research with panel members, they gained from the sharing of the collective knowledge.

Ensuring trust was an important motivation for me in accepting the teacher/learner role with Sue. When I began my research, I had to be sure that Sue, as my supervisor, was aware of the responsibility I had for the knowledge shared with me. In the research process a person may reveal something they may not have meant to share in an identifiable way (Wilson, 2004), or that should not be put into the open domain. A supervisor might unintentionally be privy to some of this knowledge. It was important that Sue was able to uphold the Responsibility to Knowledge and use discretion and respect in relation to any knowledge that was not to be made public.

Responsibility of knowledge

With Knowledge Comes Responsibility and Knowledge and Responsibility are inseparable (Rist, cited in Muller 2010). My responsibility to the knowledge shared by others has certain obligations. Far from being onerous, these obligations are a rich and inspiring part of the research methodology of my project because they ground the research in appropriate and respectful process (Muller, 2013).

As we gain knowledge our responsibility increases to use this knowledge wisely and to respect those who have assisted in our gaining of knowledge (Rist, cited in Muller, 2010). Custodians of knowledge have an obligation to ensure it is respected, nurtured, and shared where appropriate, while retaining the right not to share. One of the functions of the expert panel was to ensure the responsible sharing of the collective knowledge collated in my research project.

As my research progressed, I was conscious of the responsibility of knowledge and how this respect for knowledge saw me entrusted with more knowledge. In taking on the responsibility of teaching, I was embracing the responsibility of knowledge. By accepting the responsibility of teaching and passing on appropriate knowledge, my own knowledge increased. With increased knowledge, there is a proportionally greater responsibility to that knowledge.

Individual knowledge

Separated from responsibility, knowledge can become individualised, owned for the primary benefit of an individual. Such separation of responsibility from knowledge can lead to distortion of knowledge. Distortions, or un-validated law may be minor errors or significant distortions, such as those falsely claiming that violence/abuse is customary (Gordon, Hallahan, & Henry, 2002, p. 51–71). Without responsibility, knowledge is at best unaccountable and unconnected, and at the worst—misleading and dangerous.

While an individual's knowledge is respected and valued, there is a need to retain connectedness with the collective. An individual's knowledge is maintained within the collective body of knowledge and responsible sharing and collaboration of knowledge ensures the integrity of knowledge. As knowledge is invested in an individual their responsibility increases. They are under an obligation to use knowledge wisely and give respect to those contributing to the learning.

Respecting others' knowledge

> Language and the citing of texts are often the clearest markers of the theoretical traditions of a writer. (Tuhiwai-Smith, 1999, p. 14)

'How' and 'who' is cited can centre our knowledge or silence it, because knowledge 'can be wielded as a tool to silence the voices of people' (Reyes-Cruz, 2008, p. 652). The use of research findings are an opportunity to broadcast the otherwise silenced voices of those who shared their knowledge in the process (with their permission). In the process of decolonising knowledge, participants are not sources of data, but sources of knowledge, and the recognition of their contribution to building knowledge is required (Reyes-Cruz, 2008). I make deliberate use of citing the people I have interviewed (where appropriate) as their wisdom informs my intellectual understanding of the issues I share.

Giving credit to others respects their intellectual contribution to individual and collective learning. In this respectful way, connectedness is maintained, and the need to speak for oneself can be maintained. Naturally, there is a need to check and clarify when citing another's work.

Appreciation or appropriation

Custodians of knowledge have an obligation to ensure that it is respected, nurtured and shared when suitable, while retaining the right not to share. Colonisation has made us cautious, because our knowledge has been appropriated through research, making others 'experts' on Indigenous issues. Like prospectors, others seek to re-author our knowledge, and become the new 'owner' because knowledge is worth money and prestige in the settler society (Kincheloe & Steinberg, 2008). Sharing knowledge is not without risk as researchers have appropriated our knowledge and claimed it for their own benefit. However, Sue accepted the responsibility of knowledge. Sue does not speak for others, sharing only her journey. Respect and appreciation is evident to all those who shared their knowledge with her, or gave permission for this to occur. Sue has not claimed expert knowledge about Indigenous Australians, but she has considerable knowledge relating to how a non-Indigenous person can work and learn alongside Indigenous peoples with respect and appreciation. I am not sure if Sue is aware of the level of respect she demonstrated by her humility. Let there be no misunderstanding, in the process outlined in this chapter, there were mutual benefits. By accepting the responsibility of teaching Sue, I expanded my own understanding and knowledge. New friendships were forged and new opportunities for mutual learning were created.

INTERSECTING CIRCLES

Once Sue identified the circular motion of teacher/learner that names the mutuality inherent in the responsibility of knowledge, it became easier to identify the new and intersecting or overlapping circles. It is encouraging to hear Sue incorporate our knowledge respectfully into her work. Through the reciprocal circle of learning, Sue has become a valued friend and colleague. The circle of learning has now developed into many reciprocal circles of learning, while ours continues based on friendship and equality.

CIRCULAR AND REFORMATIVE: THE CIRCLE CONTINUES

On completion of my first doctorate I was unsuccessful in gaining employment, and when family circumstances aligned to give me time and opportunity, I enrolled full time in a second PhD. Like many other Indigenous PhD graduates, employment in academia remains elusive (Australian Government, 2012). Unfortunately, as reported by Stephen Hagan (2012), the qualifications of Indigenous academics are still viewed disrespectfully as being of lesser quality. My new research arose from my first PhD, when the people who shared their knowledge with me identified some questions they would like answered about mainstream non-Indigenous Australian culture. Due to the independent nature of a doctoral research project, this was considered ideal for respectfully asking mainstream Australians about their culture. My second doctorate, *Shifting the Lens:*

Indigenous research into mainstream Australian culture, is research initiated by Indigenous people.

Once again, I have two non-Indigenous allies, along with Sue, as my academic supervisors. With the research lens shifted, Indigenous research methodology is proving to be relevant in a different context, with many of my non-Indigenous research interviewees expressing delight in the use of circular learning in our interviews. The circular learning process continues …

Conclusion

In this chapter we tell our stories for the advancement of Indigenous social work education and practice. We separately tell our interwoven stories, pondering a revolving or circular teaching and learning process that one person (Sue) found quite unique and the other (Lorraine) wondered why. We sought to articulate and demonstrate how we worked separately on our own projects, together on joint projects, and how we conferred in respectful ways that generated progressive learning for each of us. Our quest is to decolonise and reform social work education to advance Indigenous social work, and to graduate Indigenous and non-Indigenous practitioners who have respect, skills and knowledge for working with Indigenous colleagues, clients, and communities.

References

Akerlind, G. (2007). Constraints on academics' potential for developing as a teacher. *Studies in Higher Education*, 32(1), 21–37.

Atkinson, J. (2002). *Trauma trails: recreating song lines. The trans-generational effects of trauma in Indigenous Australia.* Melbourne: Spinifex Press.

Australian Government. (2012). Review of higher education access and outcomes for Aboriginal and Torres Strait Islander People: final report. Retrieved 22 April 2013 from www.innovation.gov.au/HigherEducation/IndigenousHigherEducation/ReviewOfIndigenousHigherEducation/FinalReport/index.html.

Bennett, B., Green, S., Gilbert, S. & Bessarab, D. (2012). *Our voices: Aboriginal and Torres Strait Islander social work*. South Yarra: Palgrave Macmillan.

Bessarab, D. (2012). The supervisory yarn: embedding Indigenous epistemology in supervision. In B. Bennett S. Green S. Gilbert & D. Bessarab (Eds). *Our voices. Aboriginal and Torres Strait Islander social work* (pp. 73– 92). South Yarra: Palgrave Macmillan.

Boshier, R. (2006). Widening access by bringing education home. In A. Oduaran & H. Bhola (Eds). *Widening Access to education as social justice* (pp. 23–43). Netherlands: Springer.

Bulman, J. & Hayes, R. (2008). Promoting Indigenous participation in health promotion education through community-based participatory research. *Aboriginal and Islander Health Worker Journal*, 32(3), 10–13.

Butler, J. (1992). Teacher professional development: an Australian case study. *Journal of Education for Teaching*, 18(3), 221–38.

Cavanagh, P. & Maskell, J. (2005, December). Creatively confronting challenges: constructive roles in academic culture for non-Indigenous educators and Indigenous learners in higher education. Paper presented at the AARE Conference, University of Western Sydney, Australia.

Clark, J. (2000). Beyond empathy: an ethnographic approach to cross-cultural social work practice. Unpublished manuscript, Faculty of Social Work, University of Toronto.

de Ishtar, Z. (2004). Living on the ground research: steps toward white women researching in collaboration with Indigenous people. *Hecate*, 30(1), 72–83.

Dominelli, L. (2002). Feminist Social Work Theory and Practice. Hampshire: Palgrave.

Fullan, M. (1993). *Change forces: probing the depths of educational reform*. London, England: Palmer Press.

Gair, S., Thomson, J., & Miles, D. (2005). Reconciling Indigenous and non-Indigenous knowledges in social work education: action and legitimacy. *Journal of Social Work Education*, 41(2), 371–82.

Gair, S., Thomson, J. & Savage, D. (2005). What's stopping them? Barriers hindering Indigenous students completing a BSW at JCU, *Advances in Social Welfare Education*, 7(1), 54–66. Retrieved 17 April 2013 from eprints.jcu.edu.au/321/.

Gordon, S., Hallahan, K., & Henry, D. (2002). Putting the picture together: inquiry into the response by government agencies to complaints of family violence and child abuse in Aboriginal communities. Western Australia: Department of Premier and Cabinet.

Graveline, J. (1998). *Circlework: transforming ethnocentric consciousness.* Halifax: Fernwood.

Green, S., Bennett, B., Collins, A., Gowans, B., Hennessey, K. & Smith, K. (2012). Walking the Journey: the student experience. In B. Bennett S. Green S. Gilbert & D. Bessarab (Eds). *Our Voices: Aboriginal and Torres Strait Islander social work* (pp. 206–39). South Yarra: Palgrave Macmillan.

Hagan, S. (2012, September 5). Academics outraged over PhD 'poor fellow me' slur. *National Indigenous Times,* pp. 4–5.

Hart, M. (2008). Critical reflections on an Aboriginal approach to helping. In M. Gray J. Coates & M. Yellowbird (Eds). *Indigenous social work around the world* (pp. 129–39). Burlington: ashgate Press.

Heron, J. (1996). *Co-operative inquiry: research into the human condition.* Thousand Oaks: Sage.

Hughes, I. (2000). Ganma: Indigenous knowledge for reconciliation and community action. Paper presented to the Participatory Action Research World Congress, Ballarat, Australia. Retrieved 17 April 2013 from www.alara.net.au/files/Hughes,I-FullPaper.doc.

Kincheloe, J.L. & Steinberg, S.R. (2008). Indigenous knowledges in education. In N. Denzin Y. Lincoln & L. Tuhiwai-Smith (Eds). Handbook of critical and Indigenous methodologies (pp. 135–56). Thousand Oaks, California: Sage.

Kolb, D. (1984). *Experiential learning.* Englewood Cliffs, New Jersey: Prentice Hall.

Laenui, P. (Hayden, Burgess) (2007, June). Welcome remarks. Paper presented at the Indigenous Voices in Social Work: Not Lost in Translation Conference, University of Hawaii, Oahu.

Langton, M. (2003). Aboriginal art and film: the politics of representation. In M. Grossman (Ed.), *Blacklines: contemporary critical writing by Indigenous Australians* (pp. 109–24). Melbourne: Melbourne University Press.

Lather, P. (1998). Critical pedegogy and its complicities: a praxis of stuck places. *Educational Theory*, *48*(4), 487–98.

Martin, K. (2003). Ways of knowing, being and doing: a theoretical framework and methods for Indigenous and Indigenist research. *Journal of Australian Studies*, *76*, 203–14. Retrieved 17 April 2013 from eprints.qut.edu.au/7182/.

Martin, K. L. (2008). *Please knock before you enter: Aboriginal regulation of outsiders and the implications for researchers.* Tenerife: Post Pressed.

McLennan, V., & Khavarpour, F. (2004). Culturally appropriate health promotion: its meaning and application in Aboriginal communities. *Health Promotion Journal of Australia*, *15*(3), 237–39. Retrieved 17 April 2013 from search.informit.com.au/documentSummary;dn=454259874107813;res=IELHEA.

Muller, L. (2010). Indigenous Australian social-health theory. Unpublished doctoral dissertation. Townsville: James Cook University.

Muller, L. (2013). Forthcoming. Crows Nest: Allen & Unwin.

Nakata, M. (2007). *Disciplining the savages, savaging the discipline.* Canberra: Aboriginal Studies Press.

Nash, M., Mumford, R. & O'Donoghue, K. (2005). *Social work in action*. London: Jessica Kingsley.

Nasir, T. (2008). Two-way mentoring for Indigenous apprentices and staff. Paper presented at the AVETRA 11th Annual Conference, Adelaide, Australia. Retrieved 17 April 2013 from www.avetra.org.au/AVETRA%20WORK%2011.04.08/CS5.2%20-%20Tanyah%20Nasir.pdf.

Noble, K. & Henderson, R. (2008). Engaging with images and stories: using a learning circle approach to develop agency of beginning 'at risk' pre-service teachers. *Australian Journal of Teacher Education, 33*(1). Retrieved 22 April 2013 from ro.ecu.edu.au/ajte/vol33/iss1/4/.

Paradies, Y. (2007). Racism. In B. Carson T. Dunbar R.D. Chenhall & R. Baillie (Eds). *Social determinants of Indigenous health* (pp. 65–80). Crows Nest: Allen & Unwin.

Petersen, L. (2006). Building on strengths within communities to achieve the best outcomes for our children. *The Fiji Social Workers Journal*, 2, 3–10.

Reyes-Cruz, M. (2008). What if I just cite Graciela?: working toward decolonizing knowledge through a critical ethnography. *Qualitative Inquiry*, 14(4), 651–48.

Robertson, B. (2000). *Aboriginal and Torres Strait Islander women's task force on violence report*. Brisbane: Queensland Department of Aboriginal and Torres Strait Islander Policy and Development.

Romer, T. (2003). Learning process and the professional content in the theory of Donald Schon. *Reflective Practice*, 4(1), 85–93.

Schon, D. (1983). *The reflective practition: how professionals think in action.* New York: Basic Books.

Sherwood, J. (2010). *Do no harm: decolonising Aboriginal health research.* Unpublished thesis. University of New South Wales, Sydney, Australia.

Sinclair, R. (2004). Aboriginal social work education in Canada: decolonising pedagogy for the seventh generation, *First Peoples Child and Family Review*, 1(1), 49–61.

Sonn, C., Bishop, B. & Humphries, R. (2000). Encounters with the dominant culture: voices of Indigenous students in mainstream higher education, *Australian Psychologist*, 35(2), 128–35.

Sveiby, K.E., & Skuthorpe, T. (2006). *Treading lightly: the hidden wisdom of the world's oldest people*. Crows Nest: Allen & Unwin.

Tafoya, T. (1995). Finding harmony: balancing traditional values with western science in therapy, *Canadian Journal of Native Education*, 21(supplement), 7–27.

Tolle, E. (2000). *The power of now*. Sydney: Hodder.

Tuhiwai-Smith, L. (1999). *Decolonizing methodologies: research and Indigenous peoples*. Dunedin: University of Otago Press.

Walter, M.W., Talylor, S. & Habibis, D. (2012). Australian social work is white. In B Bennett, S. Green, S. Gilbert & D. Bessarab (Eds). *Our voices. Aboriginal and Torres Strait Islander social work* (pp. 230–47). South Yarra: Palgrave Macmillan.

Whitehead, J. (2008). Using living theory methodology in improving practice and generating educational knowledge in living theories. *Educational Journal of Living Theories, l*(1), 103–26. Retrieved 17 April 2013 from ejolts.net/node/80.

Wilson, S. (2004). *Research as ceremony: Articulating an Indigenous research paradigm*. PhD thesis. Monash University, Victoria, Australia.

Zuchowski, I., Savage, D., Miles, D. & Gair, S. (2012, October). *Decolonising field education: challenging Australian social work praxis*. Paper presented at the Australian Association of Social Work and Welfare Difference and Diversity Conference in University of South Australia, Adelaide, Australia.

3

Diversity in gender equality in Asia

Murli Desai

This chapter explores gender equality in Asia by comparing the gender measures and progress in promoting gender equality as a Millennium Development Goal in the sub-regions of East, Southeast, North, Central and South Asia. The North and Central Asian sub-regions are leading in gender equality in Asia, due to the extensive reliance on female labour under former communist rule. The sub-regions showing the next-best progress are East and Southeast, and the southern countries of South Asia. The northern countries of South Asia lag behind in gender equality as part of the so-called belt of classic patriarchy that stretches from North Africa to Bangladesh. Thus, overall human development does not necessarily lead to gender equality and countries that rank high on gender equality also have contradictions. The article therefore proposes mainstreaming gender in social work education to promote gender equality in Asia.

亞洲性別平等的多樣性

本文通過比較了性別問題措施和促進性別平等這一千年發展目標在中東、東南亞、北亞、中亞和南亞子區域的進展，來探討了亞洲的性別平等問題。由於前共產主義統治下對女性勞動力的廣泛依賴，北亞和中亞及其附屬地區已成為亞洲性別平等的領跑者。性別平等發展程度位列其後的地區為東亞，東南亞和南亞南部國家。南亞地區北部的國家，從北非延伸到孟加拉國，由於他們所謂的傳統世襲父權主義，使他們在性別平等發展上落後於他國。因此，性別平等在人類發展中並不是必然的，而且在性別平等排名靠前的國家中也存在矛盾。因此，本文在社工教育中突出性別問題來促進在亞洲的性別平等發展。

アジアにおける男女平等の多様性

この記事では、アジア地域の男女平等を、男女同権の進歩と比較しながら、その促進をアジア東部、南東部、北部、中心部、そして南部のミレニアム開発目標として調査します。アジア北部と中心部の小区域における男女の平等は、以前の共産主義の統治による広範囲におよぶ女性労働者への依存により、アジア内で先頭に立っている。小区域において次に最も良い男女の平等の進展がみられるのは東部、南東部、そして南アジア南部の国々である。南アジア北部の国々は、北アフリカからバングラデシュまで張り渡すいわゆる'古典的家父長制のベルト'が原因で男女の平等性に遅れをとっている。この様に、全体的な人間の発達が必ずしも男女平等に導くとは限らず、男女平等の地位が高い国々でも矛盾を抱えている。従ってこの記事では、男女の平等をアジアで促進する為、ソーシャルワーク教育における性(ジェンダー)の流化を提案する。

아시아 지역의 성평등

본 장에서는 '성 평등척도' 비교를 통해 '21세기 발전목표' 지역인 동, 남동, 북, 중앙, 남아시아의 남녀평등을 탐구한다. 북, 중앙 아시아인들은 공산주의 통치에서 여성 노동력에 대한 광범위한 의존을 통해 남녀평등을 이끌어냈다. 다음으로 진보를 보여줄 하위지역은 남아시아의 동, 남동, 남쪽지역 나라들이다. 남아시아의 북쪽지역 나라들의 남녀평등의 격차는 북아프리카에서 방글라데시로 이어지는 전통적인 가부장제 벨트에서 기인한다. 이와 같이, 인류 발전이 반드시 전반적인 남녀평등을 이루어지게 하는 것은 아니다. 그러므로 사회복지교육에서 성평등 문제를 주로 다루므로서 아시아 지역에서 성평등이 이루어지게 도모해야한다.

Introduction

While Asia is known for its fast economic development and explanations for it are sought in an 'Asian development model' and 'Asian values', this region is also known for the largest number of poor people in the world. In fact the fast economic growth has to a large extent been responsible for the widespread poverty through social exclusion of vulnerable groups, women being the most important one as it includes half the population. This article aims to examine gender equality in Asia by using gender measures and progress of promoting gender equality as a Millennium Development Goal (MDG) and draw implications for social policy and gender aware social work education.

Gender equality

For ages, it was believed that the different characteristics, roles and status accorded to women and men in society are determined by biology (that is, sex), that they are natural and, therefore, not changeable. However, Ann Oakley, who was among the first to use the concept of gender, said that 'sex' is a word that refers to the biological differences between male and female: the visible difference in genitalia, the related difference in procreative function. 'Gender' however is a matter of culture: it refers to the social classification into 'masculine' and 'feminine' (1972). Twentieth-century liberal feminists used the distinction between biological facts and social norms when they drew the distinction between sex (biological) and gender (historical, social and cultural) differences between women and men. They see women's subordination as resulting from gendered norms, rather than from biological sex, and aim to change these norms (Connelly, Li, MacDonald, & Parpart, 2000). Gender equality means that the different behaviour, aspirations and needs of women and men are considered, valued and favoured equally. It does not mean that women and men have to become the same, but that their rights, responsibilities and opportunities will not depend on whether they are born male or female (International Labor Organisation, 2007, p. 48).

Asian sub-regions

The chapter identifies diversity in gender equality in Asia by comparing the following Asian sub-regions:

Table 1: Countries of Asian sub-regions

Asian sub-region	Location	No. of coun-tries	Countries
East Asia	South of Mongolia and west of North Pacific Ocean	4	China, Japan, North Korea & South Korea
Southeast Asia	East of India and south of China	11	Brunei, Cambodia, Indonesia, Laos, Malaysia, Myanmar, Philippines, Singapore, Thailand, Timor-Leste & Vietnam
North Asia	East of Europe and north of Central Asia and China	2	Russia & Mongolia
Central Asia	South of Russia, east of the Caspian Sea, west of China and north of Southwest Asia	5	Kazakhstan, Kyrgyzstan, Tajikistan, Turkmenistan & Uzbekistan
South Asia	Between Southwest Asia and Southeast Asia, north of Indian Ocean	7	Bangladesh, Bhutan, India, Maldives, Nepal, Pakistan & Sri Lanka

Comparative gender measures in Asian sub-regions

The Gender-related Development Index (GDI) was introduced in the Human Development Report (HDR) on *Gender and Human Development* (United Nations Development Program, 1995) for ranking countries on a global scale by their performance in gender equality. Since 2010 HDR, Gender Inequality Index (GII) is used as an experimental composite measure of inequality in achievement between women and men. The following table reports on GDI and GII.

Table 2: Comparative gender measures in Asian sub-regions

Level of HD 2012	Countries in Asia	HDI rank 2012 1	HDI value 2007 2	GDI value 2007 3	GDI % of HDI 2007 4	GII rank 2012 5
North and Central Asia						
High	Russia	055	0.817	0.816	99.9	051
High	Kazakhstan	069	0.804	0.803	99.8	051
Medium	Turkmenistan	102	0.739	-	-	-
Medium	Mongolia	106	0.727	0.727	100.0	056
Medium	Uzbekistan	114	0.710	0.708	99.7	-
Medium	Kyrgyzstan	125	0.710	0.705	99.4	064
Medium	Tajikistan	125	0.688	0.686	99.6	057
East Asia						
V High	Japan	010	0.960	0.945	98.4	021
V High	South Korea	012	0.937	0.926	98.8	027
V High	Hong Kong	013	0.944	0.934	98.9	-
Medium	China	101	0.772	0.770	99.8	035
Southeast Asia						
V High	Singapore	018	0.944	-	-	013
V High	Brunei	030	0.920	0.906	98.5	-
High	Malaysia	064	0.829	0.823	99.2	042
Medium	Thailand	103	0.783	0.782	99.8	066
Medium	Philippines	114	0.751	0.748	99.6	077
Medium	Indonesia	121	0.734	0.726	99.0	106
Medium	Vietnam	127	0.725	0.723	99.7	048
Medium	Timor-Leste	134	0.489	-	-	-
Medium	Laos	138	0.619	0.614	99.3	100
Medium	Cambodia	138	0.593	0.588	99.2	096
Low	Myanmar	149	0.586	-	-	080

South Asia						
High	Sri Lanka	092	0.759	0.756	99.6	075
Medium	Maldives	104	0.771	0.767	99.5	064
Medium	India	136	0.612	0.594	97.1	132
Medium	Bhutan	140	0.619	0.605	97.7	092
Low	Pakistan	146	0.572	0.532	93.0	123
Low	Bangladesh	146	0.543	0.536	98.7	111
Low	Nepal	157	0.553	0.545	98.4	102

Sources: Columns 1 and 5: United Nations Development Program, 2013; Columns 2 to 4: United Nations Development Program, 2009.

GENDER-RELATED DEVELOPMENT INDEX

The Human Development Index (HDI) has three key components: Longevity measured by life expectancy at birth, knowledge measured by adult literacy and mean years of schooling and Real GDP per capita income in purchasing power parity (PPP) dollars. Table 2 shows that Asia is diverse with reference to human development ranging from very high to low, most of the countries belonging to the medium level of human development.

The GDI is HDI adjusted for gender inequality, measuring achievement in the same basic capabilities as the HDI does, but takes note of inequality in achievement between women and men. The methodology used imposes a penalty for inequality, such that the GDI falls when the achievement levels of both women and men go down or when the disparity between their achievements increases. The greater the gender disparity in basic capabilities, the lower a country's GDI compared with its HDI (The Human Development website hdr.undp.org/en/humandev/hdi/). Table 2 shows that GDI data is not available for Turkmenistan, Singapore, Timor-Leste and Myanmar. As far as the GDI percentage of HDI is concerned, the distribution of the remaining Asian countries is as follows:

- Countries with GDI Value almost same as HDI Value (99+ to 100%): All the North and Central Asian countries (with Mongolia noted for 100% congruence between the two), China, all the Southeast Asian countries except Brunei, Sri Lanka, and Maldives.
- Countries with GDI Value moderately lower than HDI Value (98+ to 99%): The East Asian countries except China, Brunei, Bangladesh and Nepal.
- Countries with GDI Value much lower than HDI Value (93+ to 98%): Bhutan, India and Pakistan.

Gender inequality index

Since 2010 HDR, the GII is used as a composite measure of inequality in achievement between women and men in three dimensions: reproductive health, empowerment and the labour market. Table 2 shows that in 2011, gender inequality is lower in countries of Singapore, Japan and South Korea where the human development is very high. Citywise, the GII rank is highest in Singapore (13) and lowest in India (132). Sub-regionwise, it is highest in East Asia and lowest in South Asia. It is more or less homogenous in North and Central Asia, ranging from 51 in Russia and Kazakhstan to 64 in Kyrgyzstan. Southeast Asia and South Asia are most diverse. In the former it ranges from 13 in Singapore to 106 in Indonesia and in the latter it ranges from 75 in Sri Lanka to 132 in India.

Conclusion

Gender inequality is lower in countries of Singapore, Japan and South Korea where the human development is very high. Gender inequality is more or less homogenous in North and Central Asia and diverse in Southeast Asia and South Asia. While in 2007, North and Central Asia and most of the Southeast Asian countries had a high level of GDI; in 2011 East Asia is leading in GII. South Asia which is most backward in the overall human development in Asia lags behind on all the three Gender Measures.

Comparative progress in gender equality in Asian sub-regions

Gender equality as a millennium development goal

The Millennium Summit placed gender equality at the heart of achieving the MDGs. The MDG-3 specifically aims to promote gender equality and empower women, targeting at gender equality in education, work and political participation.

Gender equality in education

Target 4 for MDG-3 is to eliminate gender disparity in primary and secondary education, preferably by 2005, and in all levels of education no later than 2015. Table 3 provides data on progress in gender equality in education in Asian sub-regions.

Table 3: Comparative Progress in Gender Equality in Education in Asian Sub-Regions

Level of HD 2012	Countries in Asia	Gender equality in primary school 2009 1	Gender equality in secondary school 2009 2	Gender equality in tertiary education 2009 3	Female population with at least secondary education (% ages 25 and older 2006–10 4
North and Central Asia					
High	Russia	-	-	-	93.5
High	Kazakhstan	1.01	0.98	1.45	99.3

Medium	Turkmenistan	-	-	-	-
Medium	Mongolia	0.99	1.07	1.55	83.0
Medium	Uzbekistan	0.98	0.99	0.70	-
Medium	Kyrgyzstan	1.00	1.01	1.32	81.0
Medium	Tajikistan	0.96	0.87	0.41	93.2
East Asia					
V High	Japan	1.00	1.00	0.89	80.0
V High	South Korea	0.98	0.96	0.70	79.4
V High	Hong Kong	1.02	1.03	1.03	68.7
Medium	China	1.04	1.07	1.07	54.8
Southeast Asia					
V High	Singapore	-	-	-	71.3
V High	Brunei	1.01	1.02	1.76	66.6
High	Malaysia	0.99	1.07	1.30	66.0
Medium	Thailand	0.98	1.09	1.24	29.0
Medium	Philippines	0.98	1.09	1.24	65.9
Medium	Indonesia	0.97	0.99	0.96	36.2
Medium	Vietnam	0.95	0.92	0.73	24.7
Medium	Timor-Leste	0.97	1.00	0.71	-
Medium	Laos	0.91	0.81	0.78	22.9
Medium	Cambodia	0.94	0.82	0.54	11.6
Low	Myanmar	0.98	1.02	1.37	18.0
South Asia					
High	Sri Lanka	1.00	1.02	-	72.6
Medium	Maldives	0.95	1.05	2.40	20.7
Medium	India	0.97	0.88	0.70	26.6
Medium	Bhutan	1.01	0.99	0.59	34.0

Low	Pakistan	0.84	0.79	0.85	18.3
Low	Bangladesh	1.04	1.12	0.56	30.8
Low	Nepal	0.86	0.89	0.40	17.9

Sources: Columns 1 to 3: Asian Development Bank, 2011, pp. 81–82; Column 4: United Nations Development Program, 2013.

Table 3 shows that gender equality at the primary level of education is achieved in most countries. There is less gender equality at the secondary level. At the tertiary level, some countries are behind their primary and secondary levels, whereas, some countries have ratios in favour of females.

North and Central Asia

At the primary level, all the countries of North and Central Asia have achieved gender equality up to 0.95. At the secondary level, Tajikistan has not yet achieved this ratio by 2009. At the tertiary level, Uzbekistan and Tajikistan are lagging behind. On the other hand, high ratios in favour of women are observed at this level in Kazakhstan (1.45), Kyrgyzstan (1.32) and Mongolia (1.55). As far as female population with at least secondary education (% ages 25 and older) is concerned, North and Central Asia leads, ranging from 81.0% in Kyrgyzstan to 99.3% in Kazakhstan.

East Asia

In East Asia China is doing the best with reference to gender equality in education, although it is at medium level of human development. However, although Japan and South Korea are at very high level of human development, their progress in gender equality at the tertiary level is slow. The level of education in their female population is also not so high among the countries at very high level of human development in East Asia, ranging from 68.7% in Hong Kong to 80.0% in Japan.

Southeast Asia

Cambodia and Laos lag behind in gender equality at all the three levels of education. At the secondary level, Vietnam also lags behind. At the tertiary level, Vietnam and Timor-Leste also lag behind. On the other hand, high ratios in favour of women are observed at the tertiary level in Brunei (1.76) and Thailand (1.24). Female population with at least secondary education (% ages 25 and older) in Asia is lowest in Cambodia at 11.6%. Among the countries at very high level of human development, the level of education in their female population is not so high; it is 66.6% in Brunei and 71.3% in Singapore.

South Asia

Nepal and Pakistan are lagging behind in gender equality at all the three levels of education. At the secondary level, India is also lagging behind. At the tertiary level, India, Bhutan and Bangladesh are also lagging behind. On the other hand, at this level, Maldives has a very high gender ratio of 2.40, highest in Asia.

GENDER EQUALITY IN WAGE EMPLOYMENT

MDG-3 measures the share of women in wage employment in the non-agricultural sector which measures the degree to which labour markets are open to women in the industry and service sectors. Table 4 provides the data on share of women in wage employment in the non-agricultural sector as well as overall female labour force participation in Asia.

Table 4: Comparative progress of gender equality in wage Employment in Asian sub-regions

Level of HD 2012	Countries in Asia	Share of women in wage employment (%) 2009 1	Female labour force partici-pation (% ages 15 and older) 2011 2
North and Central Asia			
High	Russia	-	56.3
High	Kazakhstan	50.0	66.6
Medium	Turkmenistan	-	46.4
Medium	Mongolia	51.1	54.3
Medium	Uzbekistan	39.4	47.7
Medium	Kyrgyzstan	50.6	55.5
Medium	Tajikistan	37.1	57.4
East Asia			
Very High	Japan	42.3	49.4
Very High	South Korea	42.1	49.2
Very High	Hong Kong	49.9	51.0
Medium	China	-	67.7
Southeast Asia			
Very High	Singapore	45.4	56.5
Very High	Brunei	30.3	55.5
High	Malaysia	39.2	43.8
Medium	Thailand	45.5	63.8
Medium	Philippines	41.9	49.7
Medium	Indonesia	32.4	51.2
Medium	Vietnam	40.4	73.2

Medium	Timor-Leste	-	38.4
Medium	Laos	32.1	76.5
Medium	Cambodia	43.5	79.2
Low	Myanmar	-	75.0
South Asia			
High	Sri Lanka	31.0	34.7
Medium	Maldives	30.0	55.7
Medium	India	18.1	29.0
Medium	Bhutan	26.8	65.8
Low	Pakistan	12.6	22.7
Low	Bangladesh	20.1	57.2
Low	Nepal	-	80.4

Sources: Column 1: Asian Development Bank, 2011, pp. 81–82; column 2: United Nations Development Program, 2013

Table 4 shows that the labour force participation of women in labour force is much higher than share of women in wage employment. This shows more women in the non-wage agricultural labour which is unorganised. This sector is unprotected as it does not provide social security and scope for unionisation or application of anti-discrimination laws and so on. It leads to increased poverty among women.

The following are sub-regionwise trends about gender equality in wage employment in Asia:

North and Central Asia

North and Central Asia lead with share of women in wage employment in Asia being 50% and above in Mongolia, Kyrgyzstan and Kazakhstan. Its labour force participation of women in general is also above 46% in all the countries and as high as 66.6% in Kazakhstan.

East Asia

In East Asia, share of women in non-agricultural wage employment is the second-highest in Asia. It ranges from 42.1% in South Korea to 49.9% in Hong Kong. Its labour force participation of women in general is above 49% and as high as 67.7% in China.

Southeast Asia

In Southeast Asia, female share in wage employment is above 45% only in Singapore and Thailand and only 30.3% in Brunei. Although Cambodia has low level of female education, the labour force participation among women in this country is the highest in this sub-region (79.2%). Laos, Myanmar and Vietnam also have above 70% of women's share in labour force in general.

South Asia

South Asia lags behind with female share in wage employment ranging from 12.6% in Pakistan to 31% in Sri Lanka. The lowest labour force participation among women in Asia is in Pakistan at 22.7% and India at 29%. Although Nepal has low level of female education, the labour force participation among women in this country is the highest in Asia (80.4%).

Gender equality in political participation

Gender equality in political participation is measured by the proportion of seats held by women in national parliament, linked to women's empowerment.

Table 5: Comparative progress of gender equality in political participation in Asian sub-regions

Level of HD 2012	Countries in Asia	Seats in national parliament (% female) 2011
North and Central Asia		
High	Russia	11.1
High	Kazakhstan	18.2

Medium	Turkmenistan	16.8
Medium	Mongolia	12.7
Medium	Uzbekistan	19.2
Medium	Kyrgyzstan	23.3
Medium	Tajikistan	17.5
East Asia		
V High	Japan	13.4
V High	South Korea	15.7
V High	Hong Kong	-
Medium	China	21.3
Southeast Asia		
V High	Singapore	23.5
V High	Brunei	-
High	Malaysia	13.2
Medium	Thailand	15.7
Medium	Philippines	22.1
Medium	Indonesia	18.2
Medium	Vietnam	24.4
Medium	Timor-Leste	38.5
Medium	Laos	25.0
Medium	Cambodia	18.1
Low	Myanmar	4.6
South Asia		
High	Sri Lanka	5.8
Medium	Maldives	6.5
Medium	India	10.9
Medium	Bhutan	13.9
Low	Pakistan	21.1
Low	Bangladesh	19.7
Low	Nepal	33.2

Source: United Nations development program, 2013.

Table 5 shows that political participation by women is low in every Asian sub-region:

North and Central Asia

Political participation of women in North and Central Asia ranges from 11.1 in Russia to 23.3% in Kyrgyzstan.

East Asia

Political participation of women is least diverse in East Asia, ranging from 13.4% in Japan to 21.3% in China.

Southeast Asia

Political participation of women in Southeast Asia is most diverse, ranging from very low of 4.6% in Myanmar to 38.5% in Timor-Leste, highest in Asia.

South Asia

Political participation of women in South Asia ranges from very low (5.3%) in Sri Lanka to 33.2% in Nepal.

CONCLUSION

The overall observations with reference to the MDG on gender equality in Asia are as follows:

Gender equality at the primary level of education is achieved in most countries. There is less gender equality at the secondary level. At the tertiary level, some countries are behind their primary and secondary levels, whereas, some countries have ratios in favour of females.

The labour force participation of women is much higher than share of women in wage employment, indicating higher levels of poverty among women.

Political participation by women is low in every sub-region.

SUB-REGIONWISE CONCLUSIONS

The progress of the Asian sub-regions for different targets of promoting gender equality as an MDG seems to be as follows:

North and Central Asia

North and Central Asia are leading in Asia with reference to gender equality in education and wage employment, although most of its countries are at a medium level of human development. In fact, high ratios in favour of women are observed at tertiary level of education in three countries. However, this sub-region lags behind the other Asian sub-regions in terms of the proportion of seats held by women in national parliament.

East Asia

China at the medium level of human development is doing better than countries at very high level of human development with reference to gender equality in education, wage employment and political participation. In East Asia, share of women in non-agricultural wage employment is the second-highest in Asia. Political participation of women is low but least diverse in East Asia.

Southeast Asia

Among the countries at very high level of human development, the level of education in their female population is not so high compared to countries at very high level of human development in East Asia or countries at medium level of human development in North and Central Asia. Southeast Asia is diverse with reference to gender equality at different levels of education, wage employment and political participation.

South Asia

Gender equality in South Asia, especially the northern countries of this sub-region, lags behind other Asian sub-regions with reference to gender equality in education and wage employment. For most of the targets, the southern South Asian countries of Maldives and Sri

Lanka are doing better on gender equality than the countries lying in the northern part of the sub-region. With reference to gender equality, these two countries are more like the countries of East and Southeast Asia. However, political participation of women in these Southern countries of South Asia is very low.

Discussion

Diversity in gender equality in Asian sub-regions

Gender equality in North and Central Asia

Gender inequality is more or less homogenous in North and Central Asia. This sub-region is leading in Asia with reference to gender equality in education and wage employment, although most of its countries are at a medium level of human development. In fact, high ratios in favour of women are observed at tertiary level of education in three countries. The explanation for high level of gender equality in these countries seems to lie in the history of communist rule when they were part of the former Soviet Union. Newman (2005) noted that in many respects, the Soviet Union remained more advanced in relation to gender than capitalist societies, in terms of higher educational attainment and professional and political status. According to Lapidus (1982), an extensive reliance on female labour had been a central feature of the Soviet pattern of industrialisation over several decades, with important consequences for virtually every aspect of economic and social life. The highest female labour force participation rates of any industrial society are to be found in the Soviet Union. Until the mid-1960s this was viewed as unambiguous evidence that socialism and sexual equality went hand in hand.

However, as Lapidus (1982) further noted, beginning in the mid-1960s, a growing array of scholarly studies, to which female economists, sociologists, and demographers were important contributors, began to document in some detail the low level of skill, mobility, and income of women workers, the heavy and conflicting demands of their dual roles, and the harmful effects of poor working conditions and inadequate social services on the health and well-being of working mothers and their families. Patriarchy is obviously prevalent in Russia today, where the HDR of UNDP Russia (2010, p. 49) notes that Russian government policy towards women is increasingly driven by the assumption that the traditional labour division between men and women (where the man is the main breadwinner, while the woman combines the tasks of earning money for the family with household duties and raising children) is the only feasible and socially acceptable paradigm. The HDR of the United Nations Development Programme Regional Bureau for Europe and CIS (2011, p. 6) notes that in Central Asia the wholesale rejection of the previous system's values is resulting in a return to traditional gender and cultural norms, which can create new sources of exclusion for women.

Gender equality in East Asia

In 2011, East Asia is leading in GII. In this sub-region, share of women in non-agricultural wage employment is the second-highest in Asia.

Although East Asia is very high on the HDI, on the GDI it falls behind. Although at very high level of human development, progress in South Korea and Hong Kong is slow/ regressing at one or more levels of education. China, at medium level of human development, is doing the best in gender equality in education, wage employment and political participation in East Asia. This fact also shows that overall human development does not necessarily lead to gender equality. According to Kabeer (2003), in East Asia, kinship structures are predominantly patrilineal: descent is traced and property transmitted through the male members. Marriage tends to be exogamous and patrilocal: women marry outside their kin and often outside their village community, leaving their own homes at marriage to join their husband's family. Households are organised along highly corporate lines, with strong conjugal bonds and cultural rules that emphasise male responsibility for protecting and provisioning women and children. Household resources and income are pooled under the management and control of the male patriarch. Female chastity is emphasised and considered essential to ensure that property is transmitted based on biological fatherhood. Female sexuality is controlled through a strong public-private divide, with women secluded in the private domain. 'Son preference' is also marked.

Gender equality in Southeast Asia

Among the countries at very high level of human development in Southeast Asia, the level of education in their female population is not so high compared to countries at very high level of human development in East Asia or countries at medium level of human development in North and Central Asia. Southeast Asia is diverse with reference to gender equality at different levels of education, wage employment and political participation.

Countries in Southeast Asia such as Cambodia (79.2%), Los (76.5%), Myanmar (75%), Vietnam (73.2%) and Thailand (63.8%) have very high levels of female labour force participation. Ester Boserup's classical study on women's role in economic development (1970) noted that traditionally female family labour made up around 50 per cent of the total agricultural force in Thailand and 75 per cent in Cambodia, both areas of female farming. Women also made up around half of the labour force engaged in trade and commerce in Burma (now Myanmar), Cambodia, Laos, the Philippines, Thailand and Vietnam.

According to Kabeer (2003), compared to East Asia, somewhat less rigid gender relations are found in Southeast Asia in the way kinship and family are organised. However, she noted that the absence of any marked restrictions on women's mobility, and some degree of symmetry in the division of labour in the household should not be taken to imply an absence of gender inequality in these societies. For example, even though Philippine women may have high status relative to women in some other countries, this needs to be assessed in relation to Philippine men to be meaningful. She also noted that it is in the relatively more egalitarian regimes of Southeast Asia—

Thailand and the Philippines—that sex tourism has emerged as a key source of income for women. Clearly, labour markets continue to reproduce gender disadvantage.

Gender equality in South Asia

South Asia lags behind other Asian sub-regions with reference to gender equality in human development and gender equality in education and wage employment. According to Kabeer (2003), like in East Asia, in South Asia also kinship structures are predominantly patrilineal and patriarchal.

However, South Asia is not a homogenous sub-region. For most of the targets, it is the northern countries of this sub-region that lag behind and the southern countries of Maldives and Sri Lanka are doing better on gender equality, more like the countries of East and Southeast Asia. Razavi and Miller (1995) noted that these northern countries of South Asia lag behind as part of the so-called belt of classic patriarchy that stretches from North Africa across the Middle East and the northern plains of the Indian subcontinent to Bangladesh. In this sub-region, kinship structures are predominantly patrilineal, marriage tends to be patrilocal and cultural rules emphasise patriarchal family management. Here, it is men who have the main responsibility for household food provisioning. This does not mean that women are absent from agricultural production, as the term 'male farming' seems to imply. In practice what it means is that women's labour contributions to household production are often subsumed under male controlled processes. Boserup (1970) noted that within South Asia, women's participation in trade traditionally varied from two to six per cent in Bangladesh, the northern plains of India and Pakistan, to around 17 per cent in the southern states of India.

Contradictions in gender equality in Asia and implications

Human development only partly determines gender equality; many countries at medium level of human development are doing better than those at the very high level of human development. The measures of human development need to be recomputed to include gender equality. Although communist rule has led to better gender equality in the former communist countries, this equality is full of contradictions. Socialist ideology by itself does not bring full gender awareness. East and Southeast Asia and the southern countries of South Asia have made progress but much remains to be done. The northern countries of South Asia are at the lowest level of human development and gender equality in Asia. Political participation by women is low in every sub-region.

The labour force participation of women is much higher than the share of women in wage employment, indicating higher level of poverty among women. According to the International Fund for Agricultural Development (IFAD), women are still one of the single-most disadvantaged groups in Asia. In many Asian countries, particularly in South Asia, women and girls are consistently discriminated against regarding their access to health, nutrition and education. In some areas gender disparities are even on the increase, as in parts of China where women are taking over a larger share of agricultural tasks as men migrate to work elsewhere (www.ifad.org/operations/projects/regions/pi/poverty.htm). Moreover, development has led to women's vulnerability to poverty as the focus in development policies has been on men, and women's work has been undervalued. Thus policies and practice for social development need to integrate a comprehensive gender policy and practice.

Social policy in Asia and, therefore the policy for women in Asia use the residual welfare, or welfare pluralism, or informal or insecure welfare approach. Even the former communist countries are shifting from universal access to privatised fee-for-service system (Cook, Kabeer & Suwannarat, 2003, p. 34). The report of a workshop organised by the UNRISD in 2007 noted that social policy is not something to be engaged in only after reaching a certain development threshold, nor is it an exclusive domain of advanced welfare states; rather, it is a key instrument for development, including social development. Policy for women must therefore be designed as gender aware policy integrated as a central component of all policies. Such a policy then has to be rights-based, in order to be comprehensive and universal. In order to deal with social exclusion of women for ages, the social policy and practice have to be inclusive and empowering women.

Gender aware social work education

Social work profession has an important role to play in planning and implementing gender policy and practice. Social work education in Asia needs to mainstream gender awareness in all its courses and field practicum as well as plan focused courses on gender aware social work covering the following modules:

Module on world status on gender equality

World Status on Gender Measures and gender equality as a Millennium Development Goal

Module on schools of feminist thought and women's movement

Liberal feminism, Marxist feminism, radical feminism, socialist feminism, postcolonial Third World feminism, postmodernist feminism, eco-feminism and women's NGOs, movement and autonomous groups

Module on United Nations policy approaches for gender aware development

Women, industrialisation and development, beginning of the United Nations activities for women, the United Nations Convention on Elimination of Discrimination against Women, Women In Development approach, Women And Development approach, Gender And Development approach and mainstreaming gender.

Module on gender-aware social work

Gender-aware social work with women and men, creating social awareness about women's rights and social action for women's rights.

Module on causes, policies and interventions for marginalisation of women by social systems

Women and marriage and family, women and culture/ religion/ caste, women and media and women and political systems.

Module on causes, policies and interventions for marginalisation of basic needs of women

Women and health, women and education, women and livelihood/ employment, women and housing, women and environment, women and sexuality and women and reproduction

Module on causes, policies and interventions for violence against and by women

Domestic violence against women, trafficking and commercial sexual exploitation of women and women and crime

Module on policies and interventions for marginalised among women

Girl child and socialisation, women in old age, women with disability and women in marginalised castes and tribes.

References

Asian Development Bank. (2011). *Key indicators for Asia and the Pacific. Manila.* Retrieved 17 April 2013 from www.adb.org/key-indicators/2011/main.

Boserup, E. (1970). *Woman's role in economic development.* New York: St Martin's Press.

Connelly, P., Li, T.M., MacDonald, M. & Parpart, J.L. (2000). Feminism and development: theoretical perspectives. In J.L. Parpart, M.P. Connelly & V.E. Barriteau (Eds). *Theoretical Perspectives on Gender and Development.* Retrieved 17 April 2013 from www.idrc.ca/es/ev-27444-201-1-DO_TOPIC.html.

Cook, S., Kabeer, N. & Suwannarat, G. (2003). Introduction. In S. Cook, N. Kabeer, & G. Suwannarat (Eds). *Social protection in Asia* (pp. 13–56). New Delhi: Har-Anand Publications.

Heywood, A. (2007). *Political ideologies: an introduction* (4th ed.) New York: Palgrave Macmillan.

International Labor Organisation. (2007). ABC of women workers' rights and gender Equality, 2nd edn. Geneva. Retrieved 17 April 2013 from www.ilo.org/wcmsp5/groups/public/---dgreports/---gender/documents/publication/wcms_087314.pdf.

Kabeer, N. (1995). *Reversed realities: gender hierarchies in development thought.* New Delhi: Kali for Women.

Kabeer, N. (2003). *Gender mainstreaming in poverty eradication and the millennium development goals: a handbook for policy-makers and other stakeholders.* Ottawa: Commonwealth Secretariat.

Lapidus, G.W. (1982). *Women, work, and family in the Soviet Union.* Armonk, NY: M. E. Sharpe. Retrieved 17 April 2013 from www.questia.com/library/book/women-work-and-family-in-the-soviet-union-by-gail-warshofsky-lapidus.jsp.

Newman, M. (2005). *Socialism: a very short introduction.* New York: Oxford University Press.

Oakley, A. (1985 [1972]). Sex, gender and society. London: Temple Smith. London: Gower.

Razavi, S. & Miller, C. (1995). *From WID to GAD: conceptual shifts in the women and development discourse.* Geneva: United Nations Research Institute for Social Development.

United Nations Development Program. (1995). *Human development report: gender and human development.* New York: Oxford University Press.

United Nations Development Program. (2009). *Human development report. Overcoming barriers: human mobility and development.* New York: Oxford University Press.

United Nations Development Program. (2013). *Human development report. The rise of the South: human progress in a diverse world.* New York.

United Nations Development Programme Regional Bureau for Europe and CIS. (2011). *Beyond transition: towards incusive societies.* Bratislava. Retrieved 17 April 2013 from hdr.undp.org/en/reports/regional/europethecis/RBEC_HDR_2011_EN.pdf.

United Nations Development Programme Russia. (2010). *Millennium Development Goals in Russia: looking into the future.* Moscow. Retrieved 17 April 2013 from hdr.undp.org/en/reports/national/europethecis/russia/Russia_NHDR_2010_EN.pdf.

United Nations Research Institute for Social Development. (2007). Conference news: poverty reduction and policy regimes: Report of the UNRISD workshop in Geneva, Geneva.

Note

This article is part of a larger Comparative Study on Diversity in Social Development in Asia carried out by the author in 2012.

4

Teaching heterosexual privilege

Mark Henrickson

Sexual and gender minorities (what English speakers call gay, lesbian, bisexual, transgender, and intersex, and their local cultural equivalents) seem to raise complex and difficult issues wherever they appear. This chapter argues that it is not sexual and gender minorities that are the problem. The real challenge to social work education is unexamined heterosexual privilege. The purpose of this chapter is to encourage social work educators, students and practitioners to examine critically their assumptions about what they believe is normal about identities, relationships, governmental recognition of relationships, fitness to raise children, and the host of other issues that have been raised by sexual and gender minority communities around the world. This is an urgent issue for social work educators because to remain uncritical about heterosexual privilege is to remain unaware and to replicate that privilege. Implications for teaching, field education, research and practice are considered.

異性戀的特權

生理性別和社會性別的少數派（在英語中他們稱之爲男同性戀，女同性戀，雙性戀，變性人和雙性人，以及在他們的文化裏具有等同意義的群體）無論在哪出現都會引起諸多複雜和困難的問題。這一章我們將討論性向和性別少數實際上並不是問題。對於社會工作教育的真正挑戰是那些異性戀所享有的未被質疑的特權。本章的目的是鼓勵社會工作教育者，學生和實踐者去批判地審視什麼是正常的身份認同，戀愛關系，政府認定的關系和健康地撫養孩子以及一系列其他的問題，同時也將討論由生理性別和社會性別少數派社區引起的問題。對于社工來說這是一個極其緊迫的問題，因爲繼續對異性戀的特權保持不批判就是沒有意識到並將重複這種特權。性向和性別的問題暗示著，之後開展的教學、實際教育、調查和實踐需要將此類問題納入考量範圍。

異性愛者の特権を教えること

性的マイノリティー（一般的にゲイ、レズビアン、バイセクシャル、トランスジェンダーまた性分化疾患とよばれる人々）は地域に関係なく、複雑で難しい問題を提起しているように思われる。この章では、性的マイノリティーが問題なのではなく、よく考察されていない異性愛の特権こそがソーシャルワーク教育にとっての本当の挑戦であると主張する。この章の目的はソーシャルワーク教育者、研究生そして実践者に彼らが‘ 普通’だと信じている素性、人間関係、人間関係に対する政府の認識、育児の適合性、そして世界中で性的マイノリティーによって引き起こされた他の問題の根源における憶測を熟考するよう奨励することである。この章の目的は、ソーシャルワークの教育関係者、学生、実践者たちに、彼らが一般に‘普通’であると信じているアイデンティティー、人間関係、またそれに対する政府の認識、育児における適性、そしてその他世界中の性的マイノリティーによって引き起こされた問題の根源に対する憶測を、批判的に吟味するよう促すことである。異性愛の特権に無批判でい続けるということは、その特権に対し無理解でい続けることであるため、これはソーシャルワークの教育関係者にとって急を要する問題である。この問題に対する教育、実地研修、研究そして実践における意味合いが検討されている。

이성애자 권리 교육

성 소수자들(게이, 레즈비언, 양성애자, 성전환자, 중성)은 어디서나 복잡하고 어려운 문제를 제기한다. 본 장에서는 이것이 성소수자들만의 문제가 아니라는 것을 주장한다. 사회복지교육에서 정말로 문제가 되는 것은 양성애자가 자동으로 가지는 특권 때문에 검토되지 않는점이 있다는 것이다. 본 장의 목적은 사회복지 교육자, 학생, 실무자들이 일반적으로 추측하고 있는 내용을 고찰해 보는데 있다.

정상이라고 추측되는 성정체성, 관계, 자녀교육에 적합한가, 법적으로 인정받는 부부형태, 성적 소수자에게 관련된 다른 일련의 문제들이 고찰되었다. 양성애자에 대한 권리는 무비판적으로 받아들여지고 있기 때문에 사회복지교육자에게 매우 시급한 이슈이다. 교육, 실습, 조사연구, 실무의 여러 측면에서 함의를 제시하였다.

Introduction

At a meeting of international social work educators a few years ago a discussion about a policy issue that involved sexual and gender minorities grew quite heated. One group, some of whom were from developed nations, proposed one view, and others, some from developing nations, held quite a different view. Finally one of the educators (from a developing nation) stood up and said, 'Why do we have to keep talking about this issue which is important only to a very few people! There are more important things that are critical in my country!' The educator was clearly frustrated about a very difficult and complex issue which appeared to be of minor importance on the scale of issues developing nations face, and was not ready to make the connection between the oppression of sexual and gender minorities with other oppressions. Sexual and gender minorities (that is, what English speakers call gay, lesbian, bisexual, transgender and intersex, as well as all their local cultural equivalents) seem to raise complex and difficult issues wherever we appear. Basic human rights and recognition for sexual and gender minorities are often labelled 'special rights' (Stone, 2012, p. 26) by those who oppose them. Heterosexuals who support sexual and gender minorities are regarded with suspicion as perhaps being 'hidden'—because, after all, why would you support such stigmatised groups unless you were one yourself?! This chapter argues that it is not sexual and gender minorities who are the problem. The real challenge to social justice and diversity is unexamined heterosexual privilege, 'the range of perks and incentives with which heterosexually identified persons are rewarded for conforming to the dominant sexuality' (Ryder, as cited in Ayers & Brown, 2005). In social work we are very accustomed to engage with issues that surround the privileges attributed by gender, race, ethnicity (Case, 2007), socioeconomic status, ability and even language. But we are so surrounded by heterosexuality and the institutions that normalise it that we rarely stop to consider the many privileges that accrue to being heterosexual. The frustrated social work educator mentioned above, I would argue, was working from a framework of uncritical heterosexual privilege.

To remain uncritical about heterosexual privilege is to remain unaware of and to replicate that privilege. If social work educators are not critical about heterosexual privilege, as we are and should be about other privileges, we will teach that privilege to students. If we are uncritical about any kind of privilege then we will participate in the oppression of people who do not have that privilege. We will pass it on to our students, and they, in turn to their clients. Replicating oppression is contrary to such basic social work principles as social justice and the dignity and worth of persons (Hess & Feldman, 2008, p. 27; Levy, 2009). Critically considering heterosexual privilege is, I propose, as important to social work educators as critically considering oppression imposed by patriarchy, race, ethnicity, class, ability or any other privileged status.

Some social workers will claim that their private religious beliefs prevent them from 'accepting' sexual and gender minorities, or that they are willing to work with them but 'don't accept their lifestyle.' While social workers recognise the many and rich contributions that religions have made to societies around the world, and the tremendous influence that religions have on both reflecting and shaping cultural and social values, social workers may not uncritically accept religious texts or discourse as justifications for their professional social work values. To do so is to move beyond the realm of 'private' beliefs and to impose those values and beliefs onto others.

Traditionalist arguments that some cultures 'do not accept' homosexuality or transgenderism can no longer be sustained: there are a number of countries in the world where consensual same-sex relationships are punishable by whipping (Malaysia) imprisonment (e.g., Myanmar, Tanzania, Uganda), torture (Uganda) or death (e.g,

Iran, Mauritania, Qatar, Saudi Arabia, Sudan, Yemen, and parts of Nigeria) (Amnesty International, 2008); such laws almost inevitably treat men more harshly than women in this regard. In 2007 Kuwait enacted a law which made it a criminal offence 'to imitate the appearance of the opposite sex' (Amnesty International, 2008); in the first year 14 people were arrested under this law, which was clearly targeted at gender and sexual minorities. Only in 2009 did an Indian court repeal Section 377 of its Penal Code (a legacy of the British Raj), which criminalised 'voluntary carnal intercourse against the order of nature'(Peletz, 2009). National contexts do not make such laws or such cultural positioning acceptable to social work, any more than allegations of infidelity justify stoning women to death. Clearly, unexamined heterosexual privilege can be not only dangerous, but in too many cases, fatal.

Heterosexual privilege is grounded in heteronormativity. Heteronormativity is the assumption that heterosexuality—that, is opposite-sex attraction and desire, and the rights and institutions that go with it, like marriage and childrearing—is normal, natural, and 'perhaps the only way to be' (Teich, 2012, p. 23), or 'natural, inevitable or desirable' (Montgomery & Stewart, 2012, p. 164). Ingraham writes that heteronormativity is the view 'that institutionalised heterosexuality constitutes the standard for legitimate and expected social and sexual relations' (cited in Montgomery & Stewart, 2012, p. 164). Heteronormativity (sometimes called heterosexism in earlier literature; Mallon, 2008, p. 388), therefore assumes that anything other than heterosexuality is deviant or abnormal. Heteronormativity is different from homophobia ('the fear of homosexuals'): homophobia is prejudiced attitudes towards sexual minorities (Herek, cited in Montgomery & Stewart, 2012, p. 164), whilst heteronormativity is the set of internalised expectations about gender and sexuality.

Heteronormativity also assumes a tidy binary of gender and sexuality boxes into which people must fit: people must be either male or female. People must be either gay (homosexual) or straight (heterosexual). Aside from the historical complexity of using such words, we now understand that gender may be more like a spectrum of possible identities, and that what is popularly understood as male or female are merely endpoints on this spectrum (Teich, 2012). Likewise, we understand that sexual identity, desire and attraction are better understood as spectra than binary boxes. Furthermore, people's locations on those spectra can change over the courses of their lives, although men are more likely to remain fixed in one orientation over their lives than are women (Diamond, 2003, 2005; Hammack, 2005; Henrickson, Neville, Jordan, & Donaghey, 2007) . Social work theory has long proposed that people and their environments are constantly interacting and that people are constantly evolving and changing through those transactions (Germain & Gitterman, 1996). In recent decades social work has made great advances in understanding oppression and cultural diversity (Dominelli, 2002), and social work educators and practitioners now take cultural and individual diversity as axiomatic. There is no reason that we should retain the essentialist belief that people's gender and sexual identities are fixed or unchanging, or should remain conformed to prehistoric paradigms; indeed, the growing literature on gender and sexual minorities over the last several decades suggests quite the opposite.

The purpose of this chapter is to encourage social work educators, students and practitioners to examine critically their assumptions about what they believe is normal about identities, relationships, governmental recognition of relationships, fitness to raise children, and the host of other issues that have been raised by sexual and gender minority communities around the world. While a number of cultures may maintain that same-sex sexual behaviours and identities, or transgendered identities are unknown or unacceptable to them, or the result of external influences, even a cursory review of history reveals that same-sex attractions and behaviours (at least) have occurred in every culture in every age (Crompton, 2003), and that, as we shall see below, in the Asia-Pacific region these attractions were historically not stigmatised. In the Asia-Pacific region what may be the result of Western influences are stigma, religious intolerance and the legacy of colonial legal prohibitions against the expressions of same-sex behaviours and romantic love (Aldrich,

2003; Leupp, 1997). Social work educators replicate stigma, intolerance and colonial attitudes when they uncritically adopt and replicate those attitudes about gender and sexuality. We know that the attitudes of social work students towards heterosexual privilege can be influenced in the classroom (Case & Stewart, 2010; Chonody, Rutledge, & Seibert, 2009). The challenge to social work educators in the Asia Pacific—and for that matter, throughout the world—is to critically examine their own understandings and attitudes about gender, sexuality and heterosexual privilege so that students and practitioners will be able to work competently with diverse communities in their various practice environments.

The Asia-Pacific context

In the Asia-Pacific context, 'sexual minorities' is a broad concept that includes a wide array of individual, social and cultural roles, behaviours and identities. The *takatāpui* of Aotearoa New Zealand (Aspin, 2005; Te Awekotuku, 2001), the *fa'afafine* of Samoa, *leitis* of Tonga, *wadna* of Fiji, *tongzhi* 同志 , *tongxin' ai*, *tongxing lian'ai* and *tongxinglian* 同性恋)of China and Chinese Taipei (Chou, 2000; Lim, 2008; Sang, 2003), *calabai*, *calalai*, and *waria* of Indonesia (Davies, 2010), *wonchung* or historical *hwarang* 화랑, or the more recent *dong-song-e-ja* and *i-van*, of Korea (Park, 2008), the *nanshoku* 男色, *shudō* 衆道, *wakashudō* 若衆道 and *dōseiaisha* 同性愛者 of Japan (Leupp, 1997), the *dogana*, *kothi* and *hijra* of India (Nanda, 1999), the *bayot*, *bakla* and *bading* of the Philippines, *tom*, *dee*, *kathoey* กะเทย of Thailand (Sinnot, 2008), *acaults*, *dzibou* and *meinmasha* of Mynamar/ Burma (Peletz, 2009) as well as Western-style urbanised lesbian, gay, bisexual and transgender individuals in internationalised cities such as Hong Kong and Singapore are only some examples. Indeed, to describe sexual and gender minorities and variations in any one culture would require a library of books in disciplines like history and anthropology rather than a single chapter in a social work anthology.

Gandhi (in Vanita, 2002) proposes that there is a rich vein of same-sex desire in South Asia, 'journeying from the ancient Sanskrit epics through medieval Puranic narratives and Urdu poetry' (p. 87), which was suppressed by British purity campaigns of the late 19th century. Leupp (1997) argues that male-male sexual partnerships are well-documented in Korea from the Silla dynasty (57 BCE-935 CE), and are documented in Japan from 985 CE; in each culture, of course, the documentation refers to royal or upper classes and does not exclude marriages with women. He argues that 'Sex between males was not only widely tolerated among the articulate classes, but positively celebrated in popular art and literature' (p. 1), and that it was not merely common but normative in Tokugawa Japan (1603–1868 CE). Leupp proposes that such liaisons declined only after Japan's modern opening to the West in 1859, when the ruling elite determined that Japan should observe Western learning in order to obtain the respect of Western nations. Male homoeroticism in China is well-documented from the Warring States period (481–221 BCE) through the Ming (1368–1644) and early Qing (1644–1911) dynasties (Vitiello, 2011), and the stories behind Lord Longyang, Emperor Ai's cut sleeve, and Mizi Xia's shared peach with Duke Ling are the stuff of legend. Indeed, the major negative response to male-male sexual attraction and behaviour comes from court historians who warned that both male and female attractions can be politically risky for the emperor:

> [B]eautiful boy favorites can be as dangerous for the sovereign and the state as beautiful concubines. An emperor's fondness for male beauty, just as his fondness for female beauty, represents a political liability in that it can degenerate into his sliding into a crazed obsession, with the consequent dereliction of his official duties. (Vitiello, 2011, p. 2)

Sang's (2003) extensive work explores relationships between women in pre-modern, republican and post-Maoist Chinese cultures (including Chinese Taipei), and suggests that changed language such as *tongxing'ai* indicates that there was significant public discourse around same-sex relationships, particularly during the May Fourth era (1915–1921 CE). This was the time when China needed to appear strong in order to achieve standing among the community of nations.

Murray (2002) has developed a typology of male same-sex attraction drawn from cultures around the Pacific; the implications of the European construction of some of these identities are developed by Wallace (2003). Some of these roles are performative or religious, some transitional, and some are egalitarian; some exclude the possibility of formalised opposite-sex relationships and some allow that possibility. There are probably at least as many different ways of conceptualising sexual identity around the Pacific as there are distinct cultures, although in the early 21st century these are being hegemonised into Westernised constructs of sexual identities. Contemporary Pasifika sexual identities are dynamic. For instance, in the last few years in Kiribati a social movement of gender minorities has emerged called 'Miss July' after the month in which Kiribati independence is observed (Kiribati On Line Community, n.d.); the Tongan word 'fakaleiti' ('in the manner of a lady') is now falling into disuse among that community in favour of 'leiti' (which implies a more authentic fully transgendered identity).

Asia-Pacific scholarship in gender and sexual minorities has increased significantly over the last decade: Laurent (2005) summarises the socio-cultural, legal and contemporary situations of sexual and gender minorities in a number of Asian countries; Henrickson (2006) considers how contemporary Māori in Aotearoa New Zealand manage to balance both cultural and sexual identities; Pitts, Smith, Mitchell and Patel (2006) describe the private lives of sexual minorities in Australia; Oswin, (2010) advocates for a queer theoretical approach to Singapore's housing policy; Bong (2011) explores the life of a bisexual woman in Malaysia; and Lam (2012) writes about Vietnam's first gay pride parade on 5 August, 2012, and asks whether Vietnam may be the first Asian nation to legalise same-sex marriages (the answer may be that Chinese Taipei/Taiwan may get there first), The AsiaPacifiQueer group, which has grown out of the Sexualities, Genders and Rights conference in Bangkok in 2005, is a group of Asian queer studies scholars who continue to challenge the Anglocentric biases in sexuality studies (Martin, Jackson, McLelland, & Yue, 2008). Yet it is also clear that 'gay and lesbian rights are not at that stage in Asia where they can be fully recognised as individual human rights' (Laurent, 2005, p. 214), and that applying English language and Western identity constructs to communities and cultures where such constructs are not necessarily indigenous is fraught and inappropriate, an argument developed by Murray (2002), and supported in the contemporary literature (Laurent, 2005).

Processes of individuation and establishing individual sexual or gender identities are discouraged by heterosexual privilege in hierarchical and collectivist cultures that value filial piety, which makes coming to terms with individual experiences of the self as different a complex process in such cultures (Walters & Old Person Jr., 2008); yet Asian countries are slowly finding their own means of expression for addressing sexual and gender minority issue (Laurent, 2005). Sexuality may play a less important role in the construction of individual identity in Asian (and Pacific) cultures than in Western Europeanised cultures in which the discovery of the self and self-fulfilment are paramount values. Asian sexuality has been described as elastic, in that often Asian sexual minorities marry opposite-sex partners and have children (Laurent, 2005) while maintaining concurrent same-sex sexual relationships. It may be construed, then, that many Asian cultures are tacitly accepting of sexual minorities, as long as family obligations for procreation—another heterosexual privilege, as well as an obligation in this context—are met. (We must wonder, however, in the age of HIV and drug-resistant gonorrhoea, whether such models of dual identity are either wise or practically sustainable.)

What all these diversities of cultures, contexts and identities have in common in the Asia Pacific, however, is their marginalisation and exclusion by heterosexual privilege.

Heterosexual privilege

Heterosexual privilege has been called both a blessing and a curse (Ayres & Brown, 2005). If it is a blessing it is because it provides heterosexual people an unquestioned place to belong, a common bond with other heterosexuals: the legal rights of marriage for instance, or the right to conceive and raise children; the rights to participate fully and openly in a society without having to disclose one's stigmatised identity; in some places tax and insurance advantages apply to opposite-sex married couples. Heterosexual privilege assumes that everyone else is also heterosexual. It is a curse, however, in that such privilege can blind one to the concealed differences of others: it makes the denial of privilege unimaginable. Privilege is that which prevents men from understanding patriarchy or their presumed power over women; it is what prevents people with lighter skin from understanding the stigmatised experiences of people with darker skin. Such privilege lulls one into complacency that everyone in the world is in fact just like you, and that the world is a safe and equitable place (Ayres & Brown, 2005).

Hicks (2008) critiques the discourses of anti-discriminatory and anti-oppressive practice in respect of sexual (and by extension, gender) minorities. He suggests that the dominant discourse of sexuality in liberal social work understands sexual minority identities as stable, fixed and positive; this means that sexual minorities come as fixed 'types' with needs that must be understood and met by social workers, and that sexual minority individuals are understood and held accountable to the identities that are attributed to them. In this way it is social work, not the sexual or gender minority individual or community, who constructs the minoritised identity, in a kind of compassionate hegemony constructed by well-intentioned social workers. This construction creates a view of sexuality as an essentially private matter that produces discord primarily when individuals are prevented from accessing legal/civil rights enjoyed by the mainstream. The solution to this discord is to amend the rights to expand access, which results in increased assimilation. Hicks calls this the new 'homonormativity' (p. 68), because these adaptive social change models are also promoted by sexual (and gender) minority rights groups. But what is important to understand about this approach is that a position of heteronormativity is adopted from which to know *about* non-heterosexuals. Heterosexuality remains the privileged and unexamined position from which to view and analyse sexual and gender minorities. Sexual and gender minorities are objectified, and remain an object of knowledge-people to know 'about'. The hegemonic point of view—heterosexuality—remains intact and is not itself interrogated.

The challenge posed by the critique of heterosexual privilege can change a discourse of privilege into one of unease, in that coming to an awareness of one's self as privileged is a very difficult and often painful process for those willing to take the political and cultural critique seriously. If we are accustomed to seeing ourselves as marginalised—for instance, being a woman in a highly patriarchal society, being from a poor or developing nation among a community of wealthy, developed nations, being a member of disadvantaged religious minority—the very idea that our self-identity as a marginalised person could in some way be privileged is alien, shocking and uncomfortable. In social work we easily use words like compassion, tolerance, and difference, words that establish norms, and tell us how to work with people who are different from those norms. Yet, the traditional vocabulary of tolerance and compassion undermine key concepts such as rights and respect (Feigenbaum, 2007). Tolerance implies that your difference makes you less than me but that I will accept you despite your difference from me. Compassion implies that I have more power than you do, and your difference marginalises you in such a way that you require my help in order to be less marginalised. In this sense, tolerance and compassion are frequently othering words used from positions of power and privilege.

Heterosexual privilege is extremely subtle because it is so much a part (probably quite literally) of the DNA of heterosexual persons that it is extremely difficult to become aware of it. It shapes identity, relationships, power and perspective; in short, it shapes everything. Feigenbaum (2007, p. 6) writes,

> Insight into hetero-privilege interpersonally provides a succinct and astute point of entry into the hazy world of unexamined dominance. Hetero-privilege consists of a tightly woven set of exclusions and disinterests that functions among straights [heterosexuals] to protects a 'prejudice [that] is deep-rooted an ancient enough to be instantly

understood—communicated keenly enough by way of the simplest glances, the merest shadow-look'. (Glave 2003/2004, p. 592)

Heterosexual privilege is constantly reinforced by the social, cultural and political structures in a society. If a legislature is willing to consider the concept of same-sex marriage, for instance, a wide array of individual, social, cultural and religious interests will oppose such concepts on the grounds of tradition. But tradition also encompasses a host of other social institutions—such as child labour, concubinage, foot-binding, human sacrifice, satī सती, slavery and human trafficking—that have previously existed in many cultures, but which most societies are (at least legislatively) no longer willing to tolerate. (This is not to suggest that some of these regressive social institutions no longer exist in practice, or are not actively promoted by underground profiteers in some regions: the analogy here is legislative tolerance.) It may be conveniently forgotten that covenants between passionate same-sex friends were traditional throughout Asia (at least among the articulate classes) centuries ago. And so hetero-privilege is self-reinforcing. 'Privilege functions best when it is doling out access, admitting and rejecting claims at whim, like a burly bouncer at the gates of justice' (Feigenbaum, 2007, p. 8).

The concepts of social justice, the dignity and worth of persons, and human rights are core to social work (Staub-Bernasconi, 2012), both as a profession and an academic discipline. If these principles are so core to social work, social work academics, researchers and lecturers do not have the option of choosing which human rights they choose to uphold, and what forms of social justice they can ignore. A discipline of inclusion may not practice any form of exclusion. While social workers can be agents for inclusion, they can also reinforce marginalisation and exclusion (Lyons & Huegler, 2012). Proactively supporting sexual and gender minorities is essential, especially in countries and cultures where being a gender or sexual minority person is unpopular or unspeakable. Even in nations where the rights of gender and sexual minorities are more legislatively secure, in one study of lesbian, gay and bisexual persons, 76.6 per cent of men and 64.4 per cent of women said that they had been verbally assaulted because of their sexuality (Queer! Faggot! Poof!), and 18.2 per cent of men and 9.2 per cent of women had been physically assaulted (queer-bashed) because of their sexual identity (Henrickson, et al., 2007). Young sexual minority students appear to select out of education because of homophobic bullying in environments which make learning more than just difficult (Henrickson, 2008), but dangerous. Sexual minority students in postgraduate programs defer disclosing their identities, and report high levels of intolerance among their academic mentors (Henrickson, 2008). Sexual minorities are at higher risk of mental disorder, suicidal ideation, substance misuse, and deliberate self harm than heterosexual people (King et al., 2008; Suicide Prevention Resource Center, 2008). Heterosexual privilege is harmful, even in societies without legal sanctions against sexual and gender minority persons.

Social work education

One of the first things that social work educators can and must do about heterosexual privilege is to become critically aware of their own attitudes and how those attitudes have been both subtly and overtly informed by their dominant social, cultural, and religious paradigms. As noted above, this is both difficult and painful as we become aware of the almost countless ways that heterosexual privilege has been reinforced by the social and cultural milieux in which we are inextricably located. 'Heterosexual people are endowed with a privilege based upon the social implications of their sexual orientation, and this privilege, if not managed effectively, can create obstacles to their constructive engagement'(Ayres & Brown, 2005, p. 3) in creating safer environments for sexual and gender minorities. There are still social workers, no doubt, (like the frustrated educator we met at the outset of this chapter) who believe that sexual and gender minority rights are an unwelcome imposition by Westernised developed nations. Yet would it not be ironic to discover that social workers who believe they are rejecting colonial and Western values by promoting heteronormative values and attempting to suppress sexual minorities are instead, through their failure to interrogate critically their heteronormativity and hetero-privilege, simply replicating those very Western colonial values?

Teaching/classroom

Martinez (2011) finds that sexual minority issues are not adequately included in social work education, and knowledge regarding subtle sexual prejudice is lacking in social work curricula. She proposes that elements that should be included in a social work curriculum include public attitudes towards lesbians and gay men; sexual prejudice, homophobia and heterosexism; homophobia as pathology; pro-gay egalitarianism; modern and aversive heterosexism, and queer consciousness. Social work educators must be mindful that sexual and gender minority students, even those who perform well, are more than likely to have experienced family, work or educational environments as hostile, and may arrive in the classroom with a history of experiences of harassment, discrimination and even violence. One of the challenges to educators is that sexual minority students may frequently be invisible, for because of heteronormativity and hetero-privilege, they must usually make a public declaration of their identities before they are identified, and the very experiences of alienation and discrimination militate against taking such risks (Rasmussen, 2004). It is essential, then, that all social work educators make an explicit statement to all students about their awareness of and inclusion of sexual and gender minorities. Encouraging the recruitment of sexual and gender minority students, academic and general staff ensures that the work of disclosure does not fall to a few isolated individuals. Nevertheless, self-disclosing one's sexual or gender minority status offers a significant opportunity for the educator and student to explore the intersection of the personal and the professional (Gates, 2011, p. 71), and offers a sense of wholeness, authenticity and integrity, and offer powerful role models for sexual and gender minority students. If educators are not self-disclosed sexual or gender minorities themselves they must acknowledge the heterosexual privilege they carry—whether they want it or not, whether they like it or not—as well as their open and accepting stance toward sexual and gender minorities. If all social work educators do this, then it is not left only to sexual or gender minority educators to disclose themselves to their students. This open attitude, and the creation of safe spaces, can be expressed in lectures, by case presentations, case examples, classroom discussions and examinations. Case examples that do not problematise minority sexual or gender identities should be developed and presented in order to normalise minority sexual identities and integrate them into classroom discussions in constructive ways. It has been demonstrated that exposing tertiary level social work students to sexual and gender minority experiences can change the attitudes of those students (Chonody, et al., 2009).

Such efforts of inclusion should not be limited to the classroom. Non-academic staff have frequent and important interactions with students, and general staff conversations can be overheard by waiting students; casual negative comments can have a long-lasting and devastating effects.

FIELD EDUCATION

Field education settings should be assessed to ensure that they are safe for sexual and gender minority students, and where necessary field supervisors should be upskilled, or alternative sites found. Every effort should be made to normalise sexual and gender identities, and to offer students opportunities to integrate their sexual or gender identities as parts of their total selves. All social work staff must work to identify, confront and change overly heteronormative assumptions and behaviours within their social work programs. The mean age when young sexual minority males experience themselves as different is 11 and females, 14 (Henrickson & Neville, 2012). Students in field education placements—particularly those in schools, orphanages, youth programs, care and protection settings, or who work with children, adolescents and young adults in any setting—must also be equipped to ensure that they clearly and specifically communicate support for sexual minority young people, even though such young people may not be apparent or self-identified.

Anti-discriminatory or anti-oppressive practice is a necessary but of itself an insufficient way of working with sexual and gender minority young people. Since sexual and gender minorities can be hidden minorities, creating supportive environments must be explicit and overt to all participants.

All of these considerations in the classroom and in field education settings are undeniably a lot of work. Imagine what it could be like to be in the role of a vulnerable student, adolescent or child facing such challenges alone.

Research

Jeyashingham (2008) advocates for more scholarship which identifies the ways day-to-day practice and social apparatuses operate to reinforce homophobia—and by extension heteronormativity—in societal and social work contexts. Although it risks perpetuating the 'sexual and gender minority as culture' discourse, and creates the possibility of a hierarchy of oppressions, Van Den Bergh and Crisp (2004) set out a useful attitudes, knowledge and skills heuristic for social work education that draws on frameworks for cultural competence with ethnic and racial minority clients, feminist and gay-affirmative practices, and sets out some proposals for affirming curriculum content. Such content should be consistent across social work educational programs within a country (Mulé, 2006), and assessed by professional regulatory bodies. Meezan and Martin (2009) have published an accessible and useful guide to research with sexual and gender minorities which should be in the reference library of every social work researcher, educator and student.

Practice

Heterosexual privilege must also not assume that every child is heterosexual. An Aotearoa New Zealand study of sexual minorities found that sexual minority young people are experiencing themselves as different and affiliating with sexual minority cultures much earlier than older generations (Henrickson, et al., 2007). This means that social work practitioners in schools, adoption, child protection and child advocacy settings, must take into account sexualities when assessing a child for care or placement. Robust anti-bullying policies and practices must be in place in schools and recreational programs, and actively enforced. Some violence against children at home may be related to the disclosure or discovery of a sexual or gender identity, relationship or behaviour that is unacceptable to the family, and finding a safe place for the child must include an assessment of safety for a child's sexual or gender minority status. This must be done without problematising the minoritised identity, but instead understanding that the heteronormative value is the problem. Temporary or permanent placement with same-sex couples or sexual minority individuals are obvious solutions, but hetero-privileging national or state laws may prohibit such solutions. Social workers must be prepared to ally with sexual and gender minority communities to reform such laws or regulations when required.

Social workers must also be mindful of the hetero-privileging paradigm in which healthcare and social services operate. Social workers are taught not to assume anything about their clients, and yet we assume heterosexual development, and a heterosexual developmental trajectory, in young people. Asking young adolescent boys 'Is there a special girl' makes all kinds of assumptions. Teaching social workers to ask neutral questions of clients like 'Are you dating anyone yet?' or in assessments, 'Are you attracted to (or in health care settings, sexually active with) men, women, both or neither?'—even of heterosexually married clients—rather than assuming an opposite-sex partner will allow a client to answer a question honestly, signal a worker's openness to hearing the answer, and will help the worker to obtain much more valuable information about the individual and their social context (Neville & Henrickson, 2006). Such questions should be framed in an open way of all clients regardless of the client's putative marriage status, or the cultural contexts and expectations.

A core professional and ethical value of social work is social justice. Social justice can transform societies and change social values and shapes social work teaching, research and practice. Although stigmatised sexual and gender minorities are frequently problematised, this chapter has proposed that a significant challenge to social justice and diversity is unexamined heterosexual privilege. This challenge does not detract or distract from equally urgent critiques based on gender, ethnicity, class, ability and other power imbalances, but it must be included with them. The moment we create hierarchies of inclusion we have begun to exclude. Heterosexual privilege is based on the assumption that heterosexuality is the normal way to be, and is reinforced by a wide array of cultural, social, political and religious institutions. Nevertheless, throughout the Asia-Pacific region and the rest of the world, heterosexual privilege is increasingly being named and challenged. No doubt in some places in the region social work educators are undertaking these challenges and engaging in a heteronormative critique. This would be encouraging, since sexual and gender minorities are at risk for an array of social problems, and are at high risk of negative social outcomes. It is important that social work educators understand and address heteronormativity in their teaching, research and practice. Through critical self-examination and awareness, and by educating ourselves about these issues, social work educators can avoid teaching heterosexual privilege that contribute to these negative outcomes. This chapter has proposed some specific ways social workers can address and change our teaching, field education, research and practice to be more inclusive, and more just.

References

Aldrich, R. (2003). *Colonialism and homosexuality*. London: Routledge.

Amnesty International. (2008). *Love, hate and the law: decriminalising homosexuality*. London: Amnesty International, International Secretariat.

Aspin, C. (2005). The place of takatapui identity within Maori society: reinterpreting Maori sexuality within a contemporary context. Paper presented at the Competing Diversities: Traditional Sexualities and Modern Western Sexual Identity Constructions Conference, Mexico City.

Ayres, I., & Brown, J.G. (2005). *Straightforward: how to mobilize heterosexual support for gay rights.* Princeton: Princeton University Press.

Bong, S.A. (2011). Beyond queer: an epistemology of bi choice. *Journal of Bisexuality*, 11(1), 39–63.

Case, K.A. (2007). Raising White privilege awareness and reducing racial prejudice: assessing diversity, course effectiveness. *Teaching of Psychology*, 34, 231–35.

Case, K.A., & Stewart, B. (2010). Changes in diversity course student prejudice and attitudes toward heterosexual privilege and gay marriage. *Teaching of Psychology*, 37(3).

Chonody, J.K., Rutledge, S.E., & Seibert, D.C. (2009). College students' attitudes toward gays and lesbians. *Journal of Social Work Education*, 45(3), 499–512.

Chou, W.-S. (2000). *Tongzhi: politics of same-sex eroticism in Chinese societies.* New York: Haworth Press.

Crompton, L. (2003). *Homosexuality and civilization.* Cambridge: Harvard University Press.

Davies, S.G. (2010). *Gender diversity in Indonesia.* London: Routledge.

Diamond, L.M. (2003). Was it a phase?: young women's relinquishment of lesbian/bisexual identities over a 5-year period. *Journal of Personality and Social Psychology*, 84(2), 352–64.

Diamond, L.M. (2005). A new view of lesbian subtypes: stable versus fluid identity trajectories over an 8-year period. *Psychology of Women Quarterly*, 29(2), 119–28.

Dominelli, L. (2002). *Anti-oppressive social work theory and practice.* Basingstoke: Palgrave Macmillan.

Feigenbaum, E. (2007). Heterosexual privilege: the political and the personal. *Hypatia*, 22(1), 1–9.

Gates, T.G. (2011). Coming out in the social work classroom: reclaiming wholeness and finding the teacher within. *Social Work Education: The International Journal*, 30(1), 70–82.

Germain, C. & Gitterman, A. (1996). *The life model of social work practice: advances in theory and practice.* New York: Columbia University Press.

Hammack, P.L. (2005). The life course development of human sexual orientation: an integrative paradigm. *Human Development*, 48(5), 267–290.

Henrickson, M. (2006). Ko wai ratou?: managing multiple identities in lesbian, gay and bisexual New Zealand Maori. *New Zealand Sociology*, 21(2), 251–73.

Henrickson, M. (2008). 'You have to be strong to be gay': bullying and educational attainment in LGB New Zealanders. *Journal of Gay and Lesbian Social Services*, 19(3/4), 67–85.

Henrickson, M. & Neville, S. (2012). Identity satisfaction over the life course in sexual minorities. *Journal of Gay and Lesbian Social Services*, 24, 80–95.

Henrickson, M., Neville, S., Jordan, C. & Donaghey, S. (2007). Lavender islands: the New Zealand study. *Journal of Homosexuality*, 53(4), 223–48.

Hess, P. M., & Feldman, N. (2008). Values and ethics in social work practice with lesbian, gay, bisexual and transgender people. In G. P. Mallon (Ed.), *Social work practice with lesbian, gay, bisexual and transgender people*, 2nd edn (pp. 25–39). New York: Routledge.

Hicks, S. (2008). Thinking through sexuality. *Journal of Social Work*, 8(1), 65–82.

Jeyasingham, D. (2008). Knowledge/Ignorance and the construction of sexuality in social work education. *Social Work Education: The International Journal*, 27(2), 138–151.

King, M., Semlyen, J., Tai, S.S., Killaspy, K., Osborn, D., Popelyuk, D. & Nazareth, I. (2008). A systematic review of mental disorder, suicide, and deliberate self harm in lesbian, gay and bisexual people. *BMC Psychiatry*, 8(70). Retrieved 17 April 2013 from www.ncbi.nlm.nih.gov/pmc/articles/PMC253365.

Kiribati On Line Community. (n.d.) Retrieved November 12, 2012, from www.kiribationlinecommunity.com/forum/topics/miss-july.

Lam, A. (2012). Will gay marriage be a reality in Vietnam, or is it a distraction?: an interview with Nguyen Qui Duc. *Huffpost Gay Voices*. Retrieved 17 April 2013 from www.huffingtonpost.com/andrew-lam/vietnam-gay-marriage_b_1734906.html.

Laurent, E. (2005). Sexuality and human rights: an Asian perspective. *Journal of Homosexuality*, 48(3–4), 163–225.

Leupp, G.P. (1997). *Male colors: the construction of homosexuality in Tokugawa Japan*. Berkelely, California: University of California Press.

Levy, D.L. (2009). Gay and lesbian identity development: an overview for social workers. *Journal of Human Behavior in the Social Environment*, 19(8), 978–93.

Lim, S.H. (2008). How to be queer in Taiwan. In F. Martin, P.A. Jackson, M. McLelland & A. Yue (Eds). *AsiaPacifiQueer* (pp. 235–50). Urbana: University of Chicago Press.

Lyons, K. & Huegler, N. (2012). Social exclusion and inclusion. In L. M. Healy & R. J. Link (Eds). *Handbook of international social work* (pp. 37–43). Oxford: Oxford University Press.

Mallon, G.P. (Ed.) (2008). *Social work practice with lesbian, gay, bisexual and transgender people*, 2nd edn. New York: Routledge.

Martin, F., Jackson, P.A., McLelland, M. & Yue, A. (Eds). (2008). *AsiaPacifiQueer: rethinking genders and sexualities*. Urbana: University of Illinois.

Martinez, P. (2011). A modern conceptualization of sexual prejudice for social work educators. *Social Work Education: The International Journal*, 30(5), 558–70.

Meezan, W. & Martin, J.I. (2009). *Handbook of research with lesbian, gay, bisexual and transgender populations*. New York: Routledge.

Montgomery, S.A. & Stewart, A.J. (2012). Privileged allies in lesbian and gay rights activism: gender, generation and resistance to heteronormativity. *Journal of Social Issues*, 68(1), 162–77.

Mulé, N.J. (2006). Equity vs. invisibility: sexual orientation issues in social work ethics and curricula standards. *Social Work Education*, 25(6), 608–22.

Murray, S.O. (2002). *Pacific homosexualities*. San José: Writers Club Press.

Nanda, S. (1999). *Neither man nor woman: the hijras of India*, 2nd edn. Belmont, CA, USA: Wadsworth.

Neville, S. & Henrickson, M. (2006). Perceptions of lesbian, gay and bisexual people of primary healthcare services. *Journal of Advanced Nursing*, 55(4), 407–15.

Oswin, N. (2010). The modern model family at home in Singapore: a queer geography. *Transactions of the Institute of British Geographers*, 35(2), 256–68.

Park, J.H. (2008). Representation, politics, ethics: rethinking homosexuality in Korean cinema. In F. Martin, P. A. Jackson, M. McLelland & A. Yue (Eds). *AsiaPacifiQueer* (pp. 197–216). Urbana: University of Chicago Press.

Peletz, M.G. (2009). *Gender pluralism: Southeast Asia since early modern times*. New York: Routledge.

Pitts, M., Smith, A., Mitchell, A. & Patel, S. (2006). Private lives: a report on the health and wellbeing of GLBTI Australians. Melbourne: Australian Research Centre in Sex, Health & Society, LaTrobe University.

Rasmussen, M.L. (2004). The problem of coming out. *Theory into Practice*, 43(2), 144–50.

Sang, T.I.D. (2003). *The emerging lesbian: female same-sex desire in modern China*. Chicago: University of Chicago Press.

Sinnot, M. (2008). The romance of the queer: the sexual and gender norms of *tom* and *dee* in Thailand. In F. Martin, P. A. Jackson, M. McLelland & A. Yue (Eds). *AsiaPacifiQueer* (pp. 131–48). Urbana: University of Chicago Press.

Staub-Bernasconi, S. (2012). Human rights and their relevance for social work as theory and practice. In L.M. Healy & R.J. Link (Eds). *Handbook of international social work* (pp. 30–36). Oxford: Oxford University Press.

Stone, A.L. (2012). *Gay rights at the ballot box.* Minneapolis: University of Minnesota Press.

Suicide Prevention Resource Center (2008). Suicide risk and prevention for lesbian, gay, bisexual, and transgender youth. Newton: Education Development Center, Inc.

Te Awekotuku, N. (2001). Hinemoa: retelling a famous romance. In A. Laurie (Ed.), *Lesbian Studies in Aotearoa/New Zealand.* New York: Harrington Park Press.

Teich, N.M. (2012). *Transgender 101: a simple guide to a complex issue.* New York: Columbia University Press.

Van Den Bergh, N., & Crisp, C. (2004). Defining culturally competent practice with sexual minorities: implications for social work education and practice. *Journal of Social Work Education*, 40(2), 221–38.

Vanita, R. (Ed.). (2002). *Queering India: same-sex love and eroticism in Indian culture and society.* New York: Routledge.

Vitiello, G. (2011). *The libertine's friend: homosexuality and masculinity in late imperial China.* Chicago: University of Chicago Press.

Wallace, L. (2003). *Sexual encounters: pacific texts, modern sexualities.* Ithica: Cornell University Press.

Walters, K., & Old Person Jr., R.L. (2008). Lesbians, gays, bisexual and transgender people of color: reconciling divided selves and communities. In G.P. Mallon (Ed.), *Social work practice with lesbian, gay, bisexual and transgender people*, 2nd edn (pp. 41–68). New York: Routledge.

5

Authentication in social work education: the balancing act

Moses Faleolo

Social work education and practice, in regard to non-Western cultures, is struggling to develop and deliver services in an effective, acceptable and culturally appropriate manner. This is because schools of social work, widespread globalisation of Western culture and its scientific knowledge have displaced and been slow to accept non-Western and Indigenous world views, local knowledge and traditional forms of helping and healing. Culturally specific knowledge, values and skills lead to an understanding of other perspectives and cultures; if a social worker's acquisition of these is hampered, then cultural competency is limited. This chapter promotes a cultural authentication approach, where social work education and practices are developed by local cultures to suit their non-Western context and where curricula in Western countries diversify, and incorporate perspectives that are representative and multicultural. It urges a rethinking of what is really universal social work by challenging the dominance of Western beliefs and values.

認證在社會工作教育中的平衡作用

摩西·法萊奧洛

考慮到非西方文化的存在，社會工作教育和實踐在不斷致力於發展和提供有效的、可被接受的、適合本地文化的服務。這是由多種原因導致：首先，提供社會工作專業學習的院校，西方文化的全球化以及非西方文化、本土的世界觀、當地的知識和傳統救助治療體系慢慢接受西方科学知识并逐渐被其取代。有關於文化方面的特定知識、價值和技能會影響個人對於其他觀點和文化的理解。如果一個社會工作者在獲取這些信息的時候有障礙，那麼其理解文化的能力也會因此被束縛。這個篇闡述的是文化認證的過程。社會工作教育和實踐的發展需要倚靠的是不僅是當地文化對非西方文化環境的適應以及多元化的西方國家課程，還包括有代表性的多元文化的綜合視角。此文章通過挑戰西方信仰和價值的主導地位，敦促大家反思到底什麼才是真正廣而適之的社會工作。

ソーシャルワーク教育の認証：均衡を取る

西洋文化圏外におけるソーシャルワークは教育、実践ともに、効率的で社会的に容認され、かつ各文化にふさわしいサービスの発展と提供が滞っている。西洋文化圏外におけるソーシャルワーク教育と実践は、効率的で、社会的に容認され、なおかつ各文化に適切なサービスの提供と発展にもがいている。これは、ソーシャルワークの教育機関や、一般に広がった西洋文化のグローバル化、またその科学的知識が、西洋以外の国固有の世界観や地方固有の知識、また伝統的なかたちの援助や治療を退け、容認することを遅らせていたためである。ソーシャルワーカーが各文化特有の知識、価値観そしてスキルを習得することは他の文化や見解を理解することにつながる。もしこれらの習得が妨げられるのならば、ソーシャルワーカーの文化的適性は制限されてしまう。この章では、ソーシャルワーク教育と実践が、地方の文化によって非西洋の環境に適したものとして発展させられ、西洋諸国のカリキュラムが多様化し、代表的で多文化的な考え方を組み入れる、文化認証アプローチ(cultural authentication approach)への働きかけを奨励する。これは西洋的な信念と価値観の優勢に異議を唱え、本当にユニバーサルなソーシャルワークとは何か、再考することを促している。

사회복지교육에서 문화고유성 모색: 형평성 법칙

비서구문화권에서는 사회복지 교육과 실천현장에서 문화적으로 적절하고 효율적인 방법으로 서비스를 제공하는데 어려움을 겪고 있다. 왜냐하면 사회복지교육기관은 대체로 서구문화의 영향을 받았고 고유의 지식, 전통적인 치유방식을 받아들이지 못했기 때문이다. 문화적으로 독특한 지식, 가치, 기술을 익혀 다른 관점과 문화를 이해하는 것, 이런 점들이 사회복지사에게 없다면 문화적인 유능성은 부족할 수밖에 없다. 본 장은 문화적 고유성 접근방식을 모색하며 사회복지교육과 실천을 위해 비서구적 방식 대신 다문화적인 측면과 고유문화를 반영하여 교과과정을 만들도록 하고 있다. 본 장은 서구의 신념과 가치가 지배하는 구조에 도전하면서 진정으로 보편적인 사회복지가 무엇인지를 생각하게 한다.

Introduction

It is essential that any social work curricula be culturally valid so as to prepare social work students comprehensively for working with diversity and multiculturalism. Asian and Pacific Island nations such as China, South Korea and Samoa have an almost homogenous ethnic population makeup and each are the dominant ethnicities within their respective countries, however, when Chinese, South Korean and Samoan nationals migrate to countries such as New Zealand (NZ), they become minority groups. In terms of their cultural capital (indigenous identity, cultural heritage, cultural knowledges and practices), Asia Pacific Island peoples are very strong in their respective homelands; but when they migrate and settle in other countries their cultural validity becomes subordinated and inferior.

Western cultural hegemony and cultural capital have both acted against the onset of cultural valid social work education. The learning base of social work knowledge and skills is predominantly Western, and this form of cultural capital is reproduced in classrooms all around the world on a daily basis. For example, according to McDermott and Nygreen (2013), Farkas (2011), and Demerath (2009) there is nothing new in American educational history about the idea of teaching low-income students of colour how to act and behave more like members of the middle class. Spring (2009), labels the approach as deculturalisation, or 'the educational process of destroying a people's culture (cultural genocide) and replacing it with a new culture' (p. 7). Some social work theories such as human development (see Clairborne & Drewery, 2010); cognitive-behavioural (see González-Prendes, 2012; Schunk and Usher, 2012), and systems and ecological perspectives (Robbins, Chatterjee, & Canda, 2012; Payne, 2011) are taught as core topics in social work education and are often unquestioned as the core contributions to social work theory learning.

These social work theories are not the only offerings. There are many other contributions, including many grounded in Asian and Pacific Island epistemologies (Faleolo, 2009a; Faleolo, 2009b; Suaali'i-Sauni, Wheeler, Saafi, Robinson, Agnew, Warren, Erick, & Hingano, 2009; Tuafuti, 2013). In an increasingly globalised century, the need for Asian and Pacific Island cultural capital and cultural validity in social work education is paramount. The 21st century social worker requires more integrated or multi-dimensional learning experiences. Samoan-based knowledges and practices (cultural capital) can be an important part of the development of cultural competency for social workers in the Asia Pacific Island region. Samoan knowledge and practices can be a partner sitting alongside Asian and Western-based offerings, each one contributing equally to practice theory, knowledge, skills and cross-cultural approaches.

I had the opportunity to present a paper entitled 'Same but different: The integration of Asian Pacific Island worldviews for social work education' at the 2012 International Conference on Social Work and Social Policy in Hanoi, Vietnam (Faleolo, 2012). My audience were representatives from various agencies and universities from the South East Asian region, America, Australia and NZ. Some were academics and researchers, and some were government employees, students, and practitioners. My ideas attracted numerous interests such as how was it possible for minority groups in NZ to have their worldviews and applications incorporated in Schools of Social Work. I mentioned that indigenous people (Māori) access inclusiveness through the Treaty of Waitangi that holds the dominant population group to account. I was also asked about how the social work teaching content was configured and the kinds of teaching activities that were provided. I referred to having a supportive management team and an environment that is accepting of cultural worldviews. This, I believe, are the main attributing factors that allow for the incorporation of cultural worldviews which is spread throughout the teaching content in both undergraduate and postgraduate programs and a variety of pedagogy styles to suit the learning development of its student population including varied assessment activities.

One of the concerns I had as I left the conference in Vietnam was that its School of Social Work was developed and modelled by American influences and very little drawn from its local context. A crucial issue and debate in contemporary social work education is social work education and practice, in regard to non-Western cultures, is struggling to develop and deliver services in an effective, acceptable and culturally appropriate manner. This is because schools of social work, widespread globalisation of Western culture and its scientific knowledge have displaced and been slow to accept non-Western and Indigenous world views, local knowledge and traditional forms of helping and healing. Culturally specific knowledge, values and skills lead to an understanding of other perspectives and cultures; if a social worker's acquisition of these is hampered, then cultural competency is limited. I believe truly indigenised and culturally relevant social work knowledge is one that is free from the restrictions and expectations of positivistic Western worldviews.

In this chapter I propose that there are three ways in which indigenous social work practice (the processes through which traditional, indigenous and local helping interventions) can be achieved. Firstly, establish a social work education curriculum where its cultural content is strongly represented, equitable, and culturally relevant for, with and by indigenous peoples. Secondly, incorporate cultural knowledge and practices into the measuring and assessing of cultural competence in social work practice. Lastly, promote the philosophical approach of authentisation and urge social workers in non-Western contexts to move away from simply adapting and modifying Western social work theory and practice to that of generating knowledge and practice models from the local context. For example, consider the importance of parables as culturally valid knowledge, for building and understanding knowledge and practices of particular cultures.

Strength, authority and equity

The first way of establishing indigenous social work is byan acknowledgement of the strength that cultural worldviews and cultural theories such as Samoan theory brings to other social work theory education, which is capable of commanding attention, and its knowledge considered as equal to other knowledge. Cultural validity is about recognising this strength, authority, and equity of Samoan ways of thinking by positioning its epistemology and methodology alongside Western ways. In other words Samoan concepts, theories, ideas, philosophies, and rationales, as well as Samoan frameworks, models, applications, modes, and techniques, are both authentic and prominent contributions to the learning and teaching of social work students. For example, Mulitalo-Lauta's concept of *Fa'asamoa*, which is partly based on his experience as a former Probation Officer (Mulitalo-Lauta, 2000; see also Faleolo, 2009b; Tuafuti, 2011; Suaali'i-Sauni et al., 2013), and Karl Pulotu-Endemann's *Fonofale Model*, which is partly based on his experience as a former Mental Health worker (Mental Health Commission, 2001; see also Seiuli, 2012; Suali'i-Sauni et al., 2013), are two contributions that accentuate the value of Samoan theorising and practice.

Mulitalo-Lauta's concept of Fa'asamoa is a holistic framework made up of five components:

1. the Samoan way;
2. the Samoan heart;
3. protocols and values;
4. social structures and social institutions; and
5. rituals and ceremonies

Taken together these provide an understanding of why Samoans think the way they think and act the way they act, and each component is relevant to social work education. For instance 'the Samoan heart' is an interesting concept, because Mulitalo-Lauta contends that Samoan social workers make decisions by using their hearts not their minds. That is, Samoan social workers follow their instincts or their gut feelings before they rationalise and calculate; or they may just follow their instincts or gut feelings alone. The

Samoan is assessing the social worker in the same fashion, using their instincts or gut feeling about the trustworthiness of the worker and the care the social worker brings into the relationship.

This leads to another component of Fa'asamoa 'the Samoan way', which is about the way that Samoan people act or particular mannerisms that are unique to Samoan people. When Samoan people avoid eye-to-eye contact with the social worker, for instance, they are showing a sign of respect, not guilt or non-compliance, because eye-to-eye contact behaviour is considered confrontational. A Samoan social worker would recognise and understand this type of behaviour instantly; a non-Samoan social worker may not.

Samoan people prefer to give even if it means that they would suffer hardship, because they believe that giving will be rewarded. But the reward is not why they give; they give because it is their duty to make sure others are comforted. Deference, or lowering oneself to elevate the other, is a common behavioural feature among Samoan people, as is living communally (two or three families in one house), and having strong spiritual beliefs.

Pulotu-Endemann's model is a holistic framework symbolised by Samoan fale or house:

The Fonofale model proposes four posts that establish the foundation of the fale or house. The foundation represents the *aiga* or family. These four posts hold up the roof, which represents cultural values and beliefs. The first of these posts is spirituality; the other three *posts* are 'physical' (the relationship between the body and medication, food and water either positively and/or negatively), 'mental' (the health of the mind including the emotional and behavioural states) and 'other' (age, sex, gender, class and other social aspects). Pulotu-Endemann's contention is that if any of the four posts become weak the entire structure or well being of the fale (or Samoan person) will collapse. The Fonofale model is not merely another way of understanding Samoan people, but for social work it is also an assessment tool, that is appropriate when working with Samoan mental health clients. In other words, the components that constitute the Fonofale model are in fact a typology which Samoan and non-Samoan social workers can use to interview Samoan clients and compile a cultural profile of the Samoan client which can be placed alongside a medical and other psychosocial assessments.

More importantly, Fa'asamoa and the Fonofale model, illustrate the emergence and acknowledgement of Samoan theorising, which predominantly draws on the experience of being a Samoan, and on Samoan approaches. These approaches translate Samoan theorising into practice or skills, and thus create a significant teleological and culturally responsive learning and teaching experience. Both concepts are easily linked to social work education. Each brings to social work education strength and authority in terms of what each theory would contribute and the importance of incorporating these types of Samoan theorising into the curriculum. Developing this linkage is what degree program and course developers undertook when reviewing their undergraduate and postgraduate content and assessment at Massey University New Zealand. Samoan theorising and applications were placed on equal par with other content, and students from all walks of life were assessed in terms of their cultural competency development. Samoan knowledge and applications were accepted as fundamental and valid forms of theory and practice within mainstream social work education.

Measuring and assessing cultural validity

The second way for indigenous social work to be achieved is through making sure that assessments are fair, feasible and practical. Indigenous social work knowledge is not only important in terms of what and how it is taught, but also about how what is taught is to be measured. This was one of the findings from a research project based on eliciting from first-year Pacific Island BASW students views on culturally valid assessment (Faleolo, Clarke, & Milne, 2008). The pilot study found that there is a need to improve the style and quality of teaching and learning and improve the initial student experiences for Pacific Island students (Koloto, Katoanga & Tatila, 2006; Hodge a& Limb, 2010; Coxon &Arini, 2011). Gay (2010) suggests that teachers should recognise cultural diversities, understand the cultural background of students and adjust their teaching and assessment accordingly. Collaborative and experiential learning are good approaches for Pacific Island students within a Pacific Island environment (Hynds & McDonald, 2010; Fletcher, Parkhill, Fa'afoi, Taleni, & O'Regan, 2009; Koloto et al, 2006). However Pacific Island students are a diverse group and teaching and assessment approaches need to allow for this diversity.

'Culturally valid assessment' is any form of assessment (essay writing, oral presentation, group work, research and role play) that a culture or group prefer and as a result that culture or group are likely to excel in. It is also being aware of cultural issues that can influence the students' performance and using this information to best support the student. The literature search for this project found that there was a lot of literature on assessment, some on culturally related educational delivery, but much less on culturally valid assessment. Exploring culturally valid assessment is important, since assessment design and events, androgogy and moderation are central to learning and will have a significant impact on student learning (Hattie & Timerley, 2007). Social and cultural issues are significant in assessment at a classroom level (May, 2010).

A critical part of this study was to allow the Pacific Island students to speak their truths. Bishop and Berryman (2006), Bensemann, Coxon, Anderson and Anae (2006), Airini, Rakena, O'Shea, Tarawa, Sauni, Ulugia-Pua, Sua-Huirua, and Curtis (2007), Congdon and Congdon (2010) and Waycott, Gray, Thompson, Sheard, Clerehan, Richardson, and Hamilton (2010) use this participatory approach to assessment. Focus group participants were asked about their experiences of assessment including what they liked and disliked, the purpose of assessment, whether they valued feedback on assessment and why, whether assessments should be the same for every student or should they be different, and what they considered as culturally appropriate and culturally valid assessment.

In terms of the participants' experiences of assessment, most students liked oral group presentations. Participants recognised and appreciated the support they received for assessments. Having approachable lecturers was important to them. They said the lecturers help them unpack what they need to do, and the Pacific Island lecturers helped them understand from a Pacific Island point of view. The findings also indicated that the purpose of assessment for students included time management, giving students direction or what to focus on, allowing students to check their progress and addressing things in their development that required improvement. Participants highly valued the feedback they received on their assessments. Participants said that feedback was essential because it provided direction on where they went wrong and where they were right. Some participants commented that feedback was important because it provided a guideline or a course of action, processes and procedures for correcting errors, and strengthening existing good points. Few participants linked feedback to the experience of reflection, which is a very important developmental skill in social work practice. Feedback, irrespective of whether it is positive or constructive, is important to students.

Participants were asked whether assessment should be the same for every student or be varied to suit the diversity of the student population. Most participants felt that assessments should be different in terms of its design and practicality. One participant suggested that the phrasing of questions in assessments be simpler or easier to understand rather than obscure and complex. Another participant commented that assessments require a 'weaving' to integrate Pacific Island values and beliefs, with Western notions of learning. In this way the participant added that assessments are different; it was not just assessing using written exercises (essays alone), but also other ways of writing such as how to write a court report, or an action plan to address a client issue. This practical assessment allows for 'reality' to be part of their learning as well as for learning to be more 'hands on'.

The group also felt that assessment tasks such as group presentations are more ideally suited to Pacific Island learners particularly the teamwork and oral feedback dynamics, because Pacific Island learners learn more by collaboration and through non written exercises. The role of referencing in essay writing was also raised: personal communications were felt to be predominant source, as opposed to academic research literature. Students argued that knowledge is not just about what is said in text books but also what is uttered through word of mouth, particularly from elders, leaders, parents and other important people in the Samoan community. The role of personal communications should be accepted as a credible source of information; this is considered culturally valid for Pacific Island people.

Few student participants acknowledged that culturally valid assessments are based on having Pacific Island-specific lecturers. The role of the Pacific Island lecturer means his or her *Pacific Islandness* is important for understanding how Pacific Island students learn, and is an important factor for considering how a culturally valid assessment is to be applied to Pacific Island students. One participant commented that the Pacific Island lecturers in the BASW degree program were able to translate into the Samoan language what they said in English during lectures and in one-to-one supervision. This enabled Pacific Island students to be clearer about the content, whereas they could not relate entirely to the content presented in the English language. Another participant said that the Pacific Island lecturers were more creative. For instance, they provided case studies which featured Māori, Samoan, Tongan and Western contexts, they utilised many different media such as PowerPoint, music, role plays, debates, and open book tests, rather than a two-hour teacher-centred lecture.

Honouring and creating pathways for the lesser known

The final way for indigenous social work to be achieved is through honouring world views, creating opportunities for alternative perspectives to be heard, and allowing for indigenous identities to contribute towards learning and education. The choice of what is to be taught and how what is learned and to be measured is integral to ensuring that voices like the Samoan voice is not lost in the translation. The majority of social work education programs (including courses and assessment practices) in NZ is heavily westernised with limited input from other cultures such as Samoa. Social work theory content throughout all of NZ tertiary institutions either features a small (e.g. one or two courses, probably an elective, and not a core paper) or no window for Samoan theoretical material to be incorporated as part of the social work education curriculum. Instead social work students are exposed to theories about human development, organisation and management, research, sociology and social policy, which are all important, but not about other perspectives like the Samoan perspective within these theories. Similarly social work students are taught skills such as communication, ethics, documentation, and group work but limited in terms of these same skills for working with other population groups like Samoan clients and their communities. Consequently there is a real struggle to get Samoan knowledge and applications accepted as valid because current social work education curricula have not been culturally responsive.

An example of one particular Samoan theory and application that should be incorporated into the social work education curriculum is the *Talanoa ile I'a*. This lesser-known theory is built from a parable, or fa'afaletui, which is a way of constructing a theory not from a research project or an idea, but from analogy or symbolism, in order to illustrate some truth or principle. The Talanoa ile I'a theory is an instructive example which conveys many lessons for teaching and learning. It guides social work students' understanding that no single version of truth is total and permanent as educators make authentic knowledge about different ethnic groups accessible to students. It enables social work students to relate personal growth to professional life, to develop strong social work skills, academic knowledge, critical thinking about society, power, inequality and change. It highlights the importance of equity, empowerment, biculturalism and multiculturalism. It also points to the value of cross-cultural social work education and the integration of Samoan and non-Samoan knowledge.

What is Talanoa ile I'a?

'Talanoa ile I'a' is a Samoan phrase that literally means 'talk to the fish'. In the Samoan language there are two words that describe talking: *tautala* and *talanoa*. For example: one day the mother turned to the father and said, 'Tatou talanoaga fa'aleaiga nane' ('Tonight we will have a family talk'), the father replied, 'O le a le mea tatou te talanoa iai?' ('What are we going to talk about?'). The mother responded saying, 'O nisi o le fanau e tautala e taimi o le tatalo' ('Some of the children are talking during prayer'). The example above describes the term talanoa as an event or forum for discussing issues as in family talks, whereas, the term tautala describes the action of talking such as sharing of opinions and knowledge in family talks. The mother wanted to have a family talk (talanoa) regarding the talking (tautala) that occurs during prayer time.

The word, '*I'a*', is the Samoan word for, 'fish'. The characteristics and attributes of fish are used as personifications of Samoan young people. For example, fish are slippery creatures, easily slipping through hands unless experienced fishermen handle them. Samoan young people (both Samoan-born and NZ-born) are not slippery creatures but are young people who undergo tricky and tremendous turmoil in their lives (socially, culturally, biologically and emotionally) as they transition from childhood to adulthood via adolescence. Such trying and demanding situations that Samoan young people experience are likely to slip away or escape from their control as they are often unsecure and unstable. Even the most experienced social work practitioner may find it difficult to hold on to the Samoan young person he/she is case managing because they tend to slip away from being helped or even backslide. Fish are silent aquatic animals: when they are captured, they struggle but their protests are voiceless. Most Samoan young people are the same: they find it difficult to disclose their issues such as sexual health problems because of fear and embarrassment. Competent parenting, effective social workers or youth workers, responsive social services, and practical policy are the keys to supporting Samoan young people through the changes in their lives. Fish roam the vast oceans in schools and live a relatively quiet lifestyle. Samoan young people are the same: they congregate in groups and move about in this big world keeping their problems a secret because generally they are afraid to express what is wrong or to speak out for themselves.

Thus the concept of Talanoa ile I'a is about two things. Firstly, it is about staging an event to hold *talanoaga* (discussion) with Samoan young people that include listening, sharing, and inviting them to express their ideas and knowledge in order to learn and understand the issues that affect them while at the same time turn their responses into solution or problem solving strategies. This in turn is the foundation of cultural validity, building knowledge and understanding of a particular culture from the voices of those who know, live and breathe the Samoan culture. Essentially honouring and creating a pathway for the lesser known to become known, acknowledged and institutionalised. Secondly, it is about the fish or Samoan young people, and their experiences. So in order to find out what are the important issues for Samoan young people we simply ask them. We talk 'to' them and not 'around' them. We treat them as people and not like objects. By talking to Samoan young people we gain important insights into their world such as how they think, what they value, believe, and whom they trust the most. We stage a talanoaga (an event or forum) in order for talking to happen, and where Samoan young people and what they have to say is highly regarded. The Samoan young people are the authority, they are the experts. Their contribution will add strength towards justifying the importance of the Samoan cultural identity. The knowledge they share will be equal to Western knowledge.

ORIGINS OF TALANOA ILE I'A

The origins of the 'Talanoa ile I'a' concept stem from works by Tamasese, Peteru and Waldegrave (1997) and Tamasese (1997) on Pacific Island Island people and poverty. At the beginning of these works is a definition of Samoan culture by His Excellency Tui Atua Tupua Tamasese Taisi Efi, former Prime Minister of (then) Western Samoa, one of the paramount matai (chief) of Samoa, and currently the Samoan Head of State. Efi uses a *fa'afaletui* or a parable to define Samoan culture as three perspectives: '*O le faautaga i tumutumu o mauga*' (the perspective of the person at the top of the mountain); '*O le faautaga i tumutumu o la'au*' (the perspective of the person at the top of the tree); and '*Ma le faautaga o le pii ama*' (the perspective of the person in the canoe who is close to the school of fish). In any big problem the three perspectives are equally necessary. The person fishing in the canoe may not have the long view of the person on the mountain or the person at the top of the tree, but they are closer to the school of fish (Tamasese, Peteru, and Waldegrave, 1997; Tamasese, 1997).

The development of the Talonoa Ile I'a theory

Efi's fa'afaletui for defining Samoan culture does not represent the perspective of the school of fish but attaches this important dimension to the perspective of the person in the canoe who is close to the school of fish. This creates the situation where a reconstruction is required of the fa'afaletui by separating out the school of fish from the perspective of the person in the canoe who is close to the school of fish, making three perspectives into *four* perspectives, and renaming the fa'afaletui as the Talanoa ile I'a theory. Thus the Talanoa ile I'a theory is not only about creating a pathway for the lesser known to become known, but is also an ecological depiction of Samoan society made up of dynamic and interactive environments.

The perspective of the school of fish or *O le faautaga o le I'a* is the everyday environment of home or school or work for Samoan young people, including their relationships with parents, siblings, caregivers, classmates, teachers, and employers. Samoan young people are in contact with these people every day in their lives, whether in the family home or at school, they are the people they trust the most. When Samoan young people come into contact with professionals and practitioners they become clients, consumers and customers. They become locked into public services by their linkages to youth workers, social workers, police officers, lawyers, doctors, judges, youth nurses and other people who are assigned to manage and resolve their issues. This interlocking of various systems with which a Samoan young person is involved—the linkages between home and school (student-teacher), home and service provider (client-professional or practitioner), service provider and community (referrer-specialist), and so on, is the perspective of the person in the canoe who is close to the school of fish or Ma le faautaga o le pii ama, in the Talanoa ile I'a theory, and indicative of its dynamic and interactive nature.

The relationship between the Samoan young person and the professional or practitioner is further extended because each professional and practitioner is a representative of their organisation and collections of organisations become larger institutions: for example, national healthcare agencies, child protection agencies and justice organisations, which interact with each other by sharing resources and services, and headed by a single person or groups as in chief executive officers, directors, general managers, boards of trustees, and district health boards. These individuals or group members are represented by the perspective of the person at the top of the tree or O le faautaga I tumutumu o la'au in the Talanoa ile I'a theory. So in effect the relationships become three-dimensional: the Samoan young person-the professional or practitioner-the Supervisor or General Manager.

The collection of agencies that form national organisations, its organisational is underpinned by overarching cultural patterns mainly influenced by government, religion, education, and the economy. For example in social and economic policy changes in New Zealand over the last century (Cheyne, O'Brien & Belgrave, 2008; Lunt, O'Brien, & Stephens, 2008; Belgrave, 2012) are lawmakers and policymakers, which are representatives from institutions such as legislative council and policy units, who have the widest-ranging influence by setting the overall cultural pattern for the rest of society to follow. These individuals set national philosophy, the direction the nation will follow, the ideas that are most important over others (what is best for the nation), and also add to the relationship with Samoan young people making it four-dimensional: the Samoan young person—the professional or practitioner—the supervisor or general manager—the policy maker or member of Parliament. The latter are represented by the person at the top of the mountain or O le faautaga I tumutumu o mauga in the Talanoa ile I'a theory, and within each dimension one acts upon the other collaboratively as Efi's faafaletui or parable states that '…all three perspectives are equally necessary' (Tamasese, Peteru, & Waldegrave, 1997; Tamasese, 1997), meaning that each is interrelated and functional, interchangeable and interdependent, electric, influential and changing, made up of dynamic interactive dimensions not as a single entity: lifeless and isolated.

The nearest Western equivalent to the Talanoa ile I'a theory in terms of its structural design is Bronfenbrenner's (1979) ecological approach to human development that identifies four different levels of environmental influence, extending from the most intimate environment to the global: microsystem, mesosystem, exosystem and macrosystem. According to Bronfenbrenner in order to understand human development, one must understand each person within the context of multiple environments.

The nearest Western equivalent to understanding the dynamic and interactive nature of the Samoan world and in particular the Talanoa ile I'a theory is Finlayson's (2000) analysis of policymaking process (see also Waycott et al., 2010; Mortensen, 2011). Finlayson describes four ways of policymaking stage: top-down; bottom-up; centre-up; and/or centre-down. From a top-down approach, the perspective of the person at the top of the mountain sets the direction, the perspective of the person at the top of the tree translates this direction into their organisations or agencies, the perspective of the person in the canoe who is close to the school of fish implements the direction or puts it into practice, and then the perspective of the school of fish receive benefits. Alternatively, the perspective of the school of fish sets the direction, the perspective of the person in the canoe who is close to the school of fish supports and advocates, the perspective of the person at the top of the tree adopts and formalises a proposal, and the perspective of the person at the top of the mountain endorses and legislates the direction as a norm, which is a bottom-up approach. Or the direction can be instigated from the perspective of the person in the canoe who is close to the school of fish to the perspective of the person at the top of the mountain' or to the perspective of the person in the canoe who is close to the school of fish (centre-up or centre-down). Even the perspective of the person in the canoe who is close to the school of fish can set the direction.

In a nutshell the structural design and dynamic nature of the Talanoa ile I'a theory distinguishes Samoan theory from Western theory. It gives greater recognition and cognisance to, the perspective of the school of fish by giving Samoan young people a pathway to have their needs acknowledged including their cultural identity. At the same time, it demonstrates how cultural validity would work in a social work education curriculum and honours the view of a lesser known contributor.

Indigenous social work theory and practice

Gay, G. (2010), Brown-Jeffy and Cooper (2011) and Scherff & Spector (2011) emphasise that cultural responsiveness, in terms of teaching, is validating because it uses the cultural knowledge, prior experiences, and performance styles of diverse students to make learning more appropriate and effective for them. The authors highlight that this type of androgogy validates indigenous identities and their perspectives in many ways such as legitimising their cultural heritages as worthy content to be taught in the formal curriculum, incorporating multicultural information or diverse worldviews, resources and materials in all subjects and skills being taught, and allows for a variety of instructional strategies and assessment events that are connected to different learning styles. For instance, the learning from the Talanoa ile I'a theory for students is significant. Social work students not only are taught the importance of learning about another culture that is different to their own but also the skills for engaging, assessing and addressing their social issues. When social workers engage Samoan clients they are able to identify and analyse cause and effects by talking directly to them, then talk to other professionals or practitioners, then talk to their supervisors or managers, and refer to policy or legislation, before making a decision on the best way to approach their needs. Social workers also learn other skills from the Talanoa ile I'a theory such as deconstructing and reconstructing theory; critical thinking (actively and skilfully appraising information to reach an answer or conclusion); integration (synthesising, comparing and contrasting); and evaluation (summarising, recommending and suggesting).

Thus, cultural responsiveness and culturally relevant pedagogy is a way for Schools of Social Work to acknowledge the local context and culture of the students, and through sensitivity to cultural nuances integrate these cultural experiences, values, and understandings into the teaching and learning environment (Efi, 2009; Brown-Jeffy & Cooper, 2011: Jabbar & Hardaker, 2012). As a Samoan man, I am partly responsible for establishing, maintaining and sustaining Samoan epistemologies and methodologies. In order to grow and foster Samoan knowledge and practices in social work education I need to keep researching and publishing literature so this body of knowledge continues to grow and advance. As a Samoan lecturer I need to be creative and interactive in order to integrate Samoan knowledge and practices with my Western knowledge and practices (formal education) so Samoan and non-Samoan social work students benefit from my teachings. However I am aware that the responsibility is shared by other parties involved in social work education: policymakers (the perspective of the person at the top of the mountain), governance and management (the perspective of the person at the top of the tree), educators and practitioners (the perspective of the person in the canoe who is close to the school of fish), the clients and the community (the perspective of the school of fish) as identified by the Talanoa ile I'a theory.

If indigenous social workers, researchers, academics and educators do not grow indigenous social work theory and practice, then Western models of social work will continue to be exported into newly established Schools of Social Work like Vietnam. Global education standards set by International Association of Schools of Social Work will influence the content, pedagogy, and assessment of social work education to the point of standardisation and local knowledge and indigenous contributions will be at the periphery. Even efforts to accommodate diversity including multiculturalism, cultural and ethnic sensitivity, cross-cultural, transcultural and anti-oppressive practices will be carefully guarded by Western interests because these approaches bring attention to, and attempt to counter, the ways that dominate cultures can marginalise and oppress minority cultures like Samoan, Chinese, and South Korean nationals living in New Zealand.

When I was charged with the responsibility of developing a Pacific Island social work course one of the first things I did was to look for literature and other teaching materials to inform its construction. It became apparent that there was a limited amount of material to be found and that what was found was a scattering of material hidden away. This motivated me to publish a book entitled *The Pacific Island voice in Social Work Education in Aotearoa New Zealand an annotated bibliography 1998–2008* in order to bring together Pacific Island literature directly relevant to social work and find out where Pacific Island contributions needed to be strong in such as human development, management, policy, social work skills and research (Faleolo, 2009a; 2009b). One of my summary points was a challenge for all Samoan practitioners and academics to write and publish more literature and other types of materials in order to grow the Pacific Island presence and culturally validate our ways of thinking and doing things in social work education (Faleolo, 2009a; 2009b). In order for cultural validity in social work education to be achieved I needed to do it.

All social work students should be examined about their understanding of other cultures than their own, and about how much their knowledge about other cultures is applied in a bicultural and multicultural context. In NZ, not all the clients that a social worker will manage will be of European or Māori backgrounds, they will also be Asian and Pacific Island. If a non-Samoan social worker comes into contact with a Samoan client he or she needs to be confident, culturally competent and effective. Provision of Samoan theory and practices for social work education not only recognise this perspective as equal to Western ways but strengthens the social work curricula by enhancing its cultural knowledge that is passed onto the social work student. The concept of Fa'asamoa and the Fonofale model enables social workers to be able to understand why Samoan clients think and behave the way they do. Samoan people use their instincts and feelings to make decisions, they avoid eye-to-eye contact with other people not because they are guilty or remorseful, but because they are avoiding confrontation and being respectful. Samoan people always approach situations and circumstances with deference, lowering himself or herself in order to elevate the other. They prefer to save face rather than ask for help. They are not individualistic, they are communal and they see the world as made up of dynamic and interactive dimensions. Altogether the Fa'asamoa and Fonofale concepts would add strength and authority to social work education curricula.

The development of cultural competency and indigenous social work theory and practice in social work education depends of having academic assessments that are real, supported and achievable. Structuring assessments where students are asked to write for essays in order to successfully complete the course is a very difficult task for Asian and Pacific Island nationals, even if support is provided. As a Samoan lecturer I have noticed that Samoan students are visual and kinesthetic learners. Setting a group presentation as an assessment task would enable Samoan learners to work collaboratively and this would be a common cultural experience. A group presentation would mean that Samoan students can still show their abilities and development as a social worker through theatre (role playing a family group conference) as opposed to essay writing. If a written assessment task is required, case notes will be understood as more relevant to what these students will need in the field of social work practice in terms of developing documentation and recording skills. Essays are only good for testing the learner's organisation and grammatical skills, which is a small area for measuring cultural competency development and does not fully reflect the abilities of all social work students.

In order for indigenous social work theory and practice in social work education to be accepted, social workers in non-Western contexts are urged to move away from simply adapting and modifying social work theory and practice to that of generating knowledge and practice models from the ground up, drawing on the values, beliefs, customs, and cultural norms of *local* and indigenous helping practices. This is the process of authentisation (Gray & Coates, 2010) whereby local culture is used as a primary source for knowledge and practiced development, and social work practice becomes culturally appropriate, relevant and authentic. It is rethinking what is regarded as universal in social work by challenging the dominance of Western beliefs and values. Such a process is necessary in order to provide professional services in a manner that is effective and consistent with local cultures but also to meet demand arising from members of non-mainstream cultures in wealthy countries like the USA and UK, as well as people from non-Western countries experiencing economic modernisation and globalisation, such as China and Vietnam.

I offer three considerations:

- Firstly, *strength*, *authority* and *equity*: acknowledging the strength that indigenous theory and practices brings to social work education, which is scholarly and equal to western and other epistemologies and methodologies such as Fa'asamoa. This alignment will mean Samoan ways of thinking and doing are equal and will become accepted as fundamental and valid forms of theory and practices within social work education. Social work curricula that feature this type of organisation and structure will be validating Samoan contributions of non-Western epistemologies generally in a globalising educational framework.
- Secondly, *measuring* and *assessing* cultural validity: making sure that assessments are fair, feasible and practical. Cultural validity

is not only important in terms of how a subject is taught but also about how what is taught is to be measured.

- Lastly, *honouring and creating pathways for the lesser-known through authentisation*: creating opportunities for alternative perspectives to be heard, and allowing for indigenous identities to contribute towards learning and education. The choices of what are to be taught, and how what is learned to be measured are integral to ensuring that the Samoan voice is not lost in social work education curricula.

REFERENCES

Airini, A., Rakena, T., O'Shea, M., Tarawa, M., Sauni, P., Ulugia-Pua, M., Sua-Huirua, T., & Curtis, E. (2007, September). Success for all in higher education: improving indigenous and minority student success in degree-level studies. Paper presented at the British Education Research Association Conference, London, England.

Belgrave, M. (2012, December). Social policy history: forty years on, forty years back. Paper presented at the Affording our Future Conference, Wellington, New Zealand.

Bishop, R., & Berryman, M. (2006). *Culture speaks: cultural relationships and classroom learning*. Wellington: Huia Press.

Bronfenbrenner, U. (1979). *The ecology of human development*. Cambridge: Harvard University Press.

Brown-Jeffy, S. & Cooper, J.E. (2011). Toward a conceptual framework of culturally relevant pedagogy: an overview of the conceptual and theoretical literature. *Teacher Education Quarterly*, 38(1), 65–84. Retrieved 17 April 2013 from www.eric.ed.gov/PDFS/EJ914924.pdf.

Claiborne, L. Bird. & Drewery, W. (2010). *Human development: family, place, culture*, 3rd edn. Sydney: McGraw-Hill.

Cheyne, C., O'Brien, M. & Belgrave, M. (2008). *Social policy in Aotearoa New Zealand: a critical introduction*, 4th edn. Auckland: Oxford University Press.

Congdon, G.J., & Congdon, S. (2011). Engaging students in a simulated collaborative action research project: an evaluation of a participatory approach to learning. *Journal of Further and Higher Education*, 35(2), 221–31.

Coxon, E., & Airini, A. (2011). Inside and around the Pacific Circle: educational places, spaces and relationships'. *Pacific Asian Education*, 23(2). Retrieved 17 April 2013 from pacificcircle-consortium.org/PAEJournal.html.

Demerath, P. (2009). *Producing success: the culture of personal advancement in an American high school.* Chicago: University of Chicago Press.

Efi, His Excellency Tui Atua Tupua Tamesese Ta'isi (2009). In search of nuance and metaphor in social policy. In Suaalii-Sauni, S., Tuagalu, I., Kirifi-Alai, N., Fuamatu, N. (Eds). *Su'esu'e Manogi: in Search of Fragrance* (pp. 79–92). Samoa: Centre for Samoan Studies, National University of Samoa.

Faleolo, M.M., Clarke, J. & Milne, J. (2008). *Culturally valid assessment: the view of Pacific Island students.* Paper for the Teaching and Learning Research Initiative. Auckland: Manukau Institute of Technology and Massey University (Unpublished).

Faleolo, M.M. (2009a). *The Pasifika 'voice' in social work education: annotated bibliography 1998–2008.* Wellington: New Zealand Council for Educational Research.

Faleolo, M.M. (2009b). Culturally valid social work education: a Samoan perspective. In C. Noble, M. Henrickson and I.Y. Han (Eds). *Social work education: voices from the Asia Pacific* (pp. 149–72). Victoria: The Vulgar Press.

Faleolo, M.M. (2012, June). Same but different: the integration of Asian and Pacific Island worldviews for social work education. Paper presented at the International Conference on Social

Work and Social Policy, Hanoi, Vietnam (to be published later in the year).

Farkas, G. (2011). Middle and high school skills, behaviors, attitudes, and curriculum enrolment, and their consequences. In G.J. Duncan & R.J. Murnane (Eds). *Whither opportunity: rising inequality, schools, and children's life chances* (pp. 71–90). New York: Russell Sage Foundation.

Finlayson, M. (2000). Policy implementation and modification. In P. Davis & T. Ashton (Ed.), *Health and Public Policy in New Zealand.* Auckland: Oxford University Press.

Fletcher, J., Parkhill, F., Fa'afoi, A., Taleni, L.T., & O'Regan, B. (2009). Pasifika students: teachers and parents voice their perceptions of what provides supports and barriers to Pasifika students' achievement in literacy and learning. *Teacher and Teacher Education*, 25(1), 24–33

Gay, G. (2010). *Culturally responsive teaching: theory, research and practice*, 2nd edn. New York: Teachers College Press.

Gray, M., & Coates, J. (2010). From 'indigenization' to cultural relevance. In M. Gray, J. Coates and M. Yellow Bird (Eds). *Indigenous social work around the world: towards culturally relevant education and practice* (pp. 13–29). Aldershot: Ashgate.

González-Prendes, A.A. (2012). Cognitive-behavioral therapy and social work values: a critical analysis. *Journal of Social Work Values and Ethics*, 9(2), 21–33.

Hattie, J. & Timperley, H. (2007). The power of feedback. *Review of Educational Research,* 77(1), 81–112.

Hodge, D.R. & Limb, G.E. (2010). Conducting spiritual assessment with native Americans enhancing cultural competency in social work practice courses. *Journal of Social Work Education*, 48(2), 265–83.

Hynds, A. & McDonald, L. (2010). Motivating teachers to improve learning for culturally diverse students in New Zealand: promoting Māori and Pacific Island student achievement. *Professional Development in Education*, 36(3), 525–40.

Jabbar, A. & Hardaker, G. (2012). The role of culturally responsive teaching for supporting ethnicdiversity in British University Business Schools. *Teaching in Higher Education*, 1–13.

Koloto, A., Katoanga, A. & Tatila, L. (2006). Critical success factors for effective use of e-Learning by Pacific Island Learners (Electronic version). Retrieved 17 April 2013 from akoaotearoa.ac.nz/download/ng/file/group-996/n4006-critical-success-factors-for-effective-use-of-e-learning-by-pacific-learners.pdf.

Lunt, N., O'Brien, M. & Stephens, R. (Eds). (2008). *New Zealand, new welfare*. Melbourne: Cengage.

McDermott, K.A. & Nygree, K. (2013). Educational new paternalism: human capital, cultural capital, and the politics of equal opportunity. *Peabody Journal of Education*, 88(1), 84–97.

May, S. (2010). Curriculum and the education of cultural and linguistic minorities. In B.McGraw, E. Baker & P. Peterson (Eds). *International encyclopaedia of education*, 3rd edn (1, 293–98). Oxford: Elsevier.

Mental Health Commission. (2001). *Pacific Island mental health services and workforce*. Wellington: Mental Health Commission.

Mortensen, A. (2011). Public health system responsiveness to refugee groups in NZ: activation from the bottom up. *Social Policy Journal of New Zealand*, 37, 123–34.

Mulitalo-Lauta, P.T.M.T. (2000). *Fa'aSamoa and social work within the New Zealand context*. Palmerston North: Dunmore Press Limited.

Payne, M. (2011). *Humanistic social work core principles in practice*. Basingstoke: Palgrave Macmillan.

Robbins, S.P., Chatterjee, P. & Canda, E.R. (2011). *Contemporary human behavior: a critical perspective for social work*, 3rd edn. Englewood Cliff: Prentice Hall.

Scherff, L., & Spector, K. (2011). *Culturally relevant pedagogy: clashes and confrontations*. Maryland: Rowman & Littlefield Education.

Schunk, D.H. & Usher, E.L. (2012). Social cognitive theory and motivation. in R.M. Ryan (Eds). *The Oxford handbook of human motivation* (pp. 13–27). New York: Oxford University Press.

Seiuli, B.M.S. (2012). Uputaua: a therapeutic approach to researching Samoan communities. *The Australian Community Psychologist*, 24(1), 24–37.

Spring, J. (2009). *Deculturalization and the struggle for equality: a brief history of the education of dominated cultures in the United States*. Boston, MA: McGraw Hill.

Suali'i-Sauni, T., Wheeler, A., Saafi, E., Robinson, G., Agnew, F., Warren, H., Erick, M. & Hingano, T. (2009). Exploration of Pacific perspectives of Pacific models of mental health service delivery in New Zealand. *Pacific Health Dialog*, 15(1), 18–27.

Tamasese, K. (1997). *Ole Taeo Afua. O le Sailiga o le tofa ma le faautaga I le mataupu o le soifua lelei faalemafaufau: ma togafitiga o le gasegase o le mafaufau e faavae I le aganuu a Samoa*. Lower Hutt: The Family Centre. (Samoan translation).

Tamasese, K., Peteru, C., & Waldegrave, C. (1997). *Ole Taeo Afua: The new morning. A qualitative investigation into Samoan perspectives on mental health and culturally appropriate services*. Lower Hutt: The Family Centre.

Tuafuti, P. (2011). Multiple challenges in research within the fa'asamoa context. *Pacific-Asian Education*, 23(2), 33–42.

Tuafuti, P. (2013, January). Fa'afaletui-Phenomenology. Paper presented at the First International Pasifika ECE Conference– A call from the deep: reclaiming our future, University of Auckland, New Zealand.

Waycott, J., Gray, K., Thompson, C., Sheard, J., Clerehan, R., Richardson, J., & Hamilton, M. (2010). Transforming assessment in higher education: a participatory approach to the development of a good practice framework for assessing student learning through social web technologies. In C.H. Steel, M.J. Keppell, P. Gerbic & S. Housego (Eds). *Curriculum, technology & transfor-*

mation for an unknown future. Proceedings ascilite Sydney 2010 (pp. 1040–50). Retrieved 17 April from ascilite.org.au/conferences/sydney10/procs/Waycott-full.pdf.

2

National voices

6

Social work definition in Japan: international definition of social work and the Japanese social work education community

Kana Matsuo

A series of structural reforms of the fundamental social welfare system in Japan during 1990s came to fruition as the 'Social Welfare Act' in 2000. Since then many social work practitioners in Japan, especially Certified Social Workers (CSWs), describe themselves as 'social workers', applying the international definition of social work which was released just around the same period. However, the question has now been raised that the definition may not fit Japanese social work practitioners. In this chapter the author reviews themes and topics in the social work education community in Japan in 2000 in the literature, and explore challenges to the definition.

日本におけるソーシャルワークの定義:　ソーシャルワークの国際定義と日本の社会福祉教育界

1990年代の日本における一連の社会福祉基礎構造改革は2000年に「社会福祉法」として結実した。この法律制定以降、日本の社会福祉の実践者たち、特に社会福祉士は、絶妙なタイミングで用意されたソーシャルワークの国際定義を盾として自分自身を説明している。しかし実践者の活動と定義は乖離しているのではないかという疑問が彼／彼女たちの間に生じている。なぜこのような乖離が生まれたのか。本稿では2000年前後の日本の社会福祉教育界における議論の焦点を文献研究により明らかにし国際定義の課題を探る。

標題：社會工作的國際定義和日本社會工作教育界

日本在20世纪90年代一系列基本社會福利系統的結構性改革在2000年結出了《社會福利法》的碩果。自此，很多日本的社會工作實踐者，特別是註冊社會工作者，使用國際上在同一時期公佈的社會工作的定義，自稱’ 社會工作者’ 。然而，社會工作的國際定義未必適合日本社會工作實踐者的問題被提出來。本文作者回顧了日本2000年社會工作教育界文獻中的主題和議題，探討對社會工作定義的挑戰。

사회복지의 국제적 정의와 일본 사회복지교육 공동체

1990년대 일본의 사회복지시스템에 대한 일련의 구조적 개혁의 결과 2000년에 이르러 사회복지법안으로 결실을 맺게 되었다. 이후 사회복지 실무자들 그 중에서도 사회복지 자격증 소지자들은 대부분 같은 기간에 발표된 국제 정의를 적용해 그들 스스로를 ‘사회복지사’로 묘사하였다. 그러나 현재 일본의 사회복지 실무자들에게 이 정의가 맞지 않을 수 있다는 의문이 제기됐다. 본 장에서 저자는 일본의 사회복지교육 공동체가 나타내고 있는 2000년대 문헌의 주제와 논제를 검토하고 사회복지를 정의 내리는 데 따르는 어려움을 탐구한다.

Introduction

On 4 November 2010, the Asian and Pacific Association for Social Work Education (APASWE) and the Japan College of Social Work (JCSW) organised a workshop in Tokyo entitled ‘International Social Work Definition Review Workshop’. The workshop was part of a series in a review project co-organised by the International Association for Schools of Social Work. Each workshop participant reported on the results of their own country’s workshop on defining social work. Many participants said something to the effect of ‘the current definition reflects Westerners’ ideas’.

Following these discussions, the Japan National Social Work Definition Review Workshop reported that Japanese educators expressed the feeling that that the current definition may not fit the Japanese community (Social Work Research Institute Asian Center for Welfare in Society, Japan College of Social Work 2011).

However, as Hare (2004) wrote, 'Throughout the next four years, numerous discussions were held at regional and general meetings of the federation across the globe' (p. 409), and there have been opportunities for inclusive international discussions held all over the world before the current definition was finally adopted.

The question is: How is the current international definition of social work treated within the context of social work education in Japan? Here one gets a glimpse of the silence behind the current discussions about the adoption of the definition. This readership is intended for people outside of Japan.

MEANING OF SOCIAL WORK AND SHAKAI FUKUSHI

We will first begin by briefly discussing the meanings of social work and *shakai fukushi* in Japan. In Japan, services that are provided to people in need are mainly referred to as *shakai fukushi* services, referring to the actual processes, skills, and methods of delivering aid, known as 'social work' in Western countries. Generally speaking, *shakai fukushi* is translated as 'social welfare' in English with various meaning of the above is included; thus 'social work' and *shakai fukushi* (social welfare) will overlap in this chapter. It is true that *shakai fukushi* has several equivalents in English, including 'well-being', 'social policy', and 'social work'. On the other hand, 'social work' also contains another meaning in Japanese, referring to 'charitable activities', especially those carried out by dedicated people before World War II.

Japanese social welfare policies and programs developed after WWII with the cooperation of the US in the General Headquarters (GHQ) leadership. These came to be known as *shakai fukushi* policies and programs. To implement these programs, educators studied social work methods rooted in Western countries, the US in particular. Those with expertise in social work had stimulated the modernisation of *shakai fukushi* services in Japan, even though it was *ue kara ataerareta mono* [given from the above] (Ichibangase

1971, p. 62). The purpose of *shakai fukushi* services were to help people solve difficulties in their daily lives (Okamura 1965).

A close study of the meaning of *shakai fukushi*/social work is not necessary for our purposes. When we describe social work education in Japan in this chapter, the concepts of social work and *shakai fukushi* will overlap.

Definition of social work in dictionaries and glossaries

There were many lengthy discussions on the meaning of social work before the current international definition was adopted. There is no doubt that the answer to this simple question reflects various particular ideals of social work. Therefore, social work has been defined differently by many social work educators, scholars, and practitioners in Japan. This section will examine how these concepts are defined in Japanese dictionaries. The following are keywords for defining social work. The author has chosen five major dictionaries that were published during the 1990s and 2000s. Although they are only a few examples, they help us understand the Japanese education community. By reviewing these definitions, several common points and differences can be found. The following are representative examples.

Common points:

- Social work is a systematic practice of social welfare.
- Social work functions as the core of the social welfare system.
- Social work is a systematic practice to help people in solving problems that they face in their daily living.
- There is no description of social work as 'consultation' (The following section will explain this point).

Points of difference:

- Social work is practiced by professional staff placed in social welfare organisations or facilities (Komatsu 1993).
- Social work supports individuals' right to life and the pursuit of happiness (Yamazaki 1996).

- Social work participates in the following areas: support for solving life problems and difficulties caused by mental health issues; intervention and support for families and small communities; organising and supporting the people in the community; administration and implementation of the local/national government's plans and policies (Akimoto, Ooshima, Shibano, Morimoto, & Yamagata 2003).
- Social work narrows its focus to the improvement of a person's ability and his/her social existence (Akimoto et al., 2003).

According to these key phrases and ideas, Japanese 'social work' seems to capture a way of helping people who face difficulties in their lives.

To further understand the Japanese definition of social work, we should examine other factors relating to social needs and social work services. In particular, we have to mention the certification program for social workers. Because of the enforcement of this program, the Japanese definition of social work changed significantly in the middle of the 1980s.

CERTIFICATION PROGRAM FOR SOCIAL WORKERS IN JAPAN

In 1987 the Ministry of Welfare (MOW) established *Shakai fukushi-shi and Kaigo fukushi-shi Ho* [the Certified Social Workers and Certified Care Workers Act] (Act No. 30 of 1987), which took effect in 1988. This act established the national qualification system for social workers. The government put the term, 'social worker', for 'shakai fukushi-shi' as its translation. Accordingly, the Certified Social Worker (CSW) was to enrol in the Center of Social Welfare Promotion and National Examination after passing an annual national examination. There were 154,010 CSWs in Japan as of 2011. (Center of Social Welfare Promotion and National Examination)

We may say that there were two contributing factors behind the establishment of the CSWs.

First, after WWII, the Ministry of Welfare established a qualification system for assigning staff in welfare offices and child welfare institutions; the staff in these offices were referred to as Social Welfare Officers and Child Welfare Officers, respectively. However, those qualifications required only a few classes, and there was neither a national examination nor any accreditation. This led to discussion about the importance of higher qualifications for social workers in places such as Europe and America.

Second, it is also clear that the socio-economic changes in Japan, where there is a progressively ageing population combined with low birth rates, converted the idea of caring into a key aspect of social welfare services. This was the significant shift that caused various social services to open their doors to communities and made necessary the establishment of professions to provide those resources to the people. The certified social worker is defined by Article 2 of the Certified Social Workers and Certified Care Workers Act in the following way:

> The certified social worker provides consultation, instruction, and advice about welfare services, with expertise and skill, to people who have physical or mental disabilities', or have any difficulties in leading their daily life because of defects or environmental reasons. The certified social worker also communicates with people who provide social services, doctors, and other medical and health care services. The certified social worker also arranges and provides other consultation services. (Author's own translation)

It is clear that the original meaning of social work became narrower because of the act, even though no dictionaries have mentioned this term as it is. After MOW established the CSW system, Japanese social work education institutions adjusted and designed curriculum and teaching materials to meet the eligibility requirements of the national examination. Another effect of this act was an explosive increase in training courses, programs, and institutions. It may also be said that the CSW system responded rapidly to improve the social work profession with breakthroughs in the development of curriculum and teaching methods (Akimoto et al., 2003).

In 2009, the act was largely revised because of the need to ensure qualified professionals. This need was reflected in *Shakai Fukushi*

Kiso Kouzou Kaikaku [The Basic Structural Reform of Social Welfare]; we shall return to this point later. There were two significant amendments in the revised act. The first was the provision relating to the obligations of CSWs, and the other was the reviewing of curriculums and qualifications. Under the new curriculum, candidates study nineteen subjects related to the social welfare system, and social policy and health care services are required subjects in order to qualify for taking the examination. Regarding social work methods and skills, the curriculum also focuses on consultation and communication with many professionals such as medical doctors, nurses, and other resources in the community.

Shakai fukushi kiso kouzou kaikaku (The basic structural reform of social welfare)

Let us now turn to the Basic Structural Reform of Social Welfare from the late 1980s to the 2000s. This will lead us further into a consideration of the trends in social work education developing around the year 2000.

The social welfare law in Japan has been targeted by several acts: they include the Public Assistance Act; the Child Welfare Act; the Social Welfare Act for the Elderly; the Services and Support for Persons with Disabilities Act; the Act on the Welfare of Persons with Physical Disabilities; the Act for the Welfare of Persons with Intellectual Disabilities; and the Mother and Child and Widows Welfare Act. The common base for social welfare services was legislated in the Social Welfare Act (Act No. 45, 1951) and it has not been reviewed since its establishment. During these past fifty years, however, there has been significant socio-economic change. Social welfare needs have also been transformed. As we mentioned above, socioeconomic change has taken place in Japan as the progressively ageing population, combined with low birth rates, have rapidly changed the nation into the 'aged society'. In this half century, the diversity of social welfare needs and the 'socialisation' of care have been key words to describe Japanese social welfare issues. Accordingly, from the late 1980s to the 2000s, the Japanese government started the Basic Structural

Reform of Social Welfare. Under this reform project, the government has emphasised the introduction of long-term care insurance, the expansion of private enterprise in providing social services, and the promotion of the decentralisation of operations relating to social welfare services. There are three main directions of the reform, and they are as follows: (1) promotion of social welfare service, (2) achievement of high-quality and efficient welfare services, and (3) establishment of regional welfare (Ministry of Health, Labour and Welfare).

During this reform process, the CSW training curriculum was also reviewed. The review focused on supporting users and cooperating with the medical and healthcare professions along with the long-term care insurance system.

It is obvious that the restructuring brought significant changes, from the previous system of *sochi seido* [services are provided in accordance with the judgment of administrative offices] to *Keiyaku* [the user makes a contract with their freely chosen welfare service; users choose services by themselves and use these services under contracts with service providers (Ministry of Health, Labour and Welfare).

This means that after the restructuring, CSWs are required to be highly skilled in communication and risk management, and to be able to put these skills into practice. They are also required to support users who are having difficulty in expressing their vision, or in choosing or designing their contract (Social Welfare and War Victims' Relief Bureau 1999).

How does the current international definition impact social work education in Japan?

As we mentioned above, 'social work' translated in the Japanese CSW system has the same meaning as *soudan enjo* [consulting]. After the revision of the curriculum in 2009, it appears that the new program more specifically focuses on training CSWs for their consultative activities (Director of Social Welfare and War Victims' Relief Bureau 2008). However, there are still objections to this interpretation in the social work community, especially among researchers who know the origins of social work. There are several teaching materials still using the term social work, which is not the subject's official name; the official term in Japan is 'consulting'. We will now review teaching materials and journals to grasp and describe social work education trends occurring around 2000.

The definition of social work on textbooks for the CSW national exam

What is social work? Many social work classes around the world begin with this question. In this section, the author addresses four major textbooks which were published after the current definition was adopted, titled *Shakai Fukushi Enjo Gijutsu Ron* [Social Work Method and Theories] and written in Japanese. The four publishers are Minerva Shobo, Japan National Council of Social Welfare, Chuohoki Publishing, and Yuhikaku Publishing. Through this analysis, we elucidate the following points where the books are similar and different.

Common points:

- All textbooks contain the current international social work definition. In addition, two textbooks (textbook 'Minerva' and 'Japan National Council of Social Welfare') introduced 'the working definition of social work practice' (Bartlett 1958), adopted by the National Association of Social Workers (NASW) in US, as a definition.
- All textbooks introduce the fact that the current definition was adopted at the conference in Montréal.
- There is no mention in any of the textbooks of the possibility of revising the current definition.
- After the revision of the curriculum, two textbooks (textbook 'Minerva' and 'Chuohoki') placed minutely detailed explanations beside each paragraph. The explanations sometimes used phrases such as 'suggestion' and 'guideline' (Kawamura 2006)

Points of difference:

- Minerva: The author, Fukuyama (2007), has briefly mentioned the background behind the 2000 revision from the view point of IFSW. The author also only released an English version, unless a Japanese translation had been released since 2001. (Fukuyama, 2007)
- Japan National Council of Social Welfare: The author, Makisato (2004), introduces three definitions that were coined by Japanese scholars Gensuke Komatsu, Yoshihiro Oota, and Jiro Matsui before the current international definition of social work appeared. These scholars are well-known pioneers in the field and are well versed in the methods of social work developed in the US. All of these definitions contain two key terms, 'life' and 'helping people face difficulties of daily life' (Makisato, 2004).
- Chuohoki: The authors explain, with a story (vignette), the ideal for the current definition since the 2006 authors also added two other definitions; they were 'Standards for Social Service Manpower' (NASW) and the definition reported by the Science Council of Japan (Kawamura 2006; Fukushima, 2010).
- Yuhikaku: The authors and editors placed greater emphasis on social work values, theories, and skills, as well as approaches from the generic social work scheme. The current definition was retranslated by Takahashi (Takahashi, 2002).

These points show that recent textbook authors have been searching for a way to capture the core of what social work is, because this question concerns various aspects of the field. We notice that the reform was the turning point in reviewing social work education. It may be said that the reform question for educators was, 'What is the specialty of social work'?

Therefore, it is possible to say that some textbooks introduced the current definition as 'a mission statement' for social work, although this appearance was very sudden. Thus, this raises another question. What trends were developing in the Japanese social work community around 2000?

Trends in journals and the social work education community around 2000

According to Akiyama (2012), in 1999 Japan did not plan to submit to IFSW any suggestion for the definition, either at an institutional or individual level (Akiyama 2012, p. 23). In the annual newsletter of the Japanese Association of Social Work Education (JASSW), there was an article regarding the Montreal International Conference and World Census, though no description regarding the current definition was adopted.

A review of the articles in major journals of social work in and around 2000 shows that the current definition did not appear at all. For example, the Japanese Society for the Study of Social Welfare has been publishing a quarterly journal known for its rigorous peer review. In 2001, the main topics in the journal were related to verifying the restructuring of the fundamental social welfare system, including such concepts as 'long-term care insurance', 'quality of social welfare services', 'information management', 'user-oriented services' and 'community work for supporting peoples independent life' (Japanese Journal of Social Welfare, 2001). However, it is important to note that this does not mean that there was no discussion regarding the 'definition of social work' itself in this period. It is useful to quote from Kuuga Hiroto (1999). Kuuga defined social work in his paper in the following way: 'Social work practice is the activity of helping clients in their daily life' (Kuuga, 1999, p. 132). He did not deny learning from social work methods of western countries, though he was looking to discover a form of Japanese-style social work. His paper might not have been intended to be part of the international discussion over a definition. He wrote that his paper was focused on self-determination in the new contract system, which was introduced as part of the reform process (p. 116).

Another example comes from an article in the journal Social Work Kenkyuu *[Studies on Social Work]* in 2000. In this article, Takata (2000) mentioned the necessity for developing proactive social work that suits the indigenous Japanese social welfare situation (Takata, 2000, p. 23).

Ten years after the reform and the adoption of the definition, social work scholars and practitioners have cautiously taken up this agenda. Watanabe reported that Japanese practitioners in social welfare institutions encounter difficulties in implementing their activities under the current international definition of social work (Japanese Society for the Study of Social Work, 2012). As we mentioned in the introduction, some educators felt that the definition may not fit Japanese social work. A fuller study and review of the current definition lies outside the scope of this chapter.

CONCLUSION

What is social work in Japan? It is clear that two factors are hidden in the background of the question. The first factor, already mentioned previously, is the relation between *shakai fukushi* and social work. The second factor is the fact that social work was an idea imported to Japan.

After the CSW program started, *shakai fukushi enjo gijutu* [social work skill] was defined the same as 'consultation' by the Japanese government, although social work had been considered by educators to be the entire range of activities involved in delivering social welfare services.

When the current international definition was installed in Japan around 2000, the reform process had been conducted, and this movement influenced a wide range of social welfare services and human resources training curriculum. The CSW curriculum was also revised and is now focused on skills needed to coordinate and network with other specific professions. That is, it is clear that social work education has reflected the direction of the social welfare system in Japan. For CSW itself, responsibilities and obligations as professional social workers came to be required, just as they are for other professions. As we mentioned in the above 'textbook' section, textbooks define social work and the profession using the current international definition, even though the definition only recently and very suddenly appeared in Japan.

It may be said, therefore, that the current international definition has been welcomed as the answer to the above question without serious debate in Japan.

On the other hand, scholars and educators still cite and rely on several contributors who use the original Japanese definition of social work as well. Those contributors had knowledge of the social work method that developed in Western countries. Some of them studied in the US or other countries, and scholars read and translated many English-language books in order to introduce them into Japanese social work education. Understanding that social work originated outside of Japan, they tried to define what social work was in Japan. Japanese practitioners have also expressed the difficulties they have faced operating in social welfare institutions.

It is important to emphasise that many Japanese scholars commonly recognise that social work supports the resolution of the difficulties faced in daily life. This is not a point of view found in the current international definition of social work. One could say that this perspective is rooted in the ideal of *shakai fukushi*. This is a valid assumption, though it is beyond the scope of the present chapter.

On 5 February 2013, Japanese organisations submitted their comments in accordance with the final version proposed by chairs of IFSW and IASSW Definition Taskforce before the IASSW Los Angeles board meeting on 24 January 2013 (Japanese Association of Psychiatric Social Workers) Nevertheless, considering the discussions of the definition reviewing, as the author mentioned in the introduction of this chapter, the Japanese social work education community seems to be waiting for a new answer.

How can we contribute to the discussion over the new international definition? The definition should not be passively accepted as a 'given' guideline or instruction. This is important not only for the Japanese, but also for people from all countries and regions. We have a responsibility to participate in this discussion with the rest of the world. We also need to distil the common essence of our senior scholars, written or spoken in their own languages, and introduce these to the international discussion. This will help us develop social work education that is based on indigenous knowledge. That is to say, we will find a definition of social work that meets a global standard.

Acknowledgements

I wish to express my gratitude to Dr Tatsuru Akimoto, President of Asian and Pacific Association for Social Work Education (APASWE), for reading the manuscript and making a number of valuable comments. My special thanks are due to Ms. Sangeeta Rubine, for her editing and help with my English.

References

(References cited in this chapter were originally written in Japanese. Original titles are cited in Japanese and translated either by the original authors or the present author for this chapter.)

Akimoto, M., Ooshima, I., Shibano, M., Morimoto, Y. & Yamagata, F. (Eds). (2003). *Gendai shakai fukushi jiten [The Yuhikaku dictionary of social welfare]*. Japan: Yuhikaku.

Akiyama, T. (2012). Social work shikaku no hitsuyousei to igi. In T. Akiyama (Ed.), *Sekai no social worker* (p. 23). Japan: Tsutusi Shobou.

Bartlett, H.M. (1958). Working definition of social work practice. *Social Work*, 3(2), 5–8.

Center of Social Welfare Promotion and National Examination. (n.d.). *Tourokusha no shikaku shuruibetsu-nendobetsu no suii [Trends qualifications of registration (by year and type)]*. Retrieved 17 April 2013 from www.sssc.or.jp/touroku/pdf/pdf_t04_2.pdf.

Director of Social Welfare and War Victims' Relief Bureau. (2008). *Daigakutou nioite kaikousuru shakai fukushi nikansuru kamokuno kakunin nikakaru shishin nitsuite [Subjects of CSW training facilities and its contents]*. Retrieved 17April 2013, from www.mhlw.go.jp/bunya/seikatsuhogo/dl/shakai-kaigo-yousei07.pdf.

Fukushima, K. (2010). Soudan enjo no teigi to kousei youso. In Shakai Fukushishi Yousei Kouza HenshuuIinkai (Ed.), *Shin shakai fukushishi yousei kouza, Vol.6: Soudan enjo no kiban to senmonshoku*, 2nd edn (pp. 20–26). Japan: Chuohoki Shuppan.

Fukuyama, K. (2007). In E. Kitajima, M. Shirasawa & H. Yonemoto (Eds). *Shin shakai fukushi yousei textbook, vol.2: shakai fukushi enjo gijutsu ron (jou) [Social work theory]*. Japan: Minerva Shobou.

Hare, I. (2004). Defining social work for the 21st century: the International Federation of Social Workers' revised definition of social work. *International Social Work*, 47 (3), 407–24.

Ichibangase, Y. (1971). *shakai fukushi heno ayumi [History of socia welfare]*. Ishiyaku Publishers.

Iwama, N. (2010). Social work. In F. Yamagata & R. Kashiwame (Eds). *Shakai fukushi yogo jiten [Dictionary of social work terms]* (pp. 245–46). Japan: Mineruva Shobou.

Japan society of social work practice (Ed.). (1993). *Kaiteiban Shakai fukushi Jissen Kihon Yogo Jiten [Dictionary of basic social work revised edition]*. Japan: Kawashima shoten.

Japanese Association of Psychiatric Social Workers (n.d.). *Progress reports in accordance with the revised definition of social work world*. Retrieved 17 April 2013 from Japanese Association of Psychiatric Social Workers: www.japsw.or.jp/backnumber/oshirase/2012/0218.html

Japanese Society for the Study of Social Welfare. (2011). *Annual Report on JSSW in fiscal year of 2011* . Retrieved 17 April 2013 from www.jssw.jp/disclosure/pdf/ga_2012_gian_1_01.pdf.

Japanese Society for the Study of Social Work. (2012). Dai 28 kai taikai houkoku gakkai shusai symposium; social work jissen niokeru 'teigi' ga motsu imi– social work no kokusai teigi no kaitei no ugoki wo keiki toshite [Report of the 28th annual conference; symposium ii social work practice and 'definition'– using the international movement toward revision as an opportunity]. *Journal of Japanese Society for the Study of Social Work*, 24, 95–124.

Kawamura, T. (2006). Shakai fukushi senmonshoku to shakai fukushi enjo katsudou. In Fukushishi Yousei Kouza Henshuu Iinkai (Ed.), *Shinpan Shakai Fukushishi Yousei Kouza, Vol.8; Shakai Fukushi Enjo Gijutsu Ron I [Social work method and theories]*, 3rd edn (pp. 41–43). Japan: Chuohoki Publishing.

Komatsu, G. (1996). Shakai fukushi enjo gijutsu: in Japanese society of social work practice (Ed.), *shakai fukushi kihon yogo jiten [Social work basic dictionary]*, (p. 83). Japan: Kawashima Shoten.

Komatsu, G. (1993). Social work. In K. Oda, T. Kyougoku, Y. Kuwabara, T. Takayama & K. Tani (Eds). *Gendai fukushigaku lexicon [The lexicon of modern welfare]* (p. 166). Japan: Yuuzankaku Shuppan.

Kouno, S. (2002). Nihon no Social Work no Rekishi [Social Work History in Japan]. In E. Kitajima, A. Soeda, S. Takahashi, & R. Watanabe (Eds). *Shakai fukushi kiso series, vol. 2: social work jissen no kiso riron [Basic theories for social work practice]* (pp. 323–38). Japan: Yuhikaku.

Kuroki, Y. (2002). Nihon no social worker no tame no kyoiku: Kenkyu kikan to senmon shoku danntai. In Y. Kuroki, R. Kobayashi, S. Sakata, & Y. Morimoto (Eds). *The Practice of Macro Social Work*. Japan: Yuhikaku.

Kuuga, H. (1999). Nihonjin no bunka to social work: Ukemiteki na taijin kankei niokeru 'shutaisei' no haaku [The Japanese culture and social work—understanding 'initiative' in the passive personal relations]. *Japanese Journal of Social Welfare*, 40(1), 113–32.

Makisato, T. (2004). Shakai fukushi enjo katsudou to shakai fukushi enjo gijutsu [Social work practice and social work skill] In Shinpan Shakai Fukushi Gakushu Sousho Hensyu Iinkai (Eds), *Shinpan shakai fukushi gakushu sousho 2004, Vol. 8: Shakai fukushi enjo gijutsu ron* (pp. 49–58). Japan: Japan National Council of Social Welfare.

Ministry of Health, Labour and Welfare (n.d.). *Annual reports on health and welfare 1998–1999: social security and national life.* Retrieved 17 April 2013 from White Papers: www.mhlw.go.jp/english/wp/wp-hw/vol1/p2c4s1.html.

Okamura, S. (1965). *Case work kiroku hou [The method of the case work record].* Japan: Seishin shobo.

Oota, Y. (2006). Shakai fukushi ni okeru enjo katsudou no igi. In Fukushishi Yousei Kouza Henshu Iinkai (Ed.), *Shinpan shakai fukushishi yousei kouza, Vol.8: shakai fukushi enjo gijutsu ron I.* Japan: Chuouhouki.

Oota, Y. (Ed.) (1999). *Social work jissen to shien katei no tenkai.* Japan: Chuohoki Shuppan.

Shakai Fukushi/Shakai Hoshou Kenkyuu Renraku Iinkai. (2003). *Social work ga tenkai dekiru shakai system zukuri heno teian.* Retrieved 17 April 2013 from www.scj.go.jp/ja/info/kohyo/18pdf/1821.pdf#page=1.

Social Welfare and War Victims' Relief Bureau. (2007). *For the bill to amend the CSW and CCW Act.* Retrieved 17 April 2013 from www1.mhlw.go.jp/houdou/1104/h0415-2_16.html.

Social Welfare and War Victims' Relief Bureau. (1999). *Shakai fukushi kiso kouzou kaikaku ni tsuite [The abstruct of the restructuring of the social welfare fundamental system].* Retrieved 17 April 2013 from www1.mhlw.go.jp/houdou/1104/h0415-2_16.html.

Social Work Research Institute Asian Center for Welfare in Society, Japan College of Social Work (2011). International definition of social work review. In proceedings of APASWE/IASSW Asian and Pacific regional workshop (pp. 33–6): Japan College of Social Work.

Takahashi, S. (2002). Hashigaki. In E. Kitajima, A. Soeda, S. Takahashi, & R. Watanabe (Eds). *Shakai fukushi kiso Series, Vol. 2:*

social work iissen no kiso [Basic theories for social work practice] (pp. iii–iv). Japan: Yuhikaku.

Takata, S. (2000). Social work kenkyu no houhou to kadai [New development of social work methods: Macro practice or community practice]. *Social Work Kenkyuu [Studies on Social Work]*, 25(4), 17–23.

Yamazaki, M. (1996). Social work. In Japanese Society of Social Work Practice (Ed.), *Shakai fukushi kihon yougo jiten [Social welfare basic dictionary]* (p. 138). Japan: Kawashima Shoten.

Yamazaki, M. (2000). Social work wo teigisuru koto [Defining social work: in the changes of time and environment]. *Social Work Kenkyuu [Studies on Social Work*], 25(4), 24–32.

7

Social work education in Vietnam: developments and progress

Richard Hugman, Bùi Thị Xuân Mai and Nguyễn Thị Thái Lan

After the earlier development of the profession in the South of Vietnam, following unification in 1975 social work was abandoned. It began to emerge again in the late 1980s and since then it has grown very rapidly. In 2004 a national curriculum for social work education was approved and 2010 social work was recognised formally as a profession. University programs have played a very strong role in this process and their number has expanded considerably. This chapter looks at the ways in which social work education is contributing to the development and modernisation of Vietnamese social work. It describes the structure and format of programs and it examines issues of indigenisation in the ways that authentically Vietnamese characteristics are being developed for social work education and professional practice.

Đào tạo công tác xã hội ở Việt Nam: Những chặng đường phát triển

Tiếp theo sự phát triển nghề nghiệp ở miền Nam Việt Nam, sau khi đất nước thống nhất vào năm 1975, nghề công tác xã hội đã bị bỏ ngỏ. Tuy nhiên vào cuối những năm 1980, nghề này đã bắt đầu phát triển trở lại và kể từ đó đến nay đã và đang lớn mạnh nhanh chóng. Vào năm 2004, Chương trình khung quốc gia đào tạo ngành công tác xã hội đã được ban hành và đến năm 2010 công tác xã hội đã được chính thức công nhận là một nghề. Chương trình đào tạo ở các trường đại học có một vai trò quan trọng trong tiến trình này và số lượng các trường đào tạo đã tăng lên đáng kể. Nội dung chương này sẽ đi tìm hiểu sự đóng góp của đào tạo công tác xã hội vào tiến trình phát triển và hiện đại hóa nghề công tác xã hội Việt Nam. Chương này cũng sẽ mô tả cấu trúc và hình thức các chương trình đào tạo và đề cập tới vấn đề làm sao xây dựng một chương trình đào tạo phù hợp với tình hình địa phương thực sự mang những bản sắc Việt Nam trong công tác đào tạo và thực hành nghề nghiệp.

越南的社會工作教育：發展和過程

在早期南越專業化發展之後，統一的的越南在1975年捨棄了社會工作專業。不過，這一專業在八十年代後期又再次開始出現之後就迅速發展。2004年，社會工作教育被認可為一個國家級課程；在2010年社會工作被正式認為為一個專業。在此過程中，大學課程扮演了一個很關鍵的角色，開設社工的學校大量增加。本章將著眼於社工教育對於越南社工發展和現代化的貢獻方式。它將描述這些大學專案的結構和課程安排。同時，本章審視了越南社會工作的本土化問題：具有真正越南特色的社會工作教育和專業實踐將如何發展。

ベトナムにおけるソーシャルワーク教育: 開発と進展

ベトナムにおけるソーシャルワークは、初期のベトナム南部に早い時期に開発されたが、その後、1975年の南北統一でソーシャルワークは見放されてしまった。1980年の終わり頃、ソーシャルワークが再び現れ始め、それ以降、急速に事業は成長した。2004年、ソーシャルワーク教育は国の教育課程として承認され、2010年にソーシャルワークは専門職として認識された。この成長過程に大学の教育課程が一役担い、これらの課程は相当に拡大した。この章では、ソーシャルワーク教育がどのような方法でベトナムのソーシャルワークの発展と近代化に貢献してきたかを調べる。ベトナムのソーシャルワーク教育の構成と形式を描写し、また、先住民文化の土着化(indigenization)の問題においてどのような方法で真のベトナム人の特性がソーシャルワーク教育と専門職としての実践を発展させたかを調査する。

베트남의 사회복지교육 : 발전 과정

남베트남에서 사회복지는 전문직으로 발전하였지만 1975년 통일 이후 중단되었다. 이후 1980년대 후반에서야 사회복지 전문직이 등장하였고 그 이후 급속도로 성장하였다. 2004년 사회복지교육에 대한 국가 교육과정이 승인되었고, 2010년에는 사회복지가 전문직으로 인정되었다. 이 과정에서 대학은 매우 중요한 역할을 했고, 대학의 숫자도 늘어났다. 본 장에서는 베트남 사회복지 발전과 근대화에 대학 교육이 기여한 측면을 살펴보았다. 또한 대학교육 프로그램의 구조와 형태를 언급하였으며 사회복지 교육과 실무가 베트남에 정착되는 과정에서 순수하게 베트남적인 특성을 담아내는 고유성의 문제를 논하였다.

A brief history of social work and social work education in Vietnam

Because the traditional Vietnamese approach to social problems and social needs was focused on people being active in their communities and assisting their neighbours, the development of professional social work has been uneven. To understand the recent history of professionalisation better, and especially the role of social work education, it is necessary to describe the phases of development in sequence as well as to note the importance of social and political change.

In her unique history of Vietnamese social work, Nguyen Thi Oanh (Oanh, 2002) begins the story before 1862. However, while this discussion draws on her scholarship, we will start nearer to the present, in the period after 1945. These were the closing years of the French colonial rule. Nevertheless this short period saw the introduction by the International Red Cross of a social work training school. This school was subsequently given to the Catholic *Daughters of Charity* and remains known by the name *Caritas*. Vietnamese social workers were trained, although as Oanh notes (2002, p. 85) this development had little impact on ordinary people and often largely served the interests of colonial administration.

Following the division of Vietnam in 1954 after the Geneva Conference, Vietnamese social work took two different paths. In the north, from 1954 to 1975 the Socialist Republic of Vietnam did not recognise professional social work as necessary. Support for vulnerable people came under the 'social protection' umbrella and training only focused on social policies and some courses in 'people mobilisation' skills (Lan, 2011). In contrast in the south the Caritas School of Social Work continued to educate social workers and this program was joined by a Vietnamese Army School of Social Work, the Buddhist Youth Service School and the United Nations sponsored national School of Social Work; the University of Da Lat also introduced social work as a discipline (Oanh, 2002, p. 86). In 1970 the Vietnam Association of Social Workers was formed and it joined the International Federation of Social Workers (IFSW), while the Caritas School and the National School of Social Work joined the Asia-Pacific Association of Social Work Education (APASWE). Oanh also notes (2002) that although in this period the social welfare system was a tool of the neo-colonial regime, many social workers also held more progressive positions and either supported or actively joined opposition to the American War (as it is known in Vietnam).

At the time of reunification in 1975 it was estimated (Oanh, 2002) there were approximately 38 Vietnamese graduate social workers, 300 trained with two-year diplomas and over 500 with other shorter forms of social work education in the country. As we will discuss in subsequent parts of this chapter, this pattern of education and training, in which graduate professionals are part of a continuum of trained social workers continues in the present Vietnamese approach. However, the knowledge and skills that had been gained before 1975 were not required under the prevailing socialist model of social welfare. While some became part of the 'mass organisations', such as the Women's Union, the Youth Union, Fatherland Association and so on, which provided social welfare for their constituency groups, many others moved into different and diverse areas of work and social life. The period 1975–1985 was one of austerity for Vietnam. From 1986 policy changed markedly as the

Vietnamese Government introduced the policy of 'renovation' (in Vietnamese *doi moi*) to create a market economy in order to promote economic development. Associated with this was also a gradual opening up of the country to outsiders, not only from other Socialist countries but also from other parts of the world. This policy has been very successful, as reflected in the rapid reduction of poverty and associated modernisation of industry and commerce. However, along with these changes social problems that had disappeared or been hidden from view very quickly re-emerged as well. In particular, issues of the welfare of children and young people, including human trafficking, and the impact of drug misuse, prostitution, the spread of HIV/AIDS have all become major challenges for the society.

Influenced through the development of external relationships, social work came to the attention of political leaders as a profession that could make a contribution to addressing these emerging issues. So in the late 1980s social workers have been slowly but increasingly invited to participate not only in health and welfare services but also in community development (Oanh, 2002, p. 90).

A major part of the reintroduction of professional social work has been the growth of social work education. While this is not the only force for change, in many respects (and especially in the north) the recognition of social work is being achieved through the creation of university level professional education and training. At the beginning of this process, social work was introduced as one subject within a Bachelor of Arts in Women's Studies at the Open University of Ho Chi Minh City (OUHCMC), followed soon after by the then College of Labour and Social Affairs (now the University of Labour and Social Affairs—ULSA) in Hanoi. In 2004 the Ministry of Education and Training (Ministry of Education and Training) approved a national curriculum in social work. This development has been enthusiastically supported by UNICEF and other INGOs, such that by 2011 there were 29 universities (4 year program) and colleges (3 year program) approved to offer these programs. Nevertheless, as we will discuss in more detail below, one of the major challenges is that there are still very few Vietnamese academics who are qualified to teach social work, especially in practice subjects.

Another major challenge was that with the officially supported creation of potentially large numbers of social work graduates there was no comparably recognised profession for them to enter. So, often encouraged by the developments in social work education, the Vietnamese Government undertook the necessary policy review that in 2010 led to the official recognition of social work as a profession within the Vietnamese political and legal system. This is 'Decision 32' of the Prime Minister's Office (32/2010/QĐ-TTg), establishing the structure of professional social work. We will return below to the implications of this policy. At the time of writing there are now demonstration projects being established by the Ministry of Labour, Invalids and Social Affairs (MOLISA), while social work graduates are finding employment in the NGO sector, in both national and international agencies.

The current situation of social work education and training in Vietnam

Training institutions and the national curriculum

Since the Ministry of Education and Training of Vietnam issued the training code for social work education in 2004, the number of universities providing the social work program increased dramatically from four in 2004 up to 23 after four years (in 2007), and to 29 in 2011 (Ministry of Education and Training, 2011). Such a number puts a considerable amount of pressure on achieving quality in training and education. In addition to the universities, many vocational training institutions including vocational schools and colleges have begun to prepare their plans to train social workers at the para-professional (pre-degree) level.

The Vietnam Government Ministry of Education and Training approved the training curriculum framework first time for university and college levels in 2004. In March 2010, the curriculum was amended on the basis of reducing the number of subjects in general knowledge and increasing the amount of time for professional knowledge, especially practice subjects and internship. It was adjusted to ensure that the most up to date theory and practice formed the basis for professional education, to maximise benefits both for students and for the beneficiaries of their work in the future (Ministry of Education and Training, 2010).

At the university level the minimum designated volume of instruction is 180 units (that is, 2,025 class hours) for programs with 4 years duration. The curriculum framework regulates approximately 59% (106 core units) of the minimum volume of the whole degree program and the remaining 41% (74 units) is open for higher education institutions themselves to design the curriculum in accordance with the orientations of their program and with a particular focus on meeting designated areas of the society's needs (Ministry of Education and Training, 2010).

At the college level the total number of units is 150 (1,687 class hours) and the duration of programs is 3 years. The curriculum framework specifies 60% (90 core units) of the minimum volume of the whole and 40% (60 units) of the volume is left open for training institutions themselves to design their own content, especially focusing on relevant skills, again in keeping with their own institution's orientation towards the needs of the society, 2010).

These changes are based on six years of experience with the 2004 curricula and the National Project on developing social work as a career approved in March 2010 (Vietnamese Government Report, 2010). It has set a requirement for more standardised learning content, updated and integrated in line with the international social work education and training standards issued by IASSW in 2004. On the basis of the Vietnamese curriculum framework, approximately 40% of the curriculum content is supplemented by each education or training institution to respond to local realities and wider social issues as well as their own specific missions.

In Vietnam, according to the education and training management system, universities and colleges are often managed by two ministries. The first of these is the Ministry of Education and Training (Ministry of Education and Training) and the second is an administrative Ministry which takes day-to-day charge. An example of this is the University of Labour & Social Affairs (ULSA), one of the universities with a large social work program, which is managed administratively by the Ministry of Labour, Invalids and Social Affairs. There are only a very few exceptions accountable solely to Ministry of Education and Training, in particular the Vietnam National University (VNU) and some open, private and semi-public universities/colleges. The VNU is a federated system of small, disciplinary focused universities, of which two are developing social work programs: University of Social Sciences and Humanities and University of Education.

In the example of the relationship between ULSA and Ministry of Labour and Social Affairs, the Ministry takes the major responsibility nationally for the development of professional social work and uses social workers; for this reason ULSA is considered as a key university in educating social workers. ULSA is located in the capital city, Hanoi, and its programs are oriented on the basis of focused content regarding social policies for disadvantageous groups, social insurance policies, and policies for special target groups, such as war veterans. By comparison, The University of Dalat, in the Central Highlands of Vietnam, is located in a locality that has low population density, small urban centres and quite a mountainous terrain. So its social work programs concentrate mainly on community and rural development.

As the oldest institution providing social work education and training, the Open University of Ho Chi Minh City (OUHCMC) is located in the largest city in the south of the country and is the largest university in the country. A former semi-private university that became a public university in 2006, the OUHCMC does not depend on an administrative ministry in charge, but is accountable directly to Ministry of Education and Training regarding educational standards. That creates great flexibility for the university to construct their training contents to meet the maximum society's needs. Its curriculum is marked by breadth. This program has some similarities with the University of Social Sciences and Humanities

(USSH), which as part of the VNU system is also not managed but is accountable directly to Ministry of Education and Training. USSH is developing its programs to lean more to a social understanding of need. Because social work is based inside the Faculty of Sociology, its programs cover many subjects which are strongly grounded in areas of sociology, such as sociologies of religion, family, crime and so on.

In recent times, it has become more widely recognised that many social work graduates do not have experience in working with specific groups such as people with HIV/AIDS, people with disabilities, children, drug addicts and so on. There is a developing national dialogue between educational institutions and employers, for example through conferences. Such dialogue with employers and service organisations is encouraging the larger universities such as ULSA, VNU and OUHCMC to pay more attention to building specialised programs for social work, such as social work for people with HIV/AIDS, people who are drug addicted and people with disabilities. The issue of mental health is getting more interest from the Vietnam Government on implementing and promoting improved quality of mental health care. Project 1215 of the Vietnamese Government approved in August 2011 aims to train 30,000 social workers in this field (Vietnamese Government Report, 2011). As a result, universities are also about to prepare specialised programs for social work training in the field of mental health care (Vietnamese Government Report, 2011).

Postgraduate training

After five years of social work undergraduate training in Vietnam, masters degrees have begun to be provided by three institutions. These are the Vietnam Academy of Social Sciences, ULSA, in 2010, in a joint program with the Philippine Women's University. The total number of students in this joint program until 2013 is about 40 students. USSH has so far provided for two cohorts with 185 students in the two-year program (Hoa & Minh, 2012). USSH has had support initially from international consultants provided through UNICEF

Vietnam and subsequently a team from the California State University at San Jose. As these programs are in their infancy they are as yet untested, although they constitute a major element of the overall policy to professionalise Vietnamese social work.

Enrichment training courses for current human services workers

National studies show that staff working in the field of social welfare lack knowledge and skills in social work. A high percentage of staff involved in helping vulnerable groups have no relevant education or training in social work, or even in related human services fields. Of those who are graduates, their majors are usually in other fields such as economics, even in agriculture or engineering (Ministry of Labour and Social Affairs, 2010; ULSA, 2007; UNICEF, 2005)

The reality shows that as a result of the impact of international integration, the introduction of professional social work trends, and the achievements of socio-economic policies, theory and practice in social services in Vietnam are being required to change. This sets a professional challenge for people working in the area of social welfare, whether within Ministry of Labour and Social Affairs, the former Committee for Population, Families and Children (now absorbed into Ministry of Labour and Social Affairs), the Women's Union, the Youth Union, the Vietnam Red Cross, or other organisations. With technical support from international organisations, many social work training exercises have been organised to equip their staff with necessary professional knowledge and skills. Nonetheless, these short-term training courses only concentrate on the supply of basic skills in order to temporarily 'fill the gap' and so do not systematically equip human services staff to become professionally qualified (Mai, 2010). Because the *Decision 32/2010/QĐ-TTg* giving approval for the Social Work Profession Development Project in Vietnam established the target that 25,000 staff must be re-trained between 2010 and 2020, short-term in-service programs clearly can only make a basic contribution (Vietnamese Government Report, 2010). At the same time, they are important as this number cannot all be provided for at college and university level institutions in this time period.

At present, many provinces and cities are running their training courses to enhance the capacities of their staff. In addition, particularly with sponsorship from UNICEF and Atlantic Philanthropy, Ministry of Education and Training and ULSA in cooperation with international institutions (such as Community and Families Service International and the Asian Social Institute) are to train 320 high-level staff in the period from 2011 to 2014. These staff are directors and deputy directors of Departments of Labour, Invalids and Social Affairs, and Social Protection Centers. In the period 2011–2012, nearly 150 people in this leadership group were trained (ULSA, 2011).

FACULTY

The lack of qualified lecturers trained in social work is a big challenge in this field in Vietnam. At present, many lecturers at social work education institutions in Vietnam do not have either MSW or PhD degrees in social work. Lecturers holding MSW degrees are mainly located at three training institutions: ULSA, The University of Dalat, and Open University HCMC. For instant, ULSA has only one lecturer who has a PhD degree in social security, three lecturers who are undertaking PhD training and about ten lecturers with MSW degrees. Many universities are recruiting faculty with BSW degrees and then encouraging them to attend MSW programs. Those early-career academics are thus involved in both teaching undergraduate BSW and participating as students in MSW programs *at the same time*.

For these reasons, universities are often making use of strategies to send their social work lecturers to pursue social work education overseas (for example, in Canada, Australia, the USA, the Philippines). What is more, although some faculty have taken MSW programs at overseas universities (for example, faculty from ULSA, The University of Da Lat and OUHCMC), most MSW programs either take the form of joint training with overseas training institutions (such as at ULSA) or purely domestic programs (such as at USSH and Vietnam Academy of Social Sciences). Nevertheless, both models are contributing to improving knowledge and skills for bachelors of social work degree holders so that they can participate in social work training and education at universities, colleges and vocational schools.

In the jointly provided MSW at ULSA, social work academics from the Philippines are invited to come and deliver lectures. In the domestic MSW programs, the lecturers are professors and associate professors who specialise in sociology and psychology and have been trained additionally in social work, with some international academics also involved.

In addition to training lecturers at universities and colleges, Ministry of Labour and Social Affairs is active in an effort to train lecturers for the vocational schools that come directly under the Ministry of Labour and Social Affairs management, because most vocational schools also do not have lecturers trained in social work. In 2012, Ministry of Labour and Social Affairs held training courses for 99 lecturers at vocational schools from three location areas: the South, the North and the Central regions of Vietnam. These lecturers were supplied with basic knowledge and skills in social work so that they can provide the most basic training for vocational students.

Training materials

Social work in Vietnam is a field marked by a significant paucity in education and training materials. Main textbooks in subjects such as 'introduction to social work', 'methods of social work' (whether working with individuals, groups and communities, counseling, social work administration, or other topics) were compiled at some large universities. ULSA and OUHCMC are the two educational institutions that have their own full textbook systems. They are the textbooks suppliers for many other universities. Additionally, specialised textbooks in working with groups such as people addicted to drug, people with disabilities, people with HIV/AIDS, and so on, are being developed in actively joint efforts with international organisations. State agencies such as Ministry of Education and Training have set out plans on specialised textbooks for training programs regarding social work working with specialised groups. In terms of training materials for vocational schools, Ministry of Labour and Social Affairs is co-operating with universities and colleges to develop a system of developing textbooks for social work training schools at two-year and three-year programs. Other advanced materials for social work training are being developed with the support from many NGOs and international organisations in Vietnam such UNICEF, Vietnam Assistance for the Handicapped (VNAH), Actionaid, Family Health International (now called FHI 360).

Teaching methods

Thanks to opportunities to work with many international experts from international organisations such as UNICEF, ILO, UNV, UNDP, Save children, CFSI, etc., and universities in Australia, Canada, the USA, Singapore, Sweden, Korea, etc., local lecturers at some universities in Vietnam have gained experience in teaching with modern methods. This creates a greater attraction for learners.

Challenges in social work education and training in Vietnam

The greatest single challenge is a lack of competent lecturers (Lan, 2011; Hoa & Minh 2012; Mai, 2012a). With the target proposed in *Decision 32/2010/QĐ-TTg* to train 35,000 social workers to 2020 (including the 25,000 who are current staff being retrained), there is a serious lack of appropriately educated and experienced faculty. At present, most universities providing social work training do not have PhD degree holder in social work; even MSW degree lecturers are very few. For example, in the Faculty of Social Work at ULSA, with the quota of recruiting nearly 400 undergraduate BSW students and 50–60 college students, there 12–14 regular lecturers, of which there are five qualified at masters level and one with a doctorate, while three are currently PhD candidates and ten MSW students. In the Social Work Division at USSH, there are 14 lecturers, of which there are two with MSW, two participating MSW programs, and one PhD candidate. Another example is the teaching staff in the Social Work Department at OUHCMC, where there are six lecturers of whom two are MSW graduates with one lecturer attending a PhD program, while this program recruited over 80 undergraduate students in 2011–2012.

As a consequence of this current faculty profile, those lecturers who have MSW and PhD degrees from overseas, such as the Philippines, Canada, the USA, Korea, and the UK, tend to lack practical experience. Thus, it takes some years to apply their learned knowledge into the context of Vietnam. Cultural factors as well as social-political-economic features, and the unclear career legal framework present difficulties for them to develop professionalism in teaching classes or supervising students on practicum placements.

In addition, many of the universities with recently established social work programs or training institutions preparing to provide social work training, do not even have any MSW qualified lecturers. They mainly use BSW graduates as lecturers.

The second challenge is the lack of a social work textbooks and reference books as well as specialised training social work materials (Lan et al, 2010; Hoa & Minh, 2010; Mai, 2012b). The number of social work textbooks is very few. Most universities do not have their own social work textbooks, except ULSA and OUHCMC (as noted above). In bookstores, it is difficult to find a Vietnamese social work textbook, unlike other fields such business administration, accounting, finance, law or sociology, which have a plenty of references in Vietnamese. The number of social work textbooks in foreign languages available in Vietnam is also very few; if any, such textbooks are donated by foreign organisations and put in the universities' libraries. However, this causes another problem as the limitations of lecturers' and students' capacities in the relevant foreign languages is an obstacle in utilising this source. So they rarely use such textbooks. Also, due to the lack competence and practical experience among teaching staff, practice skills are not addressed sufficiently in social work methods and skills textbooks. These textbooks are still very theoretical (Mai, 2012b).

The next challenge concerns the field supervisors. They are lacking in both quantity and quality (Lan, 2011, Hoa & Minh, 2012; Mai 2012a). This is one of the critical weaknesses in social work training in Vietnam in the current period (Mai, 2012a). Only universities with longer experience in social work training such as OUHCMC and ULSA have been able to set up a network of field supervisors, which now stands at over 30 agencies and centres. Most field supervisors do not have much knowledge of social work. They only have working experience, so although they understand the administration of human services they have difficulty in helping students to connect social work theories with practice. Many of them have attended training in social work supervision, but there is frequent movement to other workplaces, or they are promoted to managing positions or transferred to other fields. Therefore, there is an increasing loss of field supervisors who have knowledge and skills in social work. This is also one of the causes of inadequate practice in training programs.

Regarding education and training curricula, Vietnam is still trying to find its way in building appropriate and relevant programs. Although there is a curriculum framework set by Ministry of Education and Training, there are still many inadequacies in the allocation of training hours to different aspects of knowledge. The volume of 'basic knowledge' occupies a lot of curriculum time; meanwhile specific content from social work is equivalent to less than one-third of the total training time (excluding basic supplement subjects for social sciences and humanities, and social work). In particular, content related directly to professional skills for helping specialised groups only represents about two to three units out of a total of 180. (Mai, 2012b). The contents of some subjects are duplicated; for example, theories of social work and theories of human behavior overlap a lot. In addition, the contents of subjects for social work fieldwork and practicum with individuals, groups and communities are mainly theory taught in class rather than actual practice in the field. The duration of fieldwork and practicum only represents one-ninth of the whole training duration, which affects students' practical skills after graduation. At present, there are only programs for undergraduate training, college training, vocational training and master training; there are not any social work doctoral training programs.

In the Vietnamese context the social work profession has developed relatively recently and has only officially been recognised in the last few years, so its professional attraction is not high. Social work graduates have difficulty in getting a job because the specific regulations on the recruitment of social workers that should follow *Decision 32/2010/QĐ-TTg* are yet to become a reality. Added to this there is a continuing misunderstanding about social work at the grassroots level that social worker only need enthusiasm and dedication, so when recruiting social workers employers don't really pay attention to formal social work qualifications. Besides that, salary scale for social workers at the grassroots level is rather low in comparison with those in many other working areas, which also limits the professional attraction (Tiep, 2006).

Another challenge is the lack of an external accreditation organisation to ensure the quality of social work education and training. In many other countries independent bodies exist to assess the appropriateness and quality of the academic and professional content of programs. The Vietnamese system, in which each university or college follows the prescribed Ministry of Education and Training curriculum lacks the same level of quality assurance for each program.

In short, serious challenges remain in social work education and training, across all aspects from teaching staff, educational training curricula and low social awareness about the social work profession.

Some suggestions regarding strategy for development

Based on this description and analysis of social work education and training in Vietnam, we suggest that in the next decade it will be necessary for Vietnam to consider the following challenges and strategies.

First, in order to assure the quality of social work training, it is important that all stakeholders in Vietnamese social work together find ways to strengthen teaching capacity, by both increasing the number of social work qualified lecturers and also improving their levels of expertise at MSW and PhD level. In addition, it is necessary to find ways appropriately to apply international knowledge to Vietnam's situation and needs (Hugman et al, 2009).

From this, the second step is to continuing to study and finalise social work training curricula in accordance with international standards and the characteristics of Vietnamese society (Lan et al, 2010). This raises the question of 'indigenisation' and the possibility of developing authentic theories and practices that are both credible by international professional standards and at the same time authentically Vietnamese in terms of their cultural and social foundations (Fook & Gray, 2005; Hugman, 2010).

At the same time, third, it is crucial to set up a network of domestic schools of social work with a view to sharing experience among lecturers and students at local and national level, and in partnership with foreign education and training institutions. Discussions are already beginning about ways to establish a National Association of Schools of Social Work, and then prepare for joining the International Association of Schools of Social Work. This would provide a stronger platform for Vietnamese social work academics to continue co-operating with domestic and foreign organisations to research and develop social work training in Vietnam. In turn this might open up more join training programs with foreign schools for social work at BSW, MSW and PhD level in Vietnam. However, at this stage it remains unclear who will be able to exercise leadership in this process and how the process can be structured so as to maintain the distinctive development of Vietnamese social work and not an unintended importation of inappropriate theories and methods.

Fourth, as many countries now have accrediting and regulatory bodies that link the formal recognition of professional social work with appropriate educational qualifications, this is a further step that Vietnam has already begun to consider. The proposal to establish a National Council for Social Work Training in order to accredit and evaluate social work training programs and quality of schools of social work is already being discussed by educators and policy makers. Such a council might take responsibility to ensure quality of professional social work, such as through the accreditation of educational programs as well as issuing professional licenses or registering practitioners.

The fifth aspect of social work development to be considered is that of changes to legal documents and policies to recognise the social work profession and its role in the society. Although *Decision 32/2010/QĐ-TTg* forms the groundwork for this, there continues to be a need to implement its intentions in specific job titles and salary scales as a foundation for the recruitment and efficient use of graduates from the schools of social work.

Then, sixth, there is a continuing and pressing need to improve awareness about the roles of social work for all related government bodies, agencies and social organisation such as in health, public health, law, education so that the knowledge and skills of professionally qualified social workers can become more widely known by these professions and institutions. Related to this is the importance of adaptations and developments to law and policy concerning the areas on which social work is focused. Again, early steps have been taken in the inclusion of social work in the *Decision 1215/2011/QĐ-TTg* for community mental health, but compared to many countries Vietnam's laws concerning family, youth, health, adult offenders and so on are only just now under consideration to find appropriate ways of including social work as part of the social response to these needs.

As a conclusion, we must note that social work and social work education in Vietnam is in a period of rapid development. Consequently, social work education faces many challenges. This chapter has described and discussed the current situation, identifying the central elements to understand the processes and direction it is taking. Much has been achieved in a relatively short time and a great deal more is yet to be done as the goals that have been set for 2020 clearly show. It is time now for Vietnam social work education to look forward to building an authentic program that reflects Vietnamese culture and values based on its social-political context.

References

Gray. M. & Fook. J. (2004). The quest for a universal social work: some issues and implications. *Social Work Education*, 23(5), 625–44.

Hoa, V.T.K. & Minh, B.T. (2012). Paper presented to the Sharing of International Experiences of Social Work and Social Protection Conference, organised by Ministry of Labour and Social Affairs. Hanoi, Ministry of Labour and Social Affairs.

Hugman, R. (2010). *Understanding international social work: a critical analysis*. Basingstoke: Palgrave-Macmillan.

Hugman. R., Durst. D., Loan. L.H., Lan. N.T. & Hong. N.T. (2009). Developing social work in Vietnam: issues in professional education. *Social Work Education*, 28(2), 177–89.

Lan, N.T.T. (2011). Social work in Vietnam: historical development and current trends. In S. Stanley (Ed.), *Social work education in countries of the East: issues and challenges* (pp. 599–618). New York: Nova Publishers.

Mai, B.T.X. (2012a). Social work education in mental health. Paper presented at the National Conference to Promote the Implementation of National program on Mental disorders and Mental Illness Assistance and Rehabilitation on Community Base for 2011–2020, organised by Ministry of Labour and Social Affairs. Da Nang, Vietnam: Ministry of Labour and Social Affairs.

Mai, B.T.X. (2012b). Situation of the needs of social work education for workers working with people with disabilities in social protection centers of MOLISA. Research paper. Faculty of Social

Work, University of Labour & Social Affairs. Hanoi: Ministry of Labour and Social Affairs.

Mai, B.T.X. (2010). *An introduction to social work.* Hanoi: Labour and Social Affairs Publishing House.

Ministry of Education and Training (2004). *Decision No 35/2004/ QĐ-BGD&ĐT: issuing the national curriculum on social work education at university and college level.* Hanoi: Ministry of Education and Training.

Ministry of Education and Training (2007). *Handbook for entrance exam in 2007.* Hanoi: Ministry of Education and Training.

Ministry of Education and Training (2010). *Circular No 10/2010/ TT- BGD&ĐT: issuing the amended training curricula in social work at college and university level.* Hanoi: Ministry of Education and Training.

Ministry of Education and Training (2011). *Handbook for entrance exam in 2011.* Hanoi: Ministry of Education and Training.

Oanh. N.T. (2002). Historical development and characteristics of social work in today's Vietnam. *International Journal of Social Welfare*, 11(1), 84–91.

Social Protection Department of Ministry of Labour and Social Affairs. (2010). Report on the study on the needs of social work education and training among the staff and collaborators in the area of social work wervices in 2010. Hanoi: Ministry of Labour and Social Affairs.

Thi, T.L., Hugman. R. & Briscoe. C. (2010). Moving towards an 'indigenous' social work education in Vietnam. *Social Work Education*, 29(8), 843–54.

Tiep. N. (2006). *Scientific base for developing social work as a profession in Vietnam.* Hanoi: Ministry of Labour and Social Affairs.

UNICEF Vietnam. (2005). *A study of the human resource and training needs for the development of social work in Vietnam.* Hanoi: UNICEF Vietnam.

Vietnamese Government Report (2010). *Decision No 32/2010/ QĐ-TTg: decision on the approval of the social work profession development project 2010–2020*. Hanoi.

Vietnamese Government Report (2011). Decision 1215/2011/ QĐ-TTg approved by Prime Minister for the implementation of national program on mental disorders and mental illness assistance and rehabilitation on community base for 2011–2020. Hanoi.

8

The development of the social work profession and social work education in China: issues and prospects

Joe C. B. Leung

After the publications of a series of official documents on the need, development plans, and guidelines on developing social work workforce after 2006, local governments have encouraged the establishment of social work organisations, through the purchase of services, to deliver emerging social welfare services. Thereafter, social work positions have been thriving, particularly in coastal cities. The 2012 median- and long-term planning on the construction of the social work workforce projected the need for the number of professional direct practice social workers to half a million in 2015 and 1.45 million in 2020. Currently, China has 320 social work undergraduate educational programs and 60 MSW programs which turn out 20,000 social work graduates each year. Against this background, social work education has to be restructured to meet the new demands on practice knowledge and skills. Overall, social work education is plagued by the lack of teachers with practice experiences and poorly designed curricula.

標題：社會工作職業和社會工作教育在中國的發展：問題和前景

在出臺了一系列必要的官方檔案、發展計畫和2006年後社會工作專業人才建設規劃後，本地政府通過購買服務鼓勵社會工作機構的建立來提供緊急社會福利服務。此後，社會工作崗位，特別在沿海地區，開始迅速增長。《2012年社會工作專業人才建設中長期規劃》著眼於專業的前線社會工作者從2015年500,000人到2020年1,450,000人的人數需求增長。目前，中國有320個社會工作本科教育項目和60個社會工作碩士研究生教育項目，每年輸出20,000名社會工作專業畢業生。在此背景下，社會工作教育必須重新建構來滿足實踐知識和技能的新需求。綜上所述，社會工作教育正遭遇教師缺乏實踐經驗和課程設計不完善的困境。

中国におけるソーシャルワーク専門職と教育の発展

2006年のソーシャルワーカー事業の人員の必要性、発展計画と指針についての一連の公文書の発行後、地方政府は、新生のソーシャルワーカー事業を提供するために、サービスの買取を通して、ソーシャルワーク組織の確立に貢献した。それ以来、ソーシャルワークは沿岸の都市で活発になってきている。2012年の、また長期計画においてのソーシャルワーカーの労働人口構成によると、実際の活動に関わるソーシャルワーカーは、2015年に50万人、2020年に145万人必要であると見積られている。現在の中国では、320の学士レベルと60の修士レベルのソーシャルワークの教育プログラムがあり、毎年２万人のソーシャルワークの卒業生を出している。これらの背景と反して、ソーシャルワーク教育が実践知識と技術という新たな必要性を満たすためには再構成する必要がある。総合的にいえば、中国のソーシャルワーク教育は、実践経験のあるソーシャルワーク指導者の欠如と不充分なカリキュラム設計に悩まされている。

중국 사회복지전문직의 발전과 사회복지 교육의 태동 : 논점과 전망

2006년 이후 사회복지 인력 양성의 필요성, 발전계획, 지침서 등이 줄곧 정부문서로 나오고 있다. 지방정부에서는 사회복지관련 전문조직을 만들고, 필요한 사회복지서비스를 제공하려고 애쓰고 있다. 특히 해안도시를 중심으로 사회복지직책이 뜨고 있는데 2012년에 세운 중장기 목표에 의하면 2015년까지는 사회복지실천가를 50만 명, 2020년까지는 145만 명 필요하다고 제시하였다. 현재 중국은 320개 대학에서 사회복지 학사학위 프로그램을 가지고 있고, 60개의 대학에서 석사학위 프로그램을 가지고 있어서 매년 2만 명의 졸업생이 배출되고 있다. 그렇지만 사회복지의 지식과 기술의 새로운 도전에 직면하여 교육내용을 재구성해야

한다. 전반적으로는 교과과정이 열악하고 실무경험이 있는 교육자가 부족한 현상이 두드러지고 있다.

Introduction

In recent decades, the economic performance of China has been phenomenal. In 2010, it became the second-largest economy in the world. From another perspective, however, its per capita gross domestic product (GDP) in 2011 was only US$5,430 (nominal), ranking 91st in the world (in terms of purchasing power, it was US$8,442, ranking 94th (World Bank, December 2012). With this level of per capita GDP, China's economic wealth is similar to that of countries such as Ecuador, Jamaica, Algeria, Belize, and the Maldives. Despite its remarkable economic achievements, improvements in living standards have not been evenly distributed. Rapid industrialisation, urbanisation, and marketisation, together with a rapidly ageing society, the erosion of family values, and rising residential mobility, have triggered a wide array of social issues and led to a new set of social risks for the Chinese people. More of them have found themselves vulnerable to income loss due to social dislocation, retirement, insecure employment, and inadequate social protection (Leung & Xu, 2009). Rising social tensions have led to calls for the need to maintain social cohesion and enhance government legitimacy or, to use the Chinese expression, 'to construct a harmonious society'.

In recent years, the Chinese government has set out to develop a new social protection system with universal coverage and citizenship-based entitlement, moving towards a welfare state (China Development Research Foundation, 2012; *Economist*, September 8, 2012; Shi, 2012; World Bank, 2012). However, the development of professionally-based social care services for vulnerable populations, such as older people, the disabled, delinquents, and orphans has been limited and unevenly distributed. Long-awaited social welfare reforms to increase provision, enhance professionalisation, and design a pluralistic service delivery system are expected (Leung, 2012).

According to the *National Development Mid- and Long-term Framework on Human Capital 2010–2020* published by the Chinese government, social work is one of the six types of key strategic human resources which should receive high priority for future development. Based on the projections in the strategy, China needs to have two million social workers by 2015 and three million by 2020. Currently, China has 320 social work undergraduate programs and 60 MSW programs which produce 20,000 graduates each year. In other words, it has become one of the largest social work communities in the world. What has happened to the social work profession and social work education in recent years? What are the key challenges facing Chinese social work educators? The recent emergence of nongovernmental social work organisations (SWOs) is considered as a strategic platform for developing innovative social welfare services and creating social work jobs. As the foremost example in the development of SWOs and social work workforce, the experiences of Guangdong province are used here to illustrate the issues and prospects facing the social work profession and social work education in China.

Re-emergence of social work

Under the socialist system, there should be no social problems, including unemployment and poverty. Direct government intervention, administrative procedures, participation in labour production, ideological re-education, and political mobilisation have been adopted as the key approaches to resolving social issues and rehabilitating people with problems (Leung, 1990). Rapid economic growth and changing social structures has resulted in a wide array of social problems. These increasingly require care and treatment from professional social workers with the skills and experience to support victims of domestic violence and natural disasters, frail older people, orphans, the mentally ill, the disabled, drug addicts, juvenile delinquents, the unemployed, and the poor (Leung, 2012).

Having opened up gradually to the world during the 1980s, China has also become more active in global social work events and activities such as conferences, visits, and exchanges. Locally, the China Association of Social Work was formed in 1991, and became a member of the International Federation of Social Workers in 1992. In the 1990s, the emerging development of community-based social welfare programs, together with the adoption of the policy directive of the 'socialisation of social welfare' (or the 'small government, large society' principle) provided important impetus to the development of social care services, particularly for the frail elderly and disabled. However, the development of nongovernmental organisations (NGOs) remained largely restricted. Chinese social work was perceived mainly as a profession within the working scope of civil affairs.

Some of the regulations formulated by the Ministry of Civil Affairs on the management of residential homes for older people (2001), children's homes (2001), rehabilitation centres for people with disabilities (2001), foster care for orphans (2004), and services for homeless children (2006) prescribed a need to employ professional social workers (China Association of Social Work, 2009). However, due to poor enforcement, the functions, tasks, and job description of social workers in these settings have not been clearly outlined or substantiated (Leung, 2012). Without clear job classifications and ranks, most government departments cannot formally employ social workers or pay them a decent salary. In reality, most social workers are currently employed in NGOs or community-based organisations. Salaries in these non-civil service positions are remarkably low. On the other hand, the movement to professionalise social work has been supported by the Ministry of Civil Affairs and its departments. The Ministry may have little interest in, or capacity to, promote social work as a generic profession with positions established in settings over which other ministries have jurisdiction. The development of social work positions in medical, educational, and legal settings has therefore been slow. Overall, emerging social welfare services have tended to be staffed by untrained social workers who see their work as administrative rather than professional. Social work jobs for social work graduates have not really been available.

In 2003, the government issued a notice to encourage the development of a professional social work workforce, and encouraged local government to develop pilot projects employing social workers. After making study visits to the United States and Hong Kong in 2004 to examine their experiences of professionalisation, in the same year the Ministry of Civil Affairs recommended to the Ministry of Labor and Social Security that they enact *The Regulations on the Occupationalisation of Social Workers*. Similarly, in 2006, it encouraged the Ministry of Personnel to issue *Regulations on the Social Workers Occupational Standard System*. Both regulations envisaged the function of professional social work as implementing policy, mitigating tensions, resolving problems, maintaining social stability, promoting social justice, and building a harmonious society. Social work has been variously described as a 'shock absorber,' 'safety valve,' 'social lubricant,' and 'windshield'. Social workers apply professional knowledge and methods to providing services to individuals, families, groups, and the community in general. They can be involved in social welfare services, charity work, social assistance, and medical care for people with financial problems. Specifically, they can provide services to older people, people with disabilities or sickness, veterans, young people, and offenders (China Social Worker Association, 2009).

The 2004 and 2006 Regulations also attempted to classify social work grades based on qualifications and work experience, as well as the use of public qualifying examinations to determine professional qualifications and implement the registration of social workers. Accordingly, social workers can be divided into three levels; assistant, social worker, and senior. The first national examination for qualification at the junior or social worker grades was held in June 2008. Junior social workers are new graduates or experienced social workers with either a post-secondary professional or a university-level non-social work education. Social workers are experienced professionals with a social work degree. Junior social workers are examined in two subjects at junior level, namely 'social work integrated capacity' and 'social work practice.' As well as taking both subjects at the intermediate level, social workers are examined on the additional subject 'social work legislation and policy.' People are granted the title of social worker if they pass the examination regardless of their educational and training background. Based on the Regulations, examination syllabuses were formulated after extensive consultation with stakeholders, namely social work academics and overseas advisors. Textbooks were also published and in-service training programs introduced (Leung, 2010).

In terms of practice involving professionally trained social workers, Shanghai city has been considered as a pioneer. Several NGOs were established there in the mid-1990s to provide a community-based welfare service. Pilot social work stations were set up in schools, hospitals, and neighbourhoods. In 2003, three NGOs were set up by the government to deliver delinquency prevention services in the community. The Shanghai local government also began subsidising or directly purchasing services from these NGOs (Leung, 2007). Overall, however, the development of social work jobs was still limited.

The Sixth Plenum of the 16th Party Congress published an official policy document on constructing a harmonious socialist society in October 2006. This prescribed a strategic direction to develop a large, rational, and high-quality social work profession, supported with an effective system of training, assessment, deployment, and motivation. Furthermore in 2010, in the State Council issued the *National Development Mid-and Long-term Framework on Human Capital 2010–2020* which projected the need for two million social workers by 2015 and three million by 2020 (State Council, June 6, 2010). More importantly, these policy directions emphasised the need to strengthen social work professional education and create positions and demonstration projects. This has been regarded as a turning point in the development of social work, with the government making pledges to develop long-awaited jobs. Thereafter, the Ministry of Civil Affairs authorised pilot projects in 170 local government districts involving 260 government units. Local governments, including those of Shanghai, Beijing, Tianjin, Shenzhen, Guangzhou,

Ningbo, and Nanjing, have actively introduced social work positions as a result of the government's financial commitment. These projects cover a variety of areas including civil affairs, health care, legal services, education, and youth affairs. A new model of government and social collaboration, in which NGOs play the key role in the delivery of social services, is now being emphasised.

Two major events have helped to promote the contribution of social work. First was the Sichuan earthquake in 2008, in which social workers demonstrated (for the first time in China) the contribution they could make to the delivery of multiple services and interventions to the victims, particularly those who were vulnerable (Bian, et al., 2009; Li, et al., 2012). Second was the Foxconn suicide incident in 2010. Foxconn is a major contract manufacturer producing electronic products in Shenzhen. Poor and abusive working conditions led to 18 employees attempting suicide, 14 of whom died (Chan & Pun, 2010). In responding to the crisis, the government sent 400 social workers into Foxconn and resolved the situation through a series of group counseling sessions, support groups, and social activities. The Chinese government therefore seems now to recognise that social work can play a key role in maintaining social stability.

In October 2011, the Ministry of Civil Affairs, together with 18 other Ministries, issued a policy on strengthening the social work workforce (Ministry of Civil Affairs, November 8, 2011). This is considered to be a key policy directive guiding the future development of professional social work in China. It emphasises the need to integrate the development of a high-quality professional workforce with the development of social work positions (in terms of job design and provision of standards, job responsibility, recruitment, registration, compensation, and reward). More importantly, the cultivation of SWOs was considered as a key strategic element in developing jobs in social work. According to the 12th Five Year Plan on the development of community services and the work of civil affairs, new local initiatives include the establishment of integrated community services centres in all neighbourhoods together with incubation and training centres for social workers (Ministry of Civil Affairs, December 29, 2011a, December 29, 2011b).

Further, the publication of the Report on the Mid- and Long-term Development of the Social Work Workforce in April 2012 marked a new phase in social work development (Ministry of Civil Affairs, April 26, 2012). According to the Report, since the implementation of the examinations in 2008–2011 a total of 54,176 people, including 13,421 social workers and 40,755 assistants have qualified in China. However, it is also estimated that over 200,000 people are actually practicing as social workers. The Report revised its estimates of the requirement for qualified social workers to 0.5 and 1.5 million by 2015 and 2020, respectively. By 2020, the demand for senior social workers is expected to reach 200,000 and for top-level social workers, 30,000. Apparently, no other country in the world has such a comprehensive and long-term plan for the development of its social work profession! For the first time in January 2013, the Ministry of Civil Affairs also published ethical guidelines for social workers (Ministry of Civil Affairs January 8, 2013).

In terms of service content, social workers are involved in the following fields; social welfare, social assistance, community building, employment services, medical social service, poverty alleviation, supporting ex-servicemen, disaster relief, charity assistance, educational counseling, marriage and family life education, legal support service, labour rights advocacy, services to the elderly, and child protection. To promote public awareness of social work and create a more facilitative environment, central and local government have introduced social work festivals and award schemes for excellent individuals and projects; published textbooks, journals, good practice manuals, and casebooks; and organised local and overseas study visits, training, and exchange schemes. Under the auspices of the civil affairs departments, social worker associations have now been established in all provinces and cities to promote and coordinate this type of development.

Currently, three types of organisations employ Chinese social workers, namely government departments, community-based organisations, and SWOs. Professional social workers may be employed in civil affairs social welfare units, including homes for the aged, the disabled, the mentally ill, and orphans; or in projects involving social assistance, disaster relief, and poverty alleviation, and the relocation of homeless people. However, it is still not compulsory for civil affairs departments to employ qualified and trained social workers. At the community level, social work stations have been set up by street offices (an extension of district government) in recent years to deliver a mix of public and social administrative services including neighbourhood dispute mediation, public health and sanitation, family planning, emergency relief and social assistance, counseling delinquents, and services for the elderly. Even though street offices prefer to employ social workers, the poor salaries and job prospects they offer have discouraged graduates from taking up such posts. SWOs are defined as social organisations registered as civil non-enterprise units for the purpose of delivering social work services. Registered social workers sit on their executive boards and must comprise at least one-third of their employees. Because of government relaxation of NGO registration in recent years, SWOs have been actively involved in the state-subsidised delivery of social services (Fisher, et al., 2012; Lu, 2009; Shieh and Schwartz, 2009; Wang, 2011).

To maintain social stability and mitigate social tensions, the local governance system has to be responsive to people's needs and grievances. In 2004, the Party Document *Decisions Regarding the Strengthening of the Construction of the Governing Capacity of the Party* introduced the concept of 'strengthening social construction and management, and promoting the innovation of social management' (Communist Party of China, September 20, 2004). The Party also issued the circular *Views Concerning the Strengthening and Innovating Social Management* in 2011 to direct the development of social management through local pilots, overseas learning, and the promotion of good practice. The social management framework is summarised under the motto 'party leadership, government responsibility, society facilitation and public participation.' The 18th Party Congress in 2012 reiterated the need to strengthen social management to maintain social stability and solidarity (Hu, November 16, 2012).

To support the policy of constructing a service-oriented government, in 2012 the government issued the 12th Five Year Plan framework on the development of people-centred, sustainable, efficient, and effective public services, including the full implementation of free education, full health insurance coverage, and the promotion of low-rent housing. Admittedly, public services in China are largely inadequate, unevenly provided, and ineffectively structured (China News Centre, July 19, 2012). In facing the problem of over-reliance on the state as the major provider of public services, the Chinese government has learned over the years that it is important to, on the one hand, enlarge civil society through the formation of more civic and charitable organisations, and on the other, to strengthen the use of the 'soft' approach to addressing social issues, particularly through the use of professionals such as social workers (Leung, et al, 2012).

The Ministry of Civil Affairs published *Views Concerning the Support of Society Efforts in the Operation of Social Welfare Organisations* in 2007 and *Notice Concerning the Promotion of the Development of Non-governmental SWOs* in 2009. They recognised the urgency and importance of developing SWOs through formulating and improving their registration, monitoring and self-regulation (Ministry of Civil Affairs, October 12, 2009). Social work services are delivered by social workers according to the principle of helping people to help themselves. Such professionals are equipped with the knowledge and skills to provide assistance, counseling, mediation, behavior modification, and advocacy to those in need. In general, SWOs primarily receive government subsidies in the delivery of a variety of welfare services relating to family, home care, and youth, as well as care for the disabled. It is currently estimated that there are over 1,000 SWOs in China. Most of them are found in the coastal cities (Ministry of Civil Affairs, December 21, 2012). In 2012, the Chinese central government for the first time allocated 200 million yuan (1US$ = 6.2 yuan) to finance 377 social work projects and more than 120 training programs, with 17,700 people to be trained and 1.85 million benefiting directly (*Xinhua*, February 12, 2013).

Finally, the promotion of social work is also under the auspices of the Organisation Department of the Chinese Communist Party, and implemented through the civil affairs ministry and departments. As the chairperson of the China Association for Social Work Education, Professor Wang Sibun has identified the importance of government and party support for the professionalisation of social work (*China Development Brief*, December 12, 2006): 'In China, the biggest difference from Western countries is that social workers act as assistants for the Party to provide social work and management.'

In short, the government has launched long-term, vigorous, and comprehensive plans to introduce and expand social work. There is a growing demand for professionally trained social workers to support the thriving social welfare services sector. However, the development of social work services has been handicapped by poor pay, uneven development, and the need to professionalise the large existing population of untrained social welfare personnel engaging in social work tasks. The issue is how social work educational institutes can now respond to the thriving demand for competent practitioners at different levels.

The development of social work education

The early history of social work education can be traced back to the establishment of a program in the department of sociology of a college operated by the missionaries in Shanghai in 1914. Later, the Departments of Sociology and Sociology and Social Services in Peking University were formed, in 1922 and 1925 respectively. The establishment of these programs was assisted by professors from Princeton University of the United States. This was regarded as a response to the staff training needs of the NGOs established by American Christian missionaries in China. Before 1949, only eight universities in China offered social work programs (Leung, 1990, 1994; China Association of Social Workers, 2009; Li, et al., 2012). The social work curriculum at this point was mainly modeled after that in use in the United States.

After the establishment of the People's Republic of China in 1949, all social work education programs, together with other social science subjects, were regarded as pseudo-sciences and 'bourgeois disciplines' supporting the capitalist system. Accordingly, for almost three decades, social work education and practice were virtually nonexistent in socialist China. After the re-instatement of social sciences subjects in 1979, social work programs were re-established in a small number of universities in the late 1980s. Considered as a form of applied sociology, social work was included as a chapter in the first sociology textbook published in China in 1981. After visiting Hong Kong to learn about social work and social work education in the early 1980s, the Ministry of Civil Affairs made certain recommendations to the Ministry of Education for the establishment of social work programs. In 1989, these were launched in four universities (Leung, 2001; China Association of Social Workers, 2009).

The China Association of Social Work and the China Association for Social Work Education were formed in 1991 and 1994 respectively, to promote the development of social work professionalism and education. With the establishment of these two professional associations, China began to play a more active part in international social welfare and social work activities, such as conferences, exchanges, visits, and study tours. Western universities began to seek out collaborations with Chinese social work programs to enhance teaching capacity and curriculum design. However, throughout the 1980s and 1990s, support from the government was hesitant, and program expansion was limited. In 1994, there were still only 20 social work programs in existence.

The government's efforts from 1999 onward to expand university education led to a rapid rise in the number of social work programs to 90 in 2002, 172 in 2003, and then 200 programs in 2006, turning out 10,000 graduates each year (China Association of Social Work, 2009). This expansion was not directly due to government support as such, but the state's intention to expand university education and the relaxation of central control over the establishment of new programs at local universities (Xiong & Wang, 2007).

To train advanced social work practitioners, 33 MSW programs were established from 2010 onward. However, they did not require students to have an undergraduate degree in social work. In 2012, there were around 320 social work education programs, 60 of which offered the MSW, and the number of graduates annually had reached 20,000 (Ministry of Civil Affairs, April 26, 2012). By 2020, there will be 500 schools of social work in China. Despite currently having over 300 schools of social work, there is no overall mechanism for accreditation and curriculum standardisation. In pursuing quantity rather than quality, significant variations exist across programs. In fact, the field is full of low-quality and ill-equipped programs.

There are plenty of international publications indicating the shortcomings of social work education in China, including the poor quality of educators, curriculum design, fieldwork placements and supervisors, and reference books; (Law & Gu, 2008; Leung, 2007, 2010; Li, et al., 2012; Liu, et al., 2012; Liu, et al., 2013; Ting & Zhang, 2012; Wong, et al., 2011; Wong & Pearson, 2007; Yan & Tsui, 2007). Even though they share the same title, these 'social work' programs can have different foci and course content. Many curricula are modeled on programs delivered in Hong Kong and the United States. As such there is a tendency for course design to favour individualised clinical practice rather than the macro-practice of social development, social planning, policy analysis, and community organisations. In summary, programs are weak in practical training, particularly in human relations and social skills. Chinese degree courses have been criticised for directly incorporating Western-based programs and teachings (Shi, 2004). Restricted by the limited capacity of teachers, curricula do not often address key social issues in China, such as the plight of city migrants and their families, disaster relief and recovery, children left behind in the villages while their parents work in cities, and unemployment, not to mention human rights advocacy. With the integration of practical skills remaining limited, social work methods are often taught academically rather than professionally.

In terms of students' career interests, a 2004 survey of 1,300 social work students in Beijing and Shanghai showed that they had a strong preference for individual counseling and psychotherapy, whereas community and group work was less popular. Their preferred target groups were substance abusers, the aged, and abused children. Not surprisingly, the majority preferred to work in government rather than NGOs (Sha, et al., 2012). Given their low motivation and poor understanding of social work, coupled with the lack of formal professional positions, low pay, and lack of social status, social work graduates, particularly those from prestigious universities, tend to seek other types of jobs. It has been estimated that only about 10–30% of social work graduates actually hold professional posts in the field (Wong, et al., 2011). Mainly because of the lack of formal social work positions in the government sector and the underdeveloped NGO sector, the jobs available are limited and badly paid. All in all, social work education has developed much faster than the profession itself. In other words, it has become dissociated from field practice (Leung, 2009; Wong et al., 2011).

Meanwhile, institutions such as the Hong Kong Polytechnic University and the University of Hong Kong set up collaborative MSW programs in the early 2000s to train Chinese social work teachers and practitioners (Wong, et al., 2011). In addition, some social work educators have trained overseas and in Hong Kong then returned to teach in China. However, they have often undertaken PhD rather than MSW degrees and their direct practice experience has therefore been limited. Overall, the influence of, and assistance from Hong Kong in facilitating the development of social welfare and social work education programs has been significant. In view of the shortage of high-quality fieldwork placements and resources, many social work faculties have established SWOs. Through the purchase of services from local government, SWO projects can provide fieldwork placements for their students, as well as a research platform for developing evidence-based practice.

DEVELOPMENTS IN GUANGDONG PROVINCE

As a leader in China's economic growth and a pioneer of the reform and opening-up agenda for three decades, Guangdong province is perceived as an example for other provinces to learn from (World Bank, 2011). In 2011, the Guangdong local government published a series of policy documents to promote social organisations and the development of the social work workforce (Committee for Social Affairs of Guangdong Province, September 23, 2011a, September 23, 2011b). To support the setting up of social organisations, including SWOs, the registration procedures and tax exemption requirements have been simplified and relaxed. Through the introduction of government purchasing of services through competitive bidding, SWOs have been provided with full resources and support to assist the government in the delivery of welfare services. To ensure good-quality working conditions for employees, policy provisions include local household registration for social workers from other provinces, standardised salary schemes for social workers with different qualifications, and staff development programs (Committee for Social Affairs of Guangdong Province, September 23, 2011a; September 23, 2011b; Hong Kong Liaison Office of the International Trade Union Movement, May 2012; *Xinhua*, February 12, 2013; *Xinhuanet*, May 6, 2012).

In early 2012, Guangdong province had a total of 150 SWOs (113 in Guangzhou, 50 in Shenzhen, and seven in Dongguan). Most had been registered within the last four to five years (Shenzhen Business News Network, July 10, 2012). Through government subsidies, they primarily aim to deliver a wide array of welfare services to older people, families, the disabled, drug addicts, and delinquents. It has been estimated that by 2015 the number of SWOs in Guangdong province will reach 500, of which 50 will serve as demonstration centres (Committee for Social Affairs of Guangdong Province, September 23, 2011a).

Echoing these initiatives from the Guangdong local government, Guangzhou city, the provincial capital, introduced a policy document on the construction of the social work workforce in 2010.

This was supplemented by five other policy documents relating to the registration of social workers, the development of SWOs, the setting up and remuneration of social work positions, financial support from the government, and the assessment on the purchase of services (POS). Support available to SWOs can include special one-off grants, POS through delegation or competitive bidding, tax exemption, premises and utilities expenses, and relaxation on fee charging. The performance of SWOs receiving subsidies is assessed by a third party. Such assessment can include reviewing reports, interviews, random checks, and observations. SWOs which score with distinction on these assessments can receive appropriate rewards, such as special grants from the welfare lotteries. Those that fail cannot bid for new government contracts for two years (Guangzhou Civil Affairs Bureau, August 17, 2010).

Modeled after the arrangements in place in Hong Kong, the Guangzhou city government has decided to set up an integrative family service centre in every local community (street office) in the city, making a total of 150 such centres. A total of two million yuan a year each has been allocated. In practice, the size of, and financial subsidies given to, family service centres can vary according to the actual needs of the community. On top of the subsidies from the city government, the street offices have to provide premises and pay for any renovations and equipment needed. Each centre can employ over 20 staff, over half of whom are social workers (Guangzhou Civil Affairs Bureau, March 20, 2012). The introduction of these centres in Guangzhou represents one of the most outstanding social work projects to be launched in 2011 throughout China (*China Philanthropy Times,* March 29, 2012). Government purchasing of these services has provided a tremendous impetus to the development of SWOs.

In summary, public sector reforms have tried to separate the government from the emerging NGO sector so that social organisations can be registered more easily and have a more 'nongovernmental' image. Nevertheless, the government, through POS, has striven to set up a new system of indirect monitoring and control under the rubric of enhancing accountability. This is based on contracts, performance assessment (output indicators), and financial audits. In this relatively supportive environment and with the changing role of the government, both the number of SWOs and the scope of their services have expanded dramatically over the last three years.

According to the policy document *Constructing the Social Work Workforce*, the government has pledged to improve the quality of social workers by strengthening education in Guangdong. Initiatives to be in place by 2015 include the establishment of key training centres at different levels (4 provincial-level training and 50 city-level practice centres). The plan also includes the recruitment of 30 high-level specialists from outside the province or China itself to engage in education, training, and research. In addition, there will be various training initiatives; 30 selected young social work teachers and 100 NGO administrators will study outside China and also go on study tours; 100 social welfare administrators will attend universities; 500 social work supervisors will also be trained; and continuous professional education will be widely available (Committee on Social Affairs of Guangdong Province, September 23, 2011).

According to government estimates, Guangdong province and Guangzhou city will have 50,000 and 10,000 registered social workers, respectively, by 2015. There are now 7 universities and 2 vocational training colleges producing fewer than 600 graduates each year (Committee for Social Affairs of Guangdong Province, December 22, 2011). However, because of poor salaries and career prospects, less than one third of these graduates actually become social workers. In Guangzhou between 2008 and 2011, some 2,103 people passed the qualifying public examination but only 1,490 registered. The policy document guaranteeing the salary level of social workers does not seem to have been implemented in reality. The acute shortage of social workers is further aggravated by high turnover and dropout (Nanfeng Daily News, August 21, 2012).

Shenzhen city, in southern Guangdong province, adjacent to Hong Kong, was selected by the Chinese central government in 2007 as one of the key pilot sites for creating and developing social work positions. Through a series of policy documents guiding occupational standard assessments, education and training, social work position, salary, NGO development, and financial support, Shenzhen, within five years, appears to have overtaken Shanghai as the pioneer in terms of the variety of social work services, number of social workers and NGOs, and the systematic introduction of service purchasing. Noteworthy is the fact that before 2007, Shenzhen had hardly any NGOs, social welfare services, or social work education.

With reference to the social worker-target population ratio in Hong Kong, social workers have been placed in a variety of service settings including schools, hospitals, homes for the aged, neighbourhood centres, labour offices, centres for the disabled, and legal clinics. According to the planning ratio, there should be one social worker for every school and every hospital; for every 200 social assistance recipients; 500 older people; 10,000 factory workers; 5,000 families; 70 delinquents; and 70 drug addicts (China Association of Social Work, 2009). Innovative social work settings include the 'petition' and 'mediation' offices dealing with individual grievances and social conflicts, enterprises, family planning offices, and the army. The government has supported the establishment of SWOs. Through open bidding for new services, they can receive subsidies according to the number of social workers they employ. Social workers are recruited nationally and assigned to SWOs through service contracts. They are then placed within government organisations such as schools, hospitals, community offices, and legal departments to deliver services (Leung, 2011). These social work practice settings are under the auspices of the respective government and party authorities, including the Federation of the Disabled Person, Women's Federation, Union, Education Bureau, Health Bureau, Legal Department, Communist Youth League, Civil Affairs Bureau, and neighbourhood offices. Social worker grades and salaries have also been formulated.

Originally, 5,000 social workers were to be recruited before 2010. By the end of 2012, however, 2,700 social workers and 250 supervisors were employed by 94 SWOs in 700 projects. Some 75% were qualified. Key areas for future development include community service centres and enterprise social work. Currently, there are 160 community centres employing 5–8 social workers each. These provide multiple and integrated services to a variety of target groups including families, children, young people, the elderly, and the disabled. By 2015, there will be 700 community centres. There are also 194 social workers employed by industrial enterprises providing industrial social services such as labour dispute intervention, orientation to new workers, and activities promoting a sense of belonging (Shenzhen Social Worker Association, 2012; January 10, 2013).

From 2007 to 2012, by employing over 120 experienced social workers from Hong Kong as supervisors, social work programs have been set up in Shenzhen largely based on the Hong Kong model of operation. Such supervision supplemented with intensive in-service training and study visits to Hong Kong has quickly enhanced the quality of social workers. Within three years, a group of 320 local supervisors has been nurtured.

Overall, there are a number of issues involved:

- Social workers recruited from the north are young, inexperienced, poorly trained, and lacking in skills. Not surprisingly, the Hong Kong supervisors claimed that almost 70 per cent of their time had been devoted to education, and 20 per cent to emotional support. Administrative tasks only accounted for 10 per cent (Institute of Social Service Development, 2012).
- Practicing social workers face the problems of lack of complementary resources, services, and a legal framework. They encounter difficulties referring their users to other support services such as halfway houses for the mentally ill, shelter homes for domestic violence victims, and emergency financial support. Laws relating to social work, such as those covering child

protection and domestic violence, are largely underdeveloped (Leung, 2011).

- At present, only the Ministry of Civil Affairs and its departments are actively involved in the promotion and institutionalisation of social work services. Other ministries and departments in education, health, and labour do not seem to have an active interest in helping to develop social work under their auspices. One of the major complaints made by social workers has been that they have been assigned by other departments to carry out administrative duties, such as acting as replacement teachers or doing secretarial work (Institute of Social Service Development, 2012).
- Facing a less than satisfactory working environment, turnover rates of social workers increased from 8.2 per cent in 2008 to 18.1 per cent in 2012 (*People's Daily,* February 27, 2013). With the rapid development of job opportunities in the Pearl River Delta, experienced social workers in Shenzhen have become a key target for recruitment. Around 30 per cent of turnover can be attributed to active recruitment by the neighbouring cities.

Each of the seven universities offering social work education in Guangzhou has a distinctive curriculum tailored to its own needs and circumstances. According to Professor He Liping, professor of social work at Sun Yat Sen University, Guangzhou, interviewed by the authors in December 2012, the shortcomings of social work education include:

- The low quality of teachers, the majority of whom have no formal social work training. It is difficult to upgrade their abilities over a short period of time;
- The lack of direct practical work experiences among teachers;
- A reliance on classroom teaching, with poor integration with practice;
- The limitations placed by the teaching capacity of the staff on the courses and electives that can be offered;

- The fact that course design follows the Western model of social work methods and defines targets by age, with few programs focusing on addressing local needs such as migrants, industrial workers, rural development, and employment;
- The tendency of staff to focus on research and publication rather than teaching because of promotion criteria.

Six universities have set up their own SWOs, operated by teachers. For example, Sun Yat Sen University has three SWOs employing around 350 social workers. These provide direct practice experience for teachers as well as fieldwork placements for students. The emergence of these SWOs has gone some way to addressing the shortcomings of teachers' lack of practical experience and the need for supervised fieldwork training.

Future directions

We have witnessed an unprecedented and indeed phenomenal development of the social work profession and social work education in China. This has been primarily based on the strong leadership of the central government through the enactment of policy guidelines and plans. However, implementation of these plans has been largely dependent on the policy priorities and financial commitments of local governments. As a result, professionalisation has been uneven. Social work jobs are largely found in the coastal provinces and urban areas. Facing the rapid development of new initiatives in the south, education programs, which have been hitherto largely concentrated in northern China, can easily fail to keep up with the knowledge and skill demands of the new social work jobs. Overall, a social work community comprising professionals and teachers has been formed, though it is still unevenly distributed and poorly equipped. Despite increased promotion of the profession, the public image of social workers is still not clear and most of the Chinese public would probably still regard their work as a form of volunteering.

For decades, the field of social work was marked by the lack of integration between the profession and the education sector.

Despite the existence of thriving educational programs, the field of social work has been largely under-developed and high-quality jobs have not really been available. Hopefully, the developments in Guangdong province suggest a more optimistic future containing a wider variety of social work jobs. With better employment and career prospects in social work, professional education now requires profound reform to promote evidence-based practice and eliminate low-quality programs.

When social work was re-introduced to China in the 1990s, a lot of questions arose; can professional social work practice exist in socialist China? To what extent can Western social work, rooted in the values of democracy and individual rights, have a place in a socialist country which primarily emphasises collective interests over individuality? What is an appropriate degree of 'indigenisation' or Westernisation? The issue of whether global standards on social work education and practice can or cannot be applied or not has generated heated debate (Cheng, 2008; Gray, 2008; Hutchings & Taylor, 2007, 2008; Jia, 2007; Leung, 2007). The controversy centres on the role of Western-based social work values and knowledge in facilitating the development of social work in China. Western scholars have tended to challenge whether there can be 'genuine' social work practice in socialist China. Facing the call for 'indigenisation,' Chinese social workers seem to have reservations about directly importing Western-based social work values and knowledge, and Chinese academics have tended to reject the use of Western-based social work models to assess developments in China. On the one hand, it cannot be the case that there is only one universal brand of social work practice for use worldwide. On the other, one should also respect the uniqueness of the socioeconomic situation in China and refrain from any further polarisation that generates 'false dichotomies' (Hutchings & Taylor, 2008; Sewpaul, 2007). As Gray (2008, p. 401) puts it, the basic questions are: 'What model of social work does China need, if indeed it needs one at all? What model of social work education and practice is China developing and to what extent will Western knowledge and standards be uncritically appropriated into China?' The key question remains (Cheung, et al., 2012, p. 187):

> How do social work educators integrate social work values, knowledge, and skills into the curriculum in respect to the Chinese social, economic, political, and cultural context with an understanding that the foundation of this curriculum was originally developed from the base of a Western practice model?

Indisputably, there will be an increase in international exchange, and China will continue to take a more active role in the global social work community. There will be more opportunities for collaboration in teaching and research, as well as mutual influence. Finally, a continuous contribution to maintaining social stability and political patronage are critical factors determining the future prospects for social work in China.

References

Bian, H., Wei, K., Feng, H. & Zhang, Q. (2009). A study of social workers' involvement in the relief and reconstruction efforts following the 5.12 Wenchuan earthquake. *China Journal of Social Work*, 2(3), 211–19.

Chan, J. & Pun, N. (2010). Suicide as protest for the new generation of Chinese migrant workers: Foxconn, global capital, and the state. *The Asia-Pacific Journal*. Retrieved 17 April 2013 from japanfocus.org/-jenny-chan/3408.

Cheng, S.L. (2008). Debate, a response to the debates between Hutchings and Taylor and Jia on the global standards in China. *International Journal of Social Welfare*, 17, 396–99.

China Development Brief. (2006, 12 December). Social work: putting care into professional practice. Retrieved 17 April 2013 from www.chinadevelopmentbrief.com/node/901.

China Development Research Foundation. (2012). *constructing a social welfare system for all in China*. London: Routledge.

China News Centre. (2012, 19 July) Basic public service system planning is the necessary choice for establishing the service-oriented government. Retrieved 17 April 2013 from www.china.com.cn/news/2012-07/19/content_25952586.htm.

China philanthropy times. (2012, 29 March). Retrieved 17 April 2013 from www.gongyishibao.com.

China Association of Social Work. (2009). *Reports on development of social work in China, 1988–2008.* Beijing: Social Sciences Academic Press.

Cheung, M., Gao, J.G. & Tsui, M.S. (2012). Editorial. *China Journal of Social Work*, 5(3), 187–188.

Committee for Social Affairs of Guangdong Province (2011a, September 23). Views concerning the strengthening of the construction of social work workforce. Retrieved from www.gdshjs.org/s/2011-12/26/content_35581963.htm.

Committee on Social Affairs of Guangdong Province (2011b, September 23). Views on nurturing the development of social organisations. Retrieved 17 April 2013 from www.gdshjs.org/s/2011-12/26/content_35581447.htm.

Committee for Social Affairs of GD Province, December 22, 2011. Views on strengthening the management of social organisations. Retrieved 17 April 2013 from www.gdshjs.org/s/2011-12/22/content_35406102.htm.

Communist Party of China Data Centre (2004, 20 September). The importance of strengthening the construction of governing capacity of the Party. Retrieved 17 April 2013 from cpc.people.com.cn/GB/64162/64168/64569/65412/4429177.html.

The Economist (2012, September 8). Asian welfare states: new cradles to graves, pp. 21–23.

Fisher, K., Li, J. & Fan, L. (2012). Barriers to the supply of non-government disability services in China. *Journal of Social Policy*, 41, 161–82.

Gray, M. (2008). Some considerations on the debate on social work in China: who speaks for whom? *International Journal of Social Welfare*, 17(4), 400–06.

Hutchings, A. & Taylor, I. (2007). Defining the profession? Exploring an international definition of social work in the China context. *International Journal of Social Welfare*, 16(4), 382–90.

Hutchings, A. & Taylor, I. (2008). Correcting misconceptions about the development of social work in China: a response to Cunfu Jia. *International Journal of Social Welfare*, 17(1), 102–04.

Guangzhou Civil Affairs Bureau (2010, 17 August). Regulations on implementing the assessment of purchase of services by Guangzhou government. Retrieved 8 May 2013 from baike.baidu.com/view/8110040.htm.

Guangzhou Civil Affairs Bureau (2012, 20 March). Concerning the further improvement on constructing Integrated Family Service Centers. Retrieved 17 April 2013 from www.gzcs.gd.cn/sqfww/door/uploadfile/file_2013115103637.pdf.

Hong Kong Liaison Office of the International Trade Union Movement (2012). Social reforms launched in Guangdong Province to address new contradictions. Retrieved 17 April 2013 from www.ihlo.org/LRC?SW?010512.html

Hu, J.T. (2012, 16 November). Firmly march on the path of socialism with Chinese characteristics and strive to complete the building of a moderately prosperous society in all respects, Report to the Eighteenth National Congress of the Communist Party of China. Retrieved 17 April 2013 from www.china.org.cn/china/18th_cpc_congress/2012-11/16/content_27137540.htm.

Institute of Social Service Development (2012). Report on evaluating the effectiveness of Hong Kong supervisors in the Shenzhen Project. Hong Kong: Institute of Social Service Development.

Jia, C.F. (2007). Debate, correcting misconceptions about the development of social work in China: a response to Hutchings and Taylor. *International Journal of Social Welfare*, 17, 98–101.

Law,A. & Gu, J.X. (2008). Social work education in Mainland China: Development and issues. *Asian Social Work and Policy Review*, 2(1), 1–12.

Li, Y., Huang, C. & Han, W. (2012). Development of social work education in China: background, current status, and prospects. *Journal of Social Work Education*, 48(4), 635–53.

Liu, Y., Lam, C.M. & Yan, M.C. (2012). A challenged professional identity: the struggles of new social workers in China. *China Journal of Social Work*, 5(3), 189–200.

Liu, M.R., Sun, F., & Anderson, S. (2013). Challenges in social work field education in China: lessons from the Western experience. *Social Work Education*, 32(2), 179–96.

Leung, J. (1990). China. In T. Watts, D. Elliott & N. Mayadas (Eds). *International handbook on social work education* (pp. 403–19). Westport: Greenwood Press.

Leung, J. (1994). The development of social work education in China: issues and prospects. *Asia Pacific Journal of Social Work*, 4(2), 83–93.

Leung, J. (2007). Debate: an international definition of social work for China. *International Journal of Social Welfare*, 16(4), 391–97.

Leung, J. (2010). Social education in China, in C. Noble, M. Henrickson, and Y. Han (Eds). *Social work education: voices from the Asia Pacific region* (pp. 307–40). Carlton North: Vulgar Press.

Leung, J. (2011). A summary report on the Shenzhen Project. In Institute of Social Service Development (Ed.), *Implementation first, piloting first: the shining points of the Shenzhen Project*, (pp. 105–14). Hong Kong: Chungwah Publishers.

Leung, J. (2012). Long-term care in China: issues and prospects, *Gerontological Social Work*, 55(7), 570–86.

Leung, J. & Xu, Y.B. (2009). The development of social assistance in urban China: the residualisation of social welfare. In J. Midgley

& K.L. Tang (Eds). *Poverty and social policy responses in East Asia* (pp. 47–65). London: Routledge.

Leung, T., Yip, N.M., & Huang, R.G. (2012). Governmentality and the politicization of social work in China. *British Journal of Social Work*, 42, 1039–59.

Lu. Y.Y. (2009). *Non-governmental organizations in China: the rise of dependent autonomy.* London: Routledge.

Ministry of Civil Affairs. (2009, 12 October). Notice concerning the promotion of the development of non-governmental SWOs. Retrieved 17 April 2013 from www.mca.gov.cn/article/zwgk/fvfg/shgz/200910/20091000039649.shtml.

Ministry of Civil Affairs. (2011, 8 November). Views concerning the strengthening of the social work workforce. Retrieved 17 April 2013 from www.mca.gov.cn/article/zwgk/fvfg/shgz/201111/20111100197275.shtml.

Ministry of Civil Affairs. (2011a, 29 December). Constructing the community service system, 2011–2015. Retrieved 17 April 2013 from www.mca.gov.cn/article/zwgk/jhgh/201112/20111200248419.shtml.

Ministry of Civil Affairs. (2011b, 29 December). The development of the work of civil affairs in the 12th Five Year Plan. Retrieved 17 April 2013 from www.mca.gov.cn/article/zwgk/mzyw/201112/20111200248416.shtml.

Ministry of Civil Affairs. (2012, 29 April). The mid- and long-term development plan for social work workforce 2011–2020. Retrieved 17 April 2013 from www.mca.gov.cn/article/zwgk/fvfg/shgz/201204/20120400302330.shtml.

Ministry of Civil Affairs. (2012, 21 December). China now has over 1,000 NGO social work organizations. Retrieved 17 April 2013 from sgxh.mca.gov.cn/article/gzdt/201212/20121200397599.shtml.

Ministry of Civil Affairs. (2013, 8 January) Ethical guidelines for social workers. Retrieved 17 April 2013 from www.mca.gov.cn/article/zwgk/fvfg/shgz/201301/20130100404285.shtml.

Nanfeng Daily News. (2012, 21 August). The difficulties behind the rising demands of social workers. Retrieved 17 April 2013 from www.gdshjs.org/s/2012-08/21/content_53297185.htm.

People's Daily (2013, 27 February). Livelihood survey: why Shenzhen cannot keep its social workers. Retrieved 17 April 2013 from theory.people.com.cn/BIG5/n/2013/0227/c40531-2061322.html.

Sha, W., Wong Y.C., Lou, V., Pearson, V., & Gu, D.H. (2012). Career preferences of social work students in Beijing and Shanghai. *Social Work Education*,31(1), 4–21.

Sewpaul, V. (2007). Challenging East-West value dichotomies and essentializing discourse on culture and social work. *International Journal of Social Welfare*, 16, 398–407.

Shenzhen Business News Network. (2012, 10 July). Guangdong Social Work Association to set up research base in Shenzhen. Retrieved 17 April 2013 from www.gdshjs.org/s/2012-07/10/content_50482300.htm.

Shenzhen Social Worker Association. (2012). Reports on the development of social work in Shenzhen, 2012. Shenzhen: Author.

Shenzhen Social Worker Association. (2013, 10 January). Brief Report on Shenzhen Social Work, 2012, No. 12. Retrieved 17 April 2013 from www.szswa.org.

Shi, B.L. (2004). The new century: the choices facing social work education in China. *Journal of Beijing University of Science and Technology*, 20(1), 30–34.

Shi, S.J. (2012). Towards inclusive social citizenship? Rethinking China's social security in the trend towards urban-rural harmonization, *Journal of Social Policy*, 41(4), 789–810.

Shieh, S. & Schwartz, J. (2009). State and society responses to China's social welfare needs: an introduction to the debate. In J. Schwartz & S. Shieh (Eds). *State and society responses to social welfare needs in china* (pp. 3–12). London: Routledge.

State Council, 6 June 2010. The mid- and long-term development of human capital planning framework 2010–2020. Retrieved 17 April 2013 from www.chinanews.com/gn/news/2010/06-06/2326040.shtml.

Ting, W.F. & Zhang, H.Y. (2012). Flourishing to the spring? Social work, social work education and field education in China. *China Journal of Social Work*, 5(3), 201–22.

Wang, H. H. (2011). The evolution into NGOs in contemporary China, the two approaches and dilemmas. In P. Hsu, Y. S. Wu & S. Z. Zhao (Eds). *In search of China's development model: beyond the Beijing consensus* (pp. 204–45). London: Routledge.

Wong, Y.C. & Pearson, V. (2007). Mission possible: building social work professional identity through fieldwork placements in China. *Social Work Education*, 26(3), 292–310.

Wong, Y.C., Gu, D.H., & Chen, H.L. (2011). Social work education in China: time to take root? In S. Stanley (Ed.), *Social work education in countries of the East: issues and challenges* (pp. 73–86). New York: Nova Science.

World Bank (2011). *Reducing inequality for shared growth in China: strategy and policy options for Guangdong Province.* Washington, DC: Author.

World Bank (2012). *China 2030.* Washington, DC: Author.

World Bank (2012, December). *World development indicators database.* Retrieved 17 April 2013 from databank.worldbank.org/ddp/home.do?Step=12&id=4&CNO=2.

Xinhua. (2013, 12 February). Chinese government's NGO funding peaks in 2012. Retrieved 17 April 2013 from www.china.org.cn/china/2013-02/12/content_27947789.htm.

Xinhuanet. (2012, 6 May). Guangzhou fully implemented direct registration of social organizations. Retrieved 17 April 2013 from news.xinhuanet.com/society/2012-05/06/c_111895248.htm.

Xiong, T.G. & Wang, S.B. (2007). Development of social work education in China in the context of new policy initiatives: issues and challenges, *Social Work Education*, 26(6), 560–72.

Yan, M.C. & Tsui, M.S. (2007). The quest for western social work knowledge, literature in the USA and practice in China. *International Social Work*, 50(5), 641–53.

9

Contemporary challenges to social work education in Cambodia

Keo Chanvuthy

Cambodians are familiar with social work through the Ministry of Social Affairs, Veterans and Youth (MSAVY). Because of political and social turmoil, however, the work of MSAVY has been limited, and non-governmental organisations (NGOs) have filled the gap. This chapter identifies the many challenges NGO social work agencies face, including the shortage of professional social workers. Bachelor's and Master's level qualifications in social work were introduced at the Royal University of Phnom Penh (RUPP) only in 2008. In spite of international and local government support, many challenges exist in the recruitment and education of social workers. These challenges include an inability to promote the benefits of the RUPP course to the public; the lack of social work specialists; funding; and the lack of collaboration between NGOs and the academy. These challenges have limited the number of students, their education, and the ability to apply social work theory in practice.

柬埔寨現代社會工作教育所面臨的挑戰

柬埔寨人民是通過'社會事務、退伍軍人與青少年部門'熟悉社會工作的。然而，由於政治和社會的動盪，'社會事務、退伍軍人與青少年部門'的工作受到限制，於是非政府機構填補了這一空缺。在本章中闡述非政闡述府組織社會工作面臨的挑戰，包括專業社工人員的短缺。 皇家金邊大學在2008年開設了社會工作學士及碩士學位課程。儘管此課程得到了國際和當地政府的支持，但在招募和培養社會工作者的過程中還存在很多困難。其中包括難以讓公眾瞭解皇家金邊大學課程的優勢，社工專業人員的短缺，資金問題及非政府組織與院校之間的合作空白。這些問題影響了學生數量、教育品質及社會工作理論的實踐能力。

カンボジアにおけるソーシャルワーク教育の現代の課題

カンボジア人は社会問題・退役軍人・青少年更生省(MSAVY)を通してソーシャルワークをよく知っている。しかし、カンボジアでの政治的、社会的混乱によりMSAVYの活動が制限され、非政府組織(NGO)がその穴を埋めている。この章では、NGOが専門的なソーシャルワーカーの人員不足を含む、数々の問題に直面していることを明らかにする。学士や修士レベルのソーシャルワークの資格は、2008年に王立プノンペン大学(RUPP)にて導入されたが、国際的、また地方政府の支援にもかかわらず、ソーシャルワークの人員確保と教育にはいくつもの問題点が存在する。これらの問題の中には、RUPPの教育課程の利益をカンボジア市民に対し促進することができないということ、ソーシャルワークの専門家と資金の不足、NGOと学校との連携の欠如などが含まれる。これらの問題により、学生の数や、また、彼らの教育、社会福祉事業の理論を実践化する能力が制限されている。

캄보디아 사회복지 교육의 최근 이슈

캄보디아에서는 보건복지부(MSAVY)를 통해 사회복지 업무가 알려져왔다. 그러나, 정치사회적 혼란을 겪으면서 MSAVY의 기능이 약화되고 NGO 활동이 대신하게 되었다. 본 장은 전문인력의 부족 등 NGO 기관이 당면한 문제를 논하였다. 2008년에는 왕립프놈펜 대학에 사회복지학과가 생겼고 학사학위, 석사학위프로그램이 만들어졌다. 국제사회와 정부의 도움에도 불구하고, 캄보디아에는 사회복지교육과 실무를 담당할 전문가가 부족하다. 왕립프놈펜대학의 교육에 대해 일반에 알려지지 않은 점, 전문가 부족, 예산의 문제, NGO와 교육기관의 협조체제 부족 등의 문제를 안고있다. 이런 점이 개선되면 사회복지학생수와 교육기관이 늘고, 이론을 실천에 접목시킬 수 있을 것이다.

Introduction

Social Welfare is not a new term in Cambodia. It has been known due to the roles of Ministry of Social Affairs, Veterans and Youth (MSAVY) and its management and provision of pensions, financial support, social land concession to the retired and the disabled, widows, orphans, and elderly people throughout Cambodia. Even though MSAVY has played important roles, the lack of resources and professionalism in this field has limited its capacity to help improve the living standard of the vulnerable or the disadvantaged. Professional social workers are still in limited numbers and cannot provide a standard service due to the lack of proper training. Work at the MSAVY sometime is criticised as very slow and corrupt (Phan, 2011). Pensions or available financial support is sometimes delayed, and rehabilitation centres are criticised as not meeting the market demand. With MSAVY's limited capacity, most of MSAVY's social welfare programs have been supplanted by NGOs/INGOs, even though they face similar shortages of local professionals and resources. Local staff from both MSAVY and NGOs are recruited from any social science backgrounds. They may be provided only short training related to basic social work after their recruitment. Only since 2008 has social welfare been offered as bachelor and master degrees simultaneously at the Royal University of Phnom Penh by professional professors and lectures from U.S., Korea, and Cambodia.This study aims to provide a history of social welfare education in Cambodia as well as to outline the challenges it has faced.

Country Overview

Cambodia had gone through many civil wars for decades, suffering from the loss of many lives and the destruction of many basic social services and national infrastructure. Several scholars described 1975 as the 'Year Zero' (Ponchaud, 1978). During the Khmer Rouge period (1975 to 1979), around one million people were killed; and the number of people who died during the post-Khmer Rouge civil wars is unknown. From 1979, because of the accusation that the post-Khmer Rouge regimes were installed illegally by the Vietnamese government, sanctions were imposed on Cambodia for many more decades. In addition to the sanctions, civil wars still continued between the new government, the Khmer Rouge, and other liberation resistance whose wish it was to get rid of the Vietnamese influence. As consequence, more people died; Cambodia was isolated and poor, and depended on its own natural resources and agriculture for survival. Therefore, rehabilitation was at a very slow pace. People lived in very difficult situations, where there was a lack of nutritious food and healthcare. Necessary supplies usually came from donations and imports from its socialist allies, Vietnam and (then) Soviet Russia. Only after 1991, when all parties were open to peace negotiations and democratisation, did many countries in Europe, US, and Asia start to provide donations to Cambodia. These donations annually reached around 500 million dollars aimed to help reform and upgrade the poor standard of living of the Cambodian people.

From the general view, with foreign donations and reform by the government, the recent economy of this country is improving; according to the International Monetary Fund (IMF), the economy grew 7% (Hui, 2012), and the national per capita GDP reached as high as US$990 (Changxin, 2012). However, according to World Bank (2009), income inequality still remained a concern in Cambodia, with a total population of 13.4 million (2008 census), 80 per cent of which were rural and 30 per cent were still living under the poverty line of US$1.00 per day (Ir, Jacobs, Meesen and van Dammel, 2012; NIS, 2010). According to Changxin (2012), recently the Cambodian prime minister claimed that poverty has been reduced to only 20 per cent of the population. In addition to existing poverty, with the impact of recent climate change and the lack of proper irrigation systems, agriculture has been affected recently by flood and drought in some areas, causing more poverty and life crisis (The Cooperation Committee for Cambodia, 2007; Kem, 2011). Some people, especially the elderly, become homeless and have had to migrate to the city to beg for their survival; while others, in order to respond to the disaster, and because of the shortage of employment in rural areas, have migrated to the urban areas in order to work as the construction workers, house maids, restaurant or shop workers, and garment factory workers (Cambodia Development Resource Institute, 2007). Some who did not have a choice moved to the entertainment sectors working as beer promoters, KTV girls, or even sex workers, whose exploitation and abuse obviously exist. Some who could afford brokers' fees, migrated illegally to work in Thailand or Malaysia. However, without good preparation, monitoring, and law enforcement, many are prey to traffickers or exploitative owners. There is a recent outcry from civil society to mourn the serious abuse of legal Cambodian maids and workers in Malaysia, by their owners; some were seriously injured, while others were tortured, drugged, raped, and killed (Human Right Watch, 2011; UNIAP, 2011).

The impact of poverty not only affects adults, it also affects children; some children from poor families have had to move into the labour market at an early age. They work in construction, and as goods carriers; they have to drop out from schools and do those jobs in order to supplement their family's incomes and survival. Furthermore, since the trend of child abandonment continues to exist in society, some become street children and live on what they can scavenge or beg while others have been deceived and forced into sex workers (Cotter, 2008). While Cambodia moved quickly to modernise as well as globalise, many new social issues happen simultaneously. Violence, delinquency, and substance abuse among children and young teenagers have notably and worryingly increased from year to year (Fujimoto, n.d.; UN, 2009).

Regarding the healthcare system, because of donations from many countries, several health care centres and hospitals have been created and are able to provide primary health care services, including mental health, in many urban areas. However, due to long distances, poor transportation systems, low income, and the shortage of medicines and staffs' unwillingness to move to the countryside, several vulnerable groups do not have full access to healthcare services (WHO & Ministry of Health, 2012). Furthermore, many people are expected to pay for services in public hospitals and healthcare otherwise they will not receive attention from heath workers. According to the 2010 Cambodian Demographic Health Survey, 18 per cent of people who sought health care had to borrow money to cover the expense (Ir et al., 2012; WHO & Ministry of Health, 2012). Additionally, some people, with limited finances tend to buy medicines without prescriptions from the physicians and from pharmacies and use them at their own risk. Overall, these things have become barriers for the poor to seek proper treatment. Even though the statistic of infant, under-five and maternal mortality seems to decline year by year in Cambodia, it is still high if compared to the region. For instance, 66 out of each 1000 under-five children still die, while 83 out of each 1000 infants die during the live birth and 472 out of each 10 0000 women die during their baby delivery UNICEF, n.d).

Furthermore, the limited healthcare service is also cited as one of the causes of disability. The proportion of persons with disabilities (PWD) is 1.4 per cent of the total population (Kem, 2011). PWD are the most vulnerable group in the society; this includes women and children with disabilities. Proper training and income generation programs are not well prepared or provided to these disadvantaged groups; there is still the high degree of discrimination against this group in job recruitments, even in the governmental sector (CCC, 2006). This issue causes people with disabilities to be the poorest in Cambodia.

With all these increasing social issues, social welfare programs, including social welfare education are very much needed to provide in order to help deal with all the issues mentioned from both the state and the NGOs.

Social welfare education

Background of social welfare

Social welfare traditionally is under the responsibility of government. Usually the government arranges its national budgets to set up many projects, and via the Ministry of Social Welfare, cares for the vulnerable or disadvantaged of a country. Cambodia is no exception. The Cambodian government set up MSAVY to take responsibility for the social welfare of the people. However, the turbulence of Cambodian history is held as the cause of a dysfunctional social welfare system, which is unable to close the gap between the poor and the rich and to provide decent lives to people. During the civil war in the 1970s, only few social welfare programs were still operational in the urban areas where the people moved to in order to escape from the fighting to seek for food and medical care. The limited operational programs were due to the fact that majority of the national budget was allocated to the military, and the economy was stagnant. Very often welfare programs depended on charity: people donated money, foods, and medicines to help war refugees, the vulnerable and the disadvantaged. In 1975, when Khmer Rouge came to power, social welfare was completely absent. People lived with limited food and improper medical treatment, resulting in the loss of around one million lives. After the Khmer Rouge was toppled with the support of the Vietnamese military, the new government, still with a socialist ideology, was accused of being installed illegally by Vietnam. As a result of this accusation, economic sanctions were imposed by the west and its alliances. As a consequence the new government could provide only limited social welfare, especially to civil servants, who received some subsidy: in addition to their limited salary, these included mainly gasoline, cigarettes and rice. Because of the planned economic policy, ordinary people had to work in the collectives, and received the harvested rice according to the number of their family members. Health care service and education were provided free of charge but the services were very limited due to the lack of resources, and confined to only some urban areas. Only after Cambodia arranged a free and fair national election in 1993, with the help of the United Nations, did many donor countries start to fund programs to rehabilitate and reform Cambodia.

With donations, the Cambodian government has had more resources to provide social welfare services to people through MSAVY, with the expected aims to set up public policy services to help disadvantaged groups in society and to establish social security nets for veterans, retired civil servants, widows, and orphans. MSAVY recently highlighted the achievements of these services and programs, including the homeless social concession program, the emergency assistance program, trafficking victim rehabilitation and reintegration activities, social programs for people living with HIV/AIDS, family programs, outreach programs of to raise awareness of the rights of children, policies for orphan and child adoption, rehabilitation services for the disabled, the establishment of the organisation and national funding for social security, the policy for the elderly, and last but not least the national policy for veterans. These successful programs were reflected through many international and local celebrations: the May 15 International Family Day, the October 1 International Elderly Day, the creation of 331 elderly person's associations, and the Cambodian Veterans' Association with the national slogan: 'The nation and the people are grateful to veterans.'

In addition to these achievements, with the awareness of the importance of social work professionalism, MSAVY established the National Institute of Social Affairs on 18 October 2011 to provide a four-year Bachelor of Social Work to its own staff and the public. This institute has two faculties and one vocational training program for the disabled. The first faculty is social work consists of three departments: Department of Social Work; Department of Management of Social Protection; and Department of Sociology. The second faculty is the Faculty of Prostheses Engineering also comprising three departments: Department of Prostheses Engineering; Department of Movement Aids Engineering; and the Department of Movement Treatment. The Institute has been funded by the Cambodian government and foreign partners, and the tuition fee covers local and international professors and scholarships for some students. The tuition fee for private students is US$400 for the foundation year and US$500 for the second, third and fourth years.

If one compares Cambodia in 1993 and 2012, the physical differences can be seen clearly. However, recent studies have found that the Cambodian government, in term of social welfare, still provides limited services. According to Frederic Janssens (cited in Jaeger, 2012), the lack of public services, the core of social welfare, still remained severe. One of the causes of this dysfunction is corruption. Corruption in the public sectors actually limits the delivery of public service to the people. Even though an anti-corruption unit and anti-corruption law have been adopted, along with the arrest of some high profile officers, Cambodia is still ranked 164 out of 182 countries in the 2011 Corruption Perception Index (CPI) released by Transparency International. Only those who can afford bribes can get good service. Corruption is considered as the second largest social problem in Cambodia and affects rural people the most (Pact Cambodia, 2010), especially in term of health care accessibility. In the 2008 census, around 30 per cent of the whole population still earn less than US$1 per day and 20 per cent earn less than US$1.25, if the recent government poverty rate is used (Changxin, 2012). Therefore the poor are strongly likely not to be able to pay for the unofficial service charge. In their 2012 study with the people who sought for the healthcare, Ir et al. (2012) confirm what had been found in the 2010 *Cambodian Demographic and Health Survey* that there is still a high number of people (18 per cent) who sought health care and had to borrow money to cover their health care expense. This means that many people, especially in the rural areas, cannot even access their basic rights, the right to access healthcare and social protection.

Similarly, Fujimoto (n.d.) found that MSAVY functions mostly as a referral and registration centre more than an active policy-maker and implementer. Usually social welfare in Cambodia is offered by the NGOs and INGOs with financial support and technical assistance from outside the country. According to Fujimoto (n.d.) and Kem (2011), it is because MSAVY is the least-funded ministry. It lacks financial and human resources. The salary of the staff is very limited so even though they receive some short training from some NGOs such as SSC, well trained staffs of MSAVY often leave the ministry for other workplaces due to the higher salary that could help them to survive.

SOCIAL WORK TRAINING PROGRAM UNDER NGOs/IOs

Historically, there are increasing numbers of NGOs/IOs (international organisations) in Cambodia. International organisations started from nothing in 1975–1979 to 25 in the 1980s, and to around 300 recently. As for the NGOs, the first local NGO was created in 1991 after the peace agreement was signed and opened to UNTAC to come to help democratisation in Cambodia. Since then, the numbers of NGOs sharply increased to approximately 1,564; however only around 450 are fully operational (Coventry, 2010). According to Cho(2009), NGOs are divided into 16 specialties in accordance with their operational field: art/culture, health/sanitation, child welfare/child rights, HIV/AIDS, community development, human rights/democracy, credit/savings, mining, disability/rehabilitation, management/organisational development, disaster/rescue, education/training, water/sanitation, environment/resource, women/gender equality, and agriculture.

The increasing number of NGOs/IOs may result from the limited function of the state to provide people services especially social welfare. Therefore, according to the aforementioned categories, many NGOs and IOs have created and played important roles in this matter. The social welfare programs of those NGOs and IOs usually include medical, legal, social and economic activities. Therefore, Fujimoto (n.d.) theorised that social welfare in Cambodia actually changes from state-oriented to the third party or civil society oriented.

However, even though social welfare is not a new term, Cambodia still faces a shortage of human resources in this skill. Many NGOs/IOs, with external supports, run training courses with the purpose of creating professional social workers; some of the NGOs/IOs and their roles are mentioned below.

Social Services of Cambodia (SSC) started as an international organisation in 1992 by Ellen Menotti and a group of Cambodian American social workers. Originally, the goal of SSC was to provide training to village volunteers in social services skills, but it later included government and NGO staffs as its trainees. In 1996 SSC registered again as a local NGO, with the clear aims and commitment to influence the development of social and mental health services within the country. The training courses in SSC usually range from 6 weeks to 6 months. The training includes social work principles and practices such as counseling, a skill that trainees can use to empower their clients. Trainees are usually taught to focus on how to develop a plan with a long term developmental perspective and solutions rather than just emergencies. Even though SSC has played a crucial role, and may be the first organisation providing social work in Cambodia it also faces many difficulties. One of its problems is to try to keep experienced staff in the organisation. Usually, it will take 18 months for SSC to train its staff to be good trainers; however, with their skills in high demand, many of its trainers move to other organisations for higher payment.

The Cambodian Mental Health Development Program (CMHDP) was founded in 1994 and works mainly with psychiatric patients. The organisation trains psychiatrists and psychiatric nurses, and manages outpatient clinics and a rehabilitation centre. At the end of 2000, a total of 20 psychiatrists and 20 psychiatric nurses were trained. The outpatient clinic of CMHDP provides 2200 consultations per year. One clinic is located in Battambang, which is managed by Cambodian staff and works more or less independently from CMHDP. The rehabilitation centre is designed for chronically ill psychiatric patients, and is located in Phnom Penh. It has a day care centre where people can come to receive services three days a week. CMHDP totally serves 6000 to 7000 clients in Phnom Penh while sending its mobile team to Kampong Speu, to work in cooperation with SSC. Furthermore, CMHDP collaborates with the military hospitals to offer small scale training to medical doctors. However, CMHDP, with the limited capacity, cannot expand its services to other provinces. Usually, it is confined to Phnom Penh and some provinces such as Battambang and Kom Pong Speu.

Transcultural Psychosocial Organisation (TPO) was established in Cambodia in February 1995 as a branch of the Netherlands based TPO International. The program was created in response to the need to treat Cambodian people traumatised by civil wars and the genocidal regime between 1975 and 1979, and those who have psychosocial and mental health problems such as stress related mental disorder, anxiety, depression, and post traumatic stress disorder. According to its own research, two out of every five Cambodians identified as having a stress-related mental disorder. In other words, depression is found in 11.5 per cent of the Cambodian population, and post-traumatic stress is found in 27 per cent (Fujimoto, n.d.). From 2000, the end of the mandate of the expatriate staffs, TPO Cambodia was created as a local Non-Government Organisation. The organisation since then has been under local leadership comprised of psychiatrists, clinical psychologists, psychologists, psychiatric nurses, medical doctors, medical assistants, nurses and midwives, social workers and experienced community workers.

TPO offers many services to individuals and families to cope with trauma, for instance, awareness raising (in villages), training in counseling skills, counseling to individual persons, group work/self-help groups, clinical work (four clinics), and research (focus on how to use local resources). Its trainees include community workers, health staff and NGO staff with psychosocial skills. Furthermore, it also provides specific interventions for the family and for women and disabled people. However, TPO also has the same limitations as CMHDP: it provides services to specific places only, such as the provinces of Pursat, Battambang, BanteayMeanchey, Phnom Penh, and Kompong Thom.

Social work program under educational institutions

Sociology department

Social work was offered as an introductory course/subject in the bachelor's program in Sociology from 1994. In the second semester of third year students learn about the profession of social work, mainly related to how trained professionals can assist individuals and groups in overcoming trauma and integrating into normal lives.

As part of this, students learn to examine various theories involving social work practice with individuals, families, and communities. With only one person qualified to teach this subject, social work course was reported to be irregularly provided, especially when the staff continued his study overseas.

Social work department

The Department of Social Work at Royal University of Phnom Penh was created through an initiative from University of Washington in Seattle and received the first batch of undergraduate students in 2008. Professors and lecturers are mostly Cambodian who received financial support from University of Washington to pursue their study abroad, and from the annual recruitment by the RUPP; recently, the staff of the Social Work Department reached 14 and provides many subjects ranging from individual, family and group practice to community development and empowering, policy and governance, clinical practices, advocacy for the vulnerable or disadvantaged group.

However this undergraduate program admits only around 20 students annually, and opens no access to private students to study; furthermore, they needed four years to finish their studies before they could work in this field. Therefore, in order to respond to the immediate need for capacity-building of social workers currently working in government, civil society, and private sectors, RUPP partnered simultaneously with Ewha Womans University (EWU) in Seoul to set up a Master's Program in Social Work. In June 2007, the Memorandum of Understanding between RUPP and EWU was officially signed describing the support of EWU Graduate School of Social Welfare in establishing the Master in Social Work program at RUPP, with the purpose to provide education to future decision makers, planners, researchers, scholars in social welfare, focusing on building social work knowledge and practices, research, and education in order to enable students to play a crucial role in social work profession and in improving Cambodian social welfare.

A curriculum for this MA Social Work program was designed in collaboration with the EWU academic experts. In January 2009, EWU supported RUPP in conducting a workshop to gather all local and international stakeholders' comments on the drafted Master's program of Social Work curriculum at the RUPP Campus II. Attending the workshop were 60 participants from various NGOs and government agencies working in the field of social work and social welfare in Cambodia. Reflecting comments from the stakeholders, the curriculum was finalised, including several courses also offered by EWU. Several courses were adapted to fit the Cambodian context through comments and discussions in the workshop; those courses are foundation of social practices, social work counseling and crisis intervention, community organisation and development, poverty and employment policy, case management, social work with children and youth.

Issues in education program

Lack of trained specialists

According to the recent survey conducted among several NGOs in Cambodia on the roles of social work, Cho (2010) found that there is an agreement that social work is very important to Cambodia; social work can help not only the vulnerable and disadvantaged through social services but also develop and deal with the issues in the community and society, educate and provide clinical counseling to people. The finding actually reflects the reality especially in the terms of the deficiency of proper public service delivery; due to red tape in public institutions, social services cannot fairly provide to the poor and needy people. With low salaries, civil servants tend to be corrupt or force their clients to pay them illegally; this causes more trouble for people, especially in the case of healthcare service; people need to pay for the service if they really want it. This is the reason that 18% of the people who looked for healthcare services went into debt in order to cover the expense (WHO & Ministry of Health, 2012).

However, even NGOs also agreed that there is demand for capacity-building for the social workers and a shortage of social work professionalism in Cambodia.

Despite that many training courses have been conducted in the university and in some NGOs/IOs, many barriers still remain. First there are barriers related to the training course itself. Since the course is very new and students are required to select the course they prefer in their last year in high school, social work is unlikely to be selected by students if there is no proper orientation from the university. Additionally, while the tuition fee for social work bachelor degree is covered by the government, a small number of students are selected; the two year social work master's degree charges US$500 for one term or US$1000 for one year. This is too expensive, compared with the present economic situation of Cambodian people. Some state organisations or NGOs are willing to pay for their staff to be trained in social work but, according to Fujimoto, after the training, when the skills and experiences of their trained staffs are improved and in great demand, they leave for more highly paid jobs. This becomes a great loss which limits the functionality of those organisations. Study materials are mostly in English even though some are translated into the local language; this is a barrier for Cambodian students and the public who are not proficient in English.

In addition to this issue, it is very difficult to convince the public that the course can guarantee many job opportunities, since many working places, especially NGOs, may have different labels for social work positions even though the nature of work is the same. New graduates may not be specifically directed to relevant jobs, or are directed to jobs relevant only to social workers. Usually NGOs allow all candidates from social science field to apply for the social work position if they have some experience working with the disadvantaged or vulnerable communities even though they may not have a professional background in social work education. Therefore, the capacity of social workers in Cambodia is still substandard and needs to be built up especially in the area of child protection, HIV/AIDS, public health, drug and alcohol, domestic violence, street children, and trafficking of women.

Lack of collaboration between NGOs, academy and government

Surprisingly, while many NGOs recommend that the professional training in social work should be provided, the relevant NGOs who work in this field have limited capacity to provide internships and supervision to students. It is due to the fact that there is a shortage of staff, who are already overloaded with work or who lack the skill to help supervise students from the Social Work Department. While some students are refused an internship in some NGOs, others can get one but are allowed only to do administrative work, writing the minutes of the meeting or reading and reporting on some documents. They are rarely allowed to participate in a real project and go to real field work. Moreover, some NGOs do not have precise and concrete plans or frameworks; usually they change according to the policy set by the funding providers or by the source of funds; recently, some NGOs working to address social issues changed to working in the area of climate change or agriculture when fund was increased in these fields. Additionally, while some NGOs deal with only a single issue such as health or mental health, this model might not be applicable in a Cambodian context since mental health, for instance, might be associated with poverty. However, since the NGO deals with only mental health, then it is not effective to help empower the clients to deal with their problems. It is suggested that NGOs form partnerships to help address many different issues their clients have. However, because of competition for funds, and different systems for case management, follow-up by the sending or receiving NGOs might not be properly done or might not be done at all. Limited work due to the shortage of funding, the different nature of case management and documentation, and the shortage of follow-up are usually cited as the real causes of failure for many rehabilitation and reintegration projects in Cambodia. Overall, it is very difficult to get the right person for tutoring and supervision, a person who can truly manage social work cases and share their experience with students.

In contrast, special guests from NGOs may not be allowed in the universities, especially the public universities, because of the fear that they might make some serious criticism of the government, or simply due to the fact that the universities do not have budgets for them. In other words, the nature of the relationship between NGOs and government in Cambodia appears to be hostile, so that the university which is under the government's responsibility must make sure that there is no criticism from NGOs in the classes if they wish to give the room for the guest lecturers from NGOs. Furthermore, the state budget for the universities is still limited, covering only the basic expenses of teaching equipment, study materials production, books, field trips, and some repairs. There is no budget for any guest lecturers. If they would like to teach they have to volunteer and promise not to be involved with any political activities in the class. Therefore, all these limitations cause barriers for university students to improve their skills to be the specialists in social work. The shortage of collaboration between NGOs and the academy requires more effort to fill the gap because the collaboration can bring knowledge-sharing or exchange that can help sensitise students to necessary skills in real practices, as well as provide job opportunity for students.

While the relationship between NGOs and the Academy is not satisfactory, the same situation is also found in the relationship between social workers in the academic field and the government. As we have already seen, Cambodia still depends heavily on donations from other donor countries. As a consequence, the government has a limited budget for any social welfare program limited to the roles of social workers; as generally defined, social welfare not only provides clinical support such as counseling but also needs to seek other resources that can help rehabilitate and reintegrate clients to society. Therefore it requires significant financial expenditure on training and social activities, as well as the follow-up. While it is very difficult to seek funding from government since it also deeply depends on foreign donors, the only remaining alternative for the academic is to seek funding from foreign governments. However, because they are responding to the global financial crisis in their own countries, many foreign countries are cutting funding for developing countries. Worse than that, in the economic condition and with high inflation in Cambodia, charity is not workable; volunteerism is still not popular in Cambodia so it is not easy to convince any skilled people to provide any free services.

Future perspective

With the many barriers it has faced, it is believed that social welfare in Cambodia may progress slowly without more effort. To progress will require cooperation between the state and stakeholders such as NGOs and educational institutions. These efforts need to guarantee that social work courses have been properly oriented to the public and are able to manage their role of dealing with significant social issues. Furthermore, in this current situation, the number of students recruited by the state should be increased and the tuition fee could be decreased. It is also important that the state should have a job placement initiative in place for graduates in this field to work in the Ministry, either at the national or sub-national level. Social funds should be reserved for any NGOs or individual who wish to conduct or work to address social issues such as research, training, follow-up. There should be a campaign or awareness-raising for the public to explain how vital it could be if the public helped to provide social charity or volunteered to join social activities or community services. Corruption should be eliminated by the increase of salary and law enforcement which will guarantee that all the people will receive public services without discrimination.

References

Cambodia Development Resource Institute (2007). *Youth migration and urbanization in Cambodia*. Phnom Penh, Cambodia: Cambodia Development Resource Institute.

Changxin, L. (2012). Cambodian PM: poverty reduction target may hit two years earlier. *Xinhua*. Retrieved 17 April 2013 from www.asean-cn.org/Item/5984.aspx.

Cho, Y.H. (2009). The development path of Cambodian NGOs. *Democracy and Human Rights*, 9(3), 138–69.

Cho, Y. (2010). *How do they perceive social work?* Ewha Womans University, Seoul: Republic of Korea.

Coventry, L. (2010). *Moving from aid effectiveness to development effectiveness.* Phnom Penh: Cooperation Committee for Cambodia.

Cooperation Committee for Cambodia (2006). *The challenge of living with disability in rural Cambodia: a study of mobility impaired people in the social setting of Prey Veng District, Prey Veng Province.* Phnom Penh, Cambodia.

Cooperation Committee for Cambodia (2007). *Understanding social capital in response to floods and droughts: a study of five villages in two ecological zones of Kompong Thom Province.* Phnom Penh, Cambodia.

Cooperation Committee for Cambodia (2009). *Fostering the collective voice of NGOs in Cambodia.* Phnom Penh, Cambodia.

Cotter, K.M. (2008). Combating child sex tourism in Southeast Asia. *Denver Journal of International Law and Policy*, 37(3), 493–512. Retrieved 17 April 2013 from www.law.du.edu/.

Fujimoto, H. (n.d.). Aspects of social work with vulnerable groups in Cambodia, *Journal of Social Policy and Social Work*, 13, 5–14. Retrieved 17April 2013 from www.jcsw.ac.jp/kenkyu/hokoku/jspsw/13_fujimoto.pdf.

Hui, L. (2012). IMF: Cambodia's economy expected to grow seven percent in 2012. *Xinhua*. Retrieved 17 April 2013 from news.xinhuanet.com/english/business/2012-10/02/c_131885405.htm.

Human Rights Watch (2011). *They deceived us at every step: abuse of Cambodian domestic workers migration to Malaysia.* US: Human Rights Watch.

Ir, P., Jacobs, B., Meessen, B. & Van Damme, W. (2012). Toward a typology of health-related informal credit: an exploration of borrowing practices for paying health care by the poor in Cambodia. *BMC Journal*.Retrieved 17 April 2013 from www.biomedcentral.com/1472-6963/12/383.

Jaeger, R. (2012). *A failed state? Southeast Asia globe.* Retrieved 17 April 2013 from sea-globe.com/a-failed-state.

Kem, S. (2011). *Policy options for vulnerable groups: income growth and social protection.* Phnom Penh: Cambodia Development Resource Institute.

National Institute of Statistics (2010). *Labour and social trends in Cambodia 2010.* Phnom Penh: National Institute of Statistics.

Pact Cambodia (2010). *Corruption and Cambodian households: a quantitative household survey on perceptions, attitudes and impact of everyday forms of corrupt practices in Cambodia 2010.* Phnom Penh: Pact Cambodia.

Phan, A. (2011). Social Affairs Ministry probe reveals graft. *The Cambodia Daily.* Retrieved 17 April 2013 from www.khmer-writer.com.

Ponchaud, F. (1978). *Cambodia: year zero.* England: Penguin Books.

UNIAP (2011). *Recruitment agencies and the employment of Cambodian domestic workers in Malaysia.* Bangkok: UNIAP.

UNICEF (n.d.).*Maternal, newborn and child health and nutrition.* Phnom Penh: UNICEF.

World Health Organization & Ministry of Health of Cambodia. (2012). Health service delivery profile: Cambodia 2012. Retrieved 8 May 2013 from www.wpro.who.int/health_services/service_delivery_profile_cambodia.pdf.

10

Social work education in South Asia: a Nepalese perspective

Bala Raju Nikku

Social Work is a global profession, struggling for its identity in transition countries like Nepal. This chapter discusses briefly the evolution of social work education in the South Asia region and in Nepal in particular. Imparting social work education and training in Nepal is challenging task due to the ongoing political transitions, multicultural issues, needs of social work educators, absence of professional associations, and the lack of government recognition for the social work profession in the country. The chapter is divided in to six sections. After a general introduction, a brief discussion on social work education in the region is presented. An overview of current higher education in Nepal is presented in the third section. Section four discusses the evolution of social work education in Nepal. The main issues of social work education and the profession are discussed in the fifth section. Section six concludes the chapter.

दक्षिण एशियामा सामाजिक कार्य शिक्षा र व्यवसाय एक नेपाली परिपेक्ष्य

सामाजिक कार्य विश्वव्यापी पेशा हो, तर नेपाल जस्तो संक्रमणकालिन देशहरुमा यस पेशा आफ्नो पहिचान बनाउन संघर्षरत छ। यस अध्यायले दक्षिण एशिया, विशेषत नेपालमा सामाजिक कार्य शिक्षाको विकासको चर्चा गरेकोछ । नेपालमा भएको राजनीतिक संक्रमण, बह'सांस्कृतिक म'द्धाहरु, सामाजिक कार्य शिक्षक, व्यवसायिक संगठनको अभाव र सामाजिक कार्य पेशालाई सरकारी मान्यताको कमीले गर्दा सामाजिक कार्य शिक्षा र प्रशिक्षण नेपालमा संचालन गर्न च'नौतीप'र्ण छ । यस अध्याय छवटा खण्डमा विभाजीत छ । सक्षिप्त परिचयपछि भाग द'ईमा दक्षिण एसियामा सामाजिक कार्य शिक्षाको चर्चा गरिएको छ । नेपालमा उच्च शिक्षाको अवस्था भाग तीनमा प्रस्त'त गरीएको छ । भाग चारमा नेपालमा सामाजिक कार्य शिक्षाको श'रुवात र विकासको विश्लेषण गरीएको छ। पाचौ भागमा सामाजिक कार्य शिक्षा र पेशाको म'ख्य म'द्धाहरुमा चर्चा र छैठौ भागमा यस अध्यायको निचोड गरीएकोछ।

從尼泊爾看南亞社會工作教育

社會工作是一個全球性的行業，在一些轉型國家像尼泊爾，社會工作正在為其身份認定而努力。本章簡要討論南亞地區特別是尼泊爾的社會工作教育的發展。由於正在進行的政治過渡、多元文化問題、對社工教育者的需求、沒有專業協會以及缺乏政府認可等因素，在尼泊爾實施社會工作教育和培訓是一個非常艱難的工作。本文分為六個部分。總體概述後，是一個針對該地區的社會工作教育的簡短討論。第三部分總結了尼泊爾高等教育現狀。第四部分討論了尼泊爾社會工作教育的演變過程。社會工作教育和職業的主要問題在第五部分進行討論。第六部分總結全章。

タイトル：南アジアにおけるソーシャルワーク教育：ネパールからの視点

著者：バラ・ラジュ・ニク

ネパールのように移行期にある国ではそのアイデンティティを模索しているが、ソーシャルワークは国際的(グローバル)な専門職(プロフェション)である。この章では、南アジア地域、特にネパールにおけるソーシャルワーク教育の進展を簡単に述べる。ネパールのソーシャルワーク教育や養成研修には、継続する政情不安や多文化問題、ソーシャルワークの教育者の必要性、職能団体の不在、国内でのソーシャルワーク専門職に対する政府の認識不足などの課題が付いて回る。本章は6節に分かれていて、第1節では総合的なイントロダクション、続いて地域におけるソーシャルワーク教育の概略を説明する。現在のネパール高等教育の概要を第3節で述べ、第4節ではネパールにおけるソーシャルワーク教育の進展を説明する。第5節でソーシャルワーク教育と職業の抱える主要な課題を述べ、第6節で結論を述べる。

Social work education in South Asia

남아시아의 사회복지교육: 네팔의 관점

네팔은 과도기 국가로서 정체성을 모색하는 단계이며 이런 국가들에게 사회복지는 국제화된 학문이다. 본 장에서는 남아시아 지역과 네팔의 사회복지교육이 어떻게 시작되고 발전되었는지 간략히 설명하고자 하였다.

네팔의 사회복지교육과 실천은 정치의 변화, 다문화 문제, 사회복지교육자의 부족, 전문가 협회 조직의 부재, 사회복지전문직에 대한 정부 인식 부족 등의 문제를 갖고 있다. 이 보고서는 총 6장으로 나누어져 있다. 전반적인 소개, 네팔 사회복지교육에 대한 간단한 논의, 네팔의 고등교육에 대한 개요, 네팔의 사회복지교육의 생성과정, 사회복지교육과 전문성을 위한 주요쟁점, 결론으로 구성되어 있다.

Social work education and development: a brief framework

Although social work education is now a global enterprise, there are significant variations in the social, political, economic, and cultural environments in which it takes place in different parts of the world and, therefore, in the way it is organised, delivered, and evaluated in different countries. Thus, many of the challenges we face in social work education are country, or even institution, specific (Khinduka, 2007, p. 18).

Martinez-Brawley and Bonito Zorita (1998) argue that 'social work has always been a practice at the *fringes*. The phrase is used in its best sense and in at least two meanings: (1) that social work has been at the edges of the mainstream of scientific discourse, not because of any intrinsic deficiency in the profession but because of the nature of the practice; (2) that, in the postmodern sense, social work has been a collage where science, art, rationality and intuition, systematic and asystematic knowledge meet' (1998, p. 197).

Wherever in the world social work is practiced, there is a need to provide education for those who wish to become professional social workers. Education is not an independent and autonomous process in any society. 'The evolution of society, the transcendence of existing social structures, and how society creates itself rests in a function of education' (Jenlink, 2004, p. 225). Ritter (2008) states that the challenge is to convince social work educators how integral they are to fostering student interest in politics and inspiring them with the need to create social change through the legislative or political process (2008, p. 356).

SOCIAL WORK EDUCATION IN SOUTH ASIA

South Asia is a diverse region with countries like Nepal and Sri Lanka in transition and struggling with post conflict issues. Social work in South Asia is very diverse and disjointed. Out of eight countries of South Asia, three are land locked (Nepal, Afghanistan and Bhutan) and six are included as the least developed countries (LDCs) currently in the world. Social work education was introduced in India in 1936 whereas in the neighbouring country Nepal only in 1996. In Bhutan and Maldives fully pledged social work programs are yet to begin. In Pakistan, the first in service training course, sponsored by the Government of Pakistan and the United Nations Technical Assistance Administration (UNCTAA), trained its first 65 Pakistani social workers in 1953 (Rehmatullah, 2002, p. 1). Social work does not yet exist as a 'profession' in Afghanistan. Due to the socio-political and cultural influences, social work education in the region is very diverse and also facing an uncertain future within the academy as it has to compete with other market oriented disciplines (Nikku, 2011). Social work in south Asia show further evidence to what Hokenstad, *Khinduka and Midgley* stated in 1992:

> the universality of social work does not mean that the pattern of social work's organisation, roles, and fields of service; modes of educational preparation; or degree of social recognition are uniform throughout the world ... Yet there are impressive commonalities in the profession's roles and functions (Hokenstad, et al, 1992 p. 181).

Social work education in the South Asian region is not autonomous and free from external forces. Taking cues from Kinduka (2007), Jenlink (2004), Ritter (2008) and Martinez-Brawley and Bonito Zorita (1998), I further discuss the current status and challenges of social work education in the South Asia in general and particularly in Nepal as a case in point.

NEPAL: COUNTRY IN TRANSITION

Nepal with 30 million people is one of the least developed countries in the South Asia. The country has gone through a series of transitions and is currently rewriting its constitution and there is hope that a true republican democracy will emerge. Nepal's transition in the last 250 years from a land of many principalities to the youngest federal republic can be classified as: Nepal's Unification, Shah Regime and Instability (1769–1846); Rana Regime (1846–1950); The Democracy Project (1955–1980); Movement to Restore Democracy (1980–1990), Maoist Insurgency (1996-2006); declaring Nepal as a republic in 2008; and the exercise of rewriting the constitution (Nikku, 2012).

Social services and reforms in Nepal can be traced back through many forms of voluntary work by religious and cultural institutions such as *guthi* (clan-based association), *dharmashala* (free residences for the poor), and *patipauwa* (public resting place) in Nepal. Giving alms to the poor and disabled is widely practised even today. This practice is rooted in the concept of *Dan* (charity) in order to please the gods and to seek a better life both at present and in the next life (Nikku, 2010, p. 821).

The rapidly changing political climate in Nepal may lead to further development of higher education especially in the private sector in the recently declared republic, which replaced the centuries-old monarchy. To date there are only five universities serving the population of Nepal: the Tribhuvan University, Nepal Sanskrit University (established in the 1980s as part of a Royal Commission on Higher Education), Kathmandu University (in 1992), Purbanchal University in the eastern region (in 1994), and the Pokhara University in the western region (in 1997). These institutions were developed as regional universities in the mid- 1990s as per the recommendations of the 1992 National Education Commission. The establishment of more regional universities is in the pipeline. Among them Lumbini Buddhist University and Mid Western University have just been initiated and two autonomous medical institutions: B.P. Koirala Institute of Health Sciences and National Academy of Medical Sciences are doing particularly well.

With the changing socio, economic and political forces, private higher education in Nepal has grown in size over the last two decades and surpassed public higher education (Nikku, 2013a). Social work education is increasingly becoming an integral part of higher education systems throughout the world. However, in many countries the demand for upgrading and modernising social work curricula presents contextual challenges for social work educators (Ahmadi, 2003).

Higher education in Nepal

The functionalist theory focuses on the ways that universal education serves the needs of society. Functionalists first see education in its manifest role: conveying basic knowledge and skills to the next generation. The structural functionalists believe that higher educational credentials result in progress toward a societal stratification based on ability, a view that is shared by development agencies like the World Bank (Carnoy & Samoff, 1990). On the contrary, Reproduction theorists maintain that changes in educational attainment reinforce and legitimise ascribed hierarchies that are either tradition based or class based. Reproduction theorists further argue that in many societies the higher education facilities/institutions are dominated by the elites and that higher education, like primary and secondary education, is structured to serve the needs and perpetuate the advantaged position of the elites (Ballantine 1997; Levine, Levine & Schnell, 2001; Sijapati, 2005). In the case of Nepalese higher education, the reproductionist view was supported by Lohani (2001), a Nepali scholar, who argued that the academic programs of the new universities appear to have been orchestrated mainly by the private sector. The government policy trend is to facilitate the private sector participation in education so as to lessen the pressure on the government exchequer that finances the public education system. On the other hand, there is public discontent about increasing commercialisation and higher cost of private education (Nikku, 2009).

Within context of Nepal's political transitions and age old social welfare practices, the country is still a poverty stricken country in transition, experiencing increased privatisation and imperfect access to quality higher education, reduced national budgets, politicisation of University appointments and student party political activities which provide ample challenges and opportunities for social work education and training to take roots in Nepal.

Birth and development of social work education

An interesting coincidence is that the first Bachelor level program in social work and the Maoist insurgency both started in 1996 in Nepal. The internal conflict that shook the whole country for a decade (1996–2006) caused more than 10,000 deaths, agony and stress for thousands of families. Indeed every sector of Nepalese society, including education was affected directly or in directly by the decade long conflict and weak governance mechanisms which followed the end of this insurgency in 2008 (Nikku, 2012b).

In a poor and conflict ridden country like Nepal, the vital role that social workers could play does not need any further explanation (similarly in Sri Lanka and Afghanistan). It was opportune that formal social work training was introduced at this same time for there was a great need and opportunity for trained social workers to be involved in addressing the societal issues that emerged as a result of the conflict, in particular children, women, elder citizens and persons with disability became the most vulnerable and in need of immediate assistance. Unfortunately, due to lack of State support for social work education and training it could not play a crucial role. Despite of this formal lack of state support for social work as a profession, a few graduates from a few social work programs have been working with NGOs or have started some community based organisations and have been trying to bring changes in their own way. There remains a great need to prepare young social workers who are equipped with appropriate skills and motivation to be able to practice social work and contribute to the development processes in the country, especially now that there is relative calm. The record of professional social work education in Nepal is very embryonic. Against the lack of the above developments, an overview of current social work education system in Nepal follows.

DEVELOPMENT OF SOCIAL WORK EDUCATION

In 1996 the B.A. in Arts (Social Work) was introduced in Nepal by Kathmandu University for the first time in the country. The program was launched at St Xavier's College located in Kathmandu, an affiliate college of Kathmandu University. The credit goes to Fr. Charles Law S.J who was entrusted with the ground planning and sought assistance from Nirmala Niketan School of Social Work in India.

It was in late 1997, that Social Service as a subject was introduced at the B.A level under the Tribhuvan University (TU) constituent campus (Padma Kanya Multiple campus) located in Kathmandu. This college is meant for only girl students. Later the degree in Social Service was changed to Social Work as a subject that can be chosen as one of the major streams in addition to another major stream at the Bachelor level. The course is currently offered in six affiliated colleges of TU and is under the Faculty of Humanities and Social Sciences (FoHSS). The objective of the Faculty is to produce trained and specialised people power in both basic and applied areas of humanities, social sciences, and fine arts.

After about eight years of Kathmandu University's initiation of social work education at the bachelors level, in 2004, Dr Bala Raju Nikku (the author of this chapter) and Mr Joyson Jose (then Head of the Department of Social Work at St Xavier's College) both social work professionals from India came together and explored the opportunities with other young Nepali scholars (Pranita Bhushan Udas, Pradipta Kadambari, late Komal Magarati and

Pramod Dhungana to name a few) from different disciplines to initiate social work education under Purbanchal University, a state university located in the eastern part of the Nepal. Dr Nikku took on the cause and spent a year researching social work education models and curriculum trends in order to come up with ideas on models of social work education and an appropriate model for Nepal. As a result in the beginning of 2005 a social work subject committee was appointed by the Purbanchal University headed by Prof. M.N.Mishra, a retired professor of Public Administration of Tribhuvan University and Dr Nikku served as the secretary of the committee. The committee submitted a fully developed curriculum designed for both BSW and MSW programs based on national and international social work developments to the Purbanchal University which was subsequently approved by the University boards. As a result, the Department of Social Work at Kadambari Memorial College of Science and Management was initiated in 2005 and secured affiliation from Purbanchal University and initiated a fully developed three year BSW program. In December 2005 the MSW program was initiated at St Xavier's College, also in affiliation with Purbanchal University. This was a great initiative taken by the Purbanchal University to offer both BSW and MSW programs as it secured the long term future of social work in Nepal.

Process of social work curricula development: case of Purbanchal University

The basic aim of social work education and training is to prepare qualified social workers to help people and communities especially who are disadvantaged address and solve existing problems, as well as to participate in the development of appropriate social policies and advocate for human rights and social justice (Estes, 1992; Healy, 1992). However, these goals will not be achieved unless the social work curriculum is up-to-date and adequate and matches the new changes in societies (Soliman & Elmegied, 2010).

As the program was developing the designers saw this as an opportunity to include curricula such as children's rights. It was also an opportunity to ensure its legitimacy in the university as a whole. The team was enthusiastic and excited to work on these issues and was fortunate to receive a healthy working environment. Many other subject experts extended their input and ideas to prepare the curriculum. For example staff of Save the Children Sweden (Mr Ravi Karakara and Mr Akmal Shariff) extended support and participated in discussions to clarify doubts relating to child rights. Members from Central Child Welfare Board (especially Mr Shiva Poudel) extended their support to design a course on Juvenile Justice. The team felt that there was a need for rights based focus as Nepal was going through a serious transition and internal conflicts. Developing rights based approaches has been a journey of discovery for us by exploring new ideas, challenging established beliefs and ways of working and searching for solutions beyond the boundaries of conventional development and human rights work (Ostrom & Geidenmark, 2004). It has been an intensive process of experimentation, questioning and learning for all the committee members and university officials. Development organisations have made rapid progress in their understanding and practical application of rights based approaches (RBA).

As an end result the social work curriculum (of Purbanchal University) took a shift from clinical social work focus to a right based model. This social work curriculum and later the resource materials developed are serving as the comprehensive resources available for other social work educators, practitioners, and trainers in Nepal (Nikku & Karkara 2006; Nikku, Sah & Karkara, 2006b; Nikku, 2012a; Nikku, 2013). The course structure including relevant principles, guidelines and references could be easily adapted to the specific situations on the ground and target groups to be trained. We see this initiative/process as an opportunity but also a limitation in terms of the availability of social work educators who could deliver these specific courses as well as the whole social work program in general to the students and other audiences.

Increased opportunities to social work education

Currently these efforts of a few social work educators and increasingly supported by their graduates have at last started yielding results. Thanks to the market demands currently more than 20 affiliated private colleges of Tribhuwan University have started offering social work as one of the major options under the BA in Arts degree. In addition, social work is added as one of the course for a new five year Bachelor of Arts Bachelor of Laws (B.A.L.L.B) program under the Tribhuvan University and also to the Bachelor of Development Studies degree being offered by the Pokhara University. A new four-year Bachelors in Social Work is also being developed under the newly established Mid Western University (by the Government of Nepal in 2010) and currently is being offered from the 2012 Academic Year, though facing scarcity of educators. In addition to these educational opportunities, aspiring students can now opt for distance courses in social work through the India's Indira Gandhi National Open University's (IGNOU) overseas partner institution located in Kathmandu. In order to make available professional social work services to the current 30 million population of Nepal, there is still a huge need for institutions that can offer quality social work education and training programs throughout Nepal (Nikku, 2012b).

Main issues in social work education and practice in Nepal

There are abundant challenges for providing social work education and profession in Nepal given the historical and current political instability in the country. But there exists major opportunities that come with declaring Nepal as a federal republic, abolishing centuries of monarchy and restructuring of society. The crux is turning these challenges into opportunities for the development of social work.

Social work educators

Social work educators are the key to fostering student interest in politics and inspiring them about the need to create social change through the legislative or political process (Ritter, 2008). If developed, political social work can play a vital role in the policy processes. In addition, developing social work curriculum in line with the national, regional and global developments raises the possibility of attracting social work scholars into the profession as there are not enough trained social work educators available in the country. The reasons for this are multifold: First, until recently there were no opportunities for the social work training at Masters Level. Even now the facility is only available under a single University and in one college that is affiliated to this University. Second, there are no social work departments established within these Universities and the Universities are not investing in the promotion of the intellectual enterprise of social work. Third, there are no journals specifically focused on Social Work. Fourth, the trained MSWs from India and abroad do not like to engage themselves in social work teaching as there is a lot of demand for them from the INGO sector which pays much more than the academic institutions and lastly, ironically there is low recognition for the academics as a career in the country as a whole.

Recognition for social work profession and professionals

The lack of formal recognition for professional social workers by the government is also a major issue. There are no positions legally declared for social workers. For many governments jobs the graduate social workers cannot even compete as the training is not yet recognised by the Service Commission of Nepal. Other issues are: there is no formal association of social workers (National or Regional) formed in the country that can serve as a regulating body and could have further strengthened the profession; and there are no bodies such as the Council of Social Work Education, like in the USA, and other countries that have professional associations advocating and monitoring the scholarship and are proactive in the defense and development of social work. In the absence of these bodies there is lack of coherence in the curricula and practice standards are not enforced and ensured.

Social work trainee / volunteer

Another challenge that the social work students and faculty are facing is their working relationship with field practitioners. The social work students are placed for their field practicum in a variety of government, semi government and non governmental agencies. However, while they are accepted as students on placement, they are treated as mostly volunteers and not as trainees. This distinction creates low morale among the trainees. Some evidence suggests that there is a greater emphasis on volunteers who come from abroad compared to social work trainees who are placed in the same organisation. The fieldwork supervisors are not trained in the current curriculum model and hence there is a gap in the guidance provided to them while on placement. Also in some cases it was observed that the agencies placed higher expectations from the student trainees in terms of their contribution to the agency development than meeting the learning objectives.

Privatisation of education

It was hoped that the mushrooming of private colleges in the Kathmandu city and all over Nepal and the privatisation of professional education would have a positive influence on courses like social work. But so far the evidence shows that the competition has mostly resulted in a race to the bottom, as private colleges compete by lowering fees and offering discounts (more discounts for girl students), attractive uniforms, loose rules and free internet and Wi-Fi facilities. I foresee that a 'bubble' is forming of students with social work degrees/backgrounds but not equipped enough to carry out professional practice. Due to the lack of capacities and a host of other factors (driven by profit and loss policies), many of these private colleges offering social work as one of the two majors end up producing 'subprime' social work degrees: degrees that have little actual value for the development of Nepalese society. What will happen when graduates holding subprime degrees and insufficient social work skills are not able to find a job in an already shrinking job market in

Nepal? These systemic weaknesses need to be addressed by thinking critically about the future prospects of social work graduates in Nepal. Plans should be in place to address the students' discontent (if any) which can quickly turn to social unrest. If this happens it is against the very objectives of social work education.

Future of Nepalese social work: two steps backward?

From a single department of social work in 1996 to many colleges that are offering some form of social work and the formation of the Nepal School of Social Work in 2007 is a major accomplishment for social work education in Nepal. However this rapid growth is also producing more social work graduates than jobs and many colleges will have to close their departments due to lack of students. The students who are majoring in social work are already struggling to get their rightful jobs as there is a huge variation in their training standards and there is competition from other related disciplines like sociology, development studies, rural development and gender studies.

The colleges are yet to come together to frame policies in order to ensure minimum standards and quality in teaching social work. Lack of qualified social work educators and also lack of job security in these affiliated private colleges is another major issue. Social work educators who can inspire and instill the core values and skills that are required by the students to become change agents are needed to ensure the continuing integrity of the training and the graduates. This lack of coherence and common core standards are resulting in producing mediocre social work graduates who are not able to deliver services that are ethical and efficient. For example the University Grants Commission of Nepal is yet to respond to a request to set up a council / committee on social work education to ensure standards and legitimate powers so that this body can monitor and accredit social work programs. There is an immediate need to lobby the government so as to recognise and pass the Social Work Act of Nepal so that social work becomes a recognised profession in the real sense in the near future. To achieve all these important milestones and to step forward, Nepal needs, I believe, *social work champions* who can run an extra mile for the cause of building a profession in a transition country.

The social work profession is caught between the traditions, aspirations and political transitions. These processes are influencing the roles and functions of few trained social workers. There is an under utilisation of social work talent due to its low societal and lack of state recognition in the country. The positive side is social work education has begun but yet to gain a full university level education status.

A critical evaluation of social work education and training in Nepal is the need of the hour. I have outlined that the evolution of social work education in Nepal that shows a shift or progress from clinical and community development approaches of social work to rights based social work. The rationale is that traditional 'individual centred model of social work practice' is of only limited relevance in poverty, conflict stricken and transition countries like Nepal. This model of social work is justified on the basis that social work is and should be a contextual profession. While there is an impressive growth that took place in the development of social work education in Nepal, there is also a call for further commitment of social work professionals, practitioners and paraprofessionals in Nepal to make it further recognised by the state and valued by the society.

Way forward

Social work as a young profession in South Asia certainly requires new orientations, directions, solutions and actions to become more effective in meeting the ever growing challenges in the region. There is a need for integration of new ideas, concepts and knowledge into social work training. It will take time for social work in Nepal to grow and mature. We do not need to reinvent the wheel but continue to develop high practice standards and professional identity.

Given the restructuring of Nepalese society and lack of state resources for the higher education, the few trained social workers in Nepal have to strive further to achieve professional status for social work and they must also maintain a high level of inclusiveness. The development of social work in Nepal and South Asia should extend and expand its professional boundaries so as to provide adequate space for various existing and newly emerging human service practitioners who share similar values and social functions. Alienation of these practitioners shall further result in professional competition and rivalry for existing scarce resources and career positions. The evidence shows that there are many ways to construct social work knowledge. Recognition of practice wisdom (Goldstein, 1986) is certainly critical and crucial for the development of social work in Nepal and in the South Asia.

I argue that the promotion of social work education and practices should not only be the concerns of colleges and universities within the countries of the South Asian Region but also Global Associations like the International Association of Social Work (IASSW) and International Federation of Social Workers (IFSW) and regional associations like the Asian and Pacific Association of Social Work Education (APASWE). These organisations should play a vital role in promoting social work in the South Asian region by influencing welfare policies and also capacity build social work educators, practitioners, schools of social work and National Associations. Nurturing *social work champions* is the key to social work rejuvenation in the south Asia region.

References

Ahmadi, N. (2003). Globalisation of consciousness and new challenges for international social work. *International Journal of Social Welfare*, 12(1), 14–23.

Ballantine, J.H. (1997). *The sociology of education: a systemic analysis,* 4th edn. New Jersey: Prentice Hall.

Carnoy, M. & Samoff, J. (1990). *Education and social transition in the third world.* Princeton: Princeton University Press.

Estes, R. (1992). *Internationalizing social work education: a guide to resources for a new century*. Philadelphia: University of Pennsylvania Press.

Goldstein, H. (1986). Toward the integration of theory and practice: a humanistic approach. *Social Work,* 31(5), 352–57.

Healy, M.L. (1992). *Introducing international development content in the social work curriculum.* Washington: NASW Press.

Hokenstad, M.C., Khinduka, S.K. & Midgley, J. (1992). Social work today and tomorrow: an international perspective. In M.C. Hokenstad et al. (Eds). *Profiles in international social work* (p. 207). Washington: NASW Press.

Jenlink, E.P. (2004). Education, social creativity and the evolution of society. *World Futures: The Journal of Global Education,* 60(3), 225–40.

Khinduka, Shanti K. (2007). Toward rigor and relevance in US social work education. *Australian Social Work,* 60(1), 18–28

Levine, R.A., Levine, S.E. & Schnell, B. (2001). Improve the women: mass schooling, female literacy, and worldwide social change. *Harvard Educational Review,* 71(1), 1–50.

Lohani, B. (2001, January 11). The higher education in Nepal. *The Rising Nepal.* p. 4.

Martinez-Brawley, E. & Pazmendez-Bonito Zorita, P. (1998). At the edge of the frame: beyond science and art in social work, *Br. J. Social Work,* 28, 197–212.

Nikku, B.R. (2013a). Nepal's higher education: public vs. private? *International Higher Education,* 70(Winter), 16–18.

Nikku, B.R. (2013b). Children rights in disasters: concerns for social work—insights from South Asia and possible lessons for Africa. *International Social Work,* 56(1), 51–66.

Nikku, B.R. (2012a). Global agenda on social work and social development: voices from South Asian social work. In N. Hall. (Ed.). *Social work around the world V: building the global agenda for social work and social development* (pp. 27–41). USA: International Federation of Social Workers.

Nikku, B R. (2012b). Building social work education and the profession in a transition country: case of Nepal. *Asian Social Work and Policy Review*, 6(3), 252–64.

Nikku, B.R. (2011). Evolution of social work in Nepal: opportunities and challenges in a transition society. In Selwyn Stanley (Ed.). *Social work education in countries of the East: issues and challenge* (pp. 327–345). USA: Nova Publishers.

Nikku, B. R. (2010). Social work education in Nepal: major opportunities and abundant challenges. *Social Work Education: the International Journal,* 29(8), 818–830.

Nikku, B. R. & Karkara, R. (2006a). *Child rights: an annotated bibliography with reference to South Asia.* Nepal: Save the Children Sweden.

Nikku, B.R., Sah, N. & Karkara, R. with Sibghatullah, A. (2006b). *Child rights perspective in response to natural disasters in South Asia: a retrospective study.* Nepal: Save the Children Sweden.

Ostrom, B. & Gidenmark, E. (2004) Preface. In Joachim Theis (Ed.). *Promoting rights-based approaches: experiences and ideas from Asia and the Pacific.* Bangkok: Save the Children Sweden. Retrieved 8 May 2013 from resourcecentre.savethechildren.se/sites/default/files/documents/1833.pdf.

Rehmatullah, S. (2002). *Social Welfare in Pakistan.* London: Oxford University Press.

Ritter, J.A. (2008). A national study predicting licensed social workers' levels of political participation: the role of resources, psychological engagement, and recruitment net works, *Journal of Social Work*, 53(4), 347–57

Sijapati, B. (2005). Perils of Higher Education Reform in Nepal. *Journal of Development and Social Transformation*, (2), 25–32

Soliman, H.H. & Elmegied, H.S.A. (2010). The challenges of modernization of social work education in developing countries: the case of Egypt. *International Social Work*, 53(1), 101–14.

3

Curriculum and practicum

11

Designing advocacy and social action curriculum: reflections from the classroom

Heather Fraser

Get up, Stand up, stand up for your rights …
Get up, Stand up, don't give up the fight. (Bob Marley)

Advocacy and social action continue to be crucial to social work, particularly critical social work practice. In this chapter, I autographically reflect on 'teaching' critical social work courses in two Australian social work programs. The main focus is on how I designed and delivered curriculum for two 2008 RMIT University (Melbourne, Victoria) courses, Advocacy and Social Action and Advanced Advocacy and Social Action. However, as I explore how politics and emotions can inspire but also collide, I also draw from other more recent critical social work teaching examples related to a 2012 Flinders University (South Australia) course, Social Work Practice with Diverse Populations.

宣傳、社會行動和批判型社會工作：來自課堂教育的反饋

起來吧！站起來！為自己的權利站起來！
起來！站起來！不要放棄戰鬥！ (Bob Marley)

宣傳和社會行動對於社會工作，尤其是批判型社會工作實踐來說一直以來至關重要。本篇中，筆者將對兩個澳大利亞社會工作教學項目中關於如何'教授'批判型社會工作課程進行汇报。文章重点叙述筆者二零零八年如何在皇家墨爾本理工大學（位於墨爾本，維多利亞州）設計和教授兩門課程：《宣傳和社會行動》以及《宣傳和社會行動（高級）》。然而，筆者在探索政治和情緒如何相互促進與衝突的過程中發

現，自己從其他近期批判型社會工作教學例子中也獲益良多。這些例子源於澳大利亞南部弗林德斯大學二零一二年的一個名為《人口多樣性的社會工作實踐》課程。

権利擁護、社会活動とクリティカル・ソーシャルワーク：教室からの熟考

目覚めろ、立ち上がれ、立ち上がれ、権利のために..

目覚めろ、立ち上がれ、諦めるな、戦うことを　(ボブ・マーリー)

権利擁護と社会活動はソーシャルワーク、特に、クリティカル・ソーシャルワークにとって、重要であり続ける。この章では、オーストラリアにある二つのソーシャルワークプログラムにあるクリティカル・ソーシャルワークの教育カリキュラムを「教えること」について、提唱者本人の考えを書いてみる。２００８年に、筆者がどのようにして、二つのカリキュラム、提唱と社会的行動と進展提唱と社会的行動のコースをロイヤルメルボルン工科大学(RMIT)大学で設計し、提供したかを主な焦点を当てる。2008年、「権利擁護と社会運動コース」と「権利擁護と社会運動上級コース」というRMITの二つのカリキュラムを、私がどのようにして作り、提供したかということに主な焦点を当てる。しかし、政治と感情がどのように互いを奮い立たせ、また衝突しているのかを探求すると同時に、私はまた、2012年のフリンダース大学（南オーストラリア）にあるカリキュラム、「多様な人口におけるソーシャルワーク」の実践に関連している、クリティカル・ソーシャルワークにおいての最近のさらなる授業例から引き出してゆく。

옹호, 사회행동, 비판적 사회복지 : 수업후담

깨어나라, 자리에서 일어나라, 권리를 위해 일어나라. 깨어나라, 자리에서 일어나라, 투쟁을 포기하지 마라. (Bob Marley)

옹호와 사회행동은 사회복지영역에서 점점 중요해지고 있고, 특히 '비판사회복지실천'이라는 영역의 관점에서 중요하다. 본 장에서는 호주 사회복지대학 두 곳에서 '비판과 사회복지' 학과목을 가르친 과정을 묘사하고 있다. 우선, 2008년도에 멜번에 있는 RMIT 대학에서 '옹호와 사회행동'이라는 과목을 일반과 고급으로 나누어 두 번 개설했을 때 어떻게 교과목을 만들고 교과내용을 구성했는지에 대해 초점을 맞추었다. 이 때 당국과 부딪힌 적도 있었고 고무되기도 하였다. 또한 2012년도에 호주에 있는 Flinders University 에서 '다문화와 사회복지실천' 교과목에 비판사회복지개념을 어떻게 접목시켰는지를 포함시켰다.

INTRODUCTION

In this chapter I use autoethnography (see Plummer, 2001) and critical reflexivity (see D'Cruz, Gillingham and Melendez, 2007; Ellerman, 1998; Myerhoff and Ruby, 1992) to contribute to the important but under-researched area of social work education in the areas of advocacy and social action. Specifically, I focus on two courses taught at RMIT University (Melbourne) and one taught at Flinders University (South Australia). From these classroom reflections, I argue that advocacy and social action are not only crucial to 'good' social work, but they involve emotions as well as reason.

The chapter is organised into four parts. I start with a brief overview of autoethnography as a method, before signalling my major influences, values and inclinations. In part two, I conceptualise advocacy and social action from a critical social work perspective. In part three I provide details about the three courses I am using to describe how I have approached advocacy and social action. They are: 1) an RMIT undergraduate course literally called, Advocacy and Social Action; 2) an RMIT postgraduate course Advanced Advocacy and Social Action; and 3) a Flinders University course called Social Work with Diverse Populations. Excerpts from course guides are used to highlight curriculum design issues and show in more practical terms, how the courses are structured. In the fourth part of the chapter I identify some of the emotional and ideological challenges I have experienced teaching aspects of advocacy and social action in the classroom.

AUTOETHNOGRAPHY AND ME

> The defining feature of auto-ethnography is that it entails the scientist or practitioner performing narrative analysis to himself or herself as intimately related to a particular phenomenon (McIlveen, 2008, p. 15).

Autoethnography is a research method that draws together autobiography and ethnography. Using hindsight, personal experiences are analysed so as to illustrate wider cultural patterns of experience (Ellis, Adams & Bochner, 2011). Autoethnographers often layer their personal narratives with reference to other cultural signifiers, including academic references. Sometimes criticised for transgressing the rules for (scientific) empiricism, autoethnographers may also reveal and interrogate personal experiences in an effort to forge connections with others (such as peers, students, clients and other research participants), to allow others to 'see the world through their eyes' (Ellis, Adams & Bochner, 2011). In this chapter, I aim to show how I have seen the design and implementation of social work curricula relating to advocacy and social action.

I am a white Australian woman, who identifies as a narrative feminist and critical social worker (Fraser, 2008, 2009). I grew up Catholic and working-class, in an outer suburb of South Australia called Elizabeth. Born in 1965, I am a member of Generation X and a living example of 'a working-class kid' that made it to university through the (short-lived) government policy of free education. As a child I experienced many social problems, including those associated with poverty and violence. Apart from the trauma produced, these experiences helped prime me to a profession specialising in social problems.

Before enrolling in a Bachelor of Social Work in 1985 I knew the meaning of scarcity, shame and oppression. My student years were a struggle financially but culturally and intellectually enriching. My tendency to be outspoken, playful and irreverent, were not just tolerated but in some places, actively encouraged. My structural feminist identity flourished as I enjoyed the new-found privileges associated with higher education and better paid, more valued and independent work. These privileges reflect my European/Western context and orientation, where I (still) enjoy a considerable degree of political freedom in and outside the classroom, particularly as a woman.

I have been a social work educator for twenty years, starting as a tutor for the University of South Australia in 1992, then a field education co-ordinator at James Cook University and Monash University, followed by three years at Melbourne University teaching social policy and community work courses and an elective in anti-oppressive social work practice. In 2002–3, and then 2006–8 I taught advocacy and social action courses to RMIT students, while also teaching courses such as Critical Social Work, Critical Social Work Approaches and Introduction to Social Work. In 2007 I led the accreditation of the newly established Master of Social Work Program, allowing me to have input into the future directions of the program.

In 2004–5 I taught social work courses at the University of Manitoba, Canada: a) Anti-Oppressive Practice; b) Feminist Policies and Perspectives; and c) Narrative Analysis. Since mid-2009, I have coordinated many social work courses at Flinders University, including a third year undergraduate course, Social Work with Diverse Populations. And through my 2012 role of Accreditation Manager for the Flinders Bachelor of Social Work and Social Planning, I have been able to achieve a good understanding of the wider goals of the program.

Today I am in the process of co-authoring a book called, 'Understanding violence and abuse: an anti-oppressive practice perspective' (with Patil and Jarldorn, Fernwood Press, Winnipeg, forthcoming). I am also in the process of two other research projects, 'A gendered analysis of keeping companion animals' (with Taylor) and 'What helps and hinders women from low socio-economic backgrounds complete social science degrees?' (with Verity, Brook, Beddoe and Michell).

My interest in undervalued groups popularly known as the 'underdog' continues in my graduate supervision work where one student is studying the challenges facing offenders returning to live in the community; another focussing on grandmothers who regularly care for their grandchildren, a third student is undertaking fieldwork about 'problem wives' and their experiences of domestic violence in Bangladesh; and a fourth woman who is concentrating on the Catholic Church's attempts to shift the burden of responsibility for child sexual abuse that has occurred within its parishes.

Collectively these teaching and research activities are emotionally and intellectually stimulating but most importantly, designed to bring about some kind of social change. In a country such as Australia where most public (and private) protests are still relatively safe, advocating for change does not just have to be frightening or individually onerous. At times it can be exciting, joyous and even fun.

CONCEPTUALISING ADVOCACY AND SOCIAL ACTION FROM A CRITICAL SOCIAL WORK PERSPECTIVE

> Get up, Stand up, stand up for your rights … Get up, Stand up, don't give up the fight. (Bob Marley)

Broadly speaking, advocacy and social action are fields that involve human beings taking a stand to bring about change (Burgmann, 2000). Campaigns are often waged, such as such as trying to prevent a country hospital from closing (NSW Nurses Union, 2005). In the process, stories about whistleblowers and activists, liberators, revolutionaries and agitators may be heard. Sometimes famous people spearhead campaigns. More often, however, advocacy and social action involves ordinary people collectively deciding, 'enough is enough' and/or 'that something has to be done' (Shaw, 1996; Lakoff, 2004. This is evident through both 'old' and 'new' social movements (Mayo, 2005). Sometimes an epiphany, turning point or life changing event precipitates action (Katz, 2006). At other times, action is prompted by smaller, less noticeable but more frequent happenings that trigger new forms of awareness—and unexpected motivation and/or resistance—as expressed in Paul Kelly's song, 'From little things big things grow'. Mostly, stories are spread through local newspapers, talk back radio and word-of-mouth. Yet, sometimes 'ordinary', individuals are celebrated, as evidenced through the film, *Erin Brockovich* (Soderbergh, 2000).

However, advocacy and social action are not inevitably anti-authoritarian, adversarial or highly public in nature. Small acts, such as writing 'landfill' on the lid of a rubbish bin, is a form of social action that reminds people where their waste products are headed. The bearer of the message may remain anonymous. Similarly, social change may be ushered in through secret actions taken by anonymous individuals for the collective good, such as the leaking of news or documents that others may prefer to hide.

Advocacy and social action often involve negotiated, strategic alliances, sometimes among people (or organisations) that otherwise share little in common (Bishop, 2002; Katz, 2006; Mayo, 2005; Yeatman, 1998; Young, 1997). Consider for instance, alliances formed across religious, feminist, queer and business groups to protest the treatment of asylum seekers in Australia (Fraser & Briskman, 2005). Rather than share core values, they coalesced around the rejection of Australia's Mandatory Detention policy (Briskman, Latham & Goddard, 2008). Their alliance was issue based and temporal.

Advocacy and social action is open to being used by radicals, moderates and conservatives alike. In social work programs such as those taught at RMIT University, however, advocacy and social action have a history of being critically oriented and socially progressive. The courses are specifically designed to engage students in social change, especially change directed towards improving the health and well being of disadvantaged or oppressed people. The politically progressive orientation of Global Studies, Social Science and Planning provided the platform to teach these courses and many others, from a critical perspective.

Flinders University social work has not been tied so explicitly to critical social work perspectives, but has, nevertheless, been open to their use, and has allowed me (and at least three other faculty members I can think of) to teach from a critical social work perspective. The School of Social and Policy Studies, in which Social Work is located, also has a long history of socially progressive research and teaching (Flinders University, 2012). Again, this makes it possible for me to promote critical ideas without fearing for my employment or personal safety.

In Australia, Europe and elsewhere, critical social work is informed by and related to a range of other perspectives, such as radical, feminist, anti-discriminatory and anti-oppressive practice, and structural social work. Critical social workers are a broad coalition of people who share some common interests, values and hopes about how power might be exercised in the future, and language used to narrate different ways of being in the world (Baines, 2007; Dominelli, 2004; Pease & Fook, 1999; Ife, 2001; Thompson, 2003). Together, these perspectives have helped social work engage with social problems at their 'root causes' (such as inequality and injustice) rather than just ameliorating their worst effects (Dominelli, 2004; Fook, 1993; Fox, Piven & Cloward, 1971; Galper, 1975, 1980; Leonard, 1997; Simpkin, 1979; Throssell, 1975;).

'Critical social work' is so named because it is influenced by ideas from critical theory. From critical theory, there is an interest in and commitment to social equality with work directed towards the elimination of oppression and domination (Baines 2007). Social problems are regarded as political not just personal problems and progressive social change is seen to be both necessary and possible (Brown & Strega, 2005; Shera, 2003; Thompson, 2003; Weeks, & Quinn, 2000). Critical social work's value base and emphasis on praxis (or the interplay of theory and practice), makes for a relevant and compatible approach from within which to express social work's commitment to social justice. Social inequality and injustice are therefore, recognised from the very start of the courses, and are clearly stipulated in course guides.

Teaching advocacy, social action and diversity: a critical cocial work perspective

> We are all witness to the rape of the world. (Tracy Chapman)

Critical social work implores us to bear witness to injustice and inequality. Both inequality and injustice are recognised in the opening part of the course description for the courses (Advanced) Social Action and Advocacy,

> Over the course of the last two decades global capitalism has rapidly expanded and the Australian Welfare State—like other Welfare States—has contracted. In contrast to the post war period, public welfare has been reoriented to promote economic development rather than the protection of human rights and the satisfaction needs. Warfare, poverty, abuse, ill health and unhappiness are at an all time high, yet welfare recipients (and many others) are under more obligations to demonstrate their deservedness to receive assistance. For many, these changes have been dramatic as well as harmful. To redress these changes and to prevent the further contraction of the Welfare State, advocacy and social action are required.

Understanding advocacy and social action in contemporary Australia requires us to pay attention to differences and diversity within categories of people. Drawing ideas from modernism and postmodernism, I try to conduct analyses relating to gender, class, ethnicity, sexuality, age and ability without losing sight of individual differences in circumstances, experiences, interests and behaviour. This means that being concerned about how injustice is (re)produced interpersonally and intrapsychically, while remaining alert to the socio-cultural patterns of injustice (see DeLois & Cohen, 2000; Mullaly, 2003, 2007; and Rothkopf, 2008).

I am able to be upfront about my political orientation to teaching, but also my commitment to open and robust discussion. For instance, in the RMIT courses, I openly stated,

> that the starting point for this course is a commitment to equity, social justice and human rights. However, this does not mean that students (or staff) will necessarily agree on issues, practices or principles associated with advocacy and social action. Nor will they be expected to adhere to particular schools of thought or lines of argument.

As Hendershot (2004) and Moyer (2001) recommend, I try to avoid false dichotomies, particularly those that split the collective from the individual, the practical from the theoretical, and micro from macro politics. In the 2008 RMIT course guides this is expressed as follows,

> (Advanced) Advocacy and Social Action is a theoretical but also practical course about how to effect, understand and critique social change. It will provide students with the opportunity to analyse the possibilities and limits of advocacy and social action in and against the Australian Welfare State. Different conceptions of power and protest are part of this exploration. Some of the tools, skills and roles of advocacy will also be examined, in relation to campaigning but also everyday acts of advocacy. Throughout the course, ethical issues will be discussed.

My respect for students' rights to decipher how and why a course is being offered prompted me to advertise my philosophy of education. In both the RMIT (Advanced) Advocacy and Social Action courses and Flinders Social Work with Diverse Populations course, it looked like this,

MY PHILOSOPHY OF EDUCATION

- Education is more than memory, training or instruction. Education is also about imagination, creativity and exploration.
- Education is inherently political insofar as it involves relationships of power, including access to resources. Social work courses are 'political' given they involve relationships of power and the effect of social problems, which are not randomly distributed. Thinking about how power operates socially,

culturally, materially, psychologically and temporally is part of social work practice.

- All members of society do not currently have equal access to higher education. If we have 'made it' to university, we are likely to be enjoying some form of privilege.
- Social work courses should address students' interests and concerns but not at the expense of the needs of service users and wider communities.
- Social work courses should be taught in accordance to the AASW's Code of Ethics, but not uncritically.
- Students learn in a range of ways, including those not necessarily recognised or esteemed, such as through 'folklore' and 'anecdotes', and other knowledge bases sometimes described as 'native'.
- We learn more when we are treated respectfully—as adults—and actively encouraged to participate in our learning. Learning also involves the 'whole person', including the head, heart, gut and soul.
- 'Good' teachers remain curious about the subject matter they teach and the students they teach it to. They work hard to generate knowledge and insight among students and peers. They also take ultimate responsibility for the course design.
- Both learning and teaching involves change, challenges and risk-taking. Relationships of respect and trust are conducive to risk taking. Having the space and the atmosphere to challenge dominant beliefs is also important.
- Sometimes students and educators make mistakes. We try not to but when we do we try to be open to how the situation might be rectified.
- Course guides enunciate expectations between educators and students. Yet, they should remain sufficiently open to modifications that benefit the people engaged in the course, in that particular year. Students are responsible for reading course guides and digesting their contents. They are also responsible

for conveying feedback about the courses they are studying with care and respect. (Heather Fraser, October 2007)

The Advocacy and Social Action courses were based on a yearly theme. For instance, in 2006 the theme was Community and Trade Unions. In 2007 it was Arts and Activism, and in 2008 it was Public Welfare. Offered 'face to face' on the city campus, the 2008 courses involved twelve weekly seminars, all tied in some way to the Australian Welfare State. For the first four weeks, theoretical concepts relating to advocacy and social action were examined, particularly as they related to wide scale change. Two of these weeks were spent exploring social movements described by Mayo (2005) as 'new' and 'old'. The following five weeks focussed on advocacy and social action across the modes of social work. Worker rights and 'everyday' acts of advocacy were considered in Week 10 and in the final two weeks, students presented conference type posters and accompanying narratives. They did this after submitting critical reflections and then, either an essay on a campaign or an advocacy case study.

Student assessments for the Advocacy and Social Action courses were linked to the courses' learning objectives and outcomes:

At the completion of the course students will have developed:

A broad understanding of social action and advocacy, especially as it relates to the Australian Welfare State;

A demonstrated ability to be reflexive about their values, beliefs, attitudes and preferred communication styles/practices associated with advocacy and social action;

The capacity to analyse the complexities surrounding decisions to advocate, including ethics, organisational and legal constraints;

An awareness of the practical 'tools' of advocacy, especially as they relate to skills, tasks and personal traits needed for various campaigns and/or actions; and

An ability to apply the insights gained in the course to work settings and other contexts, including their personal lives.

The main difference between the undergraduate and postgraduate version of the Advocacy and Social Action courses were pitch and pace of material covered. However, differences between student cohorts were evident. Undergraduate students were drawn from social work but also youth work, social science, criminal justice and environment and planning. Postgraduate students came from the disciplines of social work, policy and human services, international development and environment and planning. Up to fifty students studied each course each year, and most lived in Melbourne and did paid work while studying. Many postgraduate students in particular, also juggled significant family responsibilities.

Over the five years that I taught the RMIT courses, I noticed that most of the undergraduate students were less than thirty years of age, making them Generation Y (Huntley 2006), whereas most of the postgraduates were older, either Generation X or Baby-boomer. Experientially I learned that this generational difference had implications for students' faith in the utility of large scale campaigns and wider structural change, as well as their willingness to identify as activists. Younger people did not seem so enamoured with any form of serious confrontation. It was a pattern I also noticed at Flinders University.

At Flinders University there is a mix of social work students in terms of age, ethnicity, socioeconomic status, sexuality, ability, and religion. However, the majority of students are white, heterosexual, able-bodied women from Christian backgrounds. Data from 2011 used for the 2012 Australian Association of Social Work Accreditation (AASW) showed that 98% are non-Indigenous Australians, 80% are aged between 20–40 years; 71% are from either middle or upper class backgrounds; and 76% of our students are female (with 24% male) (Flinders University, 2012).

At Flinders University, I have taught Social Work with Diverse Populations to third year undergraduate social work students since 2010, when I radically revised the course structure and content. Students do not 'visit' other groups (as a topic) each week and try to become familiar with 'their customs' so as to develop 'cultural competency'. I stopped using this conventional approach because it can feel so random, Othering and depoliticised (also see Abrams & Gibson, 2007; Hollinsworth, 2012). By examining different groups and 'their' customs—and not inspecting how difference and diversity is deployed in the current social order—white, heterosexual, middle class male identities are re-centred (Pease, 2009). Instead, the course is predicated on questions about who gets constituted as 'different' and with what effects (Abrams & Gibson, 2007; Hollinsworth, 2012). As specified in the Flinders (2010 and 2011) course guide,

> Overview of social work with diverse populations
>
> Power, privilege and oppression are the central themes of this topic and much of social work practice. Over the course of this topic we will examine the operations of privilege and oppression on the basis of class, gender, sexuality, race/ethnicity, age, ability and religion. Guided by an egalitarian social justice agenda, the topic will explore how unearned entitlements and undeserved penalties are distributed across diverse populations. Insights drawn from these analyses will form the basis of the practice interventions promoted, and then assessed.
>
> Topic aims of social work with diverse populations
>
> 1. Critically analyse the notion of diversity and diverse populations, especially as they are applied in education, health and welfare
>
> 2. Conceptualise power, privilege and oppression in relation to social workers and the practices they employ with diverse populations,
>
> 3. Examine how specific groups identified as diverse, can see the world differently from others.
>
> Learning outcomes of social work with diverse populations
>
> 4. Explain how power, privilege and oppression pattern the lives of diverse populations
>
> 5. Articulate why, and how, critical social work practices may be undertaken with diverse populations, and

6. Explicate how 'different ways of knowing, doing and being' relate to oppressed groups, especially those most likely to use social work services.

Student assessment

Privilege and oppression paper in your own life (2000 words, 50%)

Critical social work intervention paper (2000 words, 50%)

Up to 80 students enrol in the Flinders course scheduled for six three-hour lecture/workshops. Attention is first focussed on critical social work ideas about power, privilege and oppression. Associated ideas and frameworks are then applied to class, race and ethnicity, gender and sexuality, age and ability, and religion and spirituality—in that order. In the final week the topic relates to doing egalitarian social work. Core components of these 'diversity classes' are advocacy and social action, including references to past and present social movements and public campaigns.

Critical reflexivity: beyond rationality

> Be the change you want to see in the world. (Ghandi)

From a critical social work approach, advocacy and social action are not straightforward to teach or learn because they involve more than the development of knowledge and skills. Value based, partisan and goal and process oriented, advocacy and social action involve power and contest (Foucault, 2003), so cannot, therefore, escape the possibility of conflict. Conflict can take many forms, including those waged over borders, rights and resources (Mendes, 2003), but also over concepts, definitions and meanings (Hendershot, 2004), as well as strategies and techniques.

Critical reflexivity is a crucial component of courses such as Social Work with Diverse Populations and (Advanced) Advocacy and Social Action. As D'Cruz et al. (2007) explain, critical reflexivity has multiple meanings in social work. In the first variation,

> reflexivity is regarded as an individual's considered response to an immediate context and is concerned with the ability of service users to process information and create knowledge to guide life choices... In the second variation, reflexivity is defined as a social worker's self-critical approach that questions how knowledge about clients is generated and, further, how relations of power operate in this process...In the third variation, reflexivity is concerned with the part that emotion plays in social work practice.

With experience, I have learned that critical reflexivity involves not just the head but also the heart, gut and spirit (Narayan 1988). Critical reflexivity—or the active and critical interrogation of one's values, beliefs, assumptions and perceptions of experiences—calls for a pursuit far more active and dangerous than the act of gazing inwards' (Tumarkin, 2007, p. 75). It calls for courage, which Tumarkin (2007) defines using terms such as guts, grit, spine, heart and verve. As Rodriguez (2000) explains, it calls for the interrogation of privilege.

Interrogating privilege is an important part of the on campus Flinders course, Social Work with Diverse Populations. Such personal examinations rely on an engaged and trusting learning climate among students and between students and their teachers. As I did at RMIT with the Advocacy and Social Action courses, I work hard to create learning environments where robust debate is expected, valued, prepared for and responded to in respectful ways (also see, Abrams & Gibson, 2007). To maintain group energy and interest, I vary classroom activities and use multi-media. Lecture input is given in parts, interspersed with small group discussions and large group forums about power, privilege and oppression in their own lives and others. I tell stories about power, privilege and oppression in my personal and professional life. I encourage students to make their own observations of privilege in action, and bring these stories to the next class.

I make determined efforts to create space for less vocal members of the class to speak, and at their own pace. I have learned that if uncomfortable silences do occur, they do not usually last very long.

With sufficient care given to the emotional—not just intellectual—climate of the classroom, many emotions, including feelings and thoughts about vulnerability can emerge, some of which can be harnessed to enrich the collective learning experience about power, privilege and oppression.

It was in 2010 in Social Work with Diverse Populations that I first started asking students for permission to challenge them publicly about their public assertions. For instance, I might ask students, 'Can I push you on this?', or 'Are you feeling okay for me to tackle you on x or y?' Occasionally students will say, 'No please don't, not today', or words to that effect. In these instances, I quickly redirect attention to spare any potential embarrassment and allow others to jump in. For those students who do feel up to 'an arm wrestle', I give counter arguments or invite others in class to do likewise. I know that modelling good tempered responses to even the most eyebrow-raising student comments is essential if robust but safe educational environments are going to be fostered. I admit there are times when I am better at this than others, but I keep working at opening up discussions for everyone in class. For the students who hold very different, if not oppositional views to the ones I am promoting, I periodically offer them the chance to rebut what has been said. For instance, I might literally ask, 'Any rebuttals?' or 'David, do you want to respond?' Apart from helping to keep all students engaged (not just the ones who define social justice in similar ways to me), these small gestures help the growing number of students who fear conflict (of any kind), see how critical questions and analyses can be undertaken in ways that are not aggressive, adversarial and personally alienating.

Teaching *Social* Work with Diverse Populations has given me the chance to pay more attention to feelings and to more carefully construct classes to allow students to express and process their emotions. However, it was the hindsight derived from re-examining the RMIT Advocacy and Social Action curricula that led me to adopt such practices. At RMIT I was committed to helping students experience social work courses personally, emotionally, rationally and intellectually—not just have them 'delivered' as if they were pizzas. Yet, when I read over the early versions of (Advanced) Advocacy and Social Action curricula, I noticed how instrumental, task and role focussed they seemed to be. 'Knowing' and 'doing' were central, with 'feelings' left to the margins. Then, while completing a Graduate Certificate in Tertiary Teaching at RMIT I reflected on the 2007 Advocacy and Social Action student evaluations. Increasing number of students seemed to be entering these courses with little identification with advocacy and social action. My job was not only to teach about advocacy and social action, but also encourage students to open their minds and hearts to the idea of them. In the student evaluations, 'surprised' was a word mentioned most by undergraduate students who never thought they'd be interested in being an advocate or activist. 'Inspired' and 'validated' were words most by the postgraduate students that had advocacy and/or activist backgrounds. Delighted was how I felt about their engagement.

Freirian in orientation (Freire, 1970, 1990), I want students to *want* to learn about advocacy and social action. I am struck by the differences, and possible connections, between 'knowing something' and 'caring about it'. I know that when it comes to either Advocacy and Social Action or Social Work with Diverse Populations, students need to do both. I know that the degree to which they *care* affects group dynamics. When care is low or absent, indifference, passivity and fatalism can set in and become a major obstacle to learning (Freire, 1970, 1990). More appreciative of this, I decided to make more explicit, the links between the personal and political, and the rational and emotional. It is one reason why I started citing my teaching philosophy in course guides.

Whether done by self, peers, supervisors or students, teaching evaluations need to relate to content, format and process. In the RMIT Advocacy and Social Action courses, I wondered how much emphasis to place on campaigns and social movements, and how much on intra organisational and more individual forms of advocacy (Burgmann, 2000; Della Porta, 1999). I thought about how to represent intra and inter-social movement disagreements that exist, say (in)between feminists and trade unionists. I wrestled with how to deal with competing constructions of, and strategies for, advocacy and social action.

In terms of format, I tried to present the Advocacy and Social Action courses in ways that would appeal to sufficient numbers of students so the courses were viable, without sacrificing the quality of content or rigor of assessment. On the other hand, I needed to watch for over-subscription. Given the budgetary restrictions, especially in relation to employing additional staff, I sought to open up the courses to as many people as possible (including members of the public), without having so many people that interactive workshops became impossible. This is why the workshops were capped at fifty participants per course.

I aim to engage students in the courses they are studying, but also with one another. Conceptualising engagement broadly as 'the making of a connection' (with the view of) develop[ing] a partnership or relationship (Honeywill & Byth, 2006, p. 70), I have now had many years practicing how to create safe but also resilient and even playful moments in the classroom where we can (collectively) express outrage, fears and hopes. Helping students to re-evaluate their values and assumptions, and explore any stereotypes they may be carrying is part of the process.

Let me give a classroom example. It occurred in the third, 2008 postgraduate RMIT class when we were brainstorming stereotypes of activists. The class was mostly comprised of people who identified with and had experience in, advocacy and social action. Even so, some pretty ugly, anti-activist stories emerged in our collective imagination. Take for instance, the story about activists who are misguided, unemployed, unshaven and unwashed, who drop out of mainstream society, take drugs and go looking for trouble. Then there were stories about malicious, vexatious and litigious claimants, including those that loved to whine and play victim. Or the 'do gooding missionaries that promoted and dropped social causes depending on the charity dinner menu'. And let us not forget: the cowboys (and cowgirls) with big mouths and big chips on their shoulders, who saw themselves as heroes but were actually thugs and bullies, flexing their muscles largely against people in similar or worse situations than their own. It was only when images of violence, destruction and rage were mentioned that the laughter stopped and the mood of the class became sombre. This emotional change allowed students to express fears about getting involved in *any* acts of resistance, at least those likely to get the disapproval of their supervisors. The most common fear related to committing acts that could lead to 'career suicide'.

In the undergraduate RMIT classes, I participated in conversations of a different kind. By week five we were tackling the idea that was emerging about 'ignorance being bliss' and 'raised consciousness' being a burden. This discussion happened in the fourth week of class, after I asked students whether they were becoming less prepared and engaged. I wondered whether the 'gritty realist' footage of socialist, feminist, gay and black activists (shown prior) had anything to do with it. That is when I heard more than a few students speak of their distrust of organised political activity, yet, their confusion about how to join with others to promote particular issues. Unexpectedly, I also learned that the media, itself, was an issue. Accustomed to having messages broadcast quickly and across a range of media (including text messaging), they are used to slick, big budget advertising campaigns, and big blockbuster stories. In terms of visual interest and 'infotainment', some students admitted that they can be a hard audience to reach and sustain, particularly in relation to small budget community campaigns. This led us to talk about the use of music, film, theatre and culture jamming, rather than an over-reliance on (home-made) banners and street protests. One exception mentioned were the 2003, Valentine's Day Peace Rallies (in Melbourne and around the world), where music, dance, costume and theatre were interwoven with conventional protest measures.

Also a little unexpectedly, however, I discovered a great hunger for 'real', 'deep' conversations. Irrespective of gender, all students, but especially some of the younger ones, seemed to want to go beyond the virtual (and sometimes fleeting) connections they make on Facebook. Whether at RMIT or Flinders University, I saw it in the classroom. I also saw it after class, when students hung around chatting with me and/or each other. I noticed it in the stairwells or the lifts we rode to get to class. When I bumped into groups of them in the cafeteria, I felt their goodwill, and it went a long way in helping to make our classes worth attending.

I know that creating a sense of community first needs to come from me, the teacher, taking the time to foster it, in and out of the classroom. The challenge, however, is that this 'emotional work' (Hochschild, 2003) takes time, energy and a fair degree of skill but is rarely valued in the academy. In most Australian universities, intellectual and financial growth is more highly regarded than emotional growth and political awareness. Actually, I see a surprising lack of attention paid to the emotions of teaching and learning. In my fifteen years as a social work academic, I cannot remember a single reference made to the need for teachers to arrive at the classroom with energy and good humour. Yet, intuitively, I have always known how important this is. I remember this when I am preparing for class and I find myself in a low or bad mood. It helps me to constrain any impatience I might feel. It also helps me to temper any inclinations I might have become too task focussed and directive.

Ideally, I like to facilitate classes that people want to come to, even if it is early in the morning, or after a long day at work, and that if they are not able to do so, they will feel as if they are 'missing out'. Yet, like most other social work educators, I have to juggle these responsibilities with others, including those related to research and grant writing, field liaisons and community engagement. When time is short—which is often—I know how tempting it can be to assume that I will not need long to prepare. Such an assumption is dangerous because it fails to take into account the necessary emotional—not just intellectual—work that goes into teaching (Myers 1998).

While courses such as (Advanced) Advocacy and Social Action and Social Work with Diverse Populations can be motivating, empowering, and inspiring, and encourages many to become more politically engaged and 'savvy', they can also be confusing, awkward, and painful. I know this from watching students in class, marking their critical reflections, viewing their posters presentations of a campaign or piece of advocacy and reading their course evaluations. I know that for some students, developing knowledge about social issues affirms their lived experiences and life choices, but for others, or at other times, it brings them into contact with some potential threatening possibilities. This might occur for women with little former awareness of the dangers of intimate abuse start to look more closely at their relationships. While considering their experiences of privilege, wealthier students sometimes find themselves having to come to grips with the not-so-innocent aspects of their lifestyles and their involvement in global capitalism. And as questions of difference and diversity are raised, religiously oppressed students can become aware of their not-so-inclusive attitudes towards members of the gay, lesbian, bisexual and transgendered communities.

'Social locations' (or geographical places and specific socio-cultural contexts) do not determine values, knowledge and agency (personal power), but they do influence them (Foucault, 2003; Mullaly, 2003; Peel, 2003; Shera, 2003; Stretton, 2005). If nothing else, our specific social contexts, and our likely experiences of oppression and privilege, influence the types of discourses we are liable to hear, as well as the way we, and others, are likely to interpret them (Mayo, 2005; Mendes 2003; Peel, 2003; Plummer, 2003; Rothkopf, 2008). Social locations produce longstanding assumptions, including those that have not been inspected (Baines, 2007; Brown, 2003; Mullaly, 2003, 2007; Thompson, 2003; Weeks, 2003). Long held assumptions are not always easy to interrogate or relinquish (Fraser, 2009; Myers, 1998; Stretton, 2005). Realising that something you took for granted is now tied up in a series of unfair political practices does not always feel good (Galper, 1975, 1980). It can call for actions that we might prefer to avoid. Having the scales fall—or pulled—from your eyes can expand horizons but also complicate life (Myers, 1998).

Social locations mediate speaking rights (Baines, 2007; Mullaly, 2007; Peel, 2003; Stretton, 2005). While I try not to dominate the airspace in seminars and workshops, I realise my own views shape the direction of class discussions. As the teacher, I know that I enjoy more privileges with airspace. My status as the teacher gives me more opportunity to put forward preferred arguments. If I want to I can shut down (even unwittingly) the arguments with which I disagree.

I also recognise that for all my attempts to de-professionalise (Dominelli, 2004) and democratise the classroom, I know that I still have power 'over' students and their courses of study. I am aware that each year it is I and other colleagues—not the students—that decide on the courses being offered, thematically bound and critically oriented. Apart from the choice of course content and prescribed readings, I know how important student grades are. Across universities, I have noticed that my interactions with students can swiftly change the closer it gets to assignment deadlines. I also appreciate that it is me, and nobody else, that is paid to be in the classroom. Overseeing class dynamics my responsibility, as I note upfront in the course guides,

> (Advanced) Advocacy and Social Action are potentially controversial topics that can evoke a wide range of emotions. While I understand that passions may 'run high' at various points, it is important that we demonstrate respect to one another. This includes respecting others right to hold different values and opinions to your own. In the exceptional situation where aggressive or bullying behaviour is displayed, I, the lecturer will be bound to take action (Fraser, 2008).

Summary

Although advocacy and social action are important features of social work practice, they are not always easy to 'teach', nor straightforward to learn. This is because advocacy and social action cannot be emptied of emotion, nor relegated to one side of the theory/practice divide. Cutting across all fields and modes of practice, they are often riddled with stereotypes about who makes a 'good' advocate and what it takes to be an 'activist'. Using examples from two courses offered at RMIT University in Melbourne, and one offered at Flinders University in South Australia, I considered how curricula might be designed and implemented to stimulate a diverse range of students' inspiration for social change. Hopefully, this work will stimulate conversations about how advocacy and social action might be understood and taught, not just in Western contexts such as Australia, that in and of themselves contain much diversity, but many other contexts across the Asia Pacific region, and beyond.

REFERENCES

Abrams, L.S. & Gibson, P. (2007). Reframing multicultural education: teaching white privilege in the social work curriculum. *Journal of Social Work Education*, 43(1), 147–61.

Allan, J., Pease, B. & Briskman, L. (Eds) (2003). *Critical social work: an introduction to theories and practices*. Melbourne: Allen & Unwin.

Baines, D. (Ed.) (2007). *Doing anti-oppressive practice: building transformative politicized social work*. Halifax: Fernwood.

Bishop, A. (2002). *Becoming an ally: breaking the cycle of oppression*. Crows Nest: Allen & Unwin.

Briskman, L., Latham, S. & Goddard C. (2008). *Human rights overboard: seeking asylum in Australia*. Melbourne: Scribe Publications.

Brown, L. & Strega, S. (Eds) (2005). *Research as resistance: critical, Indigenous and anti-oppressive approaches*. Toronto: Canadian Scholars Press.

Burgmann, V. (2000). The point of protest: advocacy and social action in 20th century Australia. *Just Policy, Papers from the Winter School on Advocacy and Social Action*, 19/20 (September), 7–15.

D'Cruz, H., Gillingham, P. & Melendez, S. (2007). Reflexivity: a concept and its meanings for practitioners working with children and families. *Critical Social Work*, 8(1). Retrieved 17 April 2013 from www.uwindsor.ca/criticalsocialwork.

DeLois, K. & Cohen, M. (2000). A queer idea: using group work principles to strengthen learning in a sexual minorities' seminar. *Social Work with Groups*, 23(3), 53–67.

DellaPorta, D. (1999). Forms, repertoires and cycles of protest. In D. DellaPorta & M. Diani (Eds). *Social Movements, an Introduction* (pp. 165–92). Oxford: Blackwell Publishers.

Dominelli, L. (2004). *Social work: theory and practice for a changing profession.* London: Polity Press.

Ellerman, A. (1998). Can discourse analysis enable reflective social work practice? *Social Work Education*, 17(1), 35–44.

Ellis, C., Adams, T.E. & Bochner, A.P. (2011). Autoethnography: an overview. *Forum Qualitative Social Research*, 12(1). Retrieved 17 April 2013 from www.qualitative-research.net/index.php/fqs/article/view/1589/3095.

Flinders University (2012). *Bachelor of social work and social planning report to the AASW.* Unpublished report. Bedford Park, South Australia.

Fook, J. (1993). *Radical casework: a theory of practice.* Crows Nest: Allen & Unwin.

Foucault, M. (2003). *Society must be defended.* London: Penguin Books.

Fox Piven, F. & Cloward, R.A. (1971). *Regulating the poor: the functions of public welfare.* New York: Vintage books.

Fraser, H. (2009). Trying to complete socially just, politically sensitive, social work research. *Journal of Social Work*, 9(1), 87–98.

Fraser, H. (2008). *In the name of love: women's narratives of love and abuse.* Toronto: Women's Press.

Fraser, H. & Briskman, L. (2005). Through the eye of a needle: the challenge of getting justice in Australia if you're indigenous or seeking asylum. In I. Ferguson & M. Lavalette (Eds). *Globalisation, global justice and social work* (pp. 109–23). London: Routledge.

Freire, P. (1990). A critical understanding of social work. *Journal of Progressive Human Services*, 1(1), 3–10.

Freire, P. (1970). *Pedagogy of the oppressed.* New York: Continuum.

Galper, J. (1980). *Social work practice: a radical perspective.* New Jersey: Prentice Hall.

Galper, J. (1975). *The politics of social services.* New Jersey: Prentice Hall.

Hawkins, L. & Jackson, B. (2007). Partnership for people-centred development challenges and responses in a globalising world: globalization and grass roots: local to local, global to local. *New Community Quarterly*, 5(3), 55–62.

Hendershot, C. (2004). *Beyond dichotomies: reflexive engagement of critical reflexivity.* YCISS Working Paper 28 (May). Retrieved 17 April 2013 from www.yorku.ca/yciss/publications/documents/WP28-Hendershot.pdf.

Hochschild, A. (2003). *The commercialization of intimate life: notes from home and work.* Berkeley: University of California Press.

Hollinsworth, D. (2012). Forget cultural competence: ask for an autobiography. *Social Work Education: The International Journal,* 1–13. Retrieved 17 April 2013 from dx.doi.org/10.1080/02615479.2012.730513.

Honeywill, R. & Byth, V. (2006). *Neo power: how the new economic order is changing the way we live, work and play.* Melbourne: Scribe.

Huntley, R. (2006). *World according to Y: inside the new adult generation.* Crows Nest: Allen and Unwin.

Ife, J. (2001). *Human rights and social work: towards rights-based practice,* Cambridge: Cambridge University Press.

Katz, S. E. (2006). *The revolution will not be microwaved: inside America's underground food movements.* Vermont: Chelsea Green Publishing.

Lakoff, G. (2004). *Don't think like an elephant, know your values and frame the debate: the essential guide for progressives.* Vermont: Chelsea Green Publishing.

Leonard, P. (1997). *Postmodern welfare: reconstructing an emancipatory project,* London: Sage.

Martin, J. (2003). Historical development of critical social work practice. In J. Allan, B. Pease & L. Briskman (Eds). *Critical social work: an introduction to theories and practices* (pp. 17–31). Melbourne: Allen & Unwin.

Mayo, M. (2005). *Global citizens, social movements and the challenge of globalisation.* Toronto: Canadian Scholars' Press.

McIlveen, P. (2008). Autoethnography as a method for reflexive research and practice in vocational psychology. *Australian Journal of Career Development,* 17(2), 13–20.

Mendes, P. (2003). 'Defending and reforming the welfare state'. In P. Mendes (Ed). *Australia's welfare wars: the players, the politics and the ideologies* (pp. 67–81). Sydney: University of New South Wales Press.

Mowbray, M. (2000). Beyond 'a thousand tiny empowerments': advocacy and social action in Australia. *Just Policy,* 19/20, 24–31.

Moyer, B. (2001). The eight stages of social movements. In B. Moyer, J. Macalister, M.L. Finley & S. Soifer (Eds). *Doing democracy: the MAP model for organizing social movements* (pp. 42–86). Gabriola Island: New Society Publishers.

Mullaly, B. (2007). *The new structural social work.* Toronto: Oxford University Press.

Mullaly, B. (2003). Theoretical and conceptual considerations. In B. Mullaly (Ed.). *Challenging oppression: a critical social work approach* (pp. 1–26). Toronto: Oxford University Press.

Myerhoff, B. & Ruby, J. (1992). A crack in the mirror: reflexive perspectives in anthropology. In B. Myerhoff, D. Metzger, J. Ruby & V. Tufte (Eds). *Remembered lives: the work of ritual, storytelling and growing older* (pp. 307–40). Ann Arbor: University of Michigan Press.

Myers, K. (1998). Allegiances, coups and color wars: a strategy for breaking the silence on race issues in the classroom introduction. *Transformations,* 9(2), 183–195.

Narayan, U. (1988). Working together across difference: some considerations on emotions and political practice. *Hypatia*, 3(2), 31–47.

New South Wales [NSW] Nurses Union (2005). *Union news: Coraki Hospital closure threatens local community.* Retrieved 17 April 2013 from www.nswnurses.asn.au/news/2199.html.

Pease, B. (2009). *Undoing privilege: unearned advantage in a divided world*. London: Zed Books.

Pease, B. & Fook, J. (Eds). (1999). *Transforming social work practice: postmodern critical perspectives.* Crows Nest: Allen and Unwin.

Peel, M. (2003). *The lowest rung: voices of Australian poverty.* Cambridge: Cambridge University Press.

Plummer, K. (2001). *The call of life stories in ethnographic research: handbook of ethnography.* London: Sage.

Plummer, K. (2003). *Intimate citizenship, private decisions and public dialogues.* Seattle: University of Washington Press.

Rodriguez, N. (2000). Projects of whiteness in a critical pedagogy. In N. Rodriguez & L. Villaverde (Eds). *Dismantling white privilege: pedagogy, politics and whiteness* (pp. 1–19). New York: Peter Lang.

Rothkopf, D. (2008). *Superclass: the global power elite and the world they are making.* London: Little Brown Publishing.

Shaw, R. (1996). *The activist's handbook: a primer for the 1990s and beyond*. Berkeley: University of California Press.

Shera, W. (Ed) (2003). *Emerging perspectives on anti-oppressive practice.* Toronto: Canadian Scholars Press.

Simpkin, M. (1979). *Trapped within welfare: surviving social work.* London: Macmillan.

Soderbergh, S. (Director) (2000). *Erin Brockovich.* United States: Universal/MCA.

Stretton, H. (2005). *Australia fair.* Sydney: University of New South Wales Press.

Thompson, N. (2003). *Promoting equality: challenging discrimination and oppression in the human services.* London: Palgrave Macmillan.

Throssell, H. (1975). Social work overview. In H. Throssel (Ed). *Social work: radical essays* (pp. 3–23). St Lucia: University of Queensland Press.

Tumarkin, M. (2007). *Courage.* Melbourne: Melbourne University Press.

Weeks, W. & Quinn, M. (Eds) (2000). *Issues facing Australian families: human services respond,* 3rd edn. Melbourne: Longman Cheshire.

Yeatman, A. (Ed) (1998). *Activism and the policy process.* Crows Nest: Allen & Unwin.

Young, I.M. (1997). *Intersecting voices, dilemmas of gender, political philosophy, and policy.* Princeton: Princeton University Press.

12

Walking the talk in social work education

Ksenija Napan

This chapter focuses on the benefits and challenges of utilising social work values and principles when teaching, researching, evaluating and improving social work education. These values and principles are explored through their application within the social practice degree programs at Unitec, New Zealand. A range of alternative and novel teaching and assessment methods are examined and evaluated in the light of their relevance and compatibility with social work education. Special focus is placed on, group assignments, creative individual assignments, field trips, experiential learning, self and peer assessment, inquiry learning, the use of individualised learning contracts and their relevance in 'walking the talk' in social work education. In an attempt to 'walk the talk' this chapter is organised in similar stages to the way in which social work education is organised in Aotearoa New Zealand and it integrates personal, professional and political discourses relevant for the co-creation of competent social workers.

Prijeđimo s riječi na djela u edukaciji socijalnih radnika

Ovo poglavlje je usmjereno na dobrobiti i izazove pri korištenju vrijednosti i principa socijalnog rada u poučavanju, istraživanju, evaluiranju i unaprijeđivanju edukacije socijalnih radnika. Te vrijednosti i principi su istraženi kroz njihovu primjenu u dodiplomskim i poslijediplomskim edukativnim programima na Unitecu na Novom Zelandu. Alternativne i nove metode edukacije i procjene su istražene i evaluirane u relaciji sa njihovom kompatibilnošću s principima, vrijednostima i praksom socijalnog rada. Specijalna pažnja je posvećena grupnim zadacima, kreativnim individualnim zadacima, edukativnim izletima, iskustvenom učenju, samoprocjeni i kolegijalnoj procjeni, učenju propitkivanjem, idividualiziranim ugovorima namijenjenim učenju i procjeni koliko su te metode relevantne za edukaciju socijalnih radnika. U najmeri da autorica ostane vjerna primjeni principa socijalnog rada u edukaciji, ovo poglavlje je organizirano na isti način na koji je edukacija socijalnih radnika organizirana na Novom Zelandu te integrira osobne, profesionalne i političke diskurse relevantne za ko-kreaciju kompetentnih socijalnih radnika.

社會工作教育的理論聯繫實際

本章著重於在教學、研究、評估以及改進社工教育時運用社會工作的價值觀和原則的益處和挑戰。通過它們在新西蘭Unitec大學社會實踐學位課程中的應用，這些價值觀和原則得到探索。按照其與社會工作教育的相關性和兼容性，本章檢測並評價了一系列可替換和新穎的教學和評估方法。重點側重於小組任務、創造性的個人任務、實地考察、體驗式學習、自我及同伴評估、探究學習、使用個性化學習契約以及他們在社工教育中與'言出有行'的相關性。為使理論和實際相結合，本章參照新西蘭社工專業教育的組織方式劃分出幾個相似階段。它集合了與共同創造有能力的社會工作者相關的個人的、專業的和政治等方面。

タイトル：ソーシャルワーク教育の実践化

著者：セニヤ・ナパン

この章では、ソーシャルワークの指導、研究、評価、そしてソーシャルワーク教育の向上するときに活用するソーシャルワークの価値と原則のメリットと課題に焦点を当てる。これらの価値と原則はニュージーランドにあるユニテック工科大学(Unitec) における社会実践学位教育課程での適用から調査する。非伝統的で新しい様々な教授法や評価方法をソーシャルワーク教育の妥当性および適合性という観点に照らしあわせ評価する。特に、グループ課題や創作的な個人課題、現地調査、体験学習、自己及び相互評価、探究学習、個別学習契約の利用と、ソーシャルワーク教育理論の実践化との対応例について照準を合わせる。本章では、ソーシャルワーク教育がアオテアロア・ニュージーランドで組織される方法と、有能なソーシャル・ワーカーの共同生成に適切な個人、専門職、および政治論の統合の道筋について、ソーシャルワーク教育理論の実践化の試みとして整理する。

사회복지교육에서 말한 것을 실천하다

본 장에서는 사회복지 가치와 원칙을 활용하여 사회복지 교육, 조사연구, 평가에 도움을 주는데 초점을 맞추고 있다. 뉴질랜드의 Unitec University에서 사회복지 학위과정에 사회복지 가치와 원칙을 적용시켜 보았다. 다양한 교육방법과 사정방법이 사용되었고, 사회복지 교육에 연관되어 있고 필요한가를 측정하였다. 그룹과제, 창조적 개별과제, 현장학습, 경험학습, 자기분석, 걷기 등에 초점이 맞추어졌다. New Zealand의 Aotearoa에서는 사회복지 교육에 '말한 것을 실천한다.'는 방식을 응용하였다. '말한 것을 실천한다' 는 방식은 뉴질랜드의 Aotearoa에서 사회복지교육이 조직된 방식과 같으며, 개인적, 전문적, 환경적 상황을 통합하여 유능한 사회복지사를 함께 창조해내는 과정을 묘사하고 있다.

SELECTION—WELCOME TO THE PROFESSION

POSITIONING THE AUTHOR

> All of science is nothing more than the refinement of everyday thinking. (Albert Einstein)

I have joined the academic establishment because of my dissatisfaction with the way I was taught social work and my insatiable desire to change the way it was done. My Bachelor of Social Work at University of Zagreb was a five-year full-time degree which included four years of course work and one year for a research thesis. The program was mainly theoretical and encompassed five courses on various aspects of psychology and a number of social policy, economics and law papers. Only seven out of 36 subjects were directly related to social work and these were mainly taught by academics with no practical social work experience. When I completed my five years of academic study, I became aware of my mind being overloaded with theories as well as of my ignorance and lack of skills for working with people to create any kind of meaningful change. To compensate for this I enrolled in every possible counselling and psychotherapy course that was offered, believing that more learning will help me to be effective in my future profession. I was aware that the ability to relate to my future clients and to the systems they operate in was essential. Although nobody told me during my academic training that social workers in Croatia were supposed to maintain the status quo and keep the disempowered masses under control, during my first fieldwork placement I started developing a hunch that that was the case. For five years, we as students regurgitated books on radical social work, action research, ecological systems theory and we started believing that we could change the world by merely applying these theories. It was only through my fieldwork placement that I discovered that only academics had the privilege of 'playing with ideas' and social workers were far too busy filling forms and finding loopholes to place the 'old Theresa in the old people's home before she burned herself and her 25 cats in her basement flat'. Some of my colleagues who became practitioners did their best to forget everything they had learnt at university and adjusted to mediocre practice being careful not to rock the boat before they retired as old, worn out, disillusioned and 'fried' social workers. However, some followed their passion for social justice and 'managed to manage the un-manageable' by engaging in creative social work practices, which significantly improved the quality of life of people whose lives have been damaged by war, injustices or their status in the society.

My aim at the time was to learn how to help my future clients to figure out better ways of living rather than being dependent on social worker's good will. I believed that the main task of an effective social worker is to make her/himself redundant. I hoped that my wide general knowledge, political awareness of the pitfalls of socialism as well as un-sustainability of capitalism would make me open to alternative views and enable me to envisage better ways of collaborating in a way that would bring forth the world. I wanted to work 'hands on' and I wanted to change systems, practices and realities that surrounded me, but before I had even put together my curriculum vitae to start looking for a job as a social worker I got offered a position at the university where I studied. I was quite surprised with this offer, because I was an inquisitive radical student, critiquing university practices and continuously suggesting ideas that could have been interpreted as outrageous. I was also aware, that in spite of being full of creative ideas, I was very far from being competent in teaching social work just after graduating. I was the one who always asked challenging questions, trying to make links with practice. I had hair dyed in three colours and a dog who sat in on all my lectures with me. It still puzzles me that in a traditional academic setting with so many rules, regulations and boundaries, they allowed me to get away with it and even gave me a student of the year award twice! Nevertheless, they did, and on top of that, they offered me a job! Then I realised that part of the reason was that I was probably the only 'mad enthusiast' who would accept the offer. The salary was ridiculously low but it included Masters tuition in the program of my choice.

I chose the Masters of Social Psychiatry as it was a high quality radical, transdisiplinary program. During my Masters I truly engaged with my learning and it provided me with a sound theoretical base that I could rely on when practicing my newly gained counseling skills. The joy of being treated like a colleague, being allowed to dialogue with my teachers, challenge them and expand my knowledge renewed my passion to transform social work education by making it more engaging, more practical and more integrated. Most of the professors in that Master program were practitioners and that made a huge difference in terms of the integration of theory and practice. My dream of working in practice and transforming Croatian social work evolved into transforming social work education in order to transform social practices in a widest possible sense.

When accepting a job I was able to make it conditional upon continuing my engagement with practice, so I continued working for a local Centre for Social Work working with children and youth at risk in their own homes. I would work with two or three teenagers at a time. At the same time, a group of us started a support centre for youth and after a considerable success, we were invited to work at schools using drama and various experiential methods to keep teenagers out of trouble. Shortly after that, I started a part-time counseling private practice. I learnt through experience how useful it is to visit people in their own contexts and I became the first Croatian travelling counselor, attracting a number of agoraphobic, elderly and physically disabled clients who were delighted to host me in their homes. Through these interactions, I developed an interest for the field of special needs and issues of equality and social justice.

My university job allowed me a lot of freedom although now, with hindsight I wonder how I managed to do all that at once. I have to say that my main calling was transformation and innovation. I was doing it and living it and it was more than a full time job. I was also combining a lot of work—my university work was informed by my practice and my practice was often part of some innovative action research project. While I was still studying, I would spend my summer holidays in the USA working in camps for adults and children with special needs. When I got a job at the university, during the first summer break I started the first Croatian holiday camp for persons with special needs and involved students in the organisation and delivery of this service. For some persons with special needs this was their first holiday away from home or from the institutions they lived in and for some students this was their first encounter with people with special needs.

After that first summer camp students and clients were buzzing with motivation and I was encouraged by their families, and their social workers to include clients in a compulsory first-year course Social Work with Individuals. The role of clients was to act as experts in managing social workers and help our students become better practitioners. In return, students were supposed to support clients the way clients wanted to be supported. Clients were persons with chronic mental illness, multiple sclerosis, elderly people in nursing homes and persons with various special needs. Clients and students would meet during a whole academic year once a week for two hours and at the beginning would create a contract for their engagement which was a living and changeable document. Students would attend group supervision sessions once a fortnight with their client's social worker. Students would also attend two hours of theoretical lectures per week as well as two hours of collaborative practical work with fellow classmates where they would practice problem solving with one another in a peer to peer fashion, addressing either personal issues or problems that occurred during encounters with clients. Because of its intensive and challenging nature the method was named a Contact Challenge Method (Napan, 1997).

I have spent seven years teaching at the University of Zagreb doing my best to transform the social work program into one that would 'walk the social work talk'. It was not easy to do that, being the youngest staff member, but with time and persistence the Contact-Challenge method of teaching and learning social work practice came to replace the traditional first year placement. Croatian clients wholeheartedly accepted the offer and they have been helping to educate social workers in Croatia since 1990 (Napan, 1995;Urbanc, 2003).

When I moved to Aotearoa, New Zealand, I contextualised, applied and tested the Contact Challenge Method with a small group of Masters of Social Work (applied) students at Massey University, who had no previous experience in social work practice. The essence of the method is in its integrative nature; theory, practice and experience are integrated through personal, professional and political discourses, which enable students to become reflective practitioners. The Contact Challenge Method is not directly transferable to different contexts, but it is easily modifiable and contextualised within any educational program.

Although I am not directly involved in applying the Contact Challenge method at the moment, the basic values and principles that permeate it, inform my teaching. These principles are; partnership, collaboration, mutual respect, reverence for all life, inspiration, purpose and joy in lifelong learning. These seven principles will be explored in the text that follows.

SELECTING STUDENTS FOR BACHELOR OF SOCIAL WORK PROGRAMS

> Strange is our situation here on earth. Each of us comes for a short visit, not knowing why, yet sometimes seeming to a divine purpose. (Albert Einstein)

Can we apply the seven principles mentioned above when selecting students who wish to enter our program? If we can, how do we enact them through our selection processes? When selecting, what do we assess—a potential to learn, motivation, prior knowledge, skills, values, attitudes ... ?

These are the questions that often get debated in academic departments. Attitudes range from a view that everyone should be given the opportunity to study to a carefully developed processes of selection to retain only 'fit and proper' students. Social work training has been a magnet for people who have been abused or marginalised in their life (Black, Jefferies & Hatley, 1993; Barter, 1997; Hanna, 2008). Assessing when the trauma experienced will contribute to effectiveness in practice or when it will hinder professional reliability is challenging and puts social work educators in a position of being gatekeepers for the profession. In an environment when education is often perceived as a business and when the income needed from student fees is essential for financial sustainability of the program, the process of selection may become guided by different values and principles than providing a competent contingent of social work graduates.

Regardless of the political and financial context within which we operate, some of the key characteristics necessary for students to succeed in becoming effective social workers are: literacy, ability to learn, motivation to become a social worker, ability to listen, hear and follow simple instructions, ability to cooperate, critically reflect and be flexible, ability to act locally and see a bigger picture and resilience. Devising ethical and accurate processes to test if these characteristics are present in our applicants before enrolment becomes essential for effective selection in social work programs. A process that worked well for us at Unitec was as follows:

- having a paper selection first when students submit their application with a brief outline of their motivation to study.

Providing all requirements for studying at a tertiary level are satisfied, students are invited for a selection day where they are put in groups and invited to participate in a range of activities. These activities are usually some variation of the following:

- a short essay written on the spot, usually related to Te Tiriti O Waitangi (a founding document for New Zealand) and biculturalism
- a group activity which tests for prejudices and explores values and ability to cooperate as students need to reach a consensus about an ethical issue in small groups
- drawing a timeline which allows prospective students to briefly reflect on their life up to the day of their enrolment to our program
- a group activity which tests for the ability to listen and introduce their fellow applicant respectfully followed by sharing a situation when they demonstrated resilience.

These group activities are accompanied by individual brief interviews with two culturally different staff members. All these processes are collaborative and involving, meaning that students have a chance to interview staff as well. Former and present students are available to talk about the program with prospective students and answer questions they might have.

A quality of the selection process is closely related to retention and quality of our graduates. I strongly advocate the position that either we need to have a thorough selection process or an open entry with very rigorous assessment in the first year. Social workers deal with the most vulnerable people in our society and one incompetent social worker is one too many.

The selection process described above is guided by principles set out earlier:

- partnership—through reflection on Te Tiriti O Waitangi, dialogue with students, sharing how we work and by giving students a taste of activities they will be engaged in during their studies
- collaboration—through group activities where students need to demonstrate the ability to work together
- mutual respect—through respectfully introducing one another and exploring values in context through a metaphorical story
- reverence for all life—through sharing stories of resilience
- inspiration—through sharing their motivation and interest for social work and at the same time staff members presenting their interests and passion for the profession
- purpose—through drawing a time line and seeing what brings them to social work and how it fits with their past experiences and future aspirations
- joy in lifelong learning—through relaxed and friendly atmosphere where students (current, past and future) and staff exchange ideas about lifelong learning as most of our applicants are mature students with a wealth of life experiences

Although, the process is carefully planned and organised, to prospective students it appears to be lighthearted and quite enjoyable. Students generally complete a selection day feeling engaged, informed and enthused about the journey they are embarking on. Through group interactions with students, all staff have a chance to see all students in various situations and that gives them a larger picture of their values, skills and abilities to become competent social workers. All staff simply assess each student as a 'yes', 'no' or 'maybe', and only the ones who receive 'no' or 'maybe' get discussed. We aim for a consensus in finalising our decision for accepting students to the course.

The first year—developing respectful and collaborative partnerships

> No one wants advice, only collaboration. (John Steinback)

In its essence, social work is based on collaboration. Practicing collaboration while studying will increase students' ability to form collaborative and respectful partnerships with their clients. Social work clients, especially the ones who have spent a lot of time interacting with social workers hold a lot of practical wisdom in the sense of 'managing' or 'coping with' social workers as well as the insider's knowledge of their situation and their strengths and abilities. In a climate where social workers are perceived either as 'rottweillers' taking away people's children or 'do gooders' who preserve the status quo, the notion of collaborative practice becomes essential.

This is closely related to principles of human rights and dignity as well as the principle of social justice as outlined in Aotearoa New Zealand Association of Social Workers Code of Ethics (2008). True and equal partnership presumes self-determination, responsibility for one's actions, belief in people's resilience and strengths (Saleeby, 1997) and the ability to make choices even in environments where choices are very limited (Glasser, 1999). Respect presupposes trust but not blind faith; it includes a co-creative process in relating to other people where both participants engage in a dialogue with interest and curiosity, with the aim to improve the quality of life. Meaning that, when a social worker and a client discover a better way of managing life or when a teacher or a student make new links between their theory and practice, both of their lives get transformed. This is true partnership. We meet and through a trusting dialogue, we co-create a new reality abundant with new possibilities. Preferably, clients and students will experience more of these moments than social workers and teachers, however, if we believe in the idea of lifelong learning—this is exactly where and how bringing forth the world becomes reality.

For academics, this means the development of an art of teaching in a way that the body of knowledge gets enriched during this process—and not diminished or distorted. For a social worker, this means figuring out a new way of reaching a client while developing empowering contexts. A co-creative dialogue is the process that facilitates this. I use a lot of dialogical teaching, even in large classes of 70 or more, even when that may mean initially talking with 10% of the class and most of the other students listening. Eventually almost all come on board and release their inhibitions when they feel respected and appreciated. I learn their names (and expect from them to know how to pronounce mine), I show interest in them, I make a conscious intention to see their strengths and abilities, especially when these are not very visible.

I also challenge my students to bring out the best in them, hoping that this will make it easier for them to challenge me when needed, bearing in mind all cultural and contextual issues that may prevent them from doing so. I tend to live the idea of us being collaborators in the process of learning social work and pussyfooting around each other, pretending by being nice but not honest will not help us get there. My aim is to role model cooperation and partnership hoping that my students will be able to transfer and build on these principles in their social work practice, homes and communities.

PRACTICAL TEACHING TOOLS USED TO ENGENDER COLLABORATION

- learning contracts (Knowles, Holton & Swanson, 1998; Anderson, 1996)
- students choosing the format of their assignments—to reflect their learning style, culture, utilisation of prior knowledge and existing wisdom in the classroom and ensuring that learning outcomes get covered or expanded
- focus on special abilities, strengths and prior knowledge
- encouraging students to do group assignments, rewarding collaboration
- teaching collaboratively
- encouraging low contributors to participate and supporting high contributors to develop listening skills and reflection

- encouraging or requiring peer-reflection
- encouraging dialogue and agreeing to disagree
- developing respectful curiosity in difference and uniqueness.

The notion of biculturalism is so essential for New Zealand, relevant for all countries and closely linked to the principle of partnership. In my context, it manifests through:

- acknowledging Maori as Tangata Whenua (people of the land) of this country
- practising respect within a bi-cultural political context
- learning about humbleness and appreciation of unity in diversity
- developing a respectful curiosity for indigenous knowledge
- development of confidence in cultural identities by knowing and understanding influences of origins and family backgrounds.

Respect and appreciation of client's resilience and knowledge is a prerequisite for true collaboration in situations of unequal positional power. Learning and experiencing the effectiveness of indigenous models helps students develop respect and interest in practices outside of their comfort zone.

Practical teaching tools used to accomplish the principle of bicultural partnership

- employing competent Maori practitioners to be inspiring role models for our students and to share their knowledge and experience
- inviting exciting Maori guest speakers, encouraging students to submit assignments in Te Reo (Maori language)
- exploring Maori practices in class with students, encouraging Maori students to participate
- organising Noho Marae where students stay for three to four days on a Marae to learn Maori protocol and experience collectively cultural practices

- comparing and contrasting Maori practices to other indigenous models of practice as well as western concepts and effects they may have on clients, their families and communities
- promoting inquiry learning through development of genuine curiosity in various ways of perceiving reality
- exploring belief systems and how they shape practices and modelling by teaching in partnership with Maori lecturers.

The first year is essential for students to discover if they really want to become social workers. The more we as a faculty invest in them in this first year, the easier will be for them to continue their studies with integrity and motivation. Unfortunately, the first year happens in the largest classes, creates most stress on students' families and students are often unaware of supports available on campus or too busy organising their changed lives to use them effectively. The major task for educators is to perceive abilities and potential in first year students, encourage them to experiment and explore a number of areas of practice (theoretically and practically) and to create a context with clear and transparent boundaries where students can grow safely and confidently. The balance of challenge and support is essential and it is a way of showing respect.

Social work practice and social work education are permeated with issues of social control. Clarity and transparency are essential when we do not want clear boundaries to be experienced as tools of social control. Explaining the purpose for rules and regulations within a program as well as linking them with issues related to social work practice make this learning relevant, meaningful and contextualised. In this context, every conflict or disagreement becomes a welcomed learning opportunity. Social work principles can guide social work teachers when faced with challenging situations in the classroom.

MIDDLE YEARS—HEART OF THE PROGRAM

> Kaua e whakaarohia te mahinga engari te otinga. (Think not on the labour, rather reflect on the completion) (Maori proverb)

> During its history, social work has developed a dual focus. Firstly, to enable and empower individual families, groups and communities to find their own solutions to the issues and problems that beset them. Secondly to learn from specific instances of need, to inform society at large about the injustices in its midst, and to engage in action to change the structures of society that create and perpetuate injustice. (ANZASW Code of Ethics, 2008, p. 4)

Socially just social workers do not serve merely as tools of social control. For the effective pursuit of social justice, one has to have a sense of purpose in their work and to consider the impact they have on their clients, their families and communities. This sense develops through the ability to critically reflect on wider contexts where an individual social worker aims to practice and by exploring what attracts them to that particular area of practice. Ageless questions like:

- Who am I?
- Where I am coming from?
- Where am I going?
- How can I contribute?

address issues of purpose.

Reverence for life (Clark, 2008; Manton, 1955) is the core of all professions that attempt to bring forth the world. Reverence relates to respect with love and as such, it embeds love as a life force. Love transcends justice as Barnes (1994) noted, hence it includes justice and to do so it has to satisfy justice. Social justice without love lacks awareness of importance of the relationships and love without the sense of social justice can justify cruelty or become sentimental. Both love and justice need wisdom and reverence for their application in social work practice. Dialogues about issues related to love and justice become essential for the development of effective social workers. As beliefs shape actions, attention to students' beliefs through reflexive exercises will crystallise their intentions and therefore make them more accountable for their actions.

Recruiting exceptional fieldwork co-ordinators and fieldwork supervisors significantly influences the quality of learning. Unfortunately, they are a rare find. Fieldwork coordination is too often seen as a 'poor little sister' of academic teaching and this is reflected in the separation of that role from the academic teaching, less qualifications required for the role and minimal acknowledgment of practitioners who are field work supervisors and often volunteer their time to educate our students. The job of placing students becomes a difficult task and because of that, less than appropriate placements are accepted which often results in students' dissatisfaction due to the impossibility of achieving numerous learning outcomes that need to be covered in a placement portfolio.

At this stage, students begin to integrate their values, beliefs, personal experience and prior knowledge with information and skills gained during studies (Freeman & Dobbins, 2013). Critical thinking is developing and prejudicial values and beliefs are challenged. Peer support and time for reflection and discussion become essential during this early formation of a professional identity. Experiential learning, inquiry learning and whole people learning methods (Bolton, 2010; Heron, 1996; Kolb, 1984) promote inquisitive, exploratory, empowering and appreciative ways of being that attend to students in the totality of their experience and the context they are immersed in. These methods tend to integrate personal, professional and political elements as well as theory, practice and personal experience and require skillful facilitation.

Practical teaching tools used to engender purpose, reverence, inspiration, joy in lifelong learning, awareness of social justice and development of skills, values, beliefs and knowledge necessary for effective social working

- dialogues with students on current topics
- debating issues of concern
- practising justice focused teaching and learning and developing clear boundaries and rules of engagement

- developing learning contexts where mistakes are welcomed as learning opportunities
- elimination of fear from judgement
- required readings and critical reflection
- providing time and space for students to explore personal issues that may enhance or hinder their future practice
- reflective journals
- encouraging inquiry learning
- field trips to various seminars, festivals and community events
- role plays and skills training
- students working with one another on issues of concern
- exploration of ethical issues and critical debates in social work
- court visits
- time for deep reflection and critical analysis
- creative assignments using various methods to cover common learning outcomes
- assessments having a strong learning component and related to social work practice
- exploration of how beliefs shape professional practice
- personalised learning contracts
- self and peer reflection.

This is not a definitive list, it is here just as an inspiration to engender and initiate a range of alternative methods to keep this part of education relevant, exciting and alive.

THE FINAL YEAR—INTEGRATION—SOCIAL JUSTICE AND EMPOWERMENT IN ACTION

> Never doubt that a small group of thoughtful, committed citizens can change the world. Indeed, it is the only thing that ever has. (Margaret Mead)

The final year of the program consolidates knowledge, skills, values and attitudes and it shapes the professional identity of a budding social worker. Longer fieldwork placement in the final year usually secures jobs for many of our graduates, but also makes some of them aware of the fields of practice they do not want to engage with when they graduate.

Reflection on theories learnt and skills gained during the course becomes a platform for examination of values and beliefs, which will guide their practice. Inquiry learning (Heron,1996a; Napan, 2009) becomes more and more relevant. Students become more self-directed and focused on areas of their interest. Some become aware of how little they know and how vast is the area of practice they are embarking on. Comparing and contrasting various theories, models and principles as well as finding one's favourite theories or orientations characterise this stage while competent students report most joy in learning. Allowing time for self-reflection provides space to revisit some life decisions and the last year is crucial for the development of purpose for students' future direction. This sense of purpose will keep them grounded when realities around them are fragmented, it will enhance their creativity when clients appear to be stuck and will give them a sense of contributing meaningfully in a world which through a social worker's practice may not look very bright.

The Just Practice paper within a Bachelor of Social Practice program at Unitec was developed to invite and inspire the graduating class to incorporate social justice concerns into their social practice. They were invited to define their social justice intentions, purposes, aims and contexts for their practices in light of the retrospective accounts of those who have gone before them and have been acknowledged for their own 'just practice'. This was made possible by providing opportunities to bring the graduating class into close acquaintanceship with the 'lore' of just practitioners (Epston, Rennie, Napan, 2008). This course invites students, after being inspired by individual visits by just practitioners (many of whom are at the end of their careers), to co-create in small groups a virtual just practice agency that would operate according to particular group's idea of what social justice entails. The focus on creativity and possible or seemingly impossible ventures enables students to envisage and develop a focus for their future just practice.

During the last year of their studies at Unitec students undertake a group research project (Bridgman, 2008) where they inquire and apply a methodology of their choice to the topic of their interest. It is a bona fide research project, which needs to be approved by the Unitec ethics committee and gets presented to the class. In this final year, principles of collaboration, partnership, mutual respect, and reverence for all life, inspiration, purpose and joy in lifelong learning are put to the test. Working in groups under stress with deadlines and family obligations forces students to develop exceptional organising skills and good time management, so relevant for their future practice.

Another example of utilising these principles in teaching was in an elective paper called Creative Social Practice that was conducted as an Academic Co-creative Inquiry in 2008. This meant that students and myself, as a teacher, co-created the course structure, processes, content and the assessment process. Learning outcomes proposed by the course outline were personalised and modified in the light of students' interests and learning needs. Students agreed to do a presentation and a written assignment as a way of covering learning outcomes. To my surprise, students insisted for their written work to be assessed by me and not do written self and peer reflection, however as most of them produced a high quality assignments, it was obvious that a lot of self-reflection happened before submitting. They also wanted their presentations to be peer assessed, but only verbally just after presenting, and agreed that peers' feedback contributes to their final mark, but the actual grade should be assigned by me. They refused to give marks to one another saying that assigning marks destroys relationships. On the other hand, receiving a mark from me was seen as manageable as it was my job to do that. This collaborative venture unleashed students' creativity and sense of ownership of the course. Some brought in some exciting guest speakers, some elaborated on interesting integrations of their hobbies, interests and passions into their social work practice. Some produced individual assignments, some formed groups and worked collaboratively. All marking criteria were mutually agreed on and learning outcomes proposed by the course outline were covered. Most emphasised a sense of privilege while being able to dialogue about advanced, creative practices and being grateful for space provided for reflection and development of focus for application of their creative ideas.

The main challenge of collaborative work is the assessment of group assignments and ways of forming student groups. Within a Bachelor of Social Practice at Unitec, in some courses groups are self-selected, in some lecturers pre-organise them. The purpose of engaging students in doing group assignments is that when students are involved in tasks that cannot be attempted alone multiple skills are brought to bear on problems and conflicting views are aired and considered (Strauss & U, 2007; Gatfield, 1999; Young & Henquinet, 2000). Group assignments are also useful for developing skills for employability (Strauss & U, 2007). Skilful management of collaborative assessment is essential. When groups are teacher selected with no allowance for student initiated modification a rationale for this needs to be clearly explained at the beginning. For example, in the Just Practice course, students are purposefully put in groups that intentionally encompass students who major in different strands of the program (Social work, Community Development and Counselling). The groups reflect cultural, age and gender diversity and students cannot negotiate group membership as this would negate the purpose of learning how to work interdisciplinarily and with people with different backgrounds to their own. When this is explained to them, accompanied with the idea that this is a learning opportunity, they accept it and reflect on challenges they faced during the process in their assignments and take them as opportunities for learning.

Practical teaching tools used to engender smooth transition to social work practice and development of a professional identity

I find peer and self reflections extremely useful in teaching as a measure of performance and as a learning experience. These methods also allow students to explore areas of practice they feel attracted to, dare to get engaged in practices that are outside of their comfort zone, enhance their learning experience and build on their strengths. Furthermore, they mirror performance review processes in most social work agencies.

During that process, providing a space and time for exploration of beliefs and attitudes that will guide their professional practice, as well as increasing understanding of political contexts that will influence it, becomes essential as students progress through the degree. As this form of advanced teaching is personalised, small trusting groups are more suitable, however, even in large groups quite a lot of interaction and deep learning is possible (Andrade & Valtcheva, 2009). Advanced and specific questions arise at this stage and conducting teaching in an inquiry mode benefits the development of curious and competent scholars and practitioners.

As much as online components of various courses contribute to the fruitful dialogue, a balance of face-to-face and online contributions needs to be attended to for a simple reason that most social work practice is still done face-to-face.

The integration of theory and practice and the transition from study to work can be facilitated by:

- linking assignments for theoretical courses to practical social work
- involving practitioners in teaching and assessment
- using stories from practice and inviting practitioners and clients to talk about their experiences
- encouraging inquiry learning
- creative assignments by student choice focusing on the field of practice where their interests lie

- supporting students to transcend artificial divisions between theory and practice
- presenting social work theories in a very practical manner
- continuously theorising and reflecting on practice.

I have been experimenting with alternative, creative assignments for years. Students choose what kind of assignment they want to submit and outline in their learning contracts how are they going to cover the required learning outcomes. They are encouraged to think outside of the square and many use various art forms of expression. This is often accompanied with peer and self reflections that are well structured, in a written form and focussed on coverage of learning outcomes. The amount of time students put into these assignments is considerable as well as their feedback on how much they have learned while painting, making a movie, song, poem or performance while still focusing on learning outcomes related to social work.

However, the process of self and peer reflection is a challenging one. Students can do it for real and benefit from it by learning how to give a critical feedback respectfully that will prepare them for their future practice, but they can also choose to fake it—just to satisfy course requirements. We live in an environment where honest feedback can hurt, where external evaluation is perceived as more 'objective' than self-reflection. Exposing students to self and peer reflection, even though they may do it just to satisfy course requirements and not be open to receive it or honest while giving it still creates a context where reflection is encouraged and the myth of perfection deconstructed.

This is beautifully outlined in this Bachelor of Social Practice graduate's quote:

> I clearly remember my first paper and how I did not like one member of our group as she would not let me or the two other members have a say, so being the idiot I was I let it go and just backed off, but swore to myself I would never work with her again. Now two years down the track and with a lot more confidence in my own abilities I have no problems with group work, because as a group we delegate

> responsibilities and everyone does their bit and if they don't, myself and other members of the group do not hesitate to speak out. Not in a nasty way but we all make it clear that we must work equally or we will do something about it. I have never had a repeat of the problem I had in my first paper in January 2005. (Unitec BSocP Graduate, 2008)

Instead of conclusion—reflection

> By three methods we may learn wisdom: First, by reflection, which is noblest: second by imitation, which is easiest; and third by experience, which is the bitterest. (Confucius)

The main purpose of this chapter was to inspire the reader to experiment with creative methods of teaching and learning social work, explore the possible ways of integrating social work principles and values in teaching and making almost every experience a learning experience. Challenges of group, self and peer reflection have been explored and their relevance for social work practice considered. Principles of partnership, collaboration, mutual respect, and reverence for all life, inspiration, purpose and joy in lifelong learning can easily provide a meaningful context for all learning outcomes that need to be covered in a range of social work courses. Time for reflection and dialogue as well as time for experimenting with new ideas encourages development of lifelong learners and politically aware social workers who are able to see globally and act locally with integrity and competence.

All these principles are interrelated and the presence of one is embedded in others. Learning in social work never stops and practitioners either go towards specialisation in one area of practice or towards transdisciplinarity by expanding their horizons and by making meaningful links and connections with other professional areas while still staying accountable to their primary discipline.

I believe that the future of social work education is in 'high touch-high tech', integrative, whole people learning where personal, professional and political aspects are addressed. I believe that social work education needs to be informed by social work practice, the latest findings in educational research and guided by social work values and principles. It also needs to be contextualised and continuously improved according to the feedback from all stakeholders including practitioners, clients, students and researchers. Walking the talk in social work education by practising what we teach appears to be a relevant way of engaging students and creating meaningful links between personal, professional and political realities.

References

Andrade, H. & Valtcheva, A. (2009). Promoting learning and achievement through self assessment. *Theory into Practice*, 48(1), 12–19.

Aotearoa New Zealand Association of Social Workers (2008). Code of ethics. Christchurch: ANZASW National Office.

Anderson, G. (1996). *Learning contracts: a practical guide.* Sterling: Stylus Publishing, Inc.

Barnes, G. (1994). *Justice, love and wisdom—linking psychotherapy to second-order cybernetics.* Zagreb: Medicinska Naklada.

Barter, S. (1997). Social work students with personal experience of sexual abuse: implications for diploma in social work program providers. *Social Work Education*, 16(2), 113–32.

Black, P., Jefferies, D. & Hatley K. (1993). Personal history of psycho social trauma in the early life of social work and business students, *Social Work Education*, 29(2), 171–80.

Bridgman, G. (2008). Presentation to undergraduate board of studies meeting. Auckland, New Zealand: Unitec.

Bolton, G. (2010). *Reflective practice: writing and professional development*, 3rd edn. London: Sage.

Clark, G. (2008). *The man who tapped the secrets of the universe.* Minneapolis: Filiquarian Publishing LLC.

Epston, D., Rennie, G. & Napan, K. (2008). On becoming a just practictioner: experimenting with the final paper of an undergraduate program as a rite of passage. In Epston, D. (Ed.).

Down under and up over—travels with narrative therapy (pp. 81–95). Warrington: AFT Publishing.

Freeman, R. & Dobbins, K. (2013). Are we serious about enhancing courses? Using the principles of assessment for learning to enhance course evaluation, *Higher Education*, 38(2), 142–51.

Gatfield, T. (1999). Examining student satisfaction with group projects and peer-assessment. *Assessment & Evaluation in Higher Education*, 24(2), 365–77.

Glasser, W. (1999). *Choice theory: a new psychology of personal freedom*. London: Harper-Perennial.

Hanna, S. (2008). Not so strange—an application of attachment theory and feminist psychology to social work supervision. *Aotearoa New Zealand Social Work Review*, 9(3), 12–22.

Heron, J (1996). Helping whole people learn. In Boud, D. & Miller, N. (Eds). *Working with experience: animating learning* (pp. 75–95). New York: Routledge.

Heron, J. (1996a). *Co-operative inquiry: research into the human condition*. London: Sage.

Knowles, M. S., Holton, E. F. & Swanson, R. A. (1998). *The adult learner: the definitive classic in adult education and human resource development*. Waltham: Butterworth-Heinemann.

Kolb, D. A. (1984). *Experiential learning: experience as the source of learning and development*. New Jersey: Prentice Hall.

Napan, K. (1995). Experiential learning: what is a contact-challenge method? *Skolske Novine,* 24(2), 17–24.

Napan, K. (1997). The contact-challenge method: in search of effective teaching and learning social work practice. *Aotearoa New Zealand Social Work Review,* 9(1/2), 43–7.

Napan, K. (2009). Academic co-creative inquiry: creating inclusive processes for learning, refereed proceedings from educational integrity conference, University of Wollongong, 28–30/9/2009. Retrieved 17 April 2013 from ro.uow.edu.au/apcei/09/papers/24.

Saleeby, D. (1997). *The strengths perspective in social work practice*, 2nd edn. New York: Longman.

Strauss, P. & U, A. (2007). Group assessments: dilemmas facing lecturers in multicultural tertiary classrooms. *Higher Education Research and Development*, 26(2), 147–61.

Manton, J. (1955). *The Story of Albert Schweitzer*. London: Methuen & Co.

Urbanc, K. (2003). The importance of field-instruction for the development of social workers' professional identity. *Ljetopis Studijskog Centra Socijalnog Rada, University of Zagreb*, 10(1), 61–9.

Young, C.B. & Henquinet J.A. (2000). A conceptual framework for designing group projects. *Journal of Education for Business*, 76(1), 56–60.

13

Reciprocity and cultural diversity: creating successful field education placements

Louise Coventry and Marty Grace

In the Asia Pacific region, social work student placements often involve students whose cultural understandings differ from those of the agencies that can offer them placements. This chapter discusses the work of a facilitative supervisor who built learning opportunities for culturally diverse students within an Australian mainstream non government organisation. Between 2004 and 2007, ten students from culturally diverse backgrounds and varying disciplines were offered placements with a research trial that aimed to challenge dominant forms of social work and welfare practice. The facilitative approach of the supervisor and a positive orientation to learning supported a mutually fulfilling, reciprocal partnership for students, supervisor and the host agency alike. We draw on the supervisor's experiences and student evaluation materials to illustrate and discuss how this reciprocity was achieved. We conclude by discussing the implications of this experience for social work educators in the Asia Pacific region.

互利互惠和文化差異：創造成功的實習教育

在亞太地區，社會工作專業實習生對文化的理解和他們所在的實習單位經常有所差異。本篇討論了澳大利亞主流非政府組織中的社會工作督導如何在工作中為來自不同文化背景的學生創造學習機會。二零零四年至二零零七年間，十名文化和學科背景不同的學生參與了一項在實習單位進行的研究試驗，旨在挑戰社會工作和救助實踐的主流做法。順利開展督導制、主動學習的做法為學生、督導還有提供實習的機構創造相互學習，雙贏互利的關係。筆者借鑒督導者的經驗和學生們的評價材料，展現和討論實踐過程中如何達到互利互惠的目標。文章最后讨论并总结以上經驗對於亞太地區的社會工作教育者的啟示。

互恵と文化的な多様性: 成功した教育研修現場を作る事

アジア太平洋地域のソーシャルワークの研修現場では、たびたび学生側と機関側の文化の理解が異なる。この章では、オーストラリアの主流にある非政府組織(NGO)において、学習の機会を文化の異なる学生に対して築いた、あるスーパーバイザーの促進的な働きについて検討する。2004年から2007年の間に、文化背景や学問分野の違う10人の学生が主要な形のソーシャルワークと福祉実践に挑戦するという、試行研究の目的を兼ねた研修の実践を行った。スーパーバイザーの促進的な手法と学習への明確なオリエンテーションにより、学生、スーパーバイザー、主催側の機関が相互に満足できる互恵的な協力が実現した。スーパーバイザーの経験と学生の評価資料を元にどのようにして互恵的な協力が実現できたかを明らかにする。アジア太平洋地域におけるソーシャルワークの教育関係者がこの経験を生かせる方法を推論し、締めくくる。

상호작용과 문화적 다양성 : 성공적인 현장교육 장소 개발

아태지역 내 사회복지 전공 학생은 본인의 문화와 실습기관의 문화가 다른 경우가 있다. 이 장은 호주의 주요 NGO실습기관에서 학생이 다문화를 배우도록 유도하는 수퍼바이저 업무에 대해 논한다. 2004년부터 2007년까지 3년간 실습교육에 대한 리서치를 목적으로 문화배경이 다른 학생 10명을 실습기관에 배치하였고, 수퍼바이저의 지지적 접근, 문화에 대한 긍정적 오리엔테이션, 당사자들의 호환적인 파트너쉽이 주요하게 부각되었다. 당사자란, 학생, 수퍼바이저, 기관을 포함한다. 호환적 파트너쉽을 위해 수퍼바이저의 경험과 학생평가 내용이 제시되어 있으며 아태지역에서 사회복지 교육자들의 응용가능성을 제안하였다.

Introduction

Field education occupies a central place in social work education, and field education placements have recently been identified as the 'signature pedagogy' of social work (Wayne, Bogo & Raskin, 2010; Lyter, 2012). The success and quality of field education placements is a priority for students, supervisors, social work educators, and the profession itself. However, contemporary changes in educational institutions, host organisations, and the student body complicate the placement experience (Wayne, Bogo & Raskin, 2006; Reisch & Jarman-Rohde, 2000). This chapter focuses in particular on cultural diversity in field placements—situations where the supervisor and the student may be from different cultural backgrounds, and both of these backgrounds may be different from the dominant culture of the host organisation.

This chapter draws on student evaluations and supervisor reflections to illustrate how an intentional orientation towards reciprocal learning can enrich field education placements and add to the creative capacity of organisations. We discuss the learning experiences available to students, field supervisors and the host organisation and we consider what contributes to placement success including the role of supervision, the cultural imperatives of a critical practice context that rewards and values challenges to mainstream practices, a work environment that is open and inclusive, and the key skills and personal qualities of both field supervisor and student. The implications for social work educators in the Asia-Pacific region are then discussed.

Review of literature

In this section, we discuss the key terms used in this chapter: field education, facilitative supervision, collaboration, and reciprocity, as well as diversity and in particular cultural diversity.

Experiential learning has been an integral part of social work education since the founding of the first professional school of social work more than 100 years ago (Hollis & Taylor, 1951, cited in Munson

2002). Field education can be understood as learning by doing. It involves the application, under supervision, of new skills and theory in a practice setting. Australian student social workers usually undertake two field education placements, totalling 1,000 hours. While many students have previous experiences in the workplace, students nonetheless tend to have formative experiences in their field education placements (O'Donoghue, 2012). Accordingly, effective engagement with issues of cultural diversity within field education placements will most likely contribute to producing increasingly culturally competent social workers. Similarly, positive experiences of co-creating mutual learning opportunities through supervision is likely to contribute to producing social workers more confident of co-creating learning experiences with others.

The provision of supervision is central to the success and quality of field placements and an important site for the exchange of skills and knowledge (Raskin, Wayne & Bogo 2008). Kadushin's decades of work on understanding supervision has been very influential in the field of social work; he identifies three aspects of supervision: education, support and administration (Kadushin & Harkness, 2002). However, Smith (2005) notes that one of the limitations of Kadushin's model is that it assumes a deficit in the supervisee and hence does not facilitate a reciprocal approach to learning. Hair and O'Donoghue (2009) further critique Kadushin's and other influential models of supervision, highlighting the modernist assumptions underpinning these models and offering an alternative model based on social constructionism. Their approach recognises that we interpret the 'reality' of our experiences through personal, historical, cultural and social lenses, that the usefulness of a perspective is ultimately determined by those who may use it in a particular situation at a particular time, and that power differences, ever-present in all practices and relationships, enable some perspectives to be heard and others not (O'Donoghue, 2010). Hair and O'Donoghue (2009) contend that supervision should recognise the plurality and diversity of knowledge, emphasise collaboration, acknowledge that supervisees have agency in a co-constructive process, demonstrate increased sensitivity to power and the politics of empowerment and disempowerment in supervision, and explicitly recognise the influence of the social and cultural context within which supervision is immersed (p. 77).

Powell's (1993) model of supervision, influential in the field of nursing (Sloan & Watson, 2002), seems somewhat similar to Kadushin's. It includes four components: administrative, evaluative, clinical and supportive supervision. Importantly, however, Powell conceptualises the supervisor as a 'servant leader' who is self aware, proficient at the tasks at hand, operates with focus and energy, shares power, and values people by caring for them. The servant-leader-supervisor makes the organisation's mission and vision clear by, in effect, standing ahead of followers and standing behind their actions. The assumptions embedded in Powell's model include the notion that change is constant and inevitable, there are many correct ways to view the world, and the key to growth is to blend insight and behavioural change in the right amounts at the appropriate time, thus giving greater emphasis than Kadushin to the student/supervisee as co-constructor of the supervisory experience.

Other approaches that emphasise co-construction rather than the supervisor's authority use terms such as facilitation, collaboration, and partnership. Heron's (1989) model of supervision separates authoritative supervision (which is defined as prescriptive, informative and confronting) from facilitative supervision (exemplified by cathartic, catalytic and supportive interactions). Taking this idea further, supervision as collaboration and as a learning-centred partnership is the theme of more recent work on supervision, for example, that of Austin and Hopkins (2004) and Noble and Irwin (2009) and Davys and Beddoe (2010). Conceptualising supervision as collaboration and partnership seems an important distinction for the 21st century. Encouraging scrutiny of the empirical evidence base informing field education, Raskin, Wayne and Bogo (2008) note that the value of models of partnership and collaboration has already been proven. Barton, Bell and Bowles (2005) posit that the ideal relationship between student and supervisor is collaborative, non-hierarchical, and accepts difference (p. 104). If the collaborative aspects of the supervisory relationship are not acknowledged, undue emphasis is placed on the skills and personal qualities of the supervisor.

We suggest that notions of reciprocity and diversity are important to contemporary understandings of field education. The ethic of reciprocity is a fundamental moral value which requires us to treat others as we wish to be treated. The ethic appears in various guises in most philosophies and religions world-wide, including Christianity, Islam, Judaism, Hinduism and Buddhism. With roots in a wide range of religions and world cultures, it is well suited as a principle for the provision of supervision in multicultural practice settings. The idea of reciprocity facilitates a conceptual shift away from traditional, modernist educational models in which 'experts' didactically impart their hard-won skills to dutiful learners and instead invokes the notion of sharing and learning together, consistent with a constructionist view of supervision (O'Donoghue, 2003; 2010).

Reciprocal learning is facilitated when both the student and the supervisor adopt a stance of openness in relation to learning. Thus, field placement success is influenced by the willingness of both student and supervisor to bring many aspects of the personal and professional self into focus when learning. Maidment's (2003) research on problems encountered by students undertaking field placements noted that preparation for placement could usefully focus more on the process of learning and how to manage stress and less on what students might actually do while on placement. The idea of supervision as a collaborative, learning-centred partnership brings attention to the importance of both parties adopting a learning orientation, highlighting the reciprocal potential of effective field placements.

Tsui (2005) laments the lack of literature and research regarding the relationship between diversity and social work supervision. However, strategies for enhancing the cultural competence of social work practitioners and educators including field supervisors receive increasing attention in the literature. O'Donoghue and Tsui (2012) explain that cultural competence in social work supervision is a key consideration for the social work profession in New Zealand. Hair and O'Donoghue's (2009) article advances the conceptualisation of supervision relationships that can successfully encourage cultural relevance, although how this conceptualisation applies to supervision of students is left implicit.

Hair and O'Donoghue (2009) explain how a social constructionist approach can liberate supervisors from the tyranny of trying to achieve some preconceived notion of culture and cultural competence. Instead, understanding knowledge as constructed facilitates conversations within the supervisory relationship about the interweaving of various identities that shape culture. This approach is consistent with that advocated in the Universal Declaration on Cultural Diversity which states that 'each individual must acknowledge not only otherness in all its forms but also the plurality of his or her own identity, within societies that are themselves plural. Only in this way can cultural diversity be preserved as an adaptive process and as a capacity for expression, creation and innovation' (Matsuura, 2002, p. 11). The action plan outlined in the Declaration (UNESCO, 2002) supports a range of objectives including 'promoting through education an awareness of the positive value of cultural diversity and improving to this end both curriculum design and teacher education' (Objective 7) and 'incorporating, where appropriate, traditional pedagogies into the education process with a view to preserving and making full use of culturally appropriate methods of communication and transmission of knowledge' (Objective 8).

This brief review of the literature shows that contemporary approaches understand field education not as a top-down process but rather as a mutually beneficial, horizontal and collaborative process. The idea of reciprocal learning is a useful way of understanding field education and the supervisory arrangements that accompany it. The following sections take up these ideas in relation to situations involving cultural diversity, drawing on the authors' experiences and student evaluation materials to illustrate and discuss how this reciprocity was achieved in one placement setting. We conclude by discussing the implications of these experiences for social work educators in the Asia Pacific region.

Supervisor and students' reflections

Between 2004 and 2007, ten students from culturally diverse backgrounds and varying disciplines were offered placements with a research trial that aimed to challenge dominant forms of social work and welfare practice. In this chapter, we draw on the documented reflections of the supervisor (Louise Coventry) and the students (with permission). The supervisor's reflections have been tested against the views and experiences of social work educators across different universities in Victoria through personal conversation and further tested with senior staff responsible for human resource management within the host organisation. We draw on student evaluation documents where appropriate to illustrate key points. Excerpts from student evaluation reports have not been edited unless otherwise indicated, but care has been taken to avoid identifying individual students. Eight of the ten students to whom this chapter refers were able to be contacted and provided with an early copy of the chapter. Feedback provided by the students was incorporated into revised versions of the chapter. We are very grateful to all students for allowing us to report their experiences here.

About the students

Ten students were engaged in the research trial. Eight students completed a satisfactory placement. One student chose to terminate the placement before completion. Another student, who was writing an honours thesis using material generated by the research trial (without having done a placement with the organisation beforehand), chose to discontinue at an early stage.

Of the ten students, eight were studying social work, one at postgraduate level. One student was studying public policy and one was studying community development at a Technical and Further Education (TAFE) college. The students were drawn from four different universities and one TAFE college in the State of Victoria, Australia.

Seven students were female and three male. The cultural backgrounds of students were Anglo-Australian (four), Korean, Japanese, Ukrainian, Macedonian, Israeli and Nigerian. Two students spoke English as a second language; one carried an electronic dictionary in order that those using unfamiliar words could write them down for an instant translation. One student had a disability. Three were parents. The students ranged in age from approximately 20 to 40 years.

About the learning experiences for students

Here, we provide a broad overview of the learning opportunities made available to students through the research trial. The research trial primarily sought to understand how joined up governance and client centred case management makes a difference in the lives of multiply disadvantaged people. In doing this, a critical approach to mainstream practices of program design and administration was adopted. This approach, combined with a general openness to experimentation, informed the broader context of students' work. The explicit connection of theory and practice was paramount to each placement, as would be expected of most student placements.

In terms of tasks, considerable opportunities were available for students to learn about research and evaluation processes. Commonly, students undertook discrete research and evaluation projects tackling one aspect of the trial's broader agenda.

Students' conceptual and writing skills were extended during their placements. Project management skills were encouraged and developed—and some direct teaching of project management skills occurred with some students. (The supervisor's critique of contemporary social work education programs includes the view that project management skills are generally not adequately fostered.)

Most of the students' learning was, arguably, intensely personal as well as technical in nature. The supervisor initiated discussions about learning at the outset of each placement and disclosed her own learning preferences. She then worked with the students to explore their learning preferences. The supervisor pushed students to move beyond the rewording and recycling of examples borrowed from field placement manuals in articulating their learning goals and sought to draw out the deeper hopes, fears and concerns about their practice held by the students. Learning opportunities in the placement were then tailored to ensure that the students could, with support, confront and explore some of these hopes and fears.

ABOUT THE LEARNING EXPERIENCES FOR THE HOST ORGANISATION

The host organisation was exposed to considerable learning through the presence of students from diverse backgrounds. The host organisation operated in multiple sites but the research trial was based in the site where organisational management and administration tasks were performed, directly above the organisation's flagship crisis centre. At the time of the first few student placements, the organisation had a relatively homogenous staffing profile and this was especially so in the management and administration area. Traditionally, students were rarely engaged in centralised management and administrative tasks. Accordingly, there was a low visibility of students at this site and a sense among staff that student placements happened elsewhere and were not really relevant to them. The ongoing presence of students at this site over a three year period and their full involvement in staff events and activities was a new and enlightening experience for some long standing staff members.

The host organisation was in the midst of significant change and renewal during most of the three-year period when student visibility increased. One change introduced was the creation of a position expressly to manage the human resources of the organisation. The new human resource manager was supportive of student placements and provided encouragement to the supervisor. All senior staff, including the supervisor, participated in equal employment opportunity training during the same period.

The confluence of independent organisational change and the positive presence of diverse students together contributed to a stronger culture of organisational learning and development and supported a reinvigorated commitment to workplace diversity. This manifested in an increased cultural sensitivity on the part of the organisation and individual staff, increased awareness of inclusive human resource practices and an enthusiasm to continue to support the learning of diverse students. Illustrating the point, one staff member located on site, invited by a student to contribute to the student's evaluation report, wrote:

> She is always curious about the Australian way of doing things and offers frequent comparisons to Japanese culture which are interesting and helpful to understanding my own work practices and gaining insight into cross cultural workplace relationships and communication. (Organisation staff member)

About the learning experiences of the supervisor

The supervisor's personal learning was highly significant. Each of the students was able to offer a unique perspective on the work being undertaken. The nature of their questions prompted reflections on matters which, in many instances, had not previously been considered. Personal learning about other cultures was significant as students were able to explain the differences they saw between an Australian workplace and its culture and their customary ways of working. Finally, and perhaps most importantly, by being willing to speak with vulnerability and authenticity about their learning experiences and by bringing their whole selves into the work environment, the students helped the supervisor to have a very fulfilling experience of connecting with interesting people and learning more about the human condition.

Reflections

In the context of these diverse placements, reciprocity in learning and mutually fulfilling student placement experiences were achieved as a result of a combination of factors: the cultural imperatives of a critical practice context that rewards and values challenges to mainstream practices, a work environment that is open and inclusive, key skills and personal qualities on the part of both supervisor and student, and a conscious, shared orientation towards reciprocal learning.

Practice context

The research trial in which the students were engaged provided a critical environment for placements, along the lines recommended by Noble and Irwin (2009). The trial encouraged challenging questions, appropriate confrontations, and some reframing or even relearning of traditional skills, not just for students but for many other professional staff. The trial was conceptually challenging, positioning itself as part of a paradigm shift towards a new way of thinking about how welfare services could be delivered (Coventry, 2005).

This context promoted a high level of consciousness of action and lent itself to a critical application of theory and practice on the part of the student. To explain, the practice context facilitated acceptance of a plurality of perspectives and drew attention to the shared nature of the struggle to make sense of what was happening, which helped to democratise the supervision process. A state of informed not-knowing, and the creativity and openness to new ideas inherent in the practice context was instrumental in creating a welcoming space for students and the fresh ideas that they can bring. Similarly, students who may have felt 'all at sea' in the early days of a placement could be assisted to feel safe in this experience. In this way, the power distance between supervisor and student was reduced in one important way, and a language for discussing issues of power was readily accessible.

Work environment

For many years, other staff working in the same vicinity as those engaged in the (new) research trial had maintained a culture of celebration. Morning and afternoon teas, the cutting of cake, and other similar rituals were a regular, sometimes weekly occurrence, especially used to mark arrivals, departures and birthdays. These local rituals were extended to include students both as participants and, when warranted, as the guest of honour. This was important for ensuring that students felt included in the workplace. In this way, too, social exposure to other staff members often preceded professional exposure, such that students had an opportunity to make personal connections with staff that could then be drawn upon to sustain them in more challenging professional contacts with staff.

Skills and personal qualities of the supervisor

Cultural sensitivity is an important skill of a supervisor. There is no claim that the skills used were exemplary. On the contrary, the supervisor believes that she has much to learn in this regard. Having an openness to seeing that cultural differences may potentially influence attitudes and behaviours and being willing to articulate assumptions being made are first steps towards cultural sensitivity (see Hair & O'Donoghue, 2009). This openness/willingness was visible in the ways that students were supported. The supervisor wrote, for example, in relation to a student with English as a second language who was also managing a disability that:

> [Student] does not appear to find it easy to convey verbally or in writing the complexity and nuances of her thought processes or emotions. I have interpreted this as a language and expression issue, because I have also noticed a broader tendency for [student] to undersell her skills, abilities and her work. I believe that [student] has a rich inner world which she finds difficult to articulate. [Student]'s capacity to learn and reflect is nonetheless evidenced in her work and in her general demeanour. (Excerpt from supervisor's report on student placement)

Demonstrating another student's perspective is the following excerpt from a student evaluation report:

> In the early stage of the placement, I faced a situation where I could reflect on my cultural differences in working in an Australian workplace. My supervisor and I openly discussed this matter and exchanged opinions until we found the suitable approach for me to practise. I found that most negatives in Japanese workplaces could be interpreted as positives in Australian workplaces—both values and communication styles. I started experimenting with a new communication style. (Excerpt from student evaluation report)

As is apparent in the above extracts, the supervisor's approach was highly facilitative, supportive and dialectical, rather than didactic. This means that students were encouraged and supported to generate their own solutions to dilemmas:

> Throughout the placement, my supervisor has respected my autonomy in learning. (Excerpt from student evaluation report)

The supervisor was able to separate tasks from learning in conceptual terms. Supervision sessions with students mostly involved spending roughly equal amounts of time on each.

> [Student] seems to believe that she has not adequately demonstrated her planning and work management skills, partly because she feels under pressure to complete all required tasks before the end of placement. I believe that [student] has taken inadequate account of the multiple identities in her life that render complex any single identity, e.g. her identity as a high performing student. (Excerpt from supervisor's report on student placement)

The above excerpt indicates a willingness to understand students as complex individuals with many roles in addition to the role of learner. This in turn suggests that cultural sensitivity can usefully be extended to accommodate recognition of diversity in all its forms, including intrapersonal diversity—the diverse roles that one individual performs in the many facets of their life—as advocated in UNESCO's (2002) Universal Declaration on Cultural Diversity.

Students benefited considerably from the flexibility that was afforded through the placements and by the supervisor. This was explicitly acknowledged in some students' evaluation reports. Some unorthodox processes were accommodated:

> [Student] picked up an informal 'client' from within her own community during the course of the placement and sought advice and assistance in navigating the service system with the 'client'. Whilst clearly unorthodox, this event enabled [student] to more explicitly link her placement experiences of research and advocacy with her future plans to work in a casework environment'. (Excerpt from supervisor's report on student placement)

In summary, the key skills and qualities of the supervisor that contribute to successful student placements include a clarity in separating task from learning, a willingness to focus on learning first, good cultural awareness and a facilitative approach marked by generosity, patience, and flexibility.

Skills and personal qualities of the students

Like the supervisor, the students needed to acknowledge the capacity for reciprocity in learning and embrace it. This is easier said than done. One student's journey to find a way to put reciprocity at the centre of the supervisor-student relationship is depicted in the following extract from a student evaluation report:

> 'Learning-up' was a further concept introduced to me by my supervisor which is key to getting the most from supervision. It involved anticipating what would be required from me in situations such as liaison visits, supervision sessions and focus groups as well as advising these groups what I required of them. An example of this was developing my project plan that took into account when I would require feedback and informing the relevant party so they could set aside time for this. (Excerpt from student evaluation report)

We observed that students were most likely to gain the greatest benefits from placements when they had the skills and confidence to bring their own experiences and perspectives into the placement, not underselling these. Students' confidence invariably grew over the course of the placement as their appreciation of the benefits of their own contributions to the workplace, organisation and supervisor's learning deepened.

In terms of the personal qualities of the student, we found that the student's willingness to be vulnerable and authentic was especially valuable in maximising their own and other's learning. We recognise that authenticity is most likely to be present when there is a high level of trust in the student-supervisor relationship. It is important not to take this trust for granted.

What about the placements that were not successfully completed?

We learn a lot about what works from what does not work. For this reason, we now devote some attention to understanding what happened for the two students who did not proceed with their respective placement and thesis. The student who sought to write an honours thesis based on research trial data experienced delays in securing University ethics approval for this work. These delays were largely technical in nature and linked to bureaucratic processes. The unavailability of the academic supervisor at the time when the delays were most frustrating for the student had a significant impact on the student's willingness and ability to sustain momentum. This student's experience suggests that it is important to ensure that ethics approval processes are well supported and that backup supervision is arranged and available during times when a supervisor expects to be absent.

A second student had completed almost half of the placement hours when this student chose to terminate the placement. This student had a somewhat utopian view of how the placement experience could unfold. This student was attracted to the placement by the critical nature of the work, and looking for a radical experience. The management orientation of the supervisor and her attention to compliance with administrative requirements was experienced as very jarring by the student. With idealist notions unfulfilled, the student sought another placement in a 'grassroots' context. The termination process was handled well by all parties, minimising the potential for resentment on the part of either supervisor or student.

> I note that [student] has acted with considerable integrity in terminating the placement and has managed to end the placement successfully without casting blame. I experience her actions in this regard as worthy of respect. (Excerpt from supervisor's report on student placement)

This experience suggests that, in explaining the placement learning opportunities to prospective students, it is important to be realistic and grounded and avoid overselling the benefits of the placement experience. Where termination is unavoidable, it is important to invest time and energy in terminating as respectfully as possible.

Discussion

The experiences and reflections documented in this chapter have broader implications for social work educators, including field placement supervisors, throughout the Asia Pacific region. Here, we offer some practical suggestions that can inform the work of social work educators in thinking about, preparing for and managing field placements, recognising that supervision practices will significantly affect the learning experiences of the student, supervisor and host organisation.

First, we recommend that reciprocal learning be explicitly adopted as a goal of all field education placements. When reciprocity is the focus, cultural and other differences between supervisor, student and host agency are deproblematised; instead they become increasingly desirable. It is through the different perspectives of diverse people that learning is maximised. Second, we recommend that those involved in preparing for and managing field placements adopt a constructionist view of supervision, in which the starting point is the particular situation and context in which supervision is practised, and a plurality of perspectives are accommodated and valued.

A focus on reciprocity combined with a constructionist orientation suggests, in turn, that both field educators and students needs to focus firmly on personal learning processes—how learning occurs, styles or models of learning, how learning can be maximised and what is required in order for learning to lead to personal transformation and action. This contrasts with more traditional approaches to pre-placement preparation which regularly addresses supervision models and strategies for managing supervision arrangements (for field educators), and compliance with administrative requirements of the placement, for both the student and the field educator. A focus on support for learning, such as is suggested here, is consistent with recommendations made by Maidment (2003). We further suggest that support offered by social work educators to field education supervisors could usefully include opportunities for critical self-reflection. Such opportunities not only reinforce the difference between performing tasks and undertaking learning, they can build the supervisor's key skills—a facilitative supervision style, flexibility, cultural sensitivity and a commitment to reciprocity in learning.

In negotiating an appropriate placement, it is important to consider the work environment and the practice context in which the placement is scheduled to occur. We believe that placements that occur in an explicitly critical context, where a culture of challenge prevails, can be especially rewarding for students. Similarly, workplaces that have a culture of celebration and openness can be very inviting for students. It is important that local workplace rituals be extended to include celebration of the arrival and departure of the student and any other significant milestones achieved by the student. Finally, in monitoring placements, it is important to ensure that learning agreements go beyond the recycling of statements from the handbook and check that the focus is equally on tasks and on learning.

Conclusion

A focus on reciprocal learning is the key to co-creating successful and mutually rewarding field education experiences in situations involving cultural diversity. Managing diversity involves learning about the cultural and other differences between student and supervisor as part of an ongoing, shared process. It is not necessary for a student, the supervisor and the host organisation to share a culture for field education placements to be mutually beneficial. Rather, diverse cultural perspectives can enhance learning. Reciprocal learning is further supported by a facilitative approach to supervision, a critical practice context in which mainstream practices are challenged, and an inclusive work environment. The adoption of a positive learning stance can help to maximise the benefits associated with diversity at work.

Questions for discussion

When have you been in a supervisory relationship involving cultural difference?
What opportunities for learning are available in your supervisory relationships?
How could the idea of reciprocal learning be used to enhance student placement experiences in your context?

References

Austin, M. & Hopkins, K. (2004). *Supervision as collaboration in the human services: building a learning culture.* Thousand Oaks: Sage.

Barton, H., Bell, K. & Bowles, W. (2005). Help or hindrance? Outcomes of social work student placements. *Australian Social Work,* 58(3), 301–12.

Coventry, L. (2005). Experiences of YP[4]. Paper presented to National Symposium, Government and Communities in Partnership: The Next Steps, *University of Melbourne Centre for*

Public Policy, Melbourne, Australia. Retrieved 20 February 2013 from public-policy.unimelb.edu.au/events/past/2005/government_and_communities_in_partnership_the_next_steps.

Davys, A. & Beddoe, L. (2010). *Best practice in professional supervision: a guide for the helping professions.* London: Jessica Kingsley Publishers.

Hair, H. J. & O'Donoghue, K. (2009). Culturally relevant, socially just social work supervision: becoming visible through a social constructionist lens. *Journal of Ethnic and Cultural Diversity in Social Work,* 18(1–2), 70–88.

Heron, J. (1989). Six category intervention analysis. Human Potential Resource Group, University of Surrey, UK.

Kadushin, A. & Harkness, D. (2002). *Supervision in social work,* 4th edn. New York: Columbia University Press.

Lyter, S.C. (2012). Potential of field education as signature pedagogy: the field director role. *Journal of Social Work Education,* 48(1), 179–88.

Maidment, J. (2003). Problems experienced by students on field placement: using research findings to inform curriculum design and content. *Australian Social Work,* 56(1), 50–60.

Matsuura, K. (2002). Foreword, UNESC universal declaration on cultural diversity. Retrieved 3 May 2013 from unesdoc.unesco.org/images/0012/001271/127162e.pdf.

Munson, C. (2002). Handbook of clinical social work supervision, 3rd edn. New York: Haworth Press.

Noble, C. & Irwin, J. (2009). Social work supervision. *Journal of Social Work,* 9(3), 345–58.

O'Donoghue, K. (2003). *Restorying social work supervision.* Palmerston North: Dunmore press.

O'Donoghue, K. (2010). Towards the construction of social work supervision in Aotearoa New Zealand: astudy of the perspectives of social work practitioners and supervisors. PhD thesis. Massey University, Palmerston North, New Zealand.

O'Donoghue, K. (2012a). Windows on the supervisee experience: an exploration of supervisees' supervision histories. *Australian Social Work,* 65(2), 214–31.

O'Donoghue, K. & Tsui, M. (2012b). Towards a professional supervision culture: the development of social work supervision in Aotearoa New Zealand. *International Social Work,* 55(1), 5–28.

Powell, D. J. (1993). *Clinical supervision in alcohol and drug abuse counselling.* Lexington Books: New York.

Raskin, M., Wayne, J. & Bogo, M. (2008). Revisiting field education standards. *Journal of Social Work Education,* 44(2), 173–88.

Reisch, M. & Jarman-Rohde, L. (2000). The future of social work in the United States: implications for field education. *Journal of Social Work Education,* 36(2), 201–14.

Sloan, G. & Watson, H. (2002). Clinical supervision models for nursing: structure, research and limitations. *Nursing Standard,* 17(4), 41–6.

Smith, M. K. (2005). The functions of supervision. *The encyclopedia of informal education* (updated April 2008). Retrieved 22 April 2013 from www.infed.org/biblio/functions_of_supervision.htm#clinical.

Tsui, M. (2005). *Social work supervision: contexts and concepts.* Thousand Oaks: Sage.

UNESCO (2002). Universal declaration on cultural diversity. Retrieved 22 April 2013 from unesdoc.unesco.org/images/0012/001271/127160m.pdf.

Wayne, J., Bogo, M. & Raskin, M. (2006). Field notes: the need for radical change in field education. *Journal of Social Work Education,* 42(1), 161–69.

Wayne, J., Bogo, M. & Raskin, M. (2010). Field education as the signature pedagogy of social work education. *Journal of social work education*, 46(3), 327–39.

14

Field education in Fiji: practice challenges and opportunities

Kate Saxton

This chapter explores the challenges and barriers experienced by social work students studying in Fiji. As part of a movement to advance the professionalism of social work in the region, social work training is now offered as a Bachelor Degree course within Fiji. However due to the embryonic stage of 'professional social work' within Pacific Island countries, opportunities for supervised student placements are limited and many recent graduates are exposed to field education experiences without access to adequate supervision. Social work supervision is a process of critical reflection and learning which allows the social worker to link their lived practice experience with broader theoretical understandings of 'the nature of things'. Via a process of enhanced supervision, students and field educators may develop more appropriate and relevant understandings about the nature of social work in Fiji and how that translates to 'best practice' with our clients.

Na vuli cakacaka e Viti: Vakatovolei na dredre kei na katuba ni toso

Na pepa oqo e via dikeva na bolebole kei na i vakatatao era sotava na gonevuli ni vuli torocake ni veiqaravi ni Bula Raraba era vuli tiko i Viti. Me vaka ni tiki ni dua na lalawaka me vakatoroicake taki kina na tabana ni Bula Raraba ena Wasa Pasifika, esa soli tu ni kua e Viti e dua na kena koroi ni vuli torocake. Me vaka ni se tiko ena i vakatagedegede ni tauyavu na veiqaravi ni Bula Raraba ena Wasa Pasifika, e sega soti ni levu na dauniveituberi vei ira na vuli cakacaka ena tabana oqo. E na levu na gauna era vuli tara tiko na gonevuli ka sega ni qarauni se mera tuberi tiko mai vua edua na dau ni veituberi ni Bula Raraba. E rui ka bibi kina na taba ni veiqaravi ni veituberi ka ni na vakavure vakasama ka laveta na kilaka me vukea sara na kena semati na kila vaka vuli mai koronivuli ki na kila vaka vuli tara e na vanua ni cakacaka. Ni sa vakataucokotaki na cakacaka ni veituberi, sa namaki me rau bucina vata eso nai tuvatuva matau kei na vakasama veiraurau me baleta na veiqaravi ni Bula Raraba e Viti, o ira na gonevuli kei ira na dauniveituberi. Oqo e sa gaunisala ni nodra kila matua na gonevuli kei ira na dauniveituberi e Viti na veiqaravi e veiganiti vinaka vua e dua e gadreva me vukei. *(Translation by Empower Pacific staff)*

在斐濟的實地教學：實踐的挑戰與機遇

本文探討了社會工作學生們在斐濟學習時所經歷的挑戰和障礙。作為推進該地區社會工作專業化運動的一環，社會工作培訓現在在斐濟已開設了學士學位課程。但由於在太平洋島嶼國家’專業社會工作’還處在萌芽階段，學生在督導下實習的機會是有限的，許多剛畢業的學生在參與實地教學時沒法得到適當的督導。社會工作督導是一個批判性反映和學習的過程，這一過程能讓社工將他們鮮活的實踐經驗與對’事物的本質’更廣泛的理論理解聯接起來。通過這一加強督導的過程，學生以及實踐教育工作者或許能更準確的理解斐濟社會工作的性質，並知道如何將其轉化為在面對委託人時的’最佳做法’。

フィジーにおけるフィールド教育：実習における課題とその機会

ケイト・サクストン

本稿では、フィジーでソーシャルワークを学ぶ学生が経験した課題や障壁を探る。この地域におけるソーシャルワークのプロフェショナリズム（専門職への意識化）が進行する一連の動きの中で、ソーシャルワークの研修はフィジー国内でも学士課程で実施されている。しかしながら、太平洋島嶼国において「ソーシャルワーク専門職(プロフェショナル)」は胚芽期であるが故に、学生がスーパービジョンを受けて配属する機会が限られている。適切なスーパービジョンを受けることなく実習教育にさらされた卒業生も最近では数多く存在している。ソーシャルワークのスーパービジョンは、ソーシャルワーカーが生の現場の経験を「物事の本質」の広範囲にわたる理論的な理解と結びつけることができるための振り返りと学びの重要なプロセスである。学生と実習担当教員は、スーパービジョンを強化するプロセスを通し、フィジーにおけるソーシャルワークの本質についてより適切かつ適正な理解を深め、その理解を利用者への「最高の実践」に転換させていくことができるだろう。

피지의 사회복지실습교육: 도전과 기회

본장은 피지에서 학생들이 실습교육을 받을 때 경험하는 도전과 장애가 무엇인지 탐색하고 있다. 사회복지의 전문성을 고양시키려는 움직임의 일환으로 피지에서 학사학위에 사회복지가 포함되었다. 이 지역의사회복지 전문성이 초보단계이므로 수퍼비젼이 있는 실습지가 부족하고 졸업생들은 수퍼비젼이 없는 곳에서 실무를 하게 되기도 한다. 사회복지수퍼비젼은 삶의 본질에 대한 폭넓은 이해가 되도록 하기 위해 실천현장과 연계해주는 작업이며, 이를 통해 CR 즉, 비판적반영과 배움이 발생되는 과정이다. 수퍼비젼 강화체계가 있어야 학생과 실무자들이 사회복지의 본질을 보다 정확히 이해하게 되어 클라이언트를 위해 '최고의 개입'이 이루어지게 될 것이다.

Introduction

The 21st century has witnessed the expansion of social work internationally (Lavalette & Ferguson, 2007). National associations affiliated with the International Federation of Social Workers (IFSW) exist in over 80 countries, and according to the International Association of Schools of Social Work (IASSW) 2010 census there were an estimated 2000 schools of social work worldwide. Schools of social work are well established in almost all countries in Europe, Australia, North and South America, and have recently developed in Asia and Africa (Lyons, Manion & Carlson, 2006). In the Pacific Islands, social work practice is also beginning to emerge with Fiji establishing its own association of social workers—the Fiji Association of Social Workers (FASW) in 1996 and producing its first social work university graduates in 2007. Several factors have contributed to the growing social work phenomenon within the South Pacific (and indeed newly emerging economies in South East Asia and parts of Africa). These include the need for governments to respond to the rapid growth of poverty and social inequality arising from the operation of market forces, the social and personal problems caused by rapid urbanisation and alienation, the inability of informal social networks to cope with the demands of market society, significant change of tradtional family patterns, emerging social problems and the loosening of traditional support networks (Ling, 2007; Midgley, 2001). This warrants the need for a more formal system of social services, which in turn provides opportunities for professional social work to assume greater importance (Ling, 2007).

More broadly, both the spread and demand for social work services and education can be linked to globalisation and the shrinking 'global village' (Midgley, 2001). This also includes easier access, through improved communications and advancements in travel, to Western social work ideas, philosophies and practices (Lavalette & Ferguson, 2007). It is within this backdrop that I found myself called to the Pacific Islands; initially to assist in social work curriculum development in Tonga, and most recently to support the capacity of local social workers within Fiji through a process of skills transfer, policy development and mentoring. Originally from Australia, I brought with me my own ideas, cultural values and biases of how I perceived social work to be and inherent ideologies encapsulated in what it means to 'do' social work. As I have learned—at times the hard way—nothing is inherent when it comes to social work in a cross-cultural and indeed international development setting!

In order to provide a practice space which allowed for the opportunity of an organic and 'Fiji' style of social work to emerge, I have drawn from the critical social work paradigm. This school of thought requires that I that reflect critically on the influence of personal, cultural and structural processes on my own practices and on the experiences of those which I engage with (Thompson, 1997). This process of critical reflection includes analysis of the power language has in shaping knowledge (Lundy, 2004) and the role in which, as a white, middle-class, educated Anglo-Saxon, I may inadvertently participate in the control and perpetuation of discourses which seek to render minorities invisible.

The past two years have seen me working intensively within a leading NGO to assist staff in the delivery of social services to some of Fiji's most poor, vulnerable, oppressed and marginalised persons. This role has lead me to have direct interaction with over a dozen current social work students and social work graduates to which I have been involved in the provision of supervision, management and professional mentoring. Whilst I cannot separate myself from my position as an educated 'kaivalangi' (white) person, I feel it brings with it a responsibility to share my knowledge and power and advocate with and for the peoples of Fiji for whom this chapter is written. This chapter is based on the conversations, experiences and professional relationships I have had with local social work students and practitioners within Fiji, whilst written within the framework of the critical social work paradigm from which I operate.

A BRIEF OVERVIEW OF SOCIAL WORK EDUCATION IN FIJI

Whilst Fijians have been informally involved in community development and the service of 'helping' one another for generations, social work as a recognised professional vocation is a relatively new phenomenon. Amongst the i'Taukei peoples, social work often refers to community based work, whilst in the Indo-Fijian context it may refer to volunteering, usually amongst those who are retired, or nearing retirement and looking to share their experience within an non-government setting (Nickson, Kuruleca & Clarke, 2009). As recently as 1968, Fiji founded the Department of Social Welfare (DSW) which was formally established in the 1920's as the Destitute Allowance Scheme designed to assist retired Indian labourers.

The DSW was set up as the sole department legally mandated for child care and protection—although the vast majority of workers found themselves practicing in a social services domain void of clear legislative frameworks and qualification requirements (Mills, 2002). In response to inefficiencies of staff qualifications within the DSW, in 1971 the Regional Advisor on Training for the South Pacific Commission recommended the establishment of a new University Diploma of Social Services program, loosely based on its British counterpart, the Certificate of Qualification in Social Work (Yasas, 1971). The Diploma at that time was only offered to those working within the DSW. Two successive cohorts of students graduated in 1978 and 1979, before the program was abandoned (Mills, 2002).

The Diploma of Social Services was then replaced with a Diploma in Community Development, which included no core social work subjects, no fieldwork placements, and ironically no subjects in Community Development. However, bowing to pressure from 'out spoken public figures' this course was discarded in favour of the traditional Fijian strengths of the extended family, kinship and the community (including the church) which advocates argued could and should take care of the social welfare needs of Fijian communities (Mills, 2002). There is merit in this argument, as the uncritical transfer of western social work approaches to other nations does not take into account the issues of cultural relativity and the indigenisation process (Burkett & McDonald, 2005; Ling, 2007; Midgley, 2001). Whilst the ideological debates about the appropriateness of 'western'-style professional social work do (and in my opinion, should) continue within the Pacific Islands, so did the demand for formal training in social work services; albeit from workers in institutions like courts, prisons, hospitals and child protection which are largely the consequence of Fiji's former British colonial past.

As a corollary to the demise of formal social services training in Fiji the development of a well-trained social work profession was severely diminished (Mills, 2002) and yet this was juxtaposed against a growing grassroots social welfare movement which characterised Fiji in the 1990s and led to the establishment of many non-governmental organisations (NGOs) and community associations. Amongst this groundswell of concern for formal social work qualifications came the creation of the Fiji Association of Social Workers (FASW) in 1996. FASW was a key driver in voicing the need to develop training programs and the means of professional accreditation within the vast array of community and social services now operating within Fiji. This professional concern with social services training as an essential element of social development was then subsequently recognised by academic institutions. In 1997 one of Fiji's major universities launched a Postgraduate Diploma in Social Policy offered within its Sociology Faculty.

The Sociology department has also gone on to provide courses on counseling, psychology and indeed sociology itself. However social work as a standalone academic course remained elusive. Until recently, individuals wanting to study social work needed to travel outside the region, usually to a more developed country in which social problems are different in both degree and kind—as are the skills required to address them (Mills, 2002). After considerable effort and a long process of advocacy and negotiation, Fiji is the only country in the region to offer a three-year Bachelor Degree Social Work course, with 2007 seeing the first round of successful graduates. For the first time in the Pacific Islands, social work students have access to formal social work education which includes both theory and practicum- or field based placements. It is within this tumultuous, embryonic—yet exciting—backdrop of social work education that I have come to understand and encounter the challenges and opportunities facing this newly established strain of social workers within Fiji.

The role of supervision in social work education

Current first year social work students in Fiji are asked to complete a 40 hour voluntary work placement in any community based setting, followed by two supervised 65 day placements in second and third years of study respectively. Field education and placement is acknowledged as a crucial component of social work in all countries that social work education exists (Noble, 2011). Field education is the place where students have the opportunity to integrate theory with professional practice in order to develop their own professional social work identity (Tsui, 2005). It also provides a framework for developing and assessing students' competencies in a range of social work skills (AASW, 2008). Underpinning the effectiveness of field education is students having access to good quality supervision (Noble, 2011). On writing on the success of an overseas student placement in Fiji, Nickson, Kuruleca & Clarke (2009) clearly identified that having 'an experienced and available field educator in the placement agency to provide supervision' (p. 70) was a crucial component of the placement's success. The issue in Fiji as it has been relayed to me by students is that experienced and available supervisors on field placement are not the norm.

Given that social work within Fiji has only begun to be recognised as formal profession, and tertiary qualifications have only been in place for the past seven years, it is not surprising that Fiji is facing a shortage of experienced and professionally qualified social workers for which to offer supervision to students (Nickson, Kuruleca & Clarke, 2009). That is not to say that there are no competent and capable persons working in areas of social services, community development or other areas which could be termed as 'social work', as I have had the pleasure of working with many. But rather whilst persons are working within the fields of social work and other 'helping professions', most remain unaware and are unfamiliar of university expectations and conceptualisations about the purpose, role and function of social work within various agency settings. This unfamiliarity with academic notions of social work, including recognition of regular clinical supervision as a central component of professional development translates to a lack of understanding of the role and function of supervision within field education placements, and across the social services sector more broadly.

'The purpose and raison d'être for supervision is to facilitate the best possible practice and the best possible outcomes' (O'Donoghue,

2001, p. 222). In undertaking this role, the supervisor performs administrative, educational and supportive functions in interaction with the supervisee (Kadushin, 2002). Whilst many field educators and 'social work' agencies in Fiji provide administrative or managerial levels of supervision, my discussions with both recent social work graduates and current students suggest that the educational and supportive functions vary significantly from agency to agency and in many settings are non-existent. These effects of managerialism have also been apparent in a market driven social work context within Western capitalist societies which are characterised by a marked shift in emphasis from educational and professional development to conformance with organisational performance management and accountability systems (O'Donoghue & Tsui, 2011; Noble & Irwin, 2009). If organisational priorities such as performance evaluation and accountability become the focus of supervision at the expense of professional development, challenges to supervision and field education emerge (Adams, 2007).

Challenges in social work field education and supervision within Fiji

The emphasis given to administrative and/or managerial functions of social work supervision promotes hierarchical, competitive, power based relationships where the supervisor is seen to be symbolically looking over the shoulder of the practitioner as the intervention occurs (Hair & O'Donoghue, 2009; Munson, 2000). This power imbalance removes the sense of a learning-centred 'partnership' which is an essential component of professional development (Kadushin, 2002; Tsui, 2005). Ideally social work supervision should mirror a 'helping' relationship in that it is built on a trusting, caring, empathic, confidential and supportive experience (Noble & Irwin, 2009). In enacting the supportive function of supervision, the supervisor aims to sustain worker morale, help with job-related discouragement and discontent, and provide supervisees with a sense of worth as social work professionals, a sense of belonging in the agency, and a sense of security in their performance (Kadushin,

2002). In a managerially-driven supervisory setting, coupled with the hierarchical nature which typifies many Fijian relationships both within the home and the workplace, many social worker students within Fiji feel unsupported and unequal in the supervisory relationship. This issue is further compounded by the different construction of confidentiality that exists in many collectivist societies, where information is more freely shared.

The idea that the supervisor has privileged understandings of social work discounts the knowledge base of social workers and can be intentionally or unwittingly used to validate or discount, liberate or subjugate individuals, families and groups according to how knowledge and power intersect (Foucault, 1984; Hair & O'Donoghue, 2009). A critical or social constructionist approach would argue that power is inherent in all practices and relationships. Whether it is recognised or not, both the supervisor and supervisee bring with them their own perspectives or 'stories' that are multifaceted and socially constructed. Each of these stories contains the values, ideologies and discourses present in society's cultures, politics, social policies, laws, governing bodies, agencies, professions and service user groups (O'Donoghue, 2003). As power is further located within the intersectionalities of class, race, culture, ability and sexual orientation, gender identities and religion, dominant discourses become normalised within [Fijian] society and are rarely questioned. These discourses construct relationships of privilege and oppression and ultimately become the determinants of the 'haves' and 'have nots'. As a consequence social workers do not see their role in the structures of dominance, neither do they feel morally obligated to effect change (Herendez, 2008).

Noble and Irwin (2009) argue that the focus of supervision to monitor worker performance is 'at the expense of professional and intellectual growth [and] is inhibiting the possibility of new and challenging practice dialogues and learning opportunities from emerging' (p. 353). Noble (1999) regards supervision within social work as a unique opportunity to link the thinking (theory) with the doing (practice) and vice versa. By failing to provide supportive, educational and critical supervisory environments for social workers, structures of power and dominance remain internalised and social workers are less able to interrupt the perpetuation of oppression (Herendez, 2008). In this manner social work within Fiji may serve to maintain the 'status quo' and broader social work ideations of equality and social justice remain unrealised.

OPPORTUNITIES FOR CRITICAL SOCIAL WORK IN FIJI?

As social work education seeks to inform and develop practice in systematic ways, there is a need to recognise different forms of knowledge, and different ways of creating that knowledge if we are to gain a better representation of our own experiences as practitioners, and that of the many different groups with whom we work (Fook, 2003). This could be facilitated by making overt the interpretations, assumptions, knowledge, behaviours and roles of various stakeholders, the work conducted with clients, communities and agencies, and exploring how all these aspects are mediated by language, discourse, power, religion, and both organisational and socio-political politics (Brookfield, 2005). Involving opportunities for critical reflection in the supervisory relationship offers a way of exploring these influences on both ourselves and the work that we do with clients (O' Donoghue, 2003). The process whereby supervisors and supervisees develop critical consciousness or concientizacion (Freire, 1971) recognises historical and cultural prescriptions of choices for what they are, and not blindly as naturally occurring phenomenon. By presenting and discussing the ways in which gender, class, ability, ethnicity and sexual orientation construct relationships of privilege and oppression, students learn to think relationally and develop a language to address the intersections of power, privilege and oppression (Herendez, 2008).

Given the embryonic notion of social work as a professional practice within Fiji, critical reflection within field education and supervision is both an opportunity and an obstacle in and of itself. With few 'qualified' social workers to provide critically reflective supervision and supervision limited to administrative duties and an assessment of 'competence', social work students are denied the opportunity to make sense of what is happening around them, and may inadvertently be contributing to the very sources of oppression they are seeking to redress. On the contrary critical social work acknowledges and values the many sources of knowledge and is skeptical of any knowledge which may be seen as bounded in time, place and person. In this way informal, local, established traditions and practices of social work are still regarded as valid, and social work education values the contribution and the experiences of those supervisors already practicing in the field over any academic constructions of knowledge (Payne, 2001).

As Fiji continues to embark on the journey of professionalising social work through the establishment of tertiary level social work qualifications, and hopefully in time, the development of clear structures of supervisory processes, models of social work developed in Western liberal democracies are likely to be extremely influential in shaping the ways in which social work develops in the Pacific (Lavalette & Ferguson, 2007). The manifestations of a 'professional' category of social work may be seen as an application of the practice associated with 21st century Western 'professional' movement, but in a different context (Burkett & McDonald, 2005). Indeed I myself need to refrain from the impulse to espouse Western models of social work within my own process of clinical supervision within Fiji. While the impetus may be to embrace Western social work theories and methods, a pertinent issue that remains to be resolved is whether these theories and methods are suited to the local socio-cultural milieu (Ling, 2007; Midgley, 2001). If we recognise that social work has become a global profession with both a deliberate and consequential transfer of knowledge, we need to be careful in case one kind of knowledge becomes so powerful as to dominate another culture's ways of understanding (Payne, 2001). To avoid the imposition of one set of values or views over another requires critical reflection and analysis.

Critical thinking and reflection in supervision and social work practice allows Fijians to apply their own knowledge basis and develop culturally appropriate and meaningful strategies to address injustice, however this is defined. The process of linking theory with practice within the supervisory process will drive and shape local understandings of social work and assist social work students and graduates to take informed actions. By better understanding the manner in which meanings of social work knowledge is created, social workers in Fiji may find the voice to contribute understandings of what it is to do social work- Fiji style.

REFERENCES

Adams, J. (2007). *Managing people in organisations: contemporary theory and practice.* Basingstoke: Palgrave Macmillian.

Brookfield, S. (2005). *The power of critical theory for adult learning and teaching.* Maidenhead: Open University Press.

Burkett, I. & McDonald, C. (2005). Working in a different space: linking social work and social development. In I. Ferguson, M. Lavalette, E. Whitmore (Eds). *Globalisation, global justice and social work* (pp. 173–88). New York: Routledge.

Fook, J. (2003). Critical social work: the current issues. *Qualitative Social Work,* 2(2), 123–34.

Foucault, M. (1984). The politics and ethics: an interview. In P. Rabinow (Ed). *The Foucault reader* (pp. 373–80). New York: Pantheon Books.

Freire, P. (1971). *Pedagogy of the oppressed.* Middlesex: Penguin.

Hair, J. & O'Donoghue, K. (2009). Culturally relevant, socially just social work supervision: becoming visible through a social constructionist lens. *Journal of Ethnic and Cultural Diversity in Social Work,* 18(1), 70–88.

Herendez, P. (2008). The cultural context model in clinical supervision. *Training and Education in Professional Psychology,* 2(1), 10–17.

Kadashin, A. (2002). *Supervision in social work.* New York: Columbia University Press.

Lavalette, M. & Ferguson, I. (Eds). (2007). *International social work and the radical tradition.* Birmingham: Venture Press.

Ling, H. K. (2007). *Indigenising social work: research and practice in Sarawak.* Malaysia: Strategic Information and Research Development Centre (SIRC).

Lyons, K., Manion K. & Carlsen, M. (2006). *International perspectives on social work: global conditions and local practice.* New York: Palgrave Macmillan.

Lundy, C. (2004). *Social work and social justice: a structural approach to practice.* Ontario: Broadview Press Ltd.

Midgley, J. (2001). Issues in international social work: resolving critical debates in the profession. *Journal of Social Work,* 21(1), 22–35.

Mills, G. (2002). Which way for welfare in the South Pacific. *International Social Work,* 45(2), 239–50.

Munson, C. (2000). Supervision standards of practice in an era of societal restructuring. In P. Allen-Meares & C. Garvin (Eds). *The handbook of social work direct practice* (pp. 611–32). Thousand Oaks: Sage.

Nickson, A., Kuruleca, S. & Clark, M. (2009). *Fijian and Australian social work learning through field education.* In C. Noble, M. Henrickson & I.Y. Han (Eds). *Social work education: voices from the Asia-Pacific* (pp. 50–72). Carlton North: Vulgar Press.

Noble, C. (2011). Field education: supervision, curricula and teaching methods. In C. Noble & M. Henrickson (Eds). *Social work field education and supervision across Asia Pacific* (pp. 3–22). Sydney University Press.

Noble, C. (2001). Way of thinking about field education and supervision: building a critical perspective. In C. Noble & M. Henrickson (Eds). *Social work field education and supervision across Asia Pacific* (pp. 299–320). Sydney: Sydney University Press.

Noble, C. & Irwin, J. (2009). Social work supervision: an exploration of the current challenges in a rapidly changing social, economic and political environment. *Journal of Social Work,* 9, 345–59.

Noble, C. (1999). The elusive yet essential project of developing field education as a legitimate area of social work inquiry. *Issues in Social Work Education,* 19(1), 2–16.

O'Donoghue, K. & Tsui, M. (2011). Towards a professional supervision culture: the development of social work supervision in Aotearoa New Zealand. *International Social Work,* 55(1), 5–28.

O'Donoghue, K. (2003) *Re-storying social work supervision.* Wellington, New Zealand: Dunmore Press.

O'Donoghue, K. (2001). The future of social work supervision within Aotearoa/New Zealand. In L. Beddoe & J. Worral (Eds). Supervision conference 7–8 July 2000 from rhetoric to reality: keynote address and selected papers. Auckland: Auckland College of Education.

Payne, M. (2001). Knowledge bases and knowledge biases in social work. *Journal of Social Work,* 1, 133–46.

Tsui, M. (2005). *Social work supervision: contexts and concepts.* Thousand Oaks: Sage.

Yasas, F. (1971). *Training needs of welfare personal in the Social Development and Welfare Departments in Fiji including proposals for the sub regional South Pacific training course for social welfare and community work.* Suva: South Pacific Commission.

4

Policy voices

15

Social work and the Asia Pacific: from rhetoric to practice

Carolyn Noble

This chapter explores issues concerning the rapid growth of social work programs across the Asia Pacific. Referring to research which gathered responses from regions to the International Association of Schools of Social Work's (IASSW) project of developing Global Standards for Social Work Education as well as research on the experiences of students undertaking placements in many of these countries, important issues about the imposition of western influences are raised and discussed. In particular the post-colonial and critical post-modern critiques and in response the growth of cross-cultural and anti-racist educational practices are presented as a way of mitigating the dominance of the western influences as social work programs continue to be developed.

亞太地區社會工作：從空談到實踐

本章探討整個亞太地區快速增長的社會工作項目的一些有關議題。參照從區域到國際性社會工作教育學校聯合會的開發全球標準的社會工作教育項目收集來的反饋信息和針對在一些這樣的國家進行實習的學生實際經歷的研究，本章提出並討論了關於西方影響的干預這一重要議題。本章重點探討了以減弱西方影響的主導地位為目的的後殖民時期,尤其是後現代的批判及與之相應的跨文化和反種族教育實踐，而這些作為社會工作項目得到繼續發展。

タイトル：ソーシャルワークとアジア太平洋：レトリックから実践へ

著者：キャロリン·ノーブル

この章では、アジア太平洋地域で急増しているソーシャルワーク教育課程に関する問題を取り上げる。国際ソーシャルワーク教育連盟(IASSW)に各地域から寄せられたソーシャルワーク教育国際基準(グローバル・スタンダード)開発プロジェクトへの回答の集計調査および多くの国々で実施されている学生の企業派遣に関する調査を参照しながら、西欧の影響が負わせた賦課が重要な課題として取り上げられ議論されていることにも触れる。特にポストコロニアルや批判的なポストモダニズムへの批評、異文化主義・人種差別反対主義教育の実践拡大への反応は、発展を続けるソーシャルワーク教育課程中で西欧の影響の権勢を軽減させる一つの方法として提示される

아태지역의 사회복지：웅변에서 실제까지

본 장에서는 아태지역의 사회복지 교육이 빠르게 성장하고 있는 점을 탐색하였다. 국제사회복지 교육협의회(IASSW)가 주관하여 만든 국제표준화 작업에 대한 지역별 반응과 각국의 실습경험에 대한 조사연구를 바탕으로 하여 서양의 영향이 주입되고 있는 문제를 부각시켜 토의하였다. 특히 서양의 영향을 줄이는 방안으로서 근대화 과정에 대한 비판과 더불어, 문화 간 교류의 확충, 반 인종차별주의 교육의 실천 등이 모색되었다.

Introduction

Social work programs are emerging around the globe. Their growth is especially evident in countries and regions such as China and South East Asia, where there has been a significant growth in the number of schools of social work. Indeed social work programs in these and other Asia–Pacific countries seem to be more popular than they are in the western countries of its origin, where influence and raison d'etre of social work are under attack from the (aftermath) of several decades of the new right ideology. As a product of modernism, social work activity began to appear in the United Kingdom (UK) and Western Europe early 20th century, initially to tackle the many social problems that emerged after the rapid period of industrialisation, in the belief that these problems could and should be addressed by state intervention. The United States of America (USA) was an exception, focussing more on individual initiatives as a means of improving one's life chances, although its early beginnings flirted with the settlement movement's philosophy of neighbourhood renewal and community development as a way of tacking widespread poverty and disadvantage (Chenoweth & McAuliffe, 2008). Australia, Aotearoa/ New Zealand and India, as colonial countries of the UK, quickly set up social welfare programs, and other Asia Pacific countries followed, so that by the end of the 20th century most if not all countries across the region had social work programs or were planning them in order to train their own practitioners to address their own country's specific social problems (Healy, 2008). While what comes under the banner of social work as it extends its influence from country to country seems to vary, there is a common focus that underpins its rationale (Payne and Askeland, 2008). That is, social problems and social disadvantage are addressed by practitioners and scholars by applying scientific reason and knowledge from the applied social sciences, in conjunction with practice and evidence-based research developed from their own work and areas of interest, to find causes and solutions (McDonald, 2006). This is specifically a western way of addressing social issues and the ongoing debate about its relevance to a region like the Asia Pacific with all its differences and diversity remains an issue of concern (Noble, 2004, Razack, 2002). So why have so many countries across the world, especially Asian countries, adopted social work programs in such large numbers, given its western beginnings and specific western ideas and practices?

Social work: an international project

The social work literature on international social work talks confidently about social work as having a discrete set of skills, knowledge and practices that have a global unity and can therefore be translated into specific cultural settings provided that the substance of the training programs and qualifications have some cultural currency and relevance (Cox & Pawar, 2008; Harrison & Melville, 2010; Healy, 2008). Underlying this assumption is the belief that, in the main, the social work discourse is culturally neutral and is therefore ready for transportation, translation and adaptation. More important is the opening up of borders across the world as the spaces between each country shrinks and communication and access increases. As a result we have seen many developing countries begin to westernise their educational systems in order to provide choices and opportunities for their citizens in line with the standards and expectations of the developed world. Social work has been one of the more successful programs to be transported across the globe (Healy, 2008; Razack, 2002).

The underlying proposition that there is a global social work discourse that can be adapted into different cultural settings has obviously been seen as having some validity, as the growth in social work programs worldwide has been significant, if not surprising given its early beginnings as a domestic activity set up to address domestic and social issues and concerns. I say surprising because social work at the domestic level actually depends on local law, culture and welfare regimes for its work; that is it requires a local identity to function effectively (Payne & Askeland, 2008). However the focus on the domestic at the expense of the larger world picture is changing. While globalisation has, amongst other things, opened up more channels of communication previously limited by distance, language, and communication systems, it has also exposed the interconnectedness of the domestic concerns of individual countries with global activities, such as the flow of international capital and the growth of multinationals with their global financial and strategic influences. As the metaphorical shrinking of time and place has opened up previously unknown countries and cultures to new audiences and provided opportunities for social work programs to flourish, it has also exposed the many social issues associated with wars, poverty, genocide, and acts of terrorism to the national gaze. International social work can claim an important role here in creating an awareness of the impact of these global issues on national concerns giving testimony to the argument that social work was not meant to be restricted to the domestic arena but was always meant to be (in the long run) an international endeavour (Harrison & Melville, 2010; Payne & Askeland, 2008).

But I have questioned elsewhere the assumption behind the internationalising project and asked whether social work has ever been that homogeneous to assume that its generic principles and practices, well known to both academics and practitioners in the west, are actually culturally neutral as earlier assumed (Noble, 2004). Others would agree, as there is increasing evidence that some of these countries' academics and practitioners are beginning to question western model of social work and its relevance to their specific cultures and socio-political organisations (Bennett, Green, Gilbert & Bessarab, 2013; Razack, 2002). The emergence of the critical post-colonial and anti-racist critiques from ethnic and indigenous voices has been extremely influential in this development. This challenge to the western hegemony of social work by the ethnic and indigenous voices and the resulting debates and responses that followed is welcomed by some more progressive academics as well (Allan, Pease, & Briskman, 2009; Dominelli, 2002). Indeed these social work scholars would argue that the challenges posed by the post-colonial critique to the cultural hegemony of the early social work model has given it a great gift by emphasising the importance of accepting difference and locality, tradition and culture and by creating new opportunities for all cultures to question their own hegemonic structures (Allan, Pease & Briskman, 2009; Cox & Pawar, 2008; Dominelli, 2002).

However globalisation does present interesting issues for social work, even as the indigenous critique argues for the return to privileging culturally specific practices and by challenging the more powerful dominant discourse of the western social work scholarship and its assumption of white privilege and underlying racist practices. In particular the growth of global multinationals, the expansion of global manufacturing webs, the opening up of international markets, the proliferation of international defensive and economic alliances as well as the increase in mass communication and most recently the vulnerability of all countries to the global financial web and to the excesses of western capitalism are evidence that we all live in a global village whether one likes it or not! This global village is becoming more important as current world leaders come together regularly, for example at the annual G20 meetings and Association of Southeast Asian Nations (ASEAN) summits, to seek common responses to common issues that will be effective across differing national and local interests, culture and language groups, and economic systems and political ideologies and influences.

For social work, as stated earlier, the opening up of the national borders has also had a significant impact on its understanding of social problems, their causes and solutions and linking practitioners and academics in new and important ways. In particular, practitioners are now more acutely aware of the interconnectedness of events such as world poverty, the effects of war and the displacement of people to local concerns. In response social workers in the international arena have contributed to the development of global social policies informed by a human rights and social justice discourse as an important and significant response to addressing these concerns (Healy & Link, 2012; Ife, 2012). Social movement activism in the international arena has provided many practitioners with global platforms for their local individual and community-based issues (Noble, 2007; Motta & Nilsen, 2011). Social work activity in international agencies and organisations has also been able to introduce international debates about civil society and global responsibilities. For academics, the proliferation of social work programs worldwide has brought individual social workers into contact across the globe and opening up curricula to international influences. The issue of cultural relevance notwithstanding, there are a number of positives resulting from the growth of social work programs across the world such as:

- opportunities for reciprocal dialogue and learning across programs

- staff and student exchanges
- introduction of professional conversations about theoretical and program development at conferences, via the internet and access to the World Wide Web (www)
- the improvement of social work practice in dealing with social issues e.g. poverty, migration, asylum seekers, health, sexual exploitation, discrimination and foreign debt
- opening up courses for students to study abroad, and internationalising program content to include cross border conversations and collaborations
- introduction of indigenous knowledge and methodologies in social work discourse
- new awareness of the local-global linkages of social problems and the effectiveness of promoting international social policy initiatives and activism as means of addressing some of these concerns (Healy, 2008; Lyons, Hokenstad, Pawar, Huegler & Hall, 2012; Noble, 2004; Razack, 2002).

While other scholars identify tensions between the global-local divide, between westernisation and indigenous concepts of practice, multiculturalism and universalisation (Cox & Pawar, 2008) and global and national standards (Sewpaul, 2005), most would agree that this borderless world is here to stay (Harrison & Melville, 2010; Lyons et al., 2012; Payne & Askeland, 2008). Even if practitioners are not interested in extending their analysis to include international social work, it is increasingly hard for them to ignore the way the issues they face daily are connected to international political and economic events and trends (Ife, 2012; Noble, 2004).

However this development needs continuous monitoring and thoughtful analysis in its translation across cultures especially, as we know from experience, how many local and minority cultures are discounted in favour of economically more powerful colonial cultures once the two come into contact. Cox & Pawar (2008) argue that it is social work's commitment to empowerment and local community, social development as it relates to individuals, as well as socio-political and economic development, that is transferable in the international arena as it involves practices such as consciousness raising, empowering group processes and the praxis of action-reflection-action as core practice values that are of universal value. Despite these benefits, Yip (2004) who uses Asia as an example, reminds us of the inherent cultural differences in language, traditions and influences of intellectual thought such as Confucianism, Buddhism, Hinduism and Islam that separate the west from its Asian neighbours. Bennett et al. (2013) remind us of the impact on indigenous communities of the process of dispossession and the continued oppressive policies and practices of the colonial era had on their culture, land, language and ways of living in community. Differences in historical, political and cultural traditions cannot be ignored when working across borders.

Asia Pacific and social work programs and practices

I would like to take this debate forward by looking at international social work in the Asia-Pacific region in which my experience and interest lie. The rapid growth in social work programs in this region is interesting in that many of the countries developing such courses still face geographical isolation, limited access to mass communication technologies, barriers in language and cultural differences as well as access to resources and stable governments (Midgley, 2000). In fact there are still great differences between educational levels in some countries, as well as differences in levels of poverty and disadvantages and familiarity with and or, experience of a welfare state or 'safety net' services. Many countries are just emerging from recent exposures to war, famine, natural disasters and political unrest (Yip, 2004; Midgley, 2000). In addition there are great differences in economic and social development with and across the region and the way social and health problems associated with poverty, violence, unemployment, pollution, and housing are experienced and attended to (Lyons et al., 2012; Midgely, 2000).

Despite these differences most Asia-Pacific countries, including China, India, Sri Lanka, Japan, Hong-Kong China, Korea, Vietnam,

Thailand, Singapore, The Philippines, Papua New Guinea, Indonesia, Fiji and other Pacific islands, have social work programs or the beginnings of one which, when first set up, shared a common framework and reflected common core practices and knowledges. This commonality resulted from borrowing curricula from western countries with well established programs, such as the USA, Australia and Aotearoa/New Zealand. However differences in length and delivery mode, content and focus are evident. A brief summary of these differences follows. Indian social work is highly standardised with masterate qualifications while Australia, Aotearoa/New Zealand, the Philippines, Singapore, Japan, Korea, Vietnam, Thailand and Indonesia teach social work at the undergraduate level. Papua New Guinea, and other Pacific island states have adopted a more vocational, non-university approach focussing on community development and work with NGOs as specific foci of their training (Midgley, 2000). In Australia most universities offer a post graduate qualifying social work program creating a two tiered system for graduate entry practice.

The development of social work courses across the region is seen to contribute to the international cooperation between and among social workers; this interaction is essential for many reasons. First, working across borders has highlighted for all who will listen the significance of the global and the local connections: what happens in one country can and does have an impact on another's policies and practices. Likewise international policies, treaties, declaration decrees, and conventions are increasingly having a direct impact on national, regional and local policies and practices, and international contact across programs can keep this information in the forefront (Ife, 2012). Second, participating in these local-international linkages also provides opportunities for social work academics and practitioners to pay attention to social inequalities between peoples, across nations and specific regions as well as between different social and ethnic groups and drawn attention to their impact on their own local practice. Problems like HIV/AIDS, pandemics, international crime, and issues associated with mass migration, movement of refugees across countries, war, famine, genocide, trafficking in women and children, the lived experience of poverty, hunger, homelessness and unemployment can no longer be addressed at the local level (Lyons et al., 2012). International aid work and international welfare service agencies as means of seeking and employing international aid is argued to be more beneficial than working in local isolation (Healy, 2008; Lyons et al., 2012). Lastly, the growth in international conversations, research projects, and staff and student exchanges are all benefits of opening the borders, helping to promote more migratory opportunities for those interested in seeking exposure to cultural differences and using their qualifications to work abroad. As a result it is now possible for a qualified social worker to study in one country, work in another and settle in yet another; it is the same for students as well (Noble, 2004).

One development that prepares practitioners to participate in these conversations and debates at the international and or regional level as well as preparing them for the migratory aspirations of graduates is the increasing number of social work programs that are establishing international student placements as part of internationalising their curricula (Razack, 2002). International placements are one way many countries can help foster a culturally aware program, prepare students for multicultural experiences and the development of competencies, as well as providing for beginning practitioners a potentially powerful experience for learning about cultural differences as a way of preparing them for international practice, especially if these experiences are based on mutuality, equality and acceptance of differences (Healy, 2008; Noble, 2004). With the rising number of student placements and staff exchanges it is worth a look at some experiences of student placements, given the challenges posed by such a venture as the region's diversity in languages and cultural practices and traditions, access to communication technologies and geographic location would seem to pose almost insurmountable obstacles.

Social work placement in the Asia-Pacific region

The literature talks about international placements as being life-altering experiences (Healy, 2008; Razack, 2002), but from my research and experience many students have been historically cautious about undertaking this opportunity in the Asia-Pacific region despite having attractive financial assistance for such an opportunity from their universities. Being located in the Asia-Pacific region presents particular problems already outlined, such as language barriers, isolation from family and support, and familiarity of one's own cultural knowledge and comforts. However, despite these difficulties, students' resistances to such opportunities are changing and several students in the social work program I coordinated undertook the challenge and embarked on a placement abroad. Although most chose to go to English speaking countries to get the maximum experience with the minimum effort, as one student explained to me, others ventured into countries unfamiliar to them or to countries whose language and cultural heritage they shared with their family of origin.

In my previous position at the University of Western Sydney (UWS) many more students in the social work and welfare work programs undertook placements in the region especially those students who were part of the international stream of the community development degree, where an overseas placement was compulsory. In order to understand their experiences I, as the field educator at the time, undertook research with these students and university staff involved in the placements that were located in the Asia-Pacific region. Students went such countries as Indonesia, East Timor, Chile, Nepal, Thailand, Vietnam, Fiji, China and Malaysia. With only minimal support from the university all students interviewed for this study saw the benefits for their own learning and as a result undertook this experience with great excitement and anticipation despite the financial costs. Learning about other approaches to social work, especially ones located in different cultural discourses, was considered a useful and enriching experience. For their placements students were involved in such diverse programs as slum redevelopment, peace and reconciliation projects, working with street children and people with disabilities, and participating in street schools and programs for HIV/AIDS education. Working in a different culture and immersing themselves in a different way of life and welfare systems (or lack of one) enabled these students to enrich their understanding of social work practice from a cross cultural perspective by being immersed for a short time in the experience (Noble, 2003a). By immersing themselves in these experiences, students experienced first-hand the position of Other in relation to the cultural and socio-political practices, becoming for a short time the people belonging to language and cultural groups that were outside the dominant relations and therefore marginal to the existing powerbase and positions of influence (Noble, 2003a; Razack 2002).

Students undertaking placements in the region did not go unprepared. Students went on placement with a fully established syllabus and the host agency's cooperation, support and involvement in the learning and supervision of these students. In many cases the 'home' university staff accompanied their students to provide the overall supervision but more often worked in partnership with the host agency's supervisor in providing valuable learning experience for themselves as well as the students. Also, all staff and students were given the opportunity to reflect critically on their experiences after the placement was completed (Noble, 2003a). Thus the value of undertaking international placements was available for both the 'host' and home universities and agencies to explore and then reflect upon the cultural hegemony implicit in one's own program.

In focusing on students' reflections this study highlighted the importance of students having the opportunity to critique the privileged position of their own cultural heritage in a way not accessible when they were studying cross cultural theory and practice at home. Being located in a different country away from friends and family support they have little options but to immerse themselves in the experience—socially, educationally and personally. Immersing themselves in the culture of their host agency is essential if students are to get any real value for themselves and to reflect on their experience in ways that are meaningful and real. In another country, especially one which is different in culture, language and social, political and economic arrangements, students cannot escape being confronted by difference. The following comment is typical of other students who made similar points:

> Going to Indonesia was the most powerful and life changing experience of my life. I learnt more about myself, about different cultures, different lifestyles and what it was like to live in poverty (Maria) (Noble, 2003a, p. 12).

This student's comment sums up what many identified as overall challenges in undertaking a placement in a developing country:

> Challenges for me were the language barrier, but also having the courage to get on the plane and say, 'goodbye', to my family and friends for two months was a challenge as I had never been away from home before. Witnessing poverty I saw everyday was a challenge. It was a challenge not to cry...having to come to the realisation that I could not change anything in two months was a challenge. While studying, I guess I still had the ideal to save the world and that was totally gone by the time I got back. Not that I don't still want to save the world, as everyone would if they could, but knowing now that I may only be able to reach a handful of people in my lifetime (was a sadness)...but I am now (on reflection) OK with that (Laura) (Noble, 2003a, p. 14)

International placements now form a part of many social work programs and for students to be able to experience the best possible experience for all. Razack (2002) has highlighted some important considerations deemed essential for the success of such placements, such as:

- interrogate the almost universally unidirectional nature of these placements by taking into account the legacies of colonialism and being aware and sensitive to the positioning of privilege and the marginal status of agencies involved in the exchange.
- have in place a cross-culturally sensitive curriculum to inform the students learning before, during and after the placements

and as a guide for students to engage in culturally appropriate theorising about international placements.

- incorporate adequate educational space in the curriculum to interrogate and incorporate these experiences into 'home' courses before placements and to encourage their interest.
- engage in research, cross-cultural dialogue and critical reflection so as to avoid the possible dangers of domination and exploitation in the exchange.
- ensure this dialogue is ethical and appropriate to the international setting available.
- investigate whether there are *real* and/or *potential* opportunities for reciprocity in these placements and avoid placements where the experience might be unidirectional.

Social work in Asia Pacific: post-colonial and Indigenous critiques

While I have alluded to the scholarship of post-colonial social work it is a good time to summarise important concepts and critiques, especially as they relate to the Asia-Pacific region and to explore the insights of the cross-cultural, anti-racist and indigenous educational responses. The cross-cultural and indigenous responses have emerged to address and minimise the possible domination of western influences in these exchanges as well as the growth of social work programs in the region. Post-colonial theory emphasises not only the inclusion of multicultural and indigenous voices in the curricula but also proposes that cross-cultural and indigenous approaches to education should actually inform its epistemology (Dominelli, 2002; Green & Baldry, 2013; Razack, 2002).

The post-colonial critique demands that the introduction of social work programs across this region be mindful of how such colonial domination results in the suppression of indigenous cultures, languages and social structures and thus creates and maintains social injustices and socio-political inequalities as a result. It also draws attention to the dominance of the 'white voice' and 'white privilege' in contemporary social work curricula and how this domination can influence the way social problems and issues are analysed and addressed and in whose interest this activity may benefit and disadvantage (Cox & Pawar, 2008; Dominelli, 2002). While the post-colonial critique was being taken seriously by some in academia, others involved in the International Association for Schools of Social Work (IASSW) were concerned about social work programs being developed across the globe, without agreed international guidelines and professional standards. If students, practitioners and academics wanted to work and study 'across borders' then international standards were needed (Sewpaul, 2005). It was always the intention of the researchers to include a cross cultural perspective but the imperative of developing guidelines that would ensure some uniformity in social work programs was also a desired outcome.

As a consequence in 2003–2005, the International Association of Schools of Social Work (IASSW) engaged in a consultative project to develop the *Global Standards for Social Work Education* to create a common platform and identity for all programs across the globe. It was also to be used as a guiding document to help standardise the program, content and structure of social work courses worldwide, including the Asia-Pacific region, which was of interest to me and the Asian and Pacific Association of Schools of Social Work Education (APASWE) of which I was an active member. It was felt that these standards were necessary in order to create a common platform and identity and to set some benchmarks to help developing countries establish courses that would have cultural currency if, for example, students wanted to move countries and continue their study and/ or to work in this field once qualified. It was also undertaken to help developing countries argue for and get the required resources, staff and curricula content necessary for setting up such programs and for their programs to be consistent with other programs in the developed countries with well-established courses and reputations (Sewpaul, 2005).

In 2004, in the midst of this development, I surveyed several Asia-Pacific countries about their attitude to the IASSW's project of developing *Global Standards for Social Work Education* and their future usefulness as a guide to keep their standards in line with other countries with similar programs (Noble, 2004). I mention this research to draw attention to one aspect of the participant countries' responses, relevant to this focus of this chapter; that is to describe the content of their current programs and relationship with their cultural context and plans for contextualising their cultural imperatives into the broader social work discourse (read western model). All the countries who responded to the questionnaire, which included The Philippines, Hong Kong and China, Sri Lanka, India and Korea, as well as Australia and Aotearoa/New Zealand, provided similar responses. While identifying differing theoretical underpinnings such as an ecological, or strengths-based approach to a feminist and human rights and social justice focus, they all taught a mixture of the traditional practice methods of casework, group and family work, community development and organisational work but with varying degree of emphasis (Noble, 2004). Although all had a significant fieldwork component again the structure and emphasis varied according to their particular course emphasis, i.e., community development or individual change. Importantly, a small number of respondents indicated that although they were initially influenced by the western model of social work education in the delivery or establishment of new programs (for a variety of reasons), they were also aware of the importance of challenging the dominant knowledge behind these western influences. As one respondent said, 'It is up to us to work out how cultural differences can be applied to social work in our country' (Noble, 2004, p. 531). Overall, however, the respondents thought global standards would be useful and were generally supportive of the project, for as a general guide 'it was the best it could be' (Noble, 2004, p. 531). As far as I know these standards are being used across the region as benchmarks for the development of social work programs.

Interestingly, then, the challenge to the homogeneity of the social work discourse and its relevance to differing cultural context and knowledges, according to my research has been taken up in important ways in the literature from the western countries in the region, specifically from Australia and Aotearoa/New Zealand, where there is an emerging body of literature informed by a critical postmodern perspective, and which is having an important epistemological impact (Green & Baldry, 2013). Critical postmodernism promotes indigenisation and contextualisation of issues and concerns. The critical postmodern approach draws attention to the ethnocentric nature of knowledge and practice of the traditional model of social work, especially the way its practice excluded different cultures, traditions and political and social systems from its analysis and discourse (Allan et al., 2009). This critique also found resonance with the post-colonial and indigenous critique in the more progressive social work literature, giving voice to a more critical approach to social work praxis and understandings for addressing social problems (Dominelli, 2002; Mullaly, 2010; Noble, 2003). Critical postmodern social work stresses that social problems are to be addressed in the socio-political and economic context in an empowering, non-oppressive and anti-discriminatory way, simultaneously within the specific context and cultural influences of the local communities and individuals (Mullaly, 2010). Today many Australian social work programs are developing core curricula that emphasise a cross-cultural approach that places importance on respecting diversity and difference in culture and traditions, languages and philosophies and intellectual thought and debate, and attempt to engage in reciprocity and mutuality in supporting the development of a decolonised social work paradigm (Briskman, 2004; Green & Baldry, 2013; Noble, 2003; 2004). This is true for Aotearoa/New Zealand as well (see Cheyne, O'Brien & Belgrave, 2009; Connolly & Harm, 2009).

This critique has changed social work scholarship in these countries in two important ways (Allan et al., 2009). The first was to influence and support the bicultural response, especially in Aotearoa/New Zealand, which leads the way in incorporating Māori voices in social work curricula, standards and codes of practice and ethical guidelines (ANZASW, 2008; Cheyne, O'Brien & Belgrave, 2009; Connolly & Harm, 2009). What followed from this development was the identification of specific skills associated with cross-cultural practices developed in order to be able to engage more effectively with people from diverse backgrounds. The second was to spearhead the emergence of more critically reflective approach to practice which emphasises critical reflection to promote, encourage and develop contextually and culturally relevant and appropriate social work practice and educational methods (Fook & Gardner ,2007). This critical reflective scholarship has resulted in many programs adopting a more critically reflective practice claiming relevance to all settings and across all cultures and minority and marginalised groups (Briskman, 2004; Fook & Gardner, 2006). Payne & Askeland (2008) argue that as social workers become more mobile and programs expand across the world by using the process of critical reflection, the profession and the workers can be made aware of the mutuality of the learning process and what can be created locally; at the same time, for the program and the practice to still have a relationship with the larger discourse.

Educational responses—cross cultural and antiracist practice

It is important to reflect briefly on the way Australian and Aotearoa/ New Zealand scholars have taken up the challenge to address cultural biases in their programs by developing educational responses informed by critical postmodern critique and cross-cultural and indigenous practice. In this analysis, developing cultural awareness requires, it is argued, a concerted level of critical self-examination of the influences of our own cultural roots in order to be able to understand and appreciate others (Mullaly, 2010). Such an exercise often uncovers disturbing personal prejudices and unexpected levels of intolerance and racism that Bell Hooks (1990) forwarded in her groundbreaking critique of racism and racist practices. As a result of these reflections and self examinations, educational responses emerged as scholars began to grapple with the notion of providing cross culturally aware programs and strategies.

In drawing attention to the forces of assimilation and colonisation of indigenous peoples, postmodern critiques pushed anti-racist or anti-oppressive practice further by providing a 'native epistemological' response for the disconnectedness experienced by Aboriginal/Indigenous peoples from their own knowledges, voices, and historical experiences that manufactured their physical and cultural absence in the educational arena (Bennett et al., 2013, Hanohano, 1999). The recently formed National Coalition of Aboriginal and Torres Strait Islander Social Workers Association in Australia has played an important role in working to address disadvantage and discrimination in the Aboriginal and Torres Strait Islanders communities (ATSIC), and to encourage full incorporation of alternative cultural knowledge into the social work profession—especially in practice, policy, research and the educational curricula. In cooperation with the Australian Association for Social Workers (AASW), culturally specific and ASTIC practice standards and curriculum content are to be included in all social work programs in Australia from 2013 onwards. This curriculum will need to cover ATSIC society, culture, practices and issues, ways of knowing and being as well as a commitment to acknowledging the historical and contemporary disadvantages and trauma effects of past and present welfare policies and practices (ASWEAS, 2012). Aotearoa/ New Zealand as already mentioned incorporated a bicultural practice several years ago and have more recently added Maori te reo with English in its publication of the Bi-cultural Code of Ethics (ANZASW, 2008). Core courses on Māori society, language and culture have had a strong presence in both tertiary institutions and the profession for several years (Green & Baldry, 2013).

In recognising difference and identifying educational strategies in indigenous communities a cross-cultural practice which has been translated into educational practices that are mindful of cultural imperialism. These practices are designed to reduce and avoid the negative effects of western influences in the development of social work programs in the region. These educational practices are outlined below.

In educational terms it has meant that social work curricula must include:

- a deconstruction of the process of colonisation and the imposition of western epistemologies on indigenous peoples and to explore the impact of its debilitating forces of assimilation and oppression
- the exploration of Other as *a* knowledge rather than *the* knowledge
- the development of a holistic model of education that integrates spirituality, culture and traditions
- the exploration of indigenous language and knowledge in the inclusion of a tribal or native epistemology
- the uncovering of the indigenous voice by giving imagery to their pain, anguish, as well as hopes and dreams
- the exploration of strategies and alternatives as well as resistance and resilience in the educational project, that is break out from the colonial shadow
- the inclusion of the exploration of the sacred, spiritual and relationship with earth and land as part of social work practice methods
- the exploration of the connectedness with elders and traditional knowing
- the emphasis on the interconnectedness/interrelationships with *all* things
- the inclusion of texts form non-western and indigenous peoples in subject references list and as text books
- the creation of a third space where new understanding between the coloniser and the colonised positioning and identity can emerge (adapted from Briskman, 2004; Hanohano, 1999; Noble, 2003; Zubrzycki & Crawford, 2013).

Conclusion

The world is now linked in ways that it would now be impossible to unlink. We know a lot about each other and we are connected in ways that we never imagined possible a few decades ago. For social work programs there are obvious advantages for working across borders such as developing international and regional responses to the social problems we all have in common, collectively exploring the impact of foreign debt and the interrelatedness of global capital on the national and regional economic development of countries in the region, as well as more pressing problems resulting from poverty, war, and famine for increasing large numbers of people. The phrase 'we are all in this together' is a mantra adopted by world leaders. But looking at the many countries mentioned in this chapter that make up the Asia-Pacific region I am also mindful of the differences and the heterogeneity of the region. The region is characterised by many cultural and ethnic groupings, religions, and political, social and welfare systems which can provide social work with a truly international focus if the western social work discourse is open to these multifarious voices and to the possibilities of including these multi-realities into both its practice and educational approaches that this sharing can bring.

It is a vibrant region to be part of, and it is exciting to see social work programs emerging in such numbers and for curricula to be responding to these challenges. But social work educators influenced by the western approach must also be continuously mindful about issues raised by the Indigenous, post-colonial and postmodern critique. However if cross-cultural and indigenous social work as has been outlined here is used as a epistemological position for social work education programs wherever they are developed, then social work will be given an even more precious gift of truly reflecting the multi-realities of the region's culture, ways of knowing and learning and possibilities and collaboration in a mutually sustaining and equal way.

References

Allan, J., Pease, B. & Briskman, L. (2009). *Critical social work: an introduction to theories and practices*, 2nd edn. Crows Nest: Allen & Unwin.

Aotaroa New Zealand Association of Social Workers (2008). *Code of Ethics.* Christchurch: ANZASW National Office.

Australian Social Work Education Accreditation Standards (2012) Retrieved 17 April 2013 from www.aasw.asn.au/document/item/3550.

Bennett, B., Green, S., Gilbert, S. & Bessarab, D. (2013). *Our voices: Aboriginal and Torres Strait Islander social work.* South Yarra: Palgrave Macmillan.

Briskman, L. (2004). *Social work with indigenous communities.* Sydney: Federation Press.

Chenoweth, L. & McAuliffe, D. (2008). *The road to social work and human service practice.* South Melbourne: Cengage Learning.

Cheyne, C., O'Brien, M. & Belgrave, M. (2009). *Social policy in Aotearoa New Zealand: a critical introduction.* New Zealand: Oxford University Press.

Connolly, M. & Harm, L. (Eds) (2009). *Social work: contexts and practice,* 3rd edn. South Melbourne: Oxford University Press.

Cox, D. & Pawar, M. (2008). *International social work: issues, strategies and programs.* London: Sage.

Dominelli, L. (2002). Anti-oppressive practice in context. In R. Adams, L. Dominelli & M. Payne (Eds). *Social work: themes, issues and critical debates.* Hamsphire: Palgrave Macmillan.

Fook, J., & Gardner, F. (2007). *Practising critical reflection: a resource handbook.* Maidenhead. Oxford: Oxford University Press.

Green, S. & Baldry, E. (2013). Indigenous social work education in Australia. In B. Bennett, S. Green, S. Gilbert, & D. Bessarab (Eds). *Our voices: Aboriginal and Torres Strait Islander social work* (pp. 166–80). South Yarra: Palgrave Macmillan.

Hanohano, P. (1999). The spiritual imperative of native epistemology: restoring harmony and balance to education. *Canadian Journal of Native Education*, 23(2), 206–19.

Harrison, G. & Melville, R. (2010). *Rethinking social work in a global world.* New York: Palgrave Macmillan.

Healy, L. & Link, R. (Eds) (2012). *Handbook of international social work: human rights, development, and the global profession.* New York: Oxford University Press.

Healy, L. (2008). *International social work: professional action in an independent world,* 2nd edn. New York: Oxford University Press.

Hooks, B. (1990). *Yearning: race, gender and cultural politics.* Boston: South End Press.

Ife, J. (2012). *Human rights and social work: towards rights-based practice.* Cambridge: Cambridge University Press.

Lyons, K., Hokenstad, T., Pawar, M., Huegler, N. & Hall, N. (Eds) (2012). *The Sage Book of International Social Work.* London: Sage.

McDonald, C. (2006). *Challenging social work: the institutional context of practice.* Hampshire: Palgrave Macmillan.

Motta, S. & Nilsen, A. (2011). *Social movements in the global south: dispossession, development & resistance.* Hampshire: Palgrave Macmillan.

Mullaly, B. (2010). *The new structural social work.* New York: Oxford University Press.

Midgley, J. (2000). Globalisation, capitalism and social welfare. *Canadian Social Work Review*, 2(1), 13–28.

Noble, C. (2003). Discursive scholarship in anti-racist/cross cultural social work education. *Advances*, 5(1), 98–108.

Noble, C. (2003a). What am I doing here, really? Students' and teachers' reflections on international placements. In L. Dominelli (Ed). *Broadening horizons* (pp. 257–77). London: Ashgate Press.

Noble, C. (2004). Social work education, training and standards in the Asia-Pacific region: an exploration of the issues. *International Journal of Social Work Education*, 23(5), 527–36.

Noble, C. (2007). Social work, collective action and social movements. In L. Dominelli (Ed). *Revitalising communities in a globalising world.* Hampshire: Ashgate.

Payne, M. & Askeland, G. (2008). *Globalization and international social work: postmodern change and challenge.* Hampshire: Ashgate.

Razack, N. (2002). *Transforming the field: critical antiracist and anti-oppressive perspectives for the human services practicum.* Halifax: Fernwood.

Sewpaul, V. (2005). Global standards: promise and pitfalls for re-inscribing social work into civil society. *International Journal of Social Welfare,* 14(3), 210–17.

Yip, K. S. (2004). A Chinese cultural critique of the global qualifying standards for social work education. *Social Work Education: The International Journal,* 23(5), 597–612.

Zubrzycki, J. & Crawford, F. (2013). Collaboration and relationship building in Aboriginal and Torres Strait Islander social work. In B. Bennett, S. Green, S. Gilbert & D. Bessarab (Eds). *Our voices: Aboriginal and Torres Strait Islander social work* (pp. 181–205). South Yarra: Palgrave Macmillan.

16

The humanitarian perspective in social work and community welfare education

Deborah West and Dan Baschiera

Charles Darwin University, located in the Northern Territory, is Australia's most geographically isolated tertiary institution. In 2006, the social work and community welfare studies programs were re-developed to take advantage of, and focus, on our unique location in the south-east Asia region. This chapter examines the key issues raised in the curriculum development process and subsequent student feedback which provides the underlying imperatives for changes in regional social work and community welfare education. These include the cultural diversity of the region, challenges of remote service provision, political pressures, the lack of appropriate theoretical frameworks for intervention, linking of people skills and technical competencies and a clear ethical framework. It explores the practice-activism divide outlining an ethical discourse between social work and our evolving 'humanitarianism' and how this can provide a framework to consolidate and develop the knowledge base for evidence based practice in resource poor, cross cultural and remote environments.

社會工作和社會福利教育中的人道主義考量

位於北領地的查爾斯達爾文大學，是澳大利亞最偏遠的院校。 2006年，社會工作和社會福利研究計劃被重新啟動，以重點利用我們在東南亞地區的獨特位置。本章探討的是在課程開發過程及學生反饋中的重點問題。這些問題為改變地區社會工作和社會福利教育提供了基本的必要條件。這其中包括地區文化的多樣性，提供遠程服務的困難，政治上的壓力，缺乏進行干預的合適理論框架，將人的能力和技術能力相結合以及明確的道德框架等問題。從中探討了實踐積極性區分了社會工作和不斷發展的' 人道主義' 之間的道德概述，並探究了這一切如何能夠為在資源匱乏，跨越文化和偏遠環境中鞏固和發展循證實踐的知識基礎提供一個框架。

タイトル：ソーシャルワークとコミュニティ福祉教育における人道的視点

著者：デボラ・ウェスト、ダン・バスキエラ

北部準州に位置するチャールズ·ダーウィン大学は、オーストラリアの地理的に他から孤立した高等教育機関である。2006年に、ソーシャルワークおよび地域社会福祉学プログラムは、南東アジア地域に位置するこの利点に着目し再構築されている。この章では、カリキュラム開発過程で浮かび上がった主要課題と、その後の学生のフィードバックが示した地域ソーシャルワーク及び地域社会福祉学教育における変化に応じて緊急に取り組まなければならない課題を検証する。これらの課題には、地域の文化多様性、遠隔サービス提供の挑戦、政治的圧力、介入に関する適切な理論的枠組みの欠如、人々を繋げる技術や専門的能力や明確な倫理的枠組みなどが含まれる。ここでは実践行動主義を、倫理的な論議にあるソーシャルワークと我々の変わり続ける「人道主義」の間の概要に分け、そして限られた資源や異文化と人里離れた環境内で、どのようにして知識基盤を整理統合し証拠に基づく実践をいかに提供できるかという点に分けて論じる。

사회복지 인도주의적 관점과 지역사회복지 교육

Charles Darwin University는 호주에서 가장 지리적으로 고립되어 북쪽에 위치한 대학이다. 2006년부터 동남아지역이라는 지리적 특수성 때문에 사회복지교육프로그램이 다시 부각되기 시작했다. 본 장은 이 지역에 맞는 사회복지는 무엇이고 지역사회복지교육을 위해서는 교과과정에서 바꿔야하는 주요 쟁점이 무엇인가를 탐색하였다. 그러기 위해서는 문화 다양성을 고려해야 하고, 원거리 서비스 개발, 정치세력의 압력을 극복하는 일,

적절한 개입 이론 부족의 문제가 포함된다. 적절한 개입은 문화적으로 적합하고 개입기법이 뛰어나면서도 인간에게 적용할 수 있는 개입이론을 말한다. 사회복지와 인본주의 사이의 윤리적 담론을 나열하는 실무-행동주의가 할 일이 무엇인지 탐색하고 이를 통해 자원이 없고, 다문화이며, 원거리에 있는 클라이언트에게 증거기반 실천을 이행할 수 있는 지식기반을 만들 수 있게 된다.

Introduction: Northern Territory context and challenges

The Northern Territory (NT) of Australia is geographically large but with a small population spread across a range of communities. It equates to approximately one per cent of the total Australian population spread over 17 per cent of the Australian land mass. While much of the population resides in Darwin and Alice Springs, there are many smaller populations of scattered, marginalised and in accordance with established Australian measures, impoverished remote Aboriginal communities.

The population of the NT is diverse with 27 per cent identifying as Indigenous Australians and 27 per cent having at least one parent born outside of Australia (ABS, 2012). Significant populations include those from British, New Zealand, Chinese, Filipino, Greek and Italian descent. There is also an increasing community of African people within Darwin. This diversity necessitates a broad competency in cross cultural practice and in this context an informed awareness of the unique collective values of Indigenous and immigrant communities.

Given its small population NT resources are somewhat limited compared to other more populous states. Simply put there is a dearth of human service providers. In addition, delivering services to outlying communities is regularly dictated by either a limited political contract (lack of resourcing), the huge tyranny of distance and/or wet season conditions which results in road closures and limited air access. Given this environment human service workers have to be more creative and generalist in their practice. The additional resiliency skilling for humanitarian logistics compliments human service work outside of the Darwin area where the human service worker needs to maintain nominal comfort, security, competence, technical ability and sustainability in practice.

Since self government in 1978 the NT has been regarded by journalists and scholars as 'something different' within the Australian Federation (Carment, 2007). It is argued that in lacking statehood the NT has difficulties in both its political and fiscal relationship with Canberra. This in turn has compounded the logistic difficulties of delivering services across huge distances. Consequently remote Northern Australia has been marginalised with a historic cycle of limited resourcing in many sectors (Wild & Anderson, 2007). Historically this has meant a continuous breach of the political contract where Indigenous people have been disallowed self determination with a political manipulation of the collectivist/individualist divide.

Further overlaying this context is the importance of the NT, and Darwin in particular, as a Trauma and Critical Response Centre for the South East Asia Region (Department of Health and Ageing, 2006). In response to the Bali bombings the Federal Government designated the Royal Darwin Hospital as a National Critical Care and Trauma Response Centre (Dept. of Health and Ageing, 2006; National Critical Care and Trauma Response Centre, 2010). Such a designation has provided a clear focus on the need for competency and knowledge of disaster, trauma and humanitarian aid. This combined with the demographics and harsh environment, means that human service work in the NT or other remote areas is clearly different and requires some different skills than that of work in the Australian mainstream.

The pathway to remote social work in the NT has seen graduates come and go. Most stick tenaciously to mainstream roles in the major communities and very few wander into the hinterland. Most who do venture in this direction tend not to last long due to the harsh conditions of the Australian outback and difficulties socialising across the cultural divide. Urban trained human service professions are not given the practical skills and knowledge to cope in such environments. Remote service delivery needs positive patterns of adaption, in short a level of operational resiliency.

Resilience refers to the tendency to spring back, rebound or recoil, and involves the capacity to respond and endure despite adversity (Mandleco & Peery, 2000). It is linked to well-being which in turn increases meaning in a worker's life and thus enhances performance (Shearon & Parks-Sheaner, 2007). Beddoe, Davis and Adamson (2013, p. 101) acknowledge resilience as a two dimensional construct and as such state it is also about 'including the experience of adverse conditions and the presence of positive skills in coping with these conditions. An ecological lens can incorporate the important influences of individual, cultural, organisational and socio-political dimensions'.

While we agree with these definitions we have discovered that simply transferring traditional/urban social work into humanitarian delivery in remote areas does not work. As in international humanitarian disaster aid delivery operational resiliency in remote Australia is linked to a third dimension. This third dimension is a working knowledge of chaos management, vision, technical support systems, ability to survive and make do with limited infrastructure, to problem solve and generate/support the ability to work in professional isolation and/or in isolated teams.

While the core underpinnings of the human service profession remain the same there are significant differences which must be addressed in training and practice to properly prepare students for the challenges of regional or remote work. The two overlapping areas of social work and humanitarian aid are complementary and have much to offer each other in terms of preparedness and effectiveness for the chosen field of practice whether it is in social work in remote areas, international social work or humanitarian aid. This was our opening proposition as we developed our two programs: the Bachelor of Social Work and the Bachelor of Humanitarian and Community Studies.

This chapter reflects on the key issues that were raised as part of the curriculum design process but builds on that based on feedback from our students, their field education supervisors and our experiences of coordinating and teaching in the programs over a period of five years.

Ongoing curriculum development

In 2006 a process was undertaken to re-develop our social work program with a view to distinguishing it from other social work courses and our existing welfare studies course. This was in response to feedback from agencies, students and a wide variety of other stakeholders who felt that those graduating from the existing programs were not properly prepared to work in the NT or in the broader region.

The challenge faced by Charles Darwin University (CDU), was how to integrate the mutual strengths of both disciplines into effective skills for practice in the field and in particular the remote and resource poor fields that exist in the region while maintaining the integrity of both. This led to the development of the Bachelor of Social Work and the Bachelor of Humanitarian and Community Studies which share a set of units alongside their own unique units.

Shared units require clear articulation of teaching and learning outcomes and approaches which allow students in both programs to explore the theoretical and classroom based content in relation to their chosen career path whether that is in remote community development, social work or overseas aid agencies. The focus is on exploration of the application of content as opposed to content delivery. Such units include communication skills, group work, community development, culture in practice, organisational theory and practice, research methods and ethics. An additional shared unit focuses entirely on skills for regional and remote practice examining policy approaches, self-care, models of service delivery in remote areas and additional cross cultural training.

The humanitarian program also requires the completion of several technical skills units where students receive training in project management, mechanical plant, water sanitation/supply, radio telecommunications, all-terrain vehicles, power generation and safety. Much of this training is undertaken via a two week intensive on a remote cattle station. Given the diverse and often unregulated environments humanitarian workers operate in, a key aim of the training is to enable a basic familiarity with the technical requirements to enable a 'trouble shooting' level of competency. Social work students are encouraged to take such units as electives in their programs. At the same time social work students have the required units of social work theory and practice, evidence based practice, lifespan development and social policy. These units along with additional engineering units are then encouraged as electives for humanitarian studies students.

The underlying premise is that for social work to be safe and effective in remote areas training needs to incorporate humanitarian and disaster recovery skills and knowledge while humanitarian aid work needs to systematically incorporate the people skills and theoretical frameworks of social work. This combination of disciplines we hoped would generate new ways of thinking about human service work in remote and regional locations and create a shift toward a stronger operational resiliency for graduating students.

This approach was unique both within Australia and internationally. Five years on, feedback from students, field education supervisors, agencies, our observations and our own critical reflection as teachers has allowed us to identify the strengths of each program but also what needs to be improved.

A key issue that has arisen and continues to develop from working in this humanitarian space is the need to reflect further on appropriate theoretical frameworks and knowledge for work in areas of limited resources or in a disaster context. While there are many social work frameworks that are appropriate, many humanitarian students are unable to see how or why these can apply to a non-traditional environment. This leads students to question why they should be required to take units on ethics, research methods and models of practice.

Typically, students bring theory together with practice in their field placement units. However, our students are often significantly challenged not just by the 'usual' issues that arise in placement but also the incredible difference that exists in remote and international placement. 'I did not realise working across cultures and across languages would be so hard'; this in so many words has been a general and sobering comment from our humanitarian students returning from placements overseas and from within Indigenous communities. The next section of the chapter pursues these issues in greater depth making the case for both the uniqueness of remote social work and humanitarian work but also the complimentary role of the two related disciplines.

Social work helps humanitarian workers operate in cultural diversity

In Northern Australia there is a distinct cultural difference in orientation between the constructs of individualist mainstream and the Indigenous collective. This orientation is limited in research yet lies at the core of the NT's social difficulties. As DeVito (2005, p. 194) notes, 'In an individualist culture you are responsible for yourself and perhaps your immediate family; in a collectivist culture you are responsible for the entire group'. The difference in orientation is reflected in a social history of the NT with communication and value gaps that are difficult to bridge. This is evident in the drive for individualist and capitalist values from the dominant mainstream group.

Compounding this, the unique individualist construct continues to cyclically blame the victim for the end result—intergenerational unemployment, and the social stress that goes with it—leading to social exclusion. As Manuel Castells (2000, p. 71) notes: 'Social exclusion is in fact the process that disfranchises a person as labour in the context of capitalism'. If one were to incorporate Castell's argument then cultural diversity in the NT, particularly in relation to the Indigenous community, can also lead to social exclusion.

With longer term social exclusion, and as is the case for Indigenous Australians, comes the intergenerational concept of developmental trauma—identified as existing in high levels in Indigenous communities by the Northern Territory's Children's

Commissioner, Dr Howard Bath (Northern Territories Emergency Response Review Board, 2008, p. 34).

> Researchers describe development trauma disorder as a series of traumatic events during a child's developmental phase that impairs normal neurological development, particularly as it relates to a capacity to adapt to stress. This can be evident in a child's inability to form trusting relationships, anger and defiance, passivity, substance abuse and other harmful behaviours towards themselves and others.

While a range of programs have been put in place since this report (Department of Families, Housing, Community Services and Indigenous Affairs, 2012), the fundamental issues remain and only limited headway has been made.

Within this complex level of morbid socio-cultural diversity we see additional imperatives for change to the delivery of social work and welfare education in our region. These include knowledge of and ability to critique government neglect, political malfeasance, and to mitigate the social erosions of economic rationalist policies and globalisation. In the humanitarian context the Australian analysis above can also be seen in the impacts of global capitalism as the emergent global culture (globalisation). We look at the difficulties and challenges capitalism has in dealing with corporatisation, ethics, corruption and global warming.

Cultural study in human service work in northern Australia and globally therefore needs to incorporate the knowledge base social work practice and understandings if humanitarianism is to work effectively within this ongoing social history of global capitalist violence and its difficulties in constructively absorbing collective values and labour. Given that capitalist induced poverty and remoteness is also a significant factor, these issues link social work and welfare education to humanitarian mission risk management and activism along with the need to work in isolated teams.

It is a humanitarian work environment that argues strongly for the strengthening and necessary knowledge and theory social work can give to humanitarian, technical, interpersonal and cross cultural skills. As student Janine Sims so aptly put it 'The humanitarian community worker must work towards the reduction of trauma through a local and/or individual approach. What may work for one community or individual may not necessary work with another individual or community' (pers. comm.). Critical reflection would play a key role in the ability to select practices that are both appropriate and effective.

Like humanitarian work in disadvantaged parts of the world the training imperatives also need to include the ever-changing tensions between agency mandates, political pressures and constraints across vast and remote distances, while at the same time trying to interpret the cultural communication schism between the individualist and collective orientation. This is also a view by Jenny Pearson, a humanitarian working in Cambodia, in her article 'The Multi-Cultural Iceberg' (2008, p. 2).

> It is a fact that a deep and pervasive lack of cross cultural understanding still exists. The struggle to understand each other in ways that are truly meaningful continues unabated and underpins the even greater struggle to understand what is really going on inside the organisations where Cambodians and expatriates work together.

Developing humanitarian studies as an academic discipline relies strongly on the people skilling of other disciplines to assist humanitarian students to bridge their work across the cultural ravines. Social work plays a critical part in this but there is still a lot more to learn. Students continue to identify a shortfall in cross cultural understanding and meaning during debriefing sessions upon returning from their placement assignments. Additionally, anecdotal feedback from the humanitarian field indicates an ongoing lack of attention is paid to cross cultural issues in the functioning of the sector's organisations.

The sensitivities of our students have highlighted the shortfall we have in the sector. Both social work and humanitarian students identify a trend where the values of individualism tend to deny the values of a collective management system, usually over riding it because individualism is resource rich and maintains what one student defined as a 'colonial - self approach'. The basic humanitarian paradigm is that rich nations have resources while the poor and disaster impacted have not and sadly most humanitarian agencies reinforce this model. It is manifested in a power imbalance at the coal face. The humanitarian aid worker has the resources and skills and dictates the management of those resources in a top down, we are more enlightened than you approach (Ife, 2010, p. 108). It is a process which in the cut and thrust of agency delivery thwarts the collective self-determining responsibilities of a collective cultural base.

This is a point aptly described by Kate Henson one of our humanitarian students who has just completed her placement in Cambodia. In her final report she concludes:

> Lastly, Cambodia has a collective culture. Families have been brought up living in very small living spaces and sharing everything. Additionally, communities are very close. In the countryside there is still much suspicion and monks play an important role in ceremonies. Along with this there are Village Chiefs and Community Representatives who are considered powerful community members. It is difficult for Western organisations or volunteers to come into a village and really understand its culture. Thus, here, locals must be involved in the community development process. Although Westerners may have good intentions, the effects of Western workers in these isolated areas can be damaging. Solutions must come from community members themselves.

In this statement the value of teaching and challenging cross cultural constructs and providing frameworks for critique is evident. Yet, teaching in cross cultural issues is difficult as differences between people often mask some of the more profound diversities in other cultures and fundamental differences. Students must understand that they need to prepare for their real cross cultural learning which will come in the field.

The complexity of cross cultural work in meaning is also very difficult. Due to strong concrete values in remote traditional (as distinct to contemporary) Indigenous communities some Indigenous Australians have a great deal of difficulty with hypothesis and the word for 'if' in an individualist context. In a collective conditional context the word 'if' does not seem to exist in any Indigenous Australian language (Bain, 2005, p. 9). We cite this point as an example of how sensitive communication has to be to penetrate correct meanings cross culturally. In context a social worker going into a traditional community that is very concrete in its value base and states 'If there is child abuse in this community we can work on child protection' will have this statement interpreted as 'There is child abuse in this community and we will catch the culprit.' Immediately one can see the generation of chaos and accusations in a small community due to an insensitive confusion in meaning.

The distinction between remote, traditional communities and contemporary Indigenous communities is hinted at by one of our Indigenous students. Quitaysha Cartwright, in writing on chaos management makes the following distinction: 'In regards to managing chaos in a remote community I would most likely use my personal cultural experience in dealing with it. As opposed to managing a chaos in an urban based community' (pers. comm.). Fortunately Quitaysha has this personal knowledge to draw upon; however many of our other students do not and bringing them to the point of understanding can be difficult. With these challenges continuing our next step is to more clearly articulate a framework for the two disciplines to clarify our understandings and to assist students with their learning and preparation for the field.

Articulating a framework for two similar yet divergent disciplines

In the first stages of articulating this framework, several key elements demand attention: models of practice, research informed practice and ethical frameworks. These elements are vital due to requirements from the field and demands of the work environment, the underpinning philosophy of humanitarianism and feedback from students and agencies.

THE VALUE OF MODELS OF PRACTICE

One of the major challenges we have is helping students to see the relevance of models of practice. Some of the more pragmatic models do fit quite well (community development, strengths based, crisis intervention and task centred approach) while others are not appropriate. However, this is generally the case in any field of practice and it is the combination of building competence in a repertoire of models and being able to use the most appropriate one depending on the client and context that is essential. It is therefore important to provide opportunities to critique models and explore ways of working and thinking about these in application. Role plays which contextualise to a broader variety of situations become important in this context. It is also important to build new models of practice or modify others. In order to do this, students need both the foundation and structure of models and the freedom to critique them in light of humanitarian philosophy.

This exploration can be linked to the 'new humanitarianism' that questions globalisation and its damaging effects. This thinking proffers human service work with profoundly new challenges in the global context, and in turn a substantially wider knowledge base to evolve practice wisdom. James Orbinski (2002) places this view in context with a speech to graduating students:

> I want to talk to you today about humanitarianism and about citizenship. But most importantly I want to talk to you about courage and choices. In preparing for this talk over the last few days, some have said to me that students are different today: more committed to their careers and their incomes than they are to the idealism that sparks dreams of a better tomorrow for all. I don't believe this. Every one of you has imagined that life can be more just, more fair, and less cruel for others, and that you want to do something to make this

happen. This humanitarian ethos is not a lofty ideal to be discarded in the face of pragmatism or in the face of so-called political realities. Humanitarianism must be the starting point, not an afterthought. And this is most especially true for our leaders.

BUILDING RESEARCH INFORMED PRACTICE

Education and training programs have been identified as being behind the pacesetters for developments in the human service field (Edmond, McGivern, Williams, et al., 2006). The reasons for this are identified by Edmond et al. (2006, p. 379): 'Encouraging social work practitioners to rely on evidence to guide their practice is made difficult by the current paucity of scientific research underpinning many social work interventions'. This is particularly the case for those working in remote areas. As such, it is important that all social work and humanitarian students develop skills in research.

Work in this area has included developing strategic links with many agencies for students to undertake a range of research at the undergraduate level in their current course work. Thus, it has positioned itself to practice and research in the humanitarian environment.

While the BHCS is still a young degree the work of our students has led to positive commendations of their placement supervisors where the work they have done has resulted in key sanitation research, combined data collection and harnessing of workforce to build a child care centre. Recently a Nepalese student completed a placement in child protection and is planning to return to Nepal to use the experience and research informed approach he has gained to work on the profound child protection issues in his home country.

THE ETHICAL INTERSECTION BETWEEN HUMAN SERVICE AND THE NEW HUMANITARIANISM

There are many fundamental similarities between humanitarian and social work with both operating at the interface between people and their environments, (Gitterman, 1996) often dealing with the breakdown of social infrastructure and in multidisciplinary teams. Humanitarianism and social work also share values deeply based in 'humanity', social justice and human well-being (AASW, 2010). This intersection on social justice and ethics is where social work can lend a depth of ethical strength to the significant complexities of humanitarianism.

There is now an evolving billion dollar humanitarian industry, the scale of which is difficult to both quantify, and qualify. With it a new without borders humanitarianism is evolving from its traditional historical roots in order to deal with the numerous agencies, contemporary complex emergencies, conflicts, and disasters. As Arendt (2011, p. 272) states, 'We should guard against the failures of our political regimes and the possible failures in our own thinking and judgement'. Our students would agree as they are seeing the global population dislocations and are identifying the substantial need for humanitarian thinking in the way Australia thinks about human services in the future.

Despite its long operational history humanitarian ethical debate and analysis, until recently, remained in a complex limbo without much disturbance to its generally understood and designated conventions, interventions and adopted codes such as the one of political silence. A foundational humanitarian framework is described by Fiona Terry (2002, p. 19):

> Humanitarian action posits a universal ethic founded on the conviction that all people have equal dignity by virtue of their membership in humanity ... The 'humanitarian imperative' declares that there is an obligation to provide humanitarian assistance wherever it is needed, and is predicated on the right to receive, and to offer, humanitarian aid. Impartiality implies that assistance is based solely on need, without any discrimination among recipients because of nationality, race, religion or other factors. The principle of neutrality denotes a duty to refrain from taking part in hostilities or from undertaking any action that furthers the interests of one party to the conflict or compromises those of the other.

Such a humanitarian ethos emerged back in 1862 with Henri Dunant publishing his 'Memory of Solferino' advocating for the wounded soldier with the vision for an organisation akin to the Red Cross. The foundational framework of the Red Cross did dominate the humanitarian industry and locked in its conventions it lacked an evolving academic debate. This was the case until the 1970s when the *Sans Frontieres* [Without Borders] philosophy emerged from the genocide of Biafra, challenging the status quo, and the new humanitarianism emerged. The new humanitarianism is still in its ethical infancy, but its debate is already grappling with ethics in what social work already recognises as 'a highly complex and contested terrain that raises more questions than it answers' (Chenoweth & McAuliffe, 2005, p. 48).

The complexity and challenge in humanitarianism should not be understated as Joelle Tanguy (2000, p. 1) U.S. Executive Director, Medecins Sans Frontieres, eloquently describes:

> First, to be sure there is no misunderstanding, I have to acknowledge and emphasise right away that humanitarian aid is fraught with tremendous political and ethical controversies, and that steering a course of impartiality, which is our work, is a daily challenge.
>
> To make sure that aid is not fuelling conflict, to make sure that it is not turned against the very people we seek to help requires extensive political and ethical considerations that are not part of the standard medical school curriculum!
>
> Aid can be taxed, hijacked, looted, racketeered. Interventions can be manipulated to build internal or international legitimacy, to freeze military gains, to sustain ethnic cleansing, to enforce population displacements, to support famine policies. Each of these statements brings to mind the likes of the Sudan, Somalia, Bosnia, Rwanda and the Congo, Burundi and so on.

Given this history there are many reservations in the developing world regarding humanitarian intervention. There have been many instances where early humanitarian ethics have been breached and aid has delivered harm to its target population. Fiona Terry in exploring the negative consequences resulting from well intentioned humanitarian intervention identifies this ethical issue as a paradox of humanitarian action (Terry, 2002).

The global humanitarian industry provides a developmental and strategic update for the educational platform for both social work and humanitarian studies. To date it sees the ethical base in the industry tending to favour a loose ended mix of Ghandian and Kantian philosophies but driving a need for what social work refers to as applied ethics. As Reamer (1993, cited by Chenoweth & McAuliffe, 2005, p. 48) indicates, 'We are more concerned at the practice level with what is referred to as normative or applied ethics—theories that guide our conduct and assist us to make decisions based on a philosophical premise about what is morally right or wrong.'

As such social work in the past century has been working with the mix of the broader in-principle moral philosophies and meta ethics while developing the debate and professional practice toward normative or applied ethics (Chenoweth & McAuliffe, 2005).The need for a cohesive operational ethical platform is necessary for the new humanitarianism (Terry, 2002) to maintain an ethical approach in practice. The evolution of the new humanitarianism seems to be growing on the binaries of 'costs to self' (individualism) versus 'duty to others' (collectivism/universalism) and as such being used in the neo liberal agenda to erode fundamental principles of refugee protection here in Australia and to maintain the global dominance of the west (Every, 2008, p. 211). By adopting the beyond borders (and beyond politics) principles it can retain a moral philosophy of decency in humanity without conditions. With such understanding, students can then make their own decisions on the fragilities of humanitarianism once they graduate and are working in the field.

Therefore humanitarian students are required to undertake units that help them to understand and critique the issues within clear and established ethical frameworks with a view to graduating professionals well grounded in the issues, complexities, and dilemmas of practice in often chaotic and variable environments.

They will then approach these situations with a cohesive code of ethics and the set of principles that guide human service such as beneficence, non malfeasance, veracity, autonomy, equality and self-determination.

Bridging the practice-activism divide

The CDU programs explore and challenge the practice-activism divide through the course objectives, pedagogy, and texts/assignments of the two disciplines. Learning about social movements and social justice action in both disciplines is essential for students to understand what has changed as a result of organised and individual efforts over time, and to learn from the successes and challenges of both practice and activism. It is the realisation that change is not only possible and real but that they, too, can be change agents which is critical. However, in doing so they need to realise the difficulties along the way and respect fundamental cultural differences. To support this reflection students are instructed in a blend of social justice, cultural sensitivities with bottom up community capacity building and community action projects while alerted to the controls of top down programs.

The without borders humanitarian philosophy sees activism and making public any political/administrative malfeasance as crucial yet difficult. Thus the blending of a human service role with an activist humanitarian philosophy should drive an increasing and arguably needed activist debate within remote service delivery. Remote human service work needs to be positioned to address the issues that marginalise sectors of the community. A humanitarian cross cultural consciousness will help in part to bridge this practice-activism divide.

Interestingly like social work and welfare work, humanitarian responses occur where the political has failed or is in crisis. Humanitarian assistance is for those socially excluded in both the poor and extremely poor worlds. It works with people who are marginalised and victims of compounding violence, it is there for the victims of climate change, for those abandoned by decolonisation and in Australia's case social exclusion—essentially as Tanguy puts it—'those abandoned by the political contract.' (Tanguy, 2000, p. 1) Hence there is a need for both disciplines to professionally explore and close the practice-activism divide by improving on practice with research and evidence and holding the body politic more accountable, with informed activism, to its care for community mandate.

'What the world needs is change, not charity. How will the international community restore this political leadership and exercise its responsibility?' (Tanguy, 2000, p. 1). Within this profound question lies a challenge for human service work in the new humanitarianism—that of gaining an increased social justice ethos in leadership. To do so, humanitarianism will need a platform of professional ethics and a trained expertise in social justice activism to continue driving this ethos in its executive hierarchy. Additionally, practice models such as feminist and radical social work offer a structure to both critique and work to effect change.

Conclusion

This chapter has identified that there are significant benefits in the mix of social work and humanitarianism. It has explored how both disciplines are complementary and how shared education can generate an operational resiliency for work in remote areas and a solid practice framework that includes models, ethical and research theory to guide humanitarian practice. Both disciplines operate within the complex cultural diversity of northern Australia but need critical skills to start bridging the practice-activism divide to address the marginalisation of Australia's remotely scattered Indigenous communities.

We also see ethical parallels with social work and the need to formulate the new humanitarianism into a professional discipline. It is a new and open ended challenge: to ensure government service by pursuing the maintenance of the political contract with activism and to apply this with a cross cultural understanding in support for social justice and human service delivery.

References

Arendt, H. (2011). The banality of evil. In W. Buckingham, D. Burnham, C. Hill, P.J. King, J. Marenbon & M. Weeks (Eds). *The philosophy book* (p. 272). London: Dorling Kindersley.

Australian Association of Social Workers (2010). *AASW code of ethics*. Retrieved 17 April 2013 from www.aasw.asn.au/document/item/740.

Australian Bureau of Statistics (2012). *2011 Census QuickStats*. Retrieved 17 April 2013 from www.censusdata.abs.gov.au/census_services/getproduct/census/2011/quickstat/7.

Bain, M. (2005). *White men are liars: another look at Aboriginal-Western interactions*. Alice Springs: Australian Society for Indigenous Languages, Inc.

Beddoe, E., Davys, A. & Adamson, C. (2013). Educating resilient practitioners. *Social Work Education*, 32(1), 100–17.

Carment, D. (2007). *Territorianism: politics and identity in Australia*. Melbourne: Australian Scholarly Publishing.

Castells, M. (2000). *End of millennium*, 2nd edn. Malden: Blackwell Publishers.

Chenoweth, L. & McAuliffe, D. (2005). *The road to social work and human service practice*. Melbourne: Thomson.

Department of Families, Housing, Community Services and Indigenous Affairs. (2012). Stronger futures in the Northern Territories. Retrieved 22 April 2013 from www.indigenous.gov.au/stronger-futures.

DeVito, J. (2005). *Messages: building interpersonal communication skills*. New York: Pearson Education, Inc.

Duffé, B. M. (2007). *Le guide synergie qualité: propositions pour des actions humanitaires de qualité [Proposals for quality humanitarian actions]*. Coordination Sud. Retrieved 22 April 2013 from www.coordinationsud.org.

Edmond, T., Megivern, D., Williams, C., Rochman, E. & Howard, M. (2006). Intergrating evidence-based practice and field education. *Journal of Social Work Education*, 42(2), 379–80.

Every, D. (2008). A reasonable, practical and moderate humanitarianism: the co-option of humanitarianism in the Australian asylum seeker debates. *Journal of Refugee Studies*, 21(2), 210–29.

Gitterman, A. (1996). Advances in the life model of social work practice. In F.J. Turner (Ed.). *Social work treatment: interlocking theoretical perspectives*. New York: Free Press.

Ife, J. (2012). *Human rights from below: achieving rights through community development*. Melbourne: Cambridge University Press.

Mandleco, B. & Peery, C. (2000). An organisational framework for conceptualising resilience in children. *Journal of Child and Adolescent Psychiatric Nursing*, 13(3), 99–112.

National Critical Care and Trauma Response Centre. (2010). About us. Retrieved 22 April, 2013 from www.nationaltraumacentre.nt.gov.au/about-us.

Northern Territory Government. (2008). *Budget 2008–2009*. Retrieved 22 April 2013 from www.treasury.nt.gov.au/TaxesRoyaltiesAndGrants/AboutTerritoryRevenueOffice/RevenueBudgetMeasures/Pages/2008-2009-Northern-Territory-Budget.aspx.

Northern Territory Emergency Response Review Board. (2008). *Northern Territory emergency response, report of the NTER review board*. Canberra: Commonwealth of Australia.

Pearson, J. (2005). *The multi-cultural iceberg: exploring international relationships in Cambodian development organisations*. The International NGO Training and Research Centre. Retrieved 22 April 2013 from www.intrac.org/data/files/resources/101/Praxis-Note-8-The-Multi-Cultural-Iceberg.pdf.

Orbinski, J. (2002). Finding humanity in humankind. *Canadian Speeches*. Retrieved 22 April 2013 from www.highbeam.com/doc/1G1-90366614.html.

Reiff, D. (2002). Humanitarianism in crisis. *Foreign Affairs,* 81(6), 12–14.

Shearon, D.N. & Parks-Sheiner, A.C. (2007). The science behind reflective learning. Reflective learning. Unpublished research digest manuscript. Retrieved 22 April 2013 from www.logisens.com/resourceFiles/ResearchCompendiumV2_1.pdf.

Tanguy, J. (2000). *Foreign and humanitarian aid: paradox and perspectives.* Paris: Medecins Sans Frontières Publications. Retrieved 22 April 2013 from www.doctorswithoutborders.org/publications/article.cfm?id=1352.

Terry, F. (2002). *The paradox of humanitarian action: condemned to repeat?* New York: Cornell University Press.

Trudgeon, R. (2001). *Why warriors lie down and die: towards an understanding of why Aboriginal people of Arnhem Land face the greatest crisis in health and education since European contact.* Darwin, NT: Aboriginal Resource & Development Service Inc.

Wild, R. & Anderson, P. (2007). *Ampe akelyernemane meke mekarle/little children are sacred: report of the Northern Territory Board of Inquiry into the Protection of Aboriginal Children from Sexual Abuse.* Darwin: Northern Territory Government.

17

Labour migration and human rights: challenges for social work practice and education

Nilan G. Yu

This chapter examines labour migration, the problems that accompany the phenomenon, and the challenges for social work practice and education with a focus on the Asia-Pacific region. Labour migration is replete with human rights and welfare issues that social work, a discipline closely identified with human rights and social justice, needs to address. It is argued that a critical perspective highlights the role of structural forces that transcend national boundaries in creating the conditions that serve as impetus for labour migration and allow for the abuse and exploitation many labourers experience in their host countries. The challenges posed by labour migration thus draw attention to needed interventions beyond the local and national levels. The discussion in this chapter contributes to the growing body of literature on international social work and offers insights for a kind of practice requiring critical engagement with dominant ideology.

勞務移民及人權：社會工作實踐和教學中的挑戰

本章將探討勞務移民，伴隨這一現象的問題，以及重點為亞太地區的社會工作實踐及教學中的挑戰。勞務移民中充滿了人權和福利問題，作為一門與人權及社會正義緊密相連的學科，社會工作應該解決這些問題。有人認為批判的視角能突出的結構性力量的作用，它超越國界為勞務移民創造條件，成為其動力，並放任許多工人在其所處國家受到虐待和剝削。勞務移民帶來的一些難題使我們開始關注地方及國家層面之外的必要的干預措施。本章中的討論為不斷壯大的國際社會工作文獻再添一筆，並為一種主流意識形態中的強調參與的實踐提供見解。

タイトル：労働移住と人権：ソーシャルワーク実践と教育の課題

著者：ニラン G. ユー

この章では、労働移住とこの現象に伴う問題、およびアジア太平洋地域を中心としたソーシャルワーク実践と教育の課題を検討する。労働移住は人権や福祉の問題で溢れている。これらの問題は、ソーシャルワークのように人権と社会的公正密接に結びつけられる分野で対処する必要がある。批判的な視点から見て、国境を越えた構造的な力がもつ影響を浮き彫りにすることが労働移住への原動力としての役割をもち、またホスト国内で多くの労働者が経験する虐待と搾取を許容するといった状況を作り出している。労働移住によってもたらされるこれらの課題が喚起しているのは、介入の必要性が国内地域レベルを超えているという点である。この章での議論は国際ソーシャルワークの文献全体の拡大に貢献し、支配的なイデオロギーに批判的に関与するような実践の場に求められる洞察力を提供する。

이주 노동자와 인권 : 사회복지 교육과 실천의 도전

본 장에서는 이주노동자 문제를 짚어보고 아태지역의 사회복지 교육과 실천현장에서 이주노동자 문제의 현황을 다루었다. 사회복지는 인권과 사회정의를 다루는 학문으로서 이주노동자의 인권과 사회정의를 다루어야 한다. 노동자의 이주가 발생하게 되는 구조적인 힘과 이주노동자에게 학대와 착취가 자행되는 것을 방치하는 현상에 대해 언급하면서 지역과 국가를 넘어서 사회복지 분야의 개입이 필요하다는 데 초점을 두었다. 본 장은 논의를 통해 국제 사회복지 문헌 고찰과 지배적 관점을 비판적 시각으로 보게 하는 통찰력을 제시하고 있다.

Introduction

This chapter explores labour migration, the social welfare issues and problems accompanying the phenomenon and the challenges they pose for social work practice and education. It is argued here that the protection of the rights and welfare of labour migrants, many of whom come from disadvantaged populations of developing economies in the Asia-Pacific region, draws attention to needed interventions in social work spanning from the local to the international levels, constituting a particular definition of and framework for international social work. This chapter thus builds on the theory of international social work, a number of definitions for which have already been offered (see for example Gray & Webb, 2010; and Lawrence, Lyons, Simpson, & Huegler, 2009).

The chapter begins with a discussion of the philosophical base of social work and how this is linked to the issue of labour migration. A background on the trends in labour migration is then given followed by a discussion of the rights and welfare issues related to the phenomenon. The phenomenon of labour migration will then be analysed from class, gender and human rights perspectives. Drawing on the challenges for social work in view of the rights and welfare issues identified, the chapter then offers a framework for social work practice and education that represents a particular conception of international social work. While considering the personal manifestations of injustice and discrimination many labour migrants experience, the discussion in this chapter points to the need to address the structural roots of mass labour migration, particularly the stark inequality within and across economies. The approach that emerges is a form of international social work reflecting critical and vigilant engagement.

Social work and labour migration

Such is the range and variety of social work practice in various contexts that the *European Journal of Social Work* makes reference to 'the social professions' to include those that are that go beyond traditional social work practice. This notwithstanding, there is a general agreement that social work has achieved a certain level of internationalisation as to allow for the development of internationally accepted definitions such as the following definition jointly agreed upon by the International Federation of Social Workers (IFSW) and the International Association of Schools of Social Work (IASSW):

> The social work profession promotes social change, problem-solving in human relationships, and the empowerment and liberation of people to enhance wellbeing. Utilising theories of human behaviour and social systems, social work intervenes at the points where people interact with their environments. Principles of human rights and social justice are fundamental to social work. (International Federation of Social Workers, 2012)

This definition is currently under review by the IFSW and the IASSW, with a new definition in the offing. But we find a recurring theme in many conceptions of social work. Many argue that human rights and social justice are the primary motivation and justification for social work (Hawkins, 2009; Mapp, 2007). This puts the plight of migrant labourers squarely within the purview of social work. As outlined herein, labour migrants face various forms of abuse, exploitation and discrimination that represent very real and potent threats to their human rights and well-being. The international context in which the phenomenon of labour migration occurs represents a special challenge for social work practice. For this reason, discussions about international social work seem to offer the appropriate theoretical grounding for social work practice with this particular sector. We find, however, that the term international social work is used to mean different things, with varying forms of social work around the world to begin with. Like the term social work, the concept of international social work is contested and will continue to evolve (Lyons, Hokenstad, Pawar, Huegler, & Hall, 2012). The most recent definitions speak of international action involving professional exchange in practice and in education on domestic as well as international practice and policy concerns, with importance given to international perspectives and the recognition of the internationalisation of social problems (Lyons, et al., 2012).

As conceptions of international social work continue to evolve, social workers face the challenge of articulating how this emerging framework can help address the problems confronting labour migrants in what is increasingly a globalised world market. However, a critical analysis of the phenomenon of labour migration and its concomitant rights and welfare issues can identify planks for social work practice that point towards this realm. In other words, labour migration and its attendant problems, in providing a challenge for social work practice, provides an opportunity for building a framework for practice that necessarily incorporates broad international perspectives. This chapter draws on the experiences and travails of international migrant labourers, many of whom come from the Asia-Pacific region, in building a framework for social work practice. Such framework for practice that deals with issues and problems transcending national boundaries constitutes a conception of international social work and thus contributes to the theory of international social work.

THE PHENOMENON OF LABOUR MIGRATION

International labour migration began since developments in transport technology allowed labourers to venture beyond their locales to seek employment elsewhere. However, the dramatic advance of globalisation and the ever-growing inequality between different nation-states and regions in the last several decades have allowed this trend to grow exponentially. Rapid population growth and economic difficulties in developing countries push people out while demographic changes in developed countries force them to take in migrants and migrant labourers. Declining and ageing populations in developed countries result in labour shortages that lead employers and their governments to increasingly rely on migrant labour. On the other hand, unemployed and underemployed citizens of economically developing countries and their governments are enticed by the promise of economic benefits from labour migration. Overseas work often offers higher salaries compared to local employment although these are generally lower by the standards of host countries, the main motivation on the part of employers being to employ workers with as much skill for as little pay as possible.

The income and related opportunities that come with labour migration hold the promise of contributing to the development and well-being of the labourers, their families and their countries. For many, labour migration represents an enticing opportunity for a better life. Migrant labourers are able to earn more money to support their families. With many coming from the most economically underdeveloped and disadvantaged localities, labour migration comes with the promise of a way out of what, for many, would otherwise be a seemingly hopeless state of want. The allure of labour migration is cultivated as others see how the families of migrant labourers are suddenly able to build better houses and acquire possessions that represent comfort and prestige. The governments of labour sending countries, on the other hand, recognise the value of labour migration to their economy with the inflow of foreign currency in the form of remittances from migrant labourers to their families. The volume of these remittances is such that some developing countries have increasingly depended on these to bolster their economy. For some countries like the Philippines, labour export became a de facto policy as part of a national strategy to address balance of payment problems. From 1975 to 2002, the Philippines received over US$120 billion in cash remittances through the formal banking system (Morelos, 2009). According to World Bank figures, recorded remittances from foreign workers throughout the world amounted to US$251 billion in 2007, with as much as 75 per cent going to developing countries.

Today, about 192 million people or around three per cent of the world's population live outside their countries of birth (International Organisation for Migration, 2008). This is roughly around one in every 35 persons in the world and their numbers are increasing annually by almost 3 per cent. The number of Asian migrants rose from around 28 million in 1970 to almost 44 million in 2000 (Manpower, 2008b).

Not surprisingly, increase in pay and professional advancement is the primary impetus for labour migration (Manpower, 2008a). This is seen in the general pattern of worker movement towards the 'most mature economic regions' such as the United States, Western Europe and Australia as well as emerging economies such as the Gulf States and China (Manpower, 2008b, p. 5). And while it used to be the case that men were overrepresented in labour migration, a shift has been seen in recent decades such that overall migration to countries belonging some of the world's most advanced economies has become gender balanced (Manpower, 2008b).

The governments and business sectors of receiving countries benefit in economic and social terms from the presence of migrant workers. Migrant workers give their economies a needed boost in human resources to enhance their productive capacity. In the absence of labour migration, some of the more advanced economies run the risk of failing to sustain their competitive edge in the global market. While this may be the case, the dynamics of labour migration makes it so that receiving countries are not eager to commit themselves to agreements that assure a certain level of protection to migrant workers. The reluctance partly comes from the notion that the terms of employment should be mainly a matter between workers and their employers, with minimal government intervention required. Moreover, there are those who fear that any such agreement can open the floodgate for similar expectations from other labour sending countries (Go, 2007). There are, however, existing regional and international instruments that are intended to protect the rights and welfare of migrant labour such as the ASEAN Declaration on the Promotion and Protection of Rights of Migrant Workers, the UN Convention on the Protection of the Rights of All Migrant Workers and Members of their Families, the ILO Migration for Employment Convention and the ILO Migrant Workers Convention. In addition to these, there are also a few bilateral agreements covering related issues (Go, 2007).

Welfare issues in labour migration

Labour migration can pose a strain and threat to the welfare of people. In moving people out of their places of orientation, migration often cuts people off from existing social ties and networks that serve as social support to them and their families. As they move away, they lose physical proximity to friends and family who can extend a helping hand in times of need. Their tacit understanding of local resources and sources of support accumulated over years decades of experience suddenly become irrelevant as they negotiate entirely new environments. Some give up important public support entitlements afforded by their citizenship. Stripped of social support and organic knowledge of their social environment, migrants become exposed and vulnerable to threats to their well-being.

Labour migration, in and of itself, involves a number of risks and sacrifices on the part of workers. Migrant labourers, unlike immigrants, come to their countries of destination not as prospective citizens but as visitors extended a revocable privilege to stay by virtue of their utility to local employers. In the absence of the status of citizens (or citizens-to-be) and armed with very little social support and knowledge of local resources in the host environment, many migrant labourers find themselves in especially difficult circumstances. Migrant labourers often take on dangerous, demeaning and dirty jobs—the kind that local employers find difficult to fill. Often, these are jobs do not pay enough to attract local workers. While labour migration can provide an opportunity for career enhancement, in many cases, it also leads to de-skilling as labourers are forced to learn new skills to achieve higher pay in the way many doctors in the Philippines and elsewhere take up nursing for a chance to fill up openings in the new skill area in economically advanced countries. Labour migration in some kinds of work such as domestic work can put workers, most of them women, at high risk of abuse. Not a few ending up being trafficked for commercial sexual exploitation. Unskilled workers are particularly vulnerable to human trafficking, with people in the millions ending up being put into forced labour or sexual servitude such that human trafficking has now grown into the third largest illegal trade in the world, next only to arms and drug smuggling (Manpower, 2008b). The situations that many migrant labourers find themselves in their host countries thus present a number of issues related to human rights and social welfare.

Among the abusive and exploitative practices experienced by international migrant labourers are violations of contract provisions by employers including the non-payment of salaries, physical and emotional maltreatment and abuse (Garcés-Mascareñas, 2012; Mahdavi, 2011). Some are made to work very long work days. Domestic workers, for one, can be forced to serve as much as 20-hour work days which require them to begin house work very early in the day and well into the night, living socially-isolated lives (Nadeau 2007). Domestic workers are particularly at risk of this since they reside in their place of employment where they are at the beck and call of their employers. These occur within tightening state labour migration controls designed to maintain the status of labour migrants as non-citizens, enabling the subjection of some migrant labourers to what Garcés-Mascareñas (2012, p. 75) refers to as 'sanctioned bondage'. Some are locked in their apartment units by their employers to prevent them from fleeing, resulting in physical harm or even death with escape attempts made by such workers. Conceivably, a number of these virtual prisoners can go unpaid for months, be fed very little, experience physical, verbal and emotional abuse, and be subjected to sexual harassment and abuse. As a matter of practice, many employers collect the passports of migrant labourers as a way of ensuring that they have control over the latter's physical movement. This makes it extremely difficult for migrant labourers to flee to safety if they experience any abuse or threat to their lives. Seeking redress from authorities can be a gruelling experience for people who have no legal status apart from holding a privilege to stay in the country on account of their employment and whose words have to compete with those of *bona fide* citizens.

Socially isolated in unfamiliar environments and bereft of citizenship status, labour migrants are especially vulnerable to abuse and exploitation (Garcés-Mascareñas, 2012; Mahdavi, 2011). These experiences can cause serious strain on them and result in the deterioration of their mental and physical health. Such conditions represent violations of their basic rights. In the various kinds of abuses outlined above, migrant labourers can be denied their right to liberty and security as they are held in servitude, experience cruel, inhumane and degrading treatment, subjected to discriminatory treatment, and denied the right to just and favourable remuneration and effective remedy by national authorities. Their very right to life can be under threat. In this way, the welfare of migrant labourers becomes an issue not only of pertinent national labour laws but of international conventions on human rights and workers' welfare.

As they venture into new environments to find better means of providing for their and their family's needs, migrants and migrant labourers are made vulnerable to threats to their rights, welfare and security. These risks of being subjected to abuse and exploitation involve core issues in social work relating to human rights and social welfare. Some are wont to suggest that this is simply a matter of rational choice for migrant labourers. But, in doing do, they ignore the larger social realities that make labour migration a compelling choice for millions of people.

A critical understanding of labour migration

How we understand social reality and social problems has implications to how we address them. The challenges and difficulties faced by migrant labourers may be seen by some as part and parcel of the personal choices—gambles taken on calculated risks—made by individuals. Seen as such, the misfortunes that befall some migrant labourers may be regarded as mere consequences of the proverbial roll of the dice. Nothing much can and need be done about what is seen as a private issue besides, perhaps, ensuring the enforcement of applicable laws. In that sense, our understanding can limit the range of actions that can be regarded as legitimate responses to the problems and difficulties experienced by migrant labourers. Those who view labour migration as a matter of personal choice would be more inclined to intervene at the individual level, if any intervention were to be undertaken, and to expect changes at the personal level on the part of the migrant labourers, such as in being able to make more informed choices. Intervening beyond the individual level would, from this point of view, not make much sense. However, a critical understanding of labour migration sees the phenomenon beyond being a simple matter of personal choice.

Migrant labourers have varying significance in their sending and host societies. For some in their places of origin, migrant labourers may be seen as having given up and turned their backs on their homeland. For many family members they leave behind, they are a vital source of economic support. As was pointed out earlier, the level of the remittances is such that the effects are not only felt at the family and community levels but have been recognised by governments and economists as having a sizable impact on the national economies of their home countries.

In their host countries, migrant labourers may be seen by some as potential threats to the jobs and economic opportunities of locals. Local employers see them as a source of skilled labour in occupational groups with a shortage of local qualified workers or local qualified workers willing to take on the work at the salary grades being offered. Host governments may see the intake of migrant labourers as a necessary measure needed to bolster their economies. Most of these views revolve around the immediate effects or implications of labour migration. A critical understanding of labour migration would highlight how it manifests structural inequality at the global scale and how it represents threats to human rights. Such structural inequality that undermines the human rights of millions occurs along various social divisions, most notably along the lines of gender, class and national identity.

LABOUR MIGRATION, GENDER AND CLASS INEQUALITY

While one might be inclined to assume that men are more able to engage in labour migration, the fact is that women have increasingly gained representation in labour migration over the last few decades. This fact may suggest that gender inequality is not an issue in migration and labour migration but this would be a simplistic view. For one, pervasive gender inequality in their home countries pushes many women to resort to labour migration. In the case of the Philippines, some of the basic issues that impinge on labour migration include macro-level demographics and economic pressures (Sills, 2007). There is an evident connection between poverty and the decision of women to take on risky work as well as between the plight of women and the economic thrusts of their governments (International Organization for Migration, 2009). Such structural factors, as will be pointed out in the next subsection, are not confined within national economies but form part of the dominant global economic order. Gender inequality coupled with class inequality creates a situation that forces women from less privileged economic classes to take on the risks of migration and to take risky, underpaid and undervalued work. And so while women may be equally represented as men in labour migration, there is gender inequality in terms of the impetus for their engagement in labour migration and in the kind of work they find. This indicates how decisions to engage in labour migration are linked to structural inequality along the lines of gender and class. Some of the negative views of labour migrants outlined above may be drastically tempered by such an understanding of the social dynamics that, in real ways, make labour migration an existential imperative for millions of people. In this way, migrant labourers may be seen both as victims and survivors of the inequity wrought by an unequal world economic order.

Labour migration and international economic inequality

The exponential increase in labour migration goes hand-in-hand with the phenomenal expansion of the global capitalist system in the last century. The response or the lack thereof from governments in developing countries to the challenges posed by the rapid expansion of capitalism riding on the waves of globalisation had a direct bearing on the rise in labour migration. This is clearly illustrated in the case of the Philippines.

Filipinos were engaged in labour migration as early as 1500s at the beginning of the Spanish galleon trade but, for centuries, their numbers were nothing close to the scale that we see today. A drastic change in the incidence of labour migration came with the oil crisis in the 1970s as the country felt its full impact. This event forced the

Philippine government to adopt a labour export policy as a way of making use of its population's surplus labour and of increasing its foreign exchange earnings (Sills, 2007). Labour export, hand in hand with the promotion of a local business climate favourable to foreign capital, thus became the state's employment policy (Sills, 2007). The labour export policy adopted under Marcos has since been sustained by succeeding administrations up to the present (Center for Migrant Advocacy, 2009). The liberal economic framework adopted by Philippine government in responding to globalisation such as sweeping land conversion, trade liberalisation, labour contractualisation and labour export resulted in massive social and economic dislocation (Center for Migrant Advocacy, 2009). Uneven economic development and capitalist expansion forced millions of Filipinos into labour migration. The Philippines' dependency on hard currency earnings and its weak position in the global economic order provided no leverage for the Philippine government in negotiating with host states over the protection of its citizens' rights. This case illustrates how large-scale labour migration is generated in developing countries as global capitalist forces preside over the extraction of natural and human resources and the exploitation of the markets in these economies by more developed economies. It is a poignant demonstration of how structural inequality at the international level creates the kind of environment that makes labour migration an imperative for the economic and physical survival of certain populations in disadvantaged countries.

LABOUR MIGRATION AND HUMAN RIGHTS

Migrant labourers take on countless risks as they seek employment in foreign countries. Not surprisingly, many of these involve the kind of jobs only the most marginalised populations from the world's weakest national economies are constrained to take. The risks that these people are exposed to and the abuse a number of them are subjected to makes human rights a central issue in labour migration. A critical understanding of labour migration requires recognition of this phenomenon as a feature of the prevailing global economic order. The extreme inequality that exists within and across nations engenders a constraining environment that forces disadvantaged populations to take what should be unenviable choices. For those left with little choice in their home countries, labour migration becomes a tantalising source of hope for their survival even in the face of risks uncertainty.

The Universal Declaration of Human Rights (1948) requires us to view people beyond their national identity and yet many of the policies and practices of sending and host governments of migrant labourers still operate along this paradigm. If indeed, all peoples are equal, the protection extended to them must go beyond their national citizenship status. International standards demand that the rights of people be assured regardless of their gender, class, race or nationality but this is not reflected in how states relate to migrant labourers. This will remain so if the protection of human rights is attached to people's national identity.

It has been argued that structural forces, particularly social relations and orders within and between sending and host economies, create conditions that make labour migration an imperative for the survival of many migrant labourers and their families. Sending economies—usually developing countries—often are characterised by stark social inequality and, as a whole, are at a disadvantage in international relations. In this condition, they often serve as a source of vital human and natural resources for developed economies. The draining out of millions of people from these national economies is both facilitated by and results in the further gutting of these societies in a vicious cycle. This process is seen by some as the root of labour migration. It is a vital problem in that it limits people's choices and forces many to make such sacrifices that we see migrant labourers do. That such rights-threatening choices and sacrifices have to be made in the first place is seen from a critical perspective as a key challenge for action.

LABOUR MIGRATION AND INTERNATIONAL SOCIAL WORK

As pointed out earlier, our understanding of social reality and social problems has direct implications to our actions in response to them. Those who see the difficulties experienced by migrant labourers as mere consequences of the vagaries of life or ill-informed decisions may simply be inclined to counsel more forethought and judicious action on their part. Interventions, if there are any, tend to be directed and confined to assisting and supporting affected individuals and possibly their immediate family. But a critical understanding of the phenomenon points to factors beyond individuals and their immediate environments, including the preponderant influence of structural forces in engendering a complex social dynamics that fuel labour migration. From a critical perspective, we see the interconnectedness of what might be considered as personal decisions and actions and the larger society. We recognise that choices made at the personal level by individuals who opt to engage in labour migration are connected to societal and global economics and politics. In other words, there is an interconnection between the personal and political. Apart for this, we also find an interconnection between what may be deemed as local and national realities, for example, the employment situation and general state of the economy, and the global economic and political order. The immediate, personal, familial and local considerations that make labour migration an imperative for millions of people cannot be seen in isolation in what has become a highly globalised world. Thus, what might be seen by some as the need to help specific migrant labourers and their immediate families in their specific localities may require a global understanding and approach. In a way, the plight of migrant labourers presents a challenge for social work practice that point towards action at the national and international levels representing a particular conception of international social work.

Since the problems arising out of labour migration are often concretely manifested in the personal and family lives of migrant workers, it is understandable that responses to the problems arising out of the phenomenon often start at this level. Responses to the problems posed by labour migration often begin with interventions levelled at their manifestations at the individual and familial levels. Migrant labourers who suffer from breakdown of family ties, economic consequences of a failed placement, trauma arising from abuse and exploitation and/or other problems would need some form of direct support or assistance to maintain or restore their well-being. Many of the kinds of services provided by organisations catering to migrant labourers and their families are along this line. They include such things as legal assistance in repatriation and in seeking payment for unpaid services and damages, psychosocial support and reintegration planning. Clearly, such interventions can only go so far considering the deeper roots and broader context of the problems. There is a need to go beyond the individuals and their immediate families with programs and services aimed at the broader community. Such efforts include the formation of social support networks for migrant labourers and their families and the fostering of community development. The latter is done with the hope that the development of communities can make labour migration just one among many choices for local citizens. Our analysis of the dynamics of labour migration tells us that a strategic response needs to go way beyond these towards action directed at the national and international levels. If labour migration is seen beyond a matter of personal choice with the recognition of global structural forces, then actions in response to the attendant problems need to correspondingly represent such broader understanding of the phenomenon.

A key issue is the lack of state protection for migrant workers (Center for Migrant Advocacy, 2009). If the rights and welfare of migrant labourers are to be protected, the establishment of bilateral agreements covering employment and human resource development can be an important first step. Such agreements can focus on the protection of the welfare and rights of migrant workers in accordance with the labour laws of the host countries and, ideally, consistent with labour protection measures afforded to the citizens of such countries and with pertinent international conventions. It is often argued by host countries that there is no need for such agreements since prevailing labour standards and regulations would apply (Go, 2007). But it is this very assumption that provides opportunity for the abuse and discrimination that many migrant workers experience in their host countries. In the absence of explicit laws and agreements covering their rights and welfare, migrant workers become vulnerable targets of exploitative and abusive practices in their host environments where they are non-citizens. With the existence of bilateral agreements, there is at least a mechanism in place to protect their rights and welfare. The promotion of bilateral agreements between sending and receiving countries thus forms an important safeguard. Such agreements, however, have been hard to come by given the compelling political considerations of both sending and receiving countries mentioned earlier. In the case of the Philippines, the national government has been forthcoming with rhetoric but wanting in policy enforcement because of the premium placed on the goodwill of host states. This, of course, does not address the problem of labour migration at its core.

INTERNATIONAL SOCIAL WORK AS PART OF A GLOBAL STRUGGLE

Labour migration has become an inextricable part of the fabric of this globalised world. An immediate challenge is the moderation of the conditions that make labour migration risky and uncertain. But given how labour migration has become an imperative for millions, there is a need consider more fundamental issues. In thinking about the kind of practice needed to address the problems accompanying labour migration, it may be helpful to consider what Ferguson and Lavalette (2006, p. 312) refer to as 'four potential bases' for the development of a social work of resistance. For them, this involves: (1) going beyond care management towards addressing structural oppression; (2) questioning the advance of neoliberal approaches in policy and practice; (3) listening to oppressed populations and linking social work with social movements; and (4) challenging the overriding capitalist ideology that dominates the global order.

There are those who point out that a basic gap in responses to the plight of migrant labourers is the failure of sending countries to address fundamental problems in the local economy which brings about the phenomenon of mass labour migration (Center for Migrant Advocacy, 2009). Given this, an important direction for action for the protection of the rights and welfare of migrant labourers would be to work towards the promotion of a more just society where many need not be confronted with the choice between physical and economic survival on the one hand and labour migration on the other. The long term solution to the plight of migrant labourers would be the radical economic restructuring of their societies to address issues of underemployment and unemployment (Center for Migrant Advocacy, 2009). Recognising the impact of international trade on local economies and the very lives and livelihood of people at the grassroots, such solutions would emphasise the need of vigilance on the part of governments of the implications and ramifications of trade agreements that, to some, render particular economies vulnerable. Such a conception has far-reaching implications for social work practice, requiring a radical reimagining of social work from the way it is predominantly practiced in many parts of the world today, with the bases identified by Ferguson and Lavellete (2006) as a starting point.

With labour migration becoming an integral part of life in this increasingly globalised world, the protection of the rights and welfare of migrant labourers has become a vital challenge requiring a broad social movement. Alcid (2006) points to a strategic partnership between NGOs and labour unions as a promising step in that direction. The abuses migrant labourers experience often occur and are sustained in view of the absence of adequate institutional mechanisms in both the host and sending countries for the protection of their rights and welfare. There are fundamental limitations posed by nationally-bound conceptions of the rights and welfare of migrant labourers. Given the fact that the issues involved transcend national boundaries, action for the protection of their rights and welfare will have to go beyond geographical, political and juridical boundaries. The protection of the human rights and social well-being of migrant labourers necessitates a radical rethinking of how we conceptualise citizenship and citizen rights. Seen in the context of the Universal Declaration on Human Rights and international covenants on the protection of labourers, it would be a blatant omission not to consider the plight of migrant labourers as an issue of global citizenship in the context of the international community. The issues and problems confronting migrant labourers need to be seen as a collective concern at the global level in the ways such issues as genocide and large-scale environmental degradation have come to be known.

The notion of global citizenship allows us to conceive the protection of the rights and welfare of migrant labourers as not being confined and subject to what now are fast becoming imaginary national boundaries in the face of globalisation. After all, if human rights are universal and inalienable, then their enforcement should rightly be assured regardless of the national citizenship and geographic location of individuals. Nationally-defined citizenship-rights and protection would invariably fall short in assuring this unless states are prepared to transgress traditionally defined national boundaries in the protection of their citizens which, as discussed earlier, is not an option for many developing countries where many migrant labourers come from. The challenges posed by massive labour migration require a redefinition of the bounds by which we define legitimate ways of protecting the rights and welfare of millions of people throughout the world. At the same time, it also lays down a way of conceptualising social work practice that gives a particularly distinct meaning to the term international social work.

If we think about it, the problems confronting women in poverty, impoverished peasants and labourers, physically and economically displaced indigenous communities and other marginalised populations in much of the developing world are similarly linked to international issues and structures as with many problems threatening the rights and welfare of migrant labourers. This realisation bolsters the relevance of international social work as a framework for social work practice. Such conceptualisation of labour migration and social work has implications for social work education. The transnational and international dimensions of problems in labour migration call for the integration of an international perspective in the teaching of social work. This applies to many other problems social workers encounter in their practice (Wehbi, 2008). Social workers simply cannot think within the confines of their localities or even within the larger national borders where their practice is situated. Certainly, a strong human rights perspective would be an important foundation for the training of internationally-competent professionals. In the absence of recognition of universal human rights and human rights issues surrounding labour migration, the practice of social work may most likely be constrained by context-dependent constructions of citizenship rights that vary from country to country. A third important implication for social work education is the need to equip practitioners with a critical perspective, one that enables them to recognise the structural forces and dynamics manifested as personal struggles in the lives of the people they work with such as when people choose to subject themselves to a host of untold risks, abuses and uncertainties which is what millions of migrant labourers do around the world every day.

References

Alcid, M. (2006). NGO-labor union collaboration in the promotion of the rights and interests of land-based overseas Filipino workers. *Asia and Pacific Migration Journal,* 15(3), 335–57.

Center for Migrant Advocacy (2009). *The Philippines: a global model on labor migration?* Quezon City: Center for Migrant Advocacy & Friedrich Ebert Stiftung.

Ferguson, I. & Lavalette, M. (2006). Globalisation and global justice: towards a social work of resistance. *International Social Work*, 49(3), 309–18. doi:10.1177/0020872806063401.

Garcés-Mascareñas, B. (2012). *Labour migration in Malaysia and Spain*. Amsterdam: Amsterdam University Press.

Go, S. (2007). Asian labor migration: the role of bilateral labor and similar agreements. Paper presented at the regional informal workshop on labor Migration in Southeast Asia: what role for parliament. Manila, Philippines: Migrant Forum in Asia.

Gray, M. & Webb, S. A. (Eds) (2010). *International social work*. Los Angeles: Sage.

Hawkins, C. A. (2009). Global citizenship: a model for teaching universal human rights in social work education. *Critical Social Work*, 10(1), 116–31.

International Federation of Social Workers. (2012, 8 June). *Definition of social work*. Retrieved 1 April 2013 from ifsw.org/policies/definition-of-social-work/.

International Organization for Migration (2008). About migration. Retrieved January 17, 2013, from www.iom.int/jahia/Jahia/lang/en/pid/3.

International Organization for Migration (2009). *Gender and labour migration in Asia*. Geneva: International Organization for Migration.

Lawrence, S., Lyons, K., Simpson, G. & Huegler, N. (2009). *Introducing international social work*. Exeter: Learning Matters.

Lyons, K., Hokenstad, T., Pawar, M., Huegler, N. & Hall, N. (Eds) (2012). *The Sage handbook of international social work*. London: Sage Publications.

Mahdavi, P. (2011). *Gridlock: labor, migration, and human trafficking in Dubai*. Palo Alto, CA: Stanford University Press.

Manpower (2008a). *Relocating for work survey: global results 2008*. Sydney, NSW: Manpower, Inc.

Manpower (2008b). *The borderless workforce 2008*. Sydney, NSW: Manpower, Inc.

Mapp, S. C. (Ed) (2007). *Human rights and social justice in a global perspective: an introduction to international social work*. New York: Oxford University Press.

Morelos, M. (2009). Filipinos found in every country in the world. *Philippine Daily Inquirer*, 12 April, A1, A8.

Nadeau, K. (2007). A maid in servitude: Filipino domestic workers in the Middle East. *Migration Letters*, 4(1), 15–27.

Pojmann, W. (2007). Organizing women migrants: the Filipino and Cape Verdean women's associations in Rome. *Migration Letters*, 4(1), 29–39.

Sills, S. (2007). Philippine labour migration to Taiwan: social, political, demographic, and economic dimensions. *Migration Letters*, 4(1), 1–14.

The Universal Declaration of Human Rights. (1948, 10 December). Retrieved April 1 2013, from www.un.org/en/documents/udhr/.

Wehbi, S. (2008). Teaching international social work: a guiding framework. *Canadian Social Work Review*, 25(2), 117–32.

World Bank (2007). *Remittance trends 2007*, Migration and Development Brief 5. Washington, D.C.: World Bank.

18

Asylum seekers, human rights and social work

Linda Briskman

Although no region of the world is immune to asylum seeker flows, those arriving in the Asia Pacific face specific hurdles. Australia, although a signatory to the 1951 Refugee Convention, exercises its sovereign power to exclude and banish asylum seekers. There are attempts to develop a Regional Cooperation Framework, but this is lagging, and in the meantime asylum seekers languish in detention camps or restrictive community settings in Australia, Indonesia and Malaysia. Australia has introduced bi-lateral arrangements with Nauru and Manus Island to establish detention centres in those countries, seen by some as a reinvention of colonialism. Within this policy mix, this chapter argues that social workers, as moral agents, have a mandate to challenge the existing policy arrangements and to work with established social movements that strive for the human rights of asylum seekers and refugees. Examples of social work engagement are presented.

尋求庇護者，人權和社會工作

儘管世界各地都充斥著庇護尋求者，但在亞太地區的求助者會面臨特殊的障礙。澳大利亞，作為1951年’關於難民地位的公約’的簽署國，卻在使用其主權來排擠和驅逐尋求庇護者。雖然有過發展區域合作的框架的嘗試，但此計劃一再拖延，在此期間生活在澳大利亞，印度尼西亞和馬來西亞羈留營或限制社區的尋求庇護者日漸憔悴。澳大利亞與瑙魯和馬努斯島簽訂雙邊協議，在這些國家建立羈留營，此計劃卻被一些人士視為變相的移民主義。 在本章中將會討論在此政策組合下，作為道德代表的社會工作者對現有政策協議的挑戰，通過配合既定社會運動，為尋求庇護者和避難者爭取人權。最後,相關的社會工作參與案例也會例舉出來加以佐證。

亡命希望者，人権とソーシャルワーク

世界中の地域が難民運動には免疫が無いとはいえど、アジア・太平洋地域に来た亡命希望者は特定の障害に直面している。オーストラリアは1951年に難民条約に署名したが、亡命希望者を政治権力で除外、追放している。地域の連携体制を発展させようと試みるがその計画は遅れ、その間にも亡命希望者は、オーストラリアやインドネシア、マレーシアの収容施設など、制限された生活に悩みながら暮らしている。オーストラリアでは収容施設をそれらの国々に設立するために、ナウル共和国とマヌス島との相互的な協定が導入されたが、他ではその行為が植民政策の再考案とみられている。この章では、ソーシャルワーカーがこの混合した政策の中で道徳的な行いをする者として、現存する政策の協定に異議を唱え、亡命希望者と難民の人権のために取り組んでいる社会運動とともに仕事をする権限があると論ずる。ソーシャルワーカーが携わる例をここに挙げる。

망명자, 인권과 사회복지

망명자들의 유입에 영향을 받지 않는 지역은 전 세계 어디에도 없지만 아태지역 망명자들은 특정한 문제에 직면해 있다. 호주에서는 1951년에 난민협약에 서명했으나 망명자들을 제외하고 추방했다. 지역협력체제(Regional Cooperation Framework)를 발전시킬 시도가 늦어지면서 망명자들은 호주, 인도네시아, 말레이시아 등지의 임시수용소에 머물게 되었다. 호주는 수용소를 설립하겠다는 Nauru, Manus Island와 각국의 쌍방 협의를 도입했다. 본 장에서는 도덕적 행위자로서 사회복지사들이 기존 정치적 합의에 이의를 제기하고, 망명자들과 피난자들의 인권을 위한 사회운동을 해야 한다고 주장한다. 사회복지사가 어떻게 개입했는지에 대한 사례도 제시하였다

INTRODUCTION: ASYLUM SEEKING IN A GLOBAL CONTEXT

The movement of people geographically is part of human history and controlling it a relatively recent phenomenon (Hayes, 2004).

Irregular migration follows experiences of persecution, oppression and war as people seek safe haven. At the same time that the movements persist, governments tighten their borders to deter people from arriving uninvited and unannounced. By way of contrast a number of governments fulfil, to varying degrees, humanitarian obligations to the United Nations High Commissioner for Refugees (UNHCR) and take a quota of people who have applied off-shore and have often waited for many years in refugee camps for resettlement.

This chapter focuses on asylum seekers, mainly those arriving by boat, who are referred to in Australia as Irregular Maritime Arrivals. Although the terms asylum seeker and refugee are sometimes used interchangeably in this chapter to reflect the literature or context, it is important to note the distinction. The term asylum seeker denotes a person awaiting conferral of refugee status whereas a refugee is a person deemed to have met the criteria of the 1951 Refugee Convention. Asylum seekers who arrive directly in countries in order to seek refugee status are often labelled as queue jumpers, bogus claimants, invaders and illegals (Briskman & Cemlyn, 2005) and treated with suspicion and contempt.

Some irregular travellers do not arrive at their chosen destination. Weber and Pickering (2011) document the tragedy of deaths worldwide of people making irregular border crossings including by drowning, dehydration and hypothermia; deaths occur in unseaworthy vessels, unventilated lorries and environmental exposure in the United States deserts. The number of deaths enroute to Australia by drowning is alarming. One of the most publicised tragedies occurred in December 2010 on the shore of the Australian territory of Christmas Island. There a boat carrying asylum seekers crashed into rocks, claiming 50 lives, including children. Another 50 survived. This event put in motion stringent and inhumane policies that purported to stop such tragedies. But not only did boats keep coming but the measures adopted, particularly the re-introduction in 2012 of offshore processing on Nauru and Manus Island, discussed later in this chapter, created far more risks to asylum seeker well-being than the risk of drowning at sea.

Globally, immigration detention is common. Such deprivation of liberty is one of the most serious sanctions that a state can issue against a person (Briskman, Latham & Goddard, 2008). Although international data on the use of immigration detention is not readily accessible, a survey of 21 countries found an increase in the use of immigration detention, with detainees often denied their basic rights, in conditions below international standards. The survey listed detention concerns in the following regions: Asia Pacific; Canada; Central America; Western Europe; Eastern and Central Europe; South America; Middle East and North Africa; Eastern and Western Africa; Southern Africa; United States (International Detention Coalition, 2008).

Australia has one of the worst records for its treatment of asylum seekers and maintains measures that punish those who exercise their asylum seeker rights and which are aimed at deterring others from arriving. These measures, particularly immigration detention, have caused immeasurable harm to asylum seekers, including generating mental illness, and immense harm to the human rights reputation of Australia.

Hannah Arendt (1986, p. 269) disturbingly but aptly tells us that refugees have been considered as the 'the scum of the earth'. Moreover, their human rights have been obfuscated (Gosden, 2007, p. 162). For asylum seekers, human rights obligations are turned upside down with the rights of asylum seekers violated within an ideology that proclaims sovereign rights as absolute and non-negotiable in order to control national borders (Every, 2006, cited in Gosden, 2007, p. 151).

A brief introduction to Australia's asylum seeker policies precedes an overview of the Asia-Pacific context.

OVERVIEW OF ASYLUM SEEKING IN AUSTRALIA

Although increasingly tough measures exist on a global scale, Australia has stood out in its application of mandatory detention to all unauthorised arrivals, becoming a testing laboratory (Pickering,

2005) for other countries wanting to eradicate what they see as the asylum seeker scourge.

It was in 1992 that the Australian Labor Party secured in legislation the policy of mandatory detention. In subsequent years the policy was ramped up by the conservative federal government of Prime Minister John Howard (1996–2007), which meant that children, women and men were incarcerated, often in detention gaols in remote areas of Australia, on Christmas Island or, as part of the 'Pacific Solution' in Nauru or Papua New Guinea, the latter policy that has been revived by the now incumbent Labor Party. As people were branded as 'illegals', would-be terrorists and, queue jumpers by the media and government, a human rights discourse slid into a security discourse.

Many people who were eventually released from immigration detention centres on refugee visas are now so damaged that they will never repair. A psychiatrist has said that the people he has seen and treated in immigration detention were the most damaged he had seen in his psychiatric career. Another said that the detention environment was so toxic that treatment was ineffective (cited in Briskman et al. 2008).

To add to the suffering, the Howard government introduced the Temporary Protection Visa (TPV) in 1999. Until this was revoked in 2008, those released from detention were granted only temporary refugee status, creating great uncertainty and insecurity. One of the harshest provisions of the TPV was that family reunion was barred, meaning that those released were unable to apply for their families to join them, causing immense heartache and despair. The TPV, rather than deterring others from arriving as the government intended, saw women and children propelled into taking perilous journeys to join their menfolk who had come first. It is one of the reasons put forward as to why so many women and children were on the ill-fated SIEV X, a vessel bound for Australia in 2001 on which 353 people died.

The *Tampa* incident demonstrates the harsh policy reaction of the Australian government in contrast to the stance of Australia's near neighbour of New Zealand. In August 2001 the *MV Tampa*, a Norwegian vessel, came to the aid of 438 asylum seekers, mainly Afghan Hazaras, whose boat had sunk in international waters on the way to Australia. Although the captain of the *Tampa* requested medical help, the Australian government response was to send the Special Air Service to Christmas Island to intervene in order to prevent the vessel from entering Australian waters. From this the Australian government formulated the Pacific Solution, transporting the majority to a detention camp in Nauru. A new moral threshold now meant it was possible to push away unarmed people seeking refuge in Australian waters (Perera, 2002). New Zealand, on the other hand, exercised humanity by accepting 132 people from the boat as refugees. Although New Zealand displayed a welcoming response, this country too has been increasingly criticised for an increasingly harsh response to asylum seekers especially since September 11, 2001 (Briskman & Fiske, 2009).

September 11 allowed the Australian government to respond more harshly and with little outcry from the public. 'We will decide who comes to this country and under what circumstances' was an ongoing government mantra in Australia. Federal authorities were quick to link asylum seekers and the terrorist threat. Australia's Defence Minister at that time said in a radio interview:

> Look you've got to be able to manage people coming into your country, you've got to be able to control that otherwise it can be a pipeline for terrorists to come in and use your country as a staging post for terrorist activities (Reith, 2001).

The policies and practices should have been a wake-up call to social workers who witnessed, albeit often through mixed-quality media reports only, the suffering occurring in their midst. The values espoused by government in the treatment of asylum seekers, enshrined in deterrence and containment, are arguably antithetical to social work core values and beliefs. In time social workers were among those who joined advocacy movements, spurred on by shame and concern at the brutal treatment of asylum seekers in our country.

Regional prospects for change

For social workers to have knowledge about asylum seeker movements and government policies and practices, it is essential to look beyond the most publicised country of Australia to the wider Asia-Pacific region in which it is located. The first imperative is to take heed of the transit countries of Malaysia and Indonesia, staging posts for the majority of asylum seekers who travel from countries in the Middle East. The plight of asylum seekers in both countries is precarious for those without papers and without rights. The choices they face are to wait, sometimes indefinitely (through the UNHCR), for resettlement or to take a boat to Australia.

An Amnesty International report (2010) noted the lack of rights for asylum seekers and refugees in Malaysia with no formal legal status or the right to work as well as the prospect of being arrested, detained and ill-treated. An attempt to forge an asylum seeker 'people swap' between Australia and Malaysia in 2011—the exchange of 800 people who had arrived by boat in Australia for 4,000 UNHCR refugees from Malaysia over a four year period—was struck down by the High Court of Australia. If this measure had been achieved, the government believed it would serve as a deterrence measure by expelling asylum seekers from Australia and then placing them at the back of the 'queue' for processing in Malaysia (Pastore, 2013). In a 2011 visit to Australia, the United Nations High Commissioner for Human Rights, Navi Pillay, referred to the Malaysia Solution as an example of judging people by their racial, colour or religious differences (cited in Briskman, 2011).

The plight of asylum seekers in Indonesia is hidden from sight, except for some under-resourced NGOs and journalists of determination. Over the last decade, Indonesia has become 'long-term limbo' for asylum seekers from countries that include Afghanistan, Iraq, Iran, Sri Lanka, Somalia and Myanmar. According to the UNHCR, the number of refugees and asylum seekers in Indonesia reached more than 7,000 at the end of August 2012, a number considered to be an under-estimate (Sinanu & Missbach, 2012). Cassrels (2013) speaks of large numbers of asylum seekers entrapped in the West Java region of Cisarua where conditions are sub-optimal and waiting periods are long. Often lacking support and security, and at risk of arrest and uncertain futures, their expressed hopes of settlement in Australia or elsewhere increasingly diminish. Children suffer from lack of educational possibilities. Furthermore, Indonesia cooperates with Australia's policy objective to prevent asylum seekers from entering Australian territory (Nethery, Rafferty-Brown & Taylor, 2013).

Policies compete and collide. An emerging policy is a move towards regional cooperation. Menadue, Keski-Nummi and Gauthier (2011, p. 21) argue for the development of a regional approach to manage population movements. In countries close to Australia, they point out, there are significant numbers of people in refugee situations. The argument for regional cooperation contends that no one country can be expected to take sole responsibility for responding to such movements. Although at face value this proposal has merit, it can also be interpreted as a shift in responsibility from a wealthy country like Australia to less resourced countries in the region, a number of which are not signatories to the Refugee Convention. The regional process was set in train in 2002 and is known as the Bali Process. It received the support of 40 countries with a focus on combating people smuggling. In 2011, a Regional Cooperation Framework (RCF) was devised, which included in its ambit the promotion of human life and dignity (Bali Process, 2013). However at the time of writing, little progress on an agreed framework had been made.

A contrasting policy is that of offshore processing. Although the Australian Labor government supported the concept of an RCF, it nonetheless moved unilaterally to develop bi-lateral agreements with Nauru and Papua New Guinea, despite abandoning the 'Pacific Solution' in 2007. In response to what was viewed as a spate of boat arrivals, despite the relatively small number on the global stage, Australia convinced Nauru and Papua New Guinea to reopen the mothballed centres to house asylum seekers who arrived after 13 August 2012. The agreements with these countries are reminiscent of Australia's colonial past with the introduction of neo-colonialist agendas that exploit reliance on international aid (Fiske & Briskman, 2009). Ostensibly to prevent deaths at sea, in what has been proven to be flawed deterrence with boats still arriving, asylum seekers have been sent to Nauru and the Papua New Guinea site of Manus Island. Those on Manus Island include families with children. As these facilities do not have the capacity to deal with the numbers of boat arrivals since 13 August, other arrangements have been put in place for the 'excess'; in effect it has become a lottery as to who is sent offshore and who remains in Australian territory. No matter where they end up, a 'no advantage' policy will apply; that means that claims will be processed no faster than those waiting in refugee camps in other countries. For those arriving before 13 August, there have been more positive moves put in place to reduce numbers in overcrowded and damaging detention environments, with a range of 'community' options in place for those undergoing the refugee determination process.

A further development in the region concerns New Zealand. In February 2013 an agreement was reached between Australia and New Zealand, mirroring the 2001 *Tampa* arrangement, whereby the latter would take 150 already processed asylum seekers from Australia. This number is to be within the already meagre New Zealand quota of 750 people per annum. The Asia Pacific Refugee Rights Network proffered strident criticism of this measure, arguing that it will effectively reduce New Zealand's annual quota for places available via UNHCR referral at a time when 860,000 refugees are in need of resettlement but fewer than 85,000 places are available globally (APRRN, 2013).

THE DETENTION OF CHILDREN: A SOCIAL WORK CONCERN

In Australia, the incarceration of children in immigration detention has been described by two social workers as organised and ritualised abuse (Goddard & Briskman, 2004, p. 17). Although the detention of all people is scandalous, the detention of children, often for many years, has shaken to the core social workers and others in the Australian community. As at 31 December 2012, the latest date of official statistics, 1,221 children were held in closed immigration detention facilities in Australia (RCOA, 2013).

Much of the documented criticism of the detention of children occurred up until 2008 including that when notifications under child protection provisions were made, they tended to be ignored as children were bounced between the question of federal and state jurisdictions (immigration as a federal responsibility and child protection in the domain of the states). One early childhood worker explains that at the time when John Howard was Prime Minister:

> If I saw the same level of abuse, neglect and distress in the children in the service in which I work, and I failed to make a mandatory notification, I could be prosecuted. Yet I have made mandatory notifications on so many children in detention and they have gone nowhere (cited in Briskman, et al. 2008, p. 186).

A nurse who worked inside a detention centre vehemently argues that mandatory detention causes damage to children and the government's refusal to prevent this and to enforce child protection laws, makes it culpable of the torture of children (Rogalla, 2003). Research conducted on the ethics of providing services in immigration detention similarly concluded that detention, including detention of children, constitutes inhuman, degrading treatment and punishment as defined by the UN Convention against Torture (Briskman, Zion & Loff, 2012). Arguably the denial of liberty and freedom to asylum seeker children also contradicts the tenets of the Convention on the Rights of the Child.

In July 2002 after visits to Australia's immigration detention centres the Special Envoy of the UN High Commissioner for Human Rights Justice Bhagwati, handed down his report on conditions at the Woomera detention facility. In his report he spoke of the young boys and girls he met, who could not breathe the fresh air of freedom, but were confined behind spiked iron bars with gates barred and locked that prevented them from going out and playing and running in open fields. He saw gloom on their faces instead of the joy of youth, with these children growing up in an environment that affected their physical and mental growth. Many of them were traumatised and harmed themselves in utter despair (cited in NSW Council for Civil Liberties, 2007, p. 18–19).

After a visit to an immigration detention facility, Chris Goddard (2004) reflected on his previous social work practice with abused children:

> As part of my work, I have seen prisons and secure units. I have seen children dying of child abuse, with fractures too many to count. I have seen children torn apart by sexual abuse. I have seen things I had to see, that I will never forget, that I found impossible to understand. This time I have seen something that I should never have seen. I have been to see an eight-month-old girl, small for her age, smiling at her parents, soon to be walking, her every move watched by guards. I have seen an infant behind grey wires and electric fences, in a high-security prison on the edge of Australia's dead heart. I have seen her parents found guilty, without trial, of wanting freedom. I have seen parents so proud of their first-born, but so close to despair. I have seen an infant given a number. I have seen a baby girl kept in a cage.

In 2008 the Australian immigration authorities introduced a set of key detention values. One of these was the undertaking that children would not be detained in immigration detention centres. However, children continued to be detained in what became known as 'alternative places of detention' where they were subjected to similar restrictions as in detention centres. Recent compelling evidence against the detention of children comes from the advocacy group Chilout (Children Out of Detention), which has provided via facebook photos information on the dire conditions on Manus Island and also pointed out (Chilout, 2013) that:

> Families on Manus are housed in shipping containers with no air conditioning. The temperature today is due to reach 33 degrees, but will feel like 51 degrees. The risk of malaria is great so children must sleep under netting.

A role for social work

With the global emphasis of asylum seeker policy throughout the world on border protection and deterrence, social workers can invoke humanitarian concerns. They can endeavour to turn around popular discourses and to expose the suffering, drawing on their own practice wisdom. As Lester (2010) posits, a people-centred approach of human security would locate the human, rather than the state, at the centre of concern. This has an impact on social workers on the frontline and for those engaged in advocacy and activism for change.

There are inherent conflicts in conducting a human rights approach to social work when competing perspectives exist to manage migration and to provide social welfare (Robinson, 2013). Organisations in which social workers are employed may also contain examples of racism including racist attitudes and xenophobic statements (Robinson, 2013). Linda Harms Smith (2012) speaks of the complication when organisational and statutory policies are part of what is unjust and damaging. When hegemonic orders prevail, she argues, it is harder to challenge inequalities and oppressions, but if social workers wish to pursue social justice they will have to embrace their conflicted positions and engage in truth-telling, advocacy, collective action and political interventions. To overcome organisational constraints, social workers who are in less constricted work environments can assist in imparting the social change quest to practitioners caught up with the mundanity of bureaucratic procedures (Briskman, 2013). As Deborah Hayes explains, past and present movements of people around the globe are filled with painful stories, many of which are too awful to account. To tell the truths and to humanise asylum seekers means it becomes difficult to justify inferior and cruel reception. Once asylum seekers are presented in pejorative terms, it is easier for the community to absorb a dehumanising asylum system (Hayes, 2004).

The way asylum seekers have been treated in Australia is a story of shame for the nation—a narrative of brutality, misery and hard hearts. But, from the deep dark ashes of malevolent and capricious acts arose a social movement from which we can take heart. The asylum seeker advocacy movement debunked the mythology that was being perpetrated and spoke out loudly. The advocates also befriended people in detention and after their release. They saw them as brothers and sisters, daughters and sons and friends—not as threats. Organisations sprang up throughout urban and rural Australia. Some had a specific focus such as children; others focused on policy; many were involved in individual support; and an active minority engaged in direct action and resistance.

Many human services professionals were active. There were doctors and nurses, psychologists and psychiatrists who told of the harms that were being inflicted. Social work academics rose to the occasion by conducting the People's Inquiry into Detention under the auspice of the Australian Council of Heads of Schools of Social Work, a massive collective undertaking that took more than three years to complete. Through the Inquiry social work helped to re-story the perceptions of asylum seekers through accounts of their treatment during their journeys to Australia, in the processing of their claims, in immigration detention centres and after detention (Briskman, et al. 2008).

Social workers can take heart from leadership arising within their own and other human services professions, particularly when faced with the day-to-day grind of the organisational workplace, the limits on the capacity to protest and the tensions and contradictions in what is known as 'dual loyalties'—to the organisation and funding bodies and to the vulnerable groups to whom we owe a duty of care. Such tensions have the regrettable potential to diminish the focus on the vulnerable people and the commitment to enhance their lives in accordance with the spirit of social justice. As social workers, we are sometimes reluctant to position ourselves in the public domain to try and to right the wrongs that we observe. Yet we have as our basis for action as national and international social work codes of ethics that call on social workers to affirm human rights and to challenge injustice. South African social worker Tiamelo Mmatli (2008, p. 306) tells us that it is a dereliction of our professional duty not to comply with what Canadian social worker Bob Mullaly (1997) calls the promotion of political will to develop a humanised society.

The International Statement of Principles on ethics in social work proclaims that the principles of human rights and social justice are fundamental to social work (IFSW and IASSW 2004). The Australian Code of Ethics commits social workers to strive to address and redress inequity and injustice and to work toward achieving human rights (AASW, 2010).

Briskman and Cemlyn (2005) point to the need for social workers to be human rights defenders at individual, national and international levels. To date however, there is little evidence that social workers are rising to the macro challenges (Lyons, Manion & Carlsen, 2006). Hayes and Humphries (2004, p. 217) suggest that social workers in the United Kingdom have become complicit in an inferior welfare system and have been occupied with gate-keeping resources rather than meeting needs.

In social work change endeavours, we can draw upon our own ethnography because our experience in a range of fields of practice reveals the harm arising from policies that are antithetical to our common humanity. Our knowledge base and practice wisdom can open our eyes to the impact of subjugation, oppression, racism and structural disadvantage. If we take the quest towards inclusiveness and social justice sincerely, then we must reflect on our taken-for-granted and often rule-bound ways of conducting our practice and promote alternatives. Beyond direct practice we can propose an ethics of responsibility where we locate ourselves in relation to others, including strangers (Stratton & McCann, 2002).

It takes some courage to speak out in the name of a profession. Ministers of religion have been told to stick to the pulpit; health professionals have been told to dispense direct care alone; and activist lawyers have been smeared by their own profession. Social workers who ponder how far to take their concerns have a guiding principle as practice ethnographers, which can be framed as 'I know and therefore I must act'. For social workers in countries such as Australia the prospect of reprisals is minimal, and may amount to little more than public critiques from those holding opposing views. In some other countries social workers and other advocates may incur both the wrath and penalties of the state.

For those with the freedom to act, there is the question of complicity. If we do not act on what we know are we collaborators in inhumane acts? How should we behave when faced with choices of collusion, silence or advocacy? For social workers facing dual loyalties conflicts there may be a need to reconsider roles and principles. Just one example may be challenging the tenet of workplace confidentiality, so as not to collude in the information lock-up of governments and their agents (Washington, 2003, p. 18).

The role of social work educators is crucial. Academics generally have freedom to speak out, which is not always accorded to other members of the profession. Educators also have a responsibility to be role models for the next generation of social workers who they teach and influence. Hamilton and Maddison emphasise the importance of universities (2007, p. 13) as they:

> [A]re essential for producing educated, informed and questioning citizens with some capacity to scrutinise government decisions. The academics who staff these institutions require a high level of academic freedom to pursue research that may, at times, challenge a government's values and agenda.

Overriding these considerations is an obligation to redress the wrongs inflicted on human beings. As prominent Australian lawyer Julian Burnside (2007, p. 42) states:

> We must treat people decently for the sake of their humanity. The way we are treating asylum seekers diminishes us. The Universal Declaration of Human Rights should be one of our benchmarks and, indeed it is enshrined in social work codes of ethics. After the Second World War the conscience of human kind resulted in a belief that what happened to one group of people affected all members of the human family.

Social work academics need to find ways to counter criticisms. There are those for example who reject the notion that activism is an inherent a part of social work. A study by the National Association of Scholars in the United States concluded that descriptions of social work education programs were 'chock full of ideological boilerplate and statements of political commitment' (NAS, 2007). Rather than trying to defend ourselves against such accusations, social work is well placed to argue its value stance and to impress upon its critics that alternative ideologies are important in recasting the pervasive ideologies of governments in order to be closer to the heart of social work, including human rights (Trevethick, 2005, p. 32).

How we position ourselves influences the ways in which social workers cast their gaze on refugees. There can be passive or active ways of acting and we must be alert to the fact that decisions that impact on the social work agenda, are not usually made by social workers or those who share our value base. Refugees can be seen as a practice issue in dealing with torture and trauma, mental health and settlement. Another mode of working is through minimising harmful policies in order to provide better service outcomes. A third mode of intervention sees asylum seeking as a political issue requiring direct political action.

There is an inherent difficult of working across all practice boundaries requiring an exploration that draw upon a mix of ethics, theory, values, methods and ideology. Ultimately social workers need to decide whether to work in settings where the policy and practice expectations are in contradiction to personal values and professional ethics and where speaking out and protest is limited.

Conclusion

Social problems created by social policy are the business of social work and require vigilance. This chapter has grounded the discussion of social work and human rights within the Asia-Pacific region, where asylum seekers experience mistreatment in a number of countries. The challenge remains for social workers not only to engage in endeavours to challenge policies in their own fields of practice, but to extend their mandate by engaging with broader human rights violations within their own countries and though an understanding of international connectivity.

REFERENCES

Amnesty International (2010). Abused and abandoned: refugees denied rights in Malaysia ASA, June. Retrieved 23 April 2013 from www.amnesty.org/en/library/asset/ASA28/010/2010/en/2791c659-7e4d-4922-87e0-940faf54b92c/asa280102010en.pdf.

Arendt, H. (1986). *The origins of totalitarianism*. London: Andre Deutsch.

Australian Association of Social Workers [AASW] (2010). *Code of ethics*. Canberra: AASW.

Australia Pacific Refugee Rights Network (18 February 2013). *The APRRN IDC statement on New Zealand's announcement to take 150 refugees from Australia*. Retrieved 23 April 2013 from www.aprrn.info/1/.

Bali Process (2013). *About the Bali process*. Retrieved 23 April 2013 from *www.baliprocess.net/*.

Briskman, L. (2013). Courageous ethnographers or agents of the state: challenges for social work'. *Critical and Radical Social Work*, 1(1), 33–48.

Briskman, L., Zion, D. & Loff, B. (2012). Care or collusion in asylum seeker detention. *Ethics and Social Welfare*, 6(1), 37–55.

Briskman, L. (2011, 31 May). Australia's wake up call from the UN: yes, we're a racist country. *The Conversation*. Retrieved 23 April 2013 from theconversation.edu.au/australias-wake-up-call-from-the-un-yes-were-a-racist-country-1506.

Briskman, L. & Fiske, L. (2009). Working with refugees. In M. Connolly & L. Harms (Eds). *Social work: contexts and practice*, 2nd edn (pp. 135–48). South Melbourne: Oxford University Press.

Briskman, L. Latham, S. & Goddard, C. (2008). *Human rights overboard: seeking asylum in Australia*. Melbourne: Scribe.

Briskman, L. & Cemlyn, S. (2005). Reclaiming humanity for asylum seekers: social work response. *International Social Work*, 48(6), 714–24.

Burnside, J. (2007). *Watching brief: reflections on human rights, law and justice.* Melbourne: Scribe.

Cassrels, D. (2013, 16–17 March). Asylum-seekers out of sight, out of mind. *The Weekend Australian*, 24.

ChilOut Revived (2013), Children imprisoned on Manus Island. Retrieved 23 April 2013 from www.facebook.com/media/set/?set=a.480295928678920.99578.137380946303755&type=1.

Every, D. (2006). The politics of representation: a discursive analysis of refugee advocacy in the Australian parliament. PhD thesis. University of Adelaide, Adelaide, Australia.

Fiske, L, & Briskman, L. (2009). The empire strikes back: refugees, race and the reinvention of empire. In D. Bennett, J. Earnest & M. Tanji (Eds). *People, place and power: Australia and the Asia Pacific* (pp. 174–89). Perth: Black Swan Press.

Goddard, C. (2004, 13 April). Baby Ghazal's got a new name: No. 390 *The Age*. Retrieved 23 April 2013 from www.theage.com.au/articles/2004/04/12/1081621892083.html.

Goddard, C. & Briskman, L. (2004, 18 February). By any measure it's official child abuse. *Herald Sun*, 17.

Gosden, D. (2007). From humanitarianism to human rights and justice: a way to go. *Australian Journal of Human Rights*, 13(1), 149–76.

Hamilton, C. & Maddison, S. (2007). Dissent in Australia. In C. Hamilton & S. Maddison (Eds). *Silencing dissent: how the Australian government is controlling public opinion and stifling debate* (pp. 1–23). Sydney: Allen and Unwin.

Harms Smith, L. (2012). Challenging pernicious policies: working with refugees in Australia—commentary 2. In S. Banks and K. Nohr (Eds). *Practising social work ethics around the world: cases and commentaries* (pp. 200–03). London: Routledge.

Hayes, D. (2004). History and context: the impact of immigration control on welfare delivery. In D. Hayes & B. Humphries (Eds). *Social work, immigration and asylum: debates, dilemmas and ethical issues for social work and social care practice* (pp. 11–28). London: Jessica Kingsley Publishers.

Hayes, D. & Humphries, B. (2004). Conclusion. In D. Hayes & B. Humphries (Eds). *Social work, immigration and asylum: debates, dilemmas and ethical issues for social work and social care practice* (pp. 217–25). London: Jessica Kingsley Publishers.

International Detention Coalition [IDC] (2008, 10 December). A call to uphold the human rights of detainees. Media release. Retrieved 7 May 2013 from www.lhr.org.za/news/2008/international-detention-coalition-a-call-uphold-human-rights-detainees.

International Federation of Social Workers [IFSW] & International Association of Schools of Social Work [IASSW] (2004). *Ethics in social work: statement of principles.* Retrieved 23 April 2013 from ifsw.org/policies/statement-of-ethical-principles/.

Lester, E. (2010). Socio-economic rights, human security and survival migrants: Whose rights? Whose security? In A. Edwards & C. Ferstman (Eds). *Human security and non-citizens: law, policy and international affairs* (pp. 314–56). Cambridge: Cambridge University Press.

Lyons, K., Manion, K. & Carlsen, M. (2006). *International perspectives on social work: global conditions and local conditions.* Hampshire: Palgrave Macmillan.

Menadue, J., Keski-Nummi, A. & Gauthier, K. (2011). *A new approach to breaking the stalemate on refugees and asylum seekers.* Sydney: Centre for Policy Development.

Mmatli, T. (2008). Political activism as a social work strategy in Africa. *International Social Work*, 51(3), 297–310.

Mullaly, B. (1997). *Structural social work: ideology, theory and practice*, 2nd edn. Toronto: Oxford University Press.

National Association of Scholars [NAS] (2007). NAS study declares social work education to be a national academic scandal. Retrieved 7 May 2013 from www.nas.org/articles/

NAS_Study_Declares_Social_Work_Education_to_Be_a_National_Academic_Scandal.

Nethery, A., Rafferty-Brown, B. & Taylor, S. (2013). Exporting detention: Australia-funded immigration detention in Indonesia. *Journal of Refugee Studies*, 26(1), 88–109.

New South Wales Council for Civil Liberties (2007). *Shadow report prepared for the United Nations committee against torture on the occasion of its review of Australia's third periodic report under the convention against torture and other cruel, inhuman or degrading treatment or punishment.* Retrieved 7 May 2013 from www.nswccl.org.au/publications/cat_shadow.php.

Pastore, A. (2013). Why judges should not make refugee law: Australia's Malaysia solution and the refugee convention. *Chicago Journal of International Law*, 13(2), 615–47.

Perera, S. (2002). A line in the sea. *Race and Class*, 44, 23–39.

Pickering, S. (2005). *Refugees and state crime.* Sydney: Federation Press.

Reith, P. (2001, 13 September). Transcript of the Hon. Peter Reith MP radio Interview with Derryn Hinch—3AK. *Defence Ministers and Parliamentary Secretary Website.* Retrieved 7 May 2013 from www.defence.gov.au/minister/8tpl.cfm?CurrentId=999.

Refugee Council of Australia [RCOA] 2013. Strong recommendation against detention of children. *Refugee Council Monthly Bulletin*, 18 March. Sydney: Refugee Council of Australia, 2.

Robinson, K. (2013). 'Voices from the front line: social work with refugees and asylum seekers in Australia and the UK. *British Journal of Social Work.* doi:10.1093/bjsw/bct040.

Rogalla, B. (2003). Modern-day torture: government-sponsored neglect of asylum seeker children under the Australian mandatory immigration detention regime. *Journal of South Pacific Law*, 7(1). Retrieved 23 April 2013 from www.paclii.org/journals/fJSPL/vol07no1/11.shtml.

Sinanu, F. & Missbach, A. (2012, October–December). Staying stuck. *Inside Indonesia*. Retrieved 23 April 2013 from www.insideindonesia.org/feature-editions/stayingstuck?utm_source=All+Subscribers&utm_campaign=737cfea4ea-Weekly_12_Nov_2012&utm_medium=email.

Stratton, J. & McCann, S. (2002). Staring into the abyss: confronting the absence of decency in Australian refugee law and policy development. *Mots Pluriels*. Retrieved 23 April 2013 from motspluriels.arts.uwa.edu.au/MP2102jssmc.html.

Trevithick, P. (2005). *Social work skills: a practice handbook*. Berkshire: Open University Press.

Washington, S. (2003, 9–15 October). Ruddock's secret report. *Business Review Weekly*, 18.

Weber, L. and Pickering, S. (2011). *Globalization and borders: death at the global frontier*. Houndsmills: Palgrave Macmillan.

Contributors

Dan Baschiera is the coordinator of an undergraduate degree in Humanitarian and Community Studies at Charles Sturt University. He can be contacted at dan.baschiera@cdu.edu.au.

Linda Briskman PhD is professor of human rights at Swinburne University of Technology in Australia. She can be contacted at lbriskman@swin.edu.au.

Keo Chanvuthy is a lecturer with the Social Work department, Royal University of Phnom Penh, Cambodia. She can be contacted at chanvuthy_keo@yahoo.com.

Louise Coventry is a doctoral candidate at RMIT University; her research explores civil society governance in Cambodia. She can be contacted at loucoventry@gmail.com.

Murli Desai, PhD, was a professor at the Tata Institute of Social Sciences, National University of Singapore and Seoul National University. She can be contacted at murlidesai@gmail.com.

Moses Ma'alo Faleolo is finalising his PhD and is a lecturer at Massey University, Auckland (NZ). He can be contacted at M.M.Faleolo@massey.ac.nz.

Heather Fraser is a senior lecturer at Flinders University in South Australia. She can be contacted at h.fraser@flinders.edu.au.

Susan Gair is a social work scholar at James Cook University, Queensland. She can be contacted at susan.gair@jcu.edu.au.

Marty Grace is professor of social work at Victoria University, Melbourne. She can be contacted at marty.grace@vu.edu.au.

In Young Han, PhD, ACSW, LISW, CSW, is a professor of the Graduate School of Social Welfare at Ewha Womans University, Republic of Korea. She can be contacted at yhan@ewha.ac.kr.

Mark Henrickson is associate professor of social work at Massey University, Auckland, New Zealand. He can be contacted at m.henrickson@massey.ac.nz.

Jun Sung Hong, MSW, MA, is a doctoral candidate at the School of Social Work, the University of Illinois, Urbana-Champaign. He can be contacted at jhong23@illinois.edu.

Richard Hugman is professor of social work at the University of New South Wales, Sydney. He can be contacted at r.hugman@unsw.edu.au.

Joe C. B. Leung is professor at the Department of Social Work and Social Administration, the University of Hong Kong. He can be contacted at joe-leung@hku.hk.

Nguyen Thi Thai Lan is a PhD candidate at the University of New South Wales, Sydney and a social work lecturer at the University of Labour and Social Affairs, Hanoi, Vietnam. She can be contacted at lan.nguyen@unsw.edu.au.

Bui Thi Xuan Mai is Dean of the Faculty of Social Work at the University of Labour and Social Affairs in Hanoi, Vietnam. She can be contacted at buixuanmaictxh@gmail.com.

Kana Matsuo is a Joint Research Fellow at the Social Work Research Institute Asian Center for Welfare in Society and Japan College of Social Work. She can be contacted at kwani215m@gmail.com.

Lorraine Muller, BSocSc-BSW Hons, PhD, is currently working on her second PhD exploring non-Indigenous mainstream Australian culture at James Cook University. She can be contacted at Lorraine.muller@gmail.com.

Ksenija Napan, PhD, is an associate professor at the Department of Social Practice, Faculty of Social and Health Sciences at Unitec. She can be contacted at knapan@unitec.ac.nz.

Bala Raju Nikku is a visiting lecturer at School of Social Sciences, Universiti Sains Malaysia and the Founding Director of Nepal School of Social Work (NSSW). He can be contacted at nikku21@yahoo.com.

Carolyn Noble is inaugural professor of social work at Australian College of Applied Psychology, Sydney and professor emerita at Victoria University, Melbourne. She can be contacted at carolyn.noble@acap.edu.au or carolyn.noble@vu.edu.au.

Kate Saxton, PhD, has recently been working in the Pacific Islands to develop culturally relevant social work curriculum. She can be contacted at drkatesaxton@gmail.com.

Deborah West, PhD, has held a number of positions at Charles Darwin University including head of Social Work and Community Studies. She can be contacted at deborah.west@cdu.edu.au.

Nilan G. Yu, PhD, is a lecturer in social work at the School of Psychology, Social Work and Social Policy, University of South Australia. He can be contacted at nilan_yu@yahoo.com.

www.ingramcontent.com/pod-product-compliance
Lightning Source LLC
Chambersburg PA
CBHW050557270326
41926CB00012B/2088

* 9 7 8 1 7 4 3 3 2 0 3 9 6 *